BY JOSEPH KINSEY HOWARD:

MONTANA: HIGH, WIDE, AND HANDSOME

MONTANA

MARGINS

A STATE ANTHOLOGY

EDITED BY

JOSEPH KINSEY HOWARD

FORMERLY RESEARCH ASSOCIATE, THE MONTANA STUDY

NEW HAVEN

YALE UNIVERSITY PRESS

LONDON · GEOFFREY CUMBERLEGE · OXFORD UNIVERSITY PRESS

1946

Copyright, 1946, by Yale University Press

Printed in the United States of America

THE PHILIP HAMILTON MCMILLAN
MEMORIAL PUBLICATION FUND

The present volume is the thirty-fifth work published by the Yale University Press on the Philip Hamilton McMillan Memorial Publication Fund. This Foundation was established December 12, 1922, by a gift to Yale University in pursuance of a pledge announced on Alumni University Day in February, 1922, of a fund of $100,000 bequeathed to James Thayer McMillan and Alexis Caswell Angell, as Trustees, by Mrs. Elizabeth Anderson McMillan, of Detroit, to be devoted by them to the establishment of a memorial in honor of her husband.

He was born in Detroit, Michigan, December 28, 1872, prepared for college at Phillips Academy, Andover, and was graduated from Yale in the Class of 1894. As an undergraduate he was a leader in many of the college activities of his day, and within a brief period of his graduation was called upon to assume heavy responsibilities in the management and direction of numerous business enterprises in Detroit, where he was also a Trustee of the Young Men's Christian Association and of Grace Hospital. His untimely death, from heart disease, on October 4, 1919, deprived his city of one of its leading citizens and his University of one of its most loyal sons.

INTRODUCTION

PEOPLE, SURROUNDED BY SPACE

JOSEPH KINSEY HOWARD

THIS book is an attempt, limited by the checks inevitably to be encountered in such a venture, to picture life in one State, Montana, as it was and is.

It is not truly an anthology in the classical sense. "A collection of flowers of literature, that is, beautiful passages from authors," is the Webster definition; however, few anthologies are that, any more. There is some terrible writing in this book. There are flowers, too, but their appearance is incidental to the main purpose.

The heavenly blue of Plains larkspur may afford the range rider some momentary pleasure, but what he is really concerned about is the look of the new grass. If it is thick and rich, his cows will prosper; if it is thin and poor, the lovely larkspur will poison them when they turn to it for want of something better to eat.

Nor can the range rider judge the grass from the road. That's why city folk are often wrong when they say, "The country looks good." It does—from a speeding car. But the grass of the Northern Plains is bunch grass, and because it is tall it does not always follow that it is good. A dry winter and a wet spring may bring tall grass which stirs pleasingly in the wind, but the bunch is thin and the forage value of the field is low.

Much of this book is grass. Some of it is the low, untidy but sturdy stuff which isn't showy, which isn't easily visible from the road—but which makes meat. Some is true buffalo bunch: it is thick and graceful and good.

The basis of selection may seem whimsical, and perhaps it is. Nothing is more personal than an anthology, and this one's pretensions to state and regional authenticity rest wholly—allowing for those inevitable setbacks previously mentioned—upon the editor's judgment, with which few Montanans might agree. If another Montana anthologist can find a better range with thicker grass, can graze it more neatly, and can afford to pay for it, I hope he will do so. I have no desire ever to go hunting again for grass or flowers behind others' fences, though much of both remain.

The search, nevertheless, has been a grateful one. It is good to learn the resources of one's own scene.

It was exciting (though humiliating, because discovery came so late) to find a book like Van de Water's enlightened but unappreciated *Glory Hunter,* or the delightful memoirs of young Otto Maerdian; it was pleasant to be directed by a friend to a flower blooming obscurely in a country weekly, like Fred Ward's "Star in the East," and then to find a story by the same man which is the thick, common, nutritious grass—"Journey." It was gratifying to discover the real Montana, the texture of life here, the feel of dry soil, the tumult of the wild wind, the way Montanans think —to find these in the thin little books of Elliott C. Lincoln, Gwendolen Haste, and Jason Bolles, poets; and it was saddening to note that these fine voices sing no longer of my State.

The conviction that the resources of the Montana scene were culturally rich inspired this book. It was undertaken as a project of The Montana Study, with which I was associated for two years. This, an educational research experiment initiated by one of the major foundations, was designed to determine how the lives of people in a predominantly rural State could be stabilized and enriched, with particular attention to the family and the small community. It became apparent immediately that one way in which this enrichment could be promoted would be by providing opportunity for wider recognition of Montana's own glamorous tradition. Teachers reported a need for more easily accessible Montana reading materials if the school and community, as The Montana Study asserted, were to be brought into closer relation.

Baker Brownell, Northwestern University professor of philosophy, on leave, and director of The Montana Study, also made this point:

In a culture where vicarious appreciation is continually substituted for active participation in the arts, or sports, or life in general, . . . segregation of emotion from action takes place. We develop numerous techniques—much increased in modern times—whereby we get the emotions of football while sitting comfortably in the grandstand. We go to the movies and get the emotions of love without working at it. At the concert, or by radio or phonograph, we get the emotion of music without doing much of anything about it. At school, we listen and learn, but do little of significance in terms of action. Through this theory of vicarious appreciation, in short, we learn to substitute the spectator's attitude for the participative attitude and lose thereby not only the creative value of art and intellectual life but the spiritual integrity of living.*

The participative attitude toward art or literature, or toward any other human activity, can be most easily encouraged through emphasis upon native and regional values of the culture. The fully functioning community will provide even the experience of beauty for its citizens: in Montana, it will help them to interpret in music and painting, in drama and literature, the elemental values of life in this State which have been too often overlooked—space and freedom, sun and clean air, the cold majesty of the mountains and the loneliness of the plains, the gayety of a country dance, the easy friendliness of the people. These are the margins around the sometimes fretful business of earning a living. These are what Thoreau meant when he said, "I love a broad margin to my life." These are beauty, in Montana; and they give this book its title.

Too often, Mr. Brownell comments, we tend to forget "that the resources of our culture are not in purchased expertness but in ourselves and our region."

Montana is, superlatively, the country of broad physical margins. It is a State of few people, entirely surrounded by space—half a million of them distributed over 146,000 square miles, 160 acres for each person. In the United States, only the people of Wyoming and Nevada have more room. Three fourths of Montana's 1,000 communities have 200 or fewer citizens.

The first of these 1,000 communities was established just a century ago. It is Fort Benton (then Fort Lewis), head of navigation on the Missouri River, which of all American streams best merits the Pascal phrase, "A river is a road which moves." The wild Missouri was the highroad to the frontier. Its muddy turbulence terrified the first white men who saw it; its vast extent (including the portion in the Mississippi, it is 4,000 miles long and the world's greatest river), and its mysteries, challenged alike the bloodthirsty ruffian and the dedicated priest. Mike Fink, who boasted that he was the toughest of the rivermen, came up from the Ohio and Mississippi to die on the Missouri with a bullet in him at last; Father DeSmet, the gentle Belgian, fat and short of breath, scram-

* "The Value of the Humanities," *Journal of Higher Education,* November, 1945.

bled alone up an Idaho mountainside so that he might sit and look across into Montana at Red Rock Lake, ultimate source of the mighty River.

The River and its men bulk large in the story of Montana's century, so they have prominent place in this book.

That century has been one of "swiftly moving momentous change," to quote a distinguished Montana pioneer, Colonel Wilbur Fisk Sanders. "Here in Montana," he said, "we have seen the progression of the ages, from savage life to a high civilization, actually under our own observation, pass in review as under a glass case."

There are mental margins, as well as physical. These need not be permitted to contract as the physical frontier shrinks. "We should be dull students," Sanders warns, "if from this swiftly moving momentous change we could not evolve some lessons of wisdom for our own guidance, and those generations which will follow." Therefore this book is an argument for regional appreciation, not for provincialism. The regionalist weighs his area's cultural resources (which means he takes cognizance of their shortcomings, too) and their possible contribution to national or world good; but he who is provincial-minded shuns new ideas and warns "foreigners" away. The pioneers were not provincial; they yearned, says Sanders, "for the felicities which follow in the train of an old, assimilated, coherent civilization."

Provincialism would have been fatal on the frontier. To survive, the newcomers had not only to adopt some of the aboriginal customs they found here but also to seize eagerly upon anything else, from anywhere, that would work, or even that *might* work—they were not afraid to try new things. The original "white" culture, of course, was wholly "foreign." It is interesting to remark (though inclusion of the item in this book may add weight to the charge of whimsicality) that gay if illiterate French boatmen on the Upper Missouri were singing a derisive ditty about a distinguished ancestor of Winston Churchill at about the same time Napoleon was humming it, riding to an empire's doom in Russia.

Montana's *physical* isolation, until the coming of air transport, has been a seriously limiting factor in its economic development. Its *cultural* isolation has never been so complete as some Montanans and far too many in other regions thought it was. The pioneer was a proud and independent man, but he was not a fool: he was not wont to assert that the country was good enough just as he found it.

Now a note about the arrangement of this book:

Chronological classification of the materials was tried and rejected in the interest of the general reader, who might well find it tiresome. Instead, for the benefit of teacher and history student, a table of contents in which selections are listed by chronological periods will be found in the back of the book.

Next, the "toss-up" method was tried. In this process, the anthologist throws his manuscript at the ceiling, or out of the window, and picks it up blindfolded. There comes a time in the labors of all anthologists when this has great appeal. I liked it, but others objected.

Finally, an informal arrangement by subject matter was decided upon, and as a guide in selection of subjects, I adopted the speeches of Colonel Sanders, mentioned previously in this introduction. By virtue of his courage, integrity, and vision, Sanders emerges from the pages of Montana history as probably the greatest of many able men of his time. Born in New York State in 1834, he came west at twenty with his uncle, Sidney Edgerton, just appointed chief justice of Idaho Territory and soon to be the first governor of Montana Territory. Shortly after their arrival, young Sanders acted as prosecutor in the first miners' camp murder trial, that of George Ives, and subsequently filled the same role for the Vigilantes—all the time at the risk of his life in communities terrorized by as bloody a gang of cutthroats as ever flourished anywhere. He had served as a lieutenant in the Civil War and was commissioned a colonel by Edgerton during Montana Indian troubles. After statehood he became a legislator and, in 1890, United States Senator. He was Montana's most eloquent speaker during his lifetime and few have equaled him since. At the time of his death, July 7, 1905, Robert G. Ingersoll said of their encounter as opposing counsel in a notable trial: "Sanders' was the keenest blade I have ever crossed."

The Sanders speeches were too long for inclusion in this volume and lost their flavor in cutting, but Montanans, at least, could well afford to read them in Volume IV of the *Contributions to the Historical Society of Montana*. They hold remarkably discerning comment upon this State and its people—especially the pioneers, with all their virtues, but not overlooking their vices. Weighing these virtues and vices and their influence upon Montana's basic law, Sanders gave his speeches a somewhat startling prophetic quality; he forecast with astonishing accuracy some of the young State's future problems and responsibilities.

The quotations accompanying each section heading in this book come from two Sanders addresses: at the laying of the cornerstone of the State Capitol on July 4, 1889 (Montana entered the Union November 8 of that year), and at the dedication of the completed building on July 4, 1902.

Approximately two score publishers and other holders of copyrights have generously granted permission for use of their materials in this book. They are listed in the acknowledgments of sources with the index of authors in an appendix.

In addition, many individuals have contributed in one way or another. I am particularly indebted to three without whose liberal assistance this collection could not have been made. They are Dr. Harold G. Merriam of Montana State University, for many years publisher of *The Frontier,* and Mrs. Lucinda B. Scott and Mrs. Anne McDonnell, librarian and assistant librarian of the Historical Society of Montana. Much help has also been obtained from Librarian Margaret Fulmer and Assistant Bessie Sestak, Great Falls; Librarian Kathleen Campbell and Reference Librarian M. Catherine White, Montana State University; and Librarian Lois Payson of Montana State College.

For suggestions on sources, assistance on notes, or for other ideas incorporated into the book, I am grateful to these: Lew L. Callaway, pioneer and former chief justice of the Montana supreme court; M. G. O'Malley, veteran Butte reporter; Archie Clark, newspaperman and student of the frontier theater; Edmund L. Freeman, Lucia Mirrielees, and Paul Meadows of the State University faculty; Dr. F. A. Thomson of the School of Mines and Margaret M. Skinner of Northern Montana College; Ruth W. Robinson and Helen Formos, teachers; R. V. Bottomly, attorney general; Earl Talbott, old-timer, and Adelaide Howard Brownell. The fact that not all of their favorites could be squeezed into the book does not lessen my obligation to this group.

The suggestions, particularly on newspaper sources, and the assistance with many irksome details of preparing a manuscript of this kind given by Patricia Brennan, newspaper woman, are most gratefully acknowledged. So is the continued loyal championship of my literary ventures by Roberta Yerkes of Yale University Press. I am much indebted to Jean McReynolds for assistance with an onerous job of proofreading.

Finally, for their generous encouragement, for stimulation and support throughout my association with The Montana Study, I welcome an opportunity to express my gratitude to Baker Brownell, to Dr. Ernest O. Melby, former Chancellor of the University of Montana, and to the Rockefeller Foundation. A grant from the Foundation has made possible the preparation of this book. No royalties beyond those necessary to cover fees for the use of copyrighted material are being paid and none therefore accrue to the Montana Study or to the editor; this has enabled the publisher to reduce the cost of the book to the reader.

Great Falls, Montana

CONTENTS

CONTENTS

xvii

THE SPIRIT:

APPENDIX

OLD MONTANA

J. CAMPBELL CORY

Montana's legislature, whose musical and literary judgment is no better than that of most such assemblies, adopted in 1945 as the official state song a bombastic bit of doggerel which was produced by Joe Howard, musical comedy star, and Charles C. Cohan, a Butte newspaperman, in half an hour at a dinner preceding a performance by Howard in Butte. About its only virtue lies in the fact that its authors donated the copyright to a worth-while Montana charity which has profited by sales of the sheet music. In its selection, the legislature passed over the song printed here, more popular with many Montanans because of its indigenous character: it just *sounds* more like Montana, somehow. It too, however, has a serious drawback— it lacks original music and was written to be sung to the too-familiar tune of "Mandalay." Its author, a newspaperman born in Waukegan, Ill., in 1869, came to Montana from New York in 1903 and engaged in a mining venture at York, near Helena, with his brother Bob and sister Fanny, who were already here; a few years later he returned to New York, then came back to Montana, went to Alaska, and finally to Denver, where he died in 1925. His song, like the other, was written at a dinner—one given by the Rocky Mountain Club in New York City, composed of Montanans "exiled" in the metropolis. Cory wrote the song on a tablecloth or menu card. Its date is uncertain, but it was during the first decade of this century. The song appears in the outstanding collection by John A. and Alan Lomax, *Cowboy Songs and Other Frontier Ballads* (Macmillan, 1938); the official Montana state song does not. Cory's sister, Mrs. Fanny Cory Cooney of Helena, is a well-known artist who has drawn a syndicated newspaper strip for many years.

TAKE me back to Old Montana,
　　Where there's plenty room and air;
　　Where there's cottonwood an' pine trees,
　Bitterroot and prickly pear;
Where there ain't no pomp nor glitter,
　Where a shillin's called a "bit,"
Where at night the magpies twitter,
　Where the Injun fights were fit.

I

Take me where the sage is plenty,
    Where there's rattlesnakes and ticks;
Where a stack of "whites" costs twenty,
    Where they don't sell gilded bricks;
Where the old Missouri River,
    An' the muddy Yellowstone,
Make green patches in the Bad Lands
    Where old Sittin' Bull was known.

Take me where there ain't no subways,
    Nor no forty-story shacks;
Where they shy at automobiles,
    Dudes, plug-hats, an' three-rail tracks;
Where the old sun-tanned prospector
    Dreams of wealth an' pans his dirt,
Where the sleepy night-herd puncher
    Sings to steers and plies his quirt.

Take me where there's diamond hitches,
    Ropes an' brands an' ca'tridge belts;
Where the boys wear "chaps" for britches,
    Flannel shirts an' Stetson felts;
Land of alfalfa an' copper!
    Land of sapphire an' of gold!
Take me back to dear Montana,
    Let me die there when I'm old.

WAR

"Montana was battle-born."

AN INDIAN BATTLE

PETER KOCH

Indian warfare could be a comic-opera affair, or it could be savage and relentless, continuing until whole nations had been wiped out. Peter Koch tells here, in an extract from his memoir, "Life at Muscleshell in 1869 and 1870," a little about both kinds. The Koch story appears in the *Contributions to the Historical Society of Montana*, Vol. II, 1896. "This century" in the first line refers, of course, to the nineteenth. Koch was a trader at the mouth of the Musselshell (the modern spelling) during the period, and the short article about his experiences and observations contains much valuable material for the historian—Indian war, Indian whiskey, and the operations of wolfers, among other things. Subsequently a resident of Bozeman, Koch was treasurer of the Historical Society when this volume of the *Contributions* appeared.

. . .

TO the middle of this century the warfare of the Crows was directed principally against the Blackfeet and Cheyennes. The only Sioux with whom they came in contact were the Assiniboines who lived above Fort Union, north of the Missouri. Only when parties went to visit their relatives, the Gros Ventres of the river, did they come across the Arickarees and the main bands of the Sioux. But these Indians were gradually being pushed westward by the advancing civilization. The bulk of them crossed the Missouri and occupied the country of the Gros Ventres and the Mandans after nearly exterminating these tribes. The Crows used to range down to the mouth of the Yellowstone and came often to Fort Union to trade, but at the time I refer to they did not often venture below the mouth of the Big Horn or the big bend of the Muscleshell. They were carrying on a constant warfare with the Sioux, and although far inferior in numbers managed to hold their own quite well, as they were much better armed and equipped and on the whole better fighters. They realized their precarious situation, and I am confident that to this fact only did we owe it that they refrained from open depredations on the whites. The whites were enemies of the Sioux, equally with themselves, and

5

only through their help could the Crows hope to escape extermination.

Usually their warfare was not very bloody. I witnessed once a battle between a small band of River Crows who were camped at Muscleshell and a war party of about twenty-five Sioux who were discovered in the broken bluffs on the north side of the Missouri. The Crows mustered for the battle with the utmost activity and prodigious din. With great ardor and apparently an unquenchable determination to do or die did they plunge into the river and swim across. At full gallop did they charge up the heights, yelling and shooting. The Sioux were posted on the brow of the bluff. They wavered a moment then turned and fled, the Crows in close pursuit. But hardly had they gone out of sight before they returned pell-mell, their positions reversed. It was now the turn of the Sioux, and they chased the enemy half way down the bluff, when the Crows rallied and in their turn drove the Sioux. These furious charges and counter-charges were kept up through a whole afternoon with a mighty expenditure of ammunition. Not less than a thousand shots were fired and the casualties were— one Sioux horse. At last the Sioux grew tired and withdrew, and the Crows returned, singing a song of triumph and claiming a feast as a reward for their valor.

But there were exceptions to this usually bloodless character of their engagements. In the fall of 1869 a war party of thirty-two young River Crow warriors went to the Dry Fork of the Missouri to steal horses from the Sioux. They were prowling around a large camp when they were discovered. They fled, but were overtaken and compelled to take refuge on the top of a small, isolated butte, where they threw up stone breastworks. The entire Sioux camp with several thousand fighting men surrounded them. The Crows held them at bay here several days, until their ammunition and arrows were exhausted. Then, shouting their death song, they leaped from their breastworks down among their enemies, striking right and left with their knives and battle-axes. They fell, but only after killing nearly a hundred Sioux. Two only were captured alive, and such was the admiration of the Sioux for their bravery, that they permitted them to go unharmed. The next winter a party of Crows went to the battlefield and gathered the bones of the slain. I was in the Crow camp when they returned, and their expressions of grief were a more sickening sight than the slaughter

6

itself can have been. All the squaws had their faces blackened, dozens of fingers were cut off, and all related to the dead in any way slashed and stabbed their arms, breasts and thighs, until they were covered with a mixture of blood and black paint. Add to this their doleful cries and piercing screams, and it would be hard to imagine a more horrible scene.

. . .

CHARLOT'S LAST MARCH

ARTHUR L. STONE

"Manifest destiny," impelling the United States to the conquest of half of a continent, had weapons other than guns to use in extermination of the aborigines. One was starvation—the deliberate elimination of the buffalo upon which the Indian lived. Another was fraud; and it may shock some readers to learn that a man who subsequently became the President of the United States resorted to it and thus helped rob an Indian tribe of its home and wrong a great chief. The charge that James A. Garfield, negotiator of an agreement in 1872 with Charlot's people, forged the chief's name to the published copy of the treaty, was first made by Mrs. Peter Ronan, wife of the Flathead Indian agent; as stated here and in her husband's *History of the Flathead Indians* (1890) quoting the 1872 report of the Commissioner of Indian Affairs, Garfield subsequently acknowledged that Charlot had never signed. "Charlot's Last March" is from *Following Old Trails,* a collection of newspaper pieces written by Arthur L. Stone and published by subscription in Missoula in 1913 with M. J. Elrod as publisher. Stone, then editor of *The Missoulian,* in the next year founded the School of Journalism of Montana State University and became its dean. He died in 1945. This story first appeared Sept. 9, 1911.

PERHAPS there are more beautiful trails in this world than that which leads from old St. Mary's mission at Stevensville, in the heart of the Bitter Root, to the valley in which the Jocko agency nestles at the foot of the mountains which rise abruptly from its fertile slope. If there are any trails more beautiful than this, I have never seen any of them. Certainly there are few trails anywhere which possess the sad—tragic, I had almost said —associations which cluster about this road.

It was along this trail that grim old Charlot made his last march. After years of determined and, at times, defiant, struggle against the inroads of white settlement, the stern and embittered chief yielded to the inevitable and with the little remnant of his people turned his back upon the valleys which had been his ancestral home and marched to the place allotted to him on the Jocko reservation. Charlot is dead. Next Monday his people will travel

8

back over the old trail to Stevensville to join with the people of that town in their celebration of the twentieth anniversary of the departure of the Indians.

This week I spent a good deal of time along portions of this trail. The splendor of autumn was over the towering mountains, the glory of the harvest time was upon the valley. The breeze which wafted down from St. Mary's peak was tingling with the crispness of late summer. The water in the river was clear as crystal as it murmured along beneath overhanging trees. The incomparably beautiful Bitter Root landscape was never more appealing— grand mountains, rolling valleys, broad meadows, dense groves, the bluest sky that spans the earth, the brightest sun that shines upon it and the intoxicating atmosphere of this western realm.

Upon just such a morning did Charlot, chieftain and the son of chieftains, bid good-bye to the valley which had always been his home as it had been the home of his fathers. Looking over the scene the other day as I walked from the mission over toward Fort Owen, I could easily understand the bitterness which filled the heart of the old man as he marched away from all that was dear to him, to make a new home for himself and his people in a place he did not like and under conditions which were humiliating to him and which broke his old heart.

His father had refused to leave the valley. Old Victor had fought with all his Indian wily diplomacy to retain the dwelling place which he and his people loved so dearly. And with the fight against the removal of his tribe there had been interwoven a struggle for his supremacy as the titular head of the people he ruled. To both of these struggles his son had fallen heir when he inherited the symbols of tribal authority and bravely had he maintained the contest.

Deceived by the agents of the government, betrayed by the special representatives of the president, conspired against by some of his own people, trusting only the few whites who were his close neighbors—the odds were heavy against the sturdy old fellow, but he resisted steadfastly. As Victor had sought to retain his home in argument with General Stevens in 1855, so did Charlot maintain the struggle in debate with General Garfield in 1872.

But, in the end he was beaten. It was not, however, the argument of the white man which convinced him against his will. It was not the threat of the emissary of the Great Father which daunted him into submission to the government's will. It was the suffering of

9

his people, the wails of the starving children of his tribe, their destitution, their nakedness and hopelessness that touched his heart and led him into acquiescence with the will of the Great Father at Washington.

And, as he marched forth from St. Mary's with his people, with the benediction of his priest upon his head, with these memories in his mind and with the bitterness in his heart which came from a consciousness of the deceit that had been practiced against him —it is not to be wondered that he was sore and sullen.

It was the year after this exodus that I first saw and talked with Charlot. He would talk to me of everything except the Bitter Root; of his old home there was no word. I had gone to him with the approval of Mrs. Ronan, whom Charlot reverenced for her tenderness, and he knew that I was friendly. Whatever else I asked him on that Sunday afternoon in the Jocko valley, he answered readily enough. But of the Bitter Root, no word. Nor would he, to the end, have aught to say of the beautiful place he had left. It was a painful subject to him and no one who knew him ever pressed it upon him. During his later days he softened somewhat. He came to regard Fred Morgan, superintendent of the reservation, as a trusted friend and his last days were the most peaceful he had known.

But there was none of that peace in his heart when he set forth that October morning, 20 years ago, to lead his people to their new home, prescribed by the government and made necessary by the impoverished condition of his tribe. His good-bye had been said to his old friends at Stevensville; he had severed the ties. He said he would never return. As nearly as I can learn, he never did return, except once when he was brought to the valley as a witness in a lawsuit over a water right in which his old friend, Abe Mittower, was involved. It is said that he did not go to Stevensville then; he went with his friend to look over the ground on the hills.

Down the river he marched his people. Through the fields where they had played as children and had hunted as men, fields which they had never stained with white man's blood, fields upon whose bosom they had been nurtured and beneath whose breast their fathers slept, they marched in solemn train. Not in haste, not in disorder, not in an uproar, but slowly, with dignity and in silence they moved out from the mission. Out past Owen and across the river and then down the valley, ever amid scenes which had been their daily environment for a life-time, each step reluctant and each mile a pang. There was a night camp in the Missoula valley and then the march to Jocko was resumed in the morning—so deliberate was the retreat of the vanquished warrior. In the afternoon the Flatheads entered the Jocko valley. Charlot's last march was ended.

The events which led up to this departure are interesting. They reveal the utter lack of honor which characterized many of the government representatives in their dealings with the Indians; they make plain the duplicity which too often governed the negotiations with the reds; they awaken sympathy with the Indian and they furnish ample reason for the bitter hatred which Charlot bore to everything which bore a Washington postmark and to everybody who hailed from the capital. Governor Stevens understood the Indian; he dealt with him as man with man; he made promises which were intended to be kept.

It was in 1855 that Stevens concluded his treaty with the Flatheads and their kindred tribes at Council Grove, below Missoula. Victor, the father of Charlot, had ceded, in this treaty, a large area in which is now western Montana; upon yielding this region, Victor had insisted that his people retain that portion of the Bitter Root valley above Lolo Creek. But there had been an alternative clause agreed to, which empowered the President to make surveys and to determine from them whether it was better for the Flatheads to remain in the Bitter Root or to go to the Jocko reservation. Until 1872 there had been no survey made nor had the government kept its promise to send carpenters, blacksmiths, artisans and school teachers to the tribe as had been promised in the treaty.

Consequently the Indians resisted a presidential order, made in 1871, which declared that the Indians should be transferred to the Jocko valley. Congress appropriated $5,000 to defray the expenses of removal and in 1872 General Garfield was dispatched to the Bitter Root to arrange a treaty covering the removal. It was in August, 1872, that Garfield came to the valley. He said in his official report that he found the Indians unwilling to move because for 17 years the government had taken no step to carry out the provisions of the Hell Gate treaty. However, General Garfield prepared an agreement, which was published as having been signed by Charlot, first chief of the Flatheads; Arlee, second chief of the Flatheads; Adolf, third chief of the Flatheads—these as principals

—and William H. Claggett, D. G. Swain, W. F. Sanders, J. A. Vail and B. F. Potts, then governor of Montana, as witnesses.

This treaty contained the provisions that the Flatheads should move to Jocko; that the government should build 60 houses for them; that 600 bushels of wheat should be delivered to the Indians the first year; that land be broken and fenced for the Indians and they be given agricultural implements; that the $5,000 appropriated for their removal be given to the Indians; that the sum of $50,000 be paid to them in ten annual installments and that the Indians should move as soon as the houses were built for them at Jocko, except such as chose to take up land in the Bitter Root valley in the regular manner.

Charlot was outraged when he learned that it had been published that he had signed the treaty. He declared he had never signed it and that he had told the commissioner that he would not sign it, but that he would never go, alive, to the Jocko. His sense of honor was wounded, his dignity was shocked; his last bit of trust in the whites was shattered.

Meanwhile, the houses were built near the agency at Jocko. Arlee, with his personal following, who had recognized the Garfield treaty, moved to their reservation, and Arlee was designated by the government as the chief of the Flatheads. This added to the resentment of Charlot. He persisted in his declaration that he had never signed the treaty and that he was not bound by its provisions. And he held the fort at Stevensville.

Major Ronan had become agent of the Flatheads; he sympathized with Charlot, but he recognized the futility of the continued resistance of the old chief, and sought to dissuade him from his course. The Bitter Root was settling rapidly. The hunting grounds of the Flatheads were gone. They were starving. More than that, the crowding of the settlers called for their removal. The matter got to congress.

Senator Vest of Missouri and Major Maginnis, Montana's delegate in congress, were named as a special commission to investigate conditions. They visited the Jocko agency and then went to Stevensville. They investigated the conditions. They listened to Charlot's story. They heard Father Ravalli's account of the case. They concluded that Charlot was absolutely correct and they forced from General Garfield, later, the admission that Charlot had not signed the treaty. The original document on file at Washington did not bear the old man's mark. Garfield's explanation of the publication of the treaty as having been signed by Charlot was that he deemed it best to proceed as if Charlot had signed, as he felt that Charlot, when he saw the work progressing, would conclude to join with the "other chiefs" and keep the tribe unbroken. It showed how little Garfield knew Charlot.

Vest and Maginnis were much impressed by the honesty and dignity of Charlot. Their report expresses regret that Garfield committed the act of misrepresentation, as it had wronged the chief and had doubly embittered him, especially as the act of the department had placed Arlee, whom Charlot characterized as a "Renegade Nez Perce," at the head of the tribe. The commissioners talked earnestly with Charlot, urging him to accept the terms of the treaty and promised to do all they could to see that he was treated right. But the old man was too bitter and sore at heart.

In 1884, Major Ronan took Charlot and five of his sub-chiefs to Washington for conference with the president and the secretary of the interior. There were further promises made to Charlot if he would consent to the removal, but he would not yield. He was told that he might remain in the Bitter Root as long as he was friendly with the whites—this he had always been; he had saved them from dire disaster on more than one occasion. The expedition returned with no better result than a clearer understanding on Charlot's part. He had learned that Major Ronan was his friend and when, a year later, there was a distribution of supplies to the Bitter Root band, he softened considerably. Wagons, horses and plows were also issued and an attempt was made, through Ronan's influence, to give the Indians a chance to make good on their located lands.

And so time wore on. The Indians were not successful farmers and their condition became deplorable. General Carrington was sent in 1891 to try to induce Charlot to move. Arlee had died and conditions were such that it was felt that the old chief might at last consent. And this hope was, it proved, well founded. Charlot talked with Major Ronan. He also called in some of his Bitter Root friends. He consulted with Amos Buck and with the father of Dave Whaley, who gave me this account of Charlot's speech after the old chief had reached his decision:

"I will go—I and my children. My young men are becoming

13

bad; they have no place to hunt. My women are hungry. For their sake I will go. I do not want the land you promise. I do not believe your promises. All I want is enough ground for my grave. We will go over there."

Immediately the arrangements were made. Charlot's last march was begun. In the afternoon of the next day, October 17, 1891, he reached the new home of his people in the Jocko. Major Ronan had hastened ahead and was at the agency to greet the old chief, whose people also received him with proper demonstration. Mrs. Ronan, who witnessed the reception, gives this account of the end of the march from the Bitter Root:

"It was a unique and, to some minds, pathetic spectacle, when Charlot and his band of Indians marched to their future home, the Jocko reservation. Their coming had been heralded and many of the reservation Indians had gathered at the agency to give them welcome. When within a mile of the agency church, the advancing Indians spread out into a broad column. The young men kept constantly discharging their firearms, while a few of the number mounted on fleet ponies, arrayed in fantastic Indian paraphernalia, with long blankets partially draping the forms of the warriors and steeds, rode back and forth in front of the advancing caravan, shouting and firing their guns until they neared the church, where a large banner of the Sacred Hearts of Mary and Jesus was erected on a tall pole. Near the sacred emblem stood a valiant soldier of Jesus Christ, Rev. Ph. Canistrelli, S.J. With outstretched hands the good priest blessed and welcomed the forlorn looking pilgrims. Chief Charlot's countenance retained its habitual expression of stubborn pride and gloom, as he advanced on foot, shaking hands with all who had come to greet him. After the handshaking was over all assembled in the agency chapel to the benediction of the most Holy Sacrament. The 'O Salutaris' and 'Tantum Ergo' chanted by those untutored children of the forest, told better than any other words could of the patient teachings of the Jesuit fathers. Every word of the beautiful Latin verses sounded as distinct as if coming from cultivated voices. If the poor creatures reflected on the meaning of these words:

> 'Bella premunt hostilia,
> Da robur, fer auxilium,

they must have felt that the touching sentiment truly expressed the feelings of their hearts. After the benediction, the good and learned Father Canistrelli, who has spent many years laboring among the Indians, striving to enlighten their hearts, addressed them in their own language. The good words seemed to console and comfort them, if the peaceful expression of their countenances indexed aright their minds."

Such was the end of Charlot's last march. At its end he did not find immediately the peace which had been promised him. To the last he nursed his grievances and they were many. Genuine wrongs he had and he brooded over them until they magnified and multiplied. He never loved the Jocko. He was never reconciled to this change of homes. Some satisfaction he found in the better condition of his people and that was all. He distrusted all whites. Had it not been for the indorsement which I brought him at first from Mrs. Ronan and the subsequent recommendation which Major Catlin gave me—the major had been one of Charlot's trusted Stevensville friends—I doubt if any of the several visits which I made at the Jocko cabin would have been as pleasant and as satisfactory as they were. But I gained an insight into the old man's heart that always gives me sympathy even with his utter stubbornness. If the whites had been as honest with him as he was with them, his last days would have been happier.

As I walked along the route of his last march the other day I could not help thinking of this thing. The beauty of the valley which he loved so much and all of the associations which gathered about its scenes must have been constant visions before his sightless eyes during those last bitter years. And the memory of that last sad march down the valley must have been a painful thought for him. Next Monday his people will march again over the old trail, but it will be a travesty of that march of 20 years ago.

15

THE INDIAN AND TAXATION

A FLATHEAD CHIEF

The Indian orator was probably Charlot, whose story is told in the preceding selection—hereditary chief of the Flatheads, properly called the Salish. A treaty signed in 1855 granted the Salish the right to remain in their ancestral home, the Bitterroot Valley, until the Federal Government needed the land. This was inconclusive; and when Charlot refused to move in 1872, the Indian commissioners conspired to make Arlee the chief. Arlee moved to the Flathead reservation with a portion of the tribe, and Charlot never spoke to him again. In 1891, after years of near-starvation, Charlot sadly led the two hundred who remained in his band north. In the interim they had refused to pay taxes on the land they occupied in the Bitterroot. Several conferences were held on this issue; at one of them this speech was given and a translation appeared in *The Weekly Missoulian* on April 26, 1876. The name of the speaker does not appear, and the eloquent and bitter address is attributed only to "a Flathead Chief." Charlot was the spokesman, however, at most such meetings with the whites. Note the angry reference at the start of the second paragraph to earth burial. Plains Indians considered the practice both unclean and blasphemous: one did not dig in the sacred earth ("the bosom of my Mother," one Indian prophet called it) to inter the dead; instead, tree burial and dissolution in the air was favored.

YES, my people, the white man wants us to pay him. He comes in his intent, and says we must pay him—pay him for our own, for the things we have from our God and our forefathers; for things he never owned and never gave us. What law or right is that? What shame or what charity? The Indian says that a woman is more shameless than a man; but the white man has less shame than our women. Since our forefathers first beheld him, more than seven times ten winters have snowed and melted. Most of them like those snows have dissolved away. Their spirits went whither they came; his, they say, go there too. Do they meet and see us here? Can he blush before his maker, or is he forever dead? Is his prayer his promise—a trust of the wind? Is it a sound without sense? Is it a thing whose life is a foul thing?

And is he not foul? He has filled graves with our bones. His horses, his cattle, his sheep, his men, his women have a rot. Do not his breath, his gums stink? His jaws lose their teeth and he stamps them with false ones, yet he is not ashamed. No, no! His course is destruction; he spoils what the Spirit who gave us this country made beautiful and clean. But that is not enough: he wants us to pay him, besides his enslaving our country. Yes, and our people, besides, that degradation of a tribe who never were his enemies.

What is he? Who sent him here? We were happy when he first came; since we often saw him, always heard him and of him. We first thought he came from the Light; but he comes like the dusk of the evening now, not like the dawn of the morning. He comes like a day that has passed, and night enters our future with him.

"To take and to lie" should be burnt on his forehead, as he burns the sides of my horses, stolen by him, with his name. Had Heaven's Chief burnt him with some mark to refuse him, we might have refused him. No; we did not refuse him in his weakness; in his poverty we fed, we cherished him—yes, befriended him, and showed him the fords and defiles of our land. Yet we did not think his face was concealed with hair, and that he often smiled like a rabbit in his own beard. A long-tailed, skulking thing, fond of flat lands, and soft grass and woods.

Did he not feast us with our own cattle, on our own land— yes, on our plain by the cold spring? Did he not invite our hands to his papers? Did he not promise before the Sun and before the Eye that put fire in it, and in the name of both, and in the name of his own Chief—promise us what he promised: to give us what he has not given, to do what he knew he would never do? Now, because he lied, and because he yet lies, without friendship, manhood, justice, or charity, he wants us to give him money, pay him more. When shall he be satisfied? A roving skulk, first; a natural liar, next; and withal a murderer, a tyrant!

To confirm his purpose, to make the trees and stones and his own people hear him, he whispers soldiers, lockhouses and iron chains. My people, we are poor; we are fatherless. The white man fathers this doom on us and on the few that may see a few days more. He, the cause of our ruin, is his own snake which he says stole upon his mother in her own country to lie to her. He says his story is that man was rejected and cast off. Why did we not reject him forever? He says one of his virgins had a Son nailed to death on two cross sticks to save him. Were all of them dead then, when

17

that young man died, we would be all safe now and our country our own.

But he lives to persist; yes, the rascal is also an unsatisfied beggar, and his hangman and swine follow his walk. Pay him money? Did he inquire, how? No, no; his meanness ropes his charity, his avarice wives his envy, his race breeds to extort. Did he speak at all like a friend? He saw a few horses and some cows, and so many tons of rails . . . His envy thereon baited to the quick. Why thus? Because he himself says he is in a big debt, and wants us to help pay it. His avarice put him in debt, and he wants us to pay him for it and be his fools. Did he ask how many a helpless widow, how many a fatherless child, how many a blind and naked thing fare a little from that little we have? Did he—in a destroying night when the mountains and the firmament put their faces together to freeze us—did he inquire if we had a spare rag of a blanket to save our lost and perishing steps to our fires? No, no; cold he is, you know, and merciless. Four times in one shivering night I last winter knew the old one-eyed Indian, Kenneth, the gray man of full seven tens of winters, was refused shelter in four of the white man's houses on his way on that bad night; yet the aged, blinded man was turned out to his fate. No, no; he is cold and merciless, haughty and overbearing. Look at him, and he looks at you—how? His fishy eyes scan you as the why-oops do the shelled blue cock. He is cold, and stealth and envy are with him, and fit him as do his hands and feet.

We owe him nothing! He owes us more than he will pay us—yet he says there is a God!

I know another aged Indian, with his only daughter and wife alone in their lodge. He had a few beaver skins and four or five poor horses—all he had. The night was bad and held every stream in thick ice; the earth was white; the stars burned nearer us as if to pity us, but the more they burned the more stood the hair of the deer on end with cold, nor heeded they the frost bursting the willows. Two of the white man's people came to the lodge, lost and freezing pitifully. They fared well inside that lodge. The old wife and only daughter unbound and cut off their frozen shoes, gave them new ones and crushed sage-bark rind to keep their feet smooth and warm. They gave them warm soup, boiled deer meat and boiled beaver. They were saved; their safety returned to make them live. After a while they would not stop; they would go. They went away. Mind you: remember well! At midnight they returned, murdered the old father and his daughter and her mother asleep, took the beaver skins and horses, and left. Next day the first and only Indian they met, a fine young man, they killed, put his body under the ice and rode away on his horse.

Yet they say *we* are not good! Will he tell his own crimes? No, no; his crimes to us are left untold. But the desolater bawls and cries the dangers to the country from us, the few left of us. Other tribes kill and ravish his women, stake his children and eat his steers; and he gives them blankets and sugar for it. We, the poor Flatheads who never troubled him, he wants now to distress and make poorer!

I have no more to say, my people. But this much I have said, and I close, to hear your minds about this payment.

He never begot laws nor rights to ask it. His laws never gave us a blade of grass nor a tree, nor a duck, nor a grouse, nor a trout. No; like the wolverine that steals your cache, how often does he come? You know he comes as long as he lives, and takes more and more—and dirties what he leaves.

PRIMITIVE AMERICAN COMMANDOS

JOHN C. EWERS

This is reprinted from *The Masterkey,* published by the Southwest Museum, Los Angeles, July, 1943. Its author, John C. Ewers, for several years prior to his enry into naval service was the curator of the Museum of the Plains Indian at Browning, Montana. He brought to that new institution—he was its first curator—not only technical skill in his professional field of anthropology but also great enthusiasm for preservation and public diffusion of the values of Plains Indian culture. In addition to many contributions to professional journals and two handbooks published by the Department of the Interior, *The Blackfeet* and *Blackfeet Crafts,* he is the author of a definitive work on Indian art, *Plains Indian Painting,* published in 1939 by Stanford University Press. After serving in Japan, Ewers left the Navy in May, 1946, and became associate curator of ethnology of the United States National Museum, a division of the Smithsonian Institution.

NO phase of modern warfare has more fascination for the civilian than the Commando raid. We know the Commando as a small raiding party, carefully organized to accomplish specific objectives rather than the destruction of a large enemy force, striking swiftly and quietly in a surprise night raid, rapidly carrying out its planned assignments in enemy territory, and as quickly making a well-timed withdrawal and return to its base.

Most of us think of these Commandos as efficient cogs in the complex modern war machine, perfected to meet the particular needs of present-day warfare. But to a small number of wrinkled old warriors, living on the Indian reservations of the Great Plains in the United States and Canada, Commando tactics are not new. They and their fathers, and their fathers' fathers for many generations back, used these same basic principles in their intertribal wars during the days when great herds of buffalo blackened the plains.

White fur-traders regarded the Blackfoot tribes (Piegan, Bloods, and Northern Blackfoot) as the most numerous and most warlike Indians of the northwestern Plains. For more than 130 years after the first trader described them in 1754, these Indians continued to send out raiding parties westward across the Rockies against the Kutenai, Flatheads, and Nez Perces; southward against the Shoshone and Crows; and eastward against the Assiniboin, Sioux, and Cree. Not until 1885—less than sixty years ago—were these war expeditions discontinued.

Their theater of war was an immense region of rolling plains and lofty mountains stretching from the North Saskatchewan River in Canada southward almost to Great Salt Lake; extending westward across the Rockies into the present Idaho, and eastward more than 500 miles over the plains from the base of the mountains. In area it was greater than pre-war Germany and Italy combined, excluding Italy's African possessions that have since been taken from her by the Allies.

Blackfoot children were brought up to look upon war as opportunity. The warpath was man's surest road to fame and fortune. Even today full-blood Blackfoot parents whose sons are in the armed forces of the United States are comforted by the age-old tribal saying, "It is better for a man to be killed in battle than to die of old age or sickness." There was no selective service for the Blackfoot. All warriors were volunteers.

The great majority of Blackfoot war-parties were organized for the purpose of capturing horses from enemy camps. Horses were their wealth. They needed fast horses to hunt buffalo, and strong, healthy horses to transport their tipis and household effects as they moved camp from place to place in pursuit of buffalo. They dearly loved horse-races. With horses in place of money they could obtain any material thing they desired. With horses a man could make desirable gifts to the parents of the girl of his choice to obtain their approval of marriage. With horses he could purchase powerful sacred bundles through which supernatural aid was gained for himself and his household. Through the wise distribution of horses a man added to his social prestige. The Blackfoot never seemed to have enough horses. The surest way to add to their herds was to capture horses from other tribes. This, of course, meant war. But to a hardy, courageous, aggressive people the stakes were worth the risks involved.

Horse-raiding parties were the primitive Commandos of the Plains. These parties were usually small, often numbering no more than 10 or 15 men. Each party was led by an experienced warrior. Other men who had faith in his judgment and in the power of his sacred medicine to bring success volunteered to join his party. Most members of the raiding party were seasoned warriors—men from 18 to 40 years of age. But boys in their middle 'teens joined the parties to learn the art of war. They carried supplies and equipment, did the cooking and other chores for the warriors.

For a day or more after a party was organized the men and their relatives were busy preparing weapons, clothing, food, and equipment for the trip. Then, at a time determined by the leader, the men set out. Generally they went on foot, even though the distance to enemy camps was often as great as 200 or 300 miles. They walked briskly, but stopped frequently to smoke, eat, repair moccasins, and talk. Twenty-five miles was a good day's march. Consequently war-parties were generally away from home for weeks, often months. Those setting out in winter often did not return until spring.

At first they traveled by day and slept at night. Each party was a self-sufficient unit, carrying all their weapons, ammunition, clothing, and bedding. They took some food along too—thin dried strips of buffalo meat or meat pounded and mixed with mint or berries in the form of a highly concentrated popular food known as pemmican, carried in rawhide bags. They counted on replenishing their meat supply enroute, before they got too near the enemy to make hunting dangerous.

When the leader believed they were within two or three days' journey from their objective, the enemy camp, they stopped to make their last hunt, using noiseless bows and arrows to kill the game. Generally the leader chose a spot in a heavily timbered area near a stream or on a height, where the party quickly built a war-lodge from fallen timbers. This ingenious structure looked something like a tipi built of logs and poles covered with bark or brush, with a long, angling, covered entrance, and surrounded by a breastwork of stones or thick logs. While the main body hunted, prepared food, and hid out in and near this little fort, the leader sent two or three of the shrewdest men ahead to locate the enemy camp. The scouts moved very cautiously. Usually they covered their heads and upper bodies with wolfskins to disguise their human forms. They looked for horse-tracks, footprints, decaying animal carcasses, fire-hearths, or disturbances of wild animals as signs of the nearness of other human beings. Silently they approached the enemy camp, noted its size and number of horses, and the physical details of the surrounding country. Then they returned to their party.

Thereafter the party moved more swiftly, always by night, hiding out in the daytime, until they neared the enemy camp. Near the top of a hill overlooking the camp or in a wooded area within sight of the enemy village, but out of sight of the enemy, they halted. The warriors painted themselves, sang their war-songs, prayed to their spirit-helpers for success, and donned their feather bonnets or good-luck ornaments. The leader explained his plan of attack and designated a meeting-place after horses were taken. There the packs and food-pouches were left. But in case they might be too hurried to pick them up on their way home, they carried small rawhide pouches of dried meat or pemmican at their belts. These contained their war lunches—emergency rations for the long journey homeward.

The rush for horses was usually made late at night when the enemy, unaware of any danger to their horses, were sleeping soundly. Usually the leader and a few of his ablest men entered the camp to cut loose the best horses picketed in front of the tipis. The Blackfoot considered it a high honor to take these fine animals almost from under the noses of their sleeping owners. Armed with their weapons and ropes, these picked men silently crept into the enemy camp. They threw bits of meat to the enemy dogs to quiet them, located the picketed horses, cut the rawhide picket-lines with their knives, slipped their war-bridles on the horses, and slowly, quietly rode them out of camp. If all went well, they returned to the camp for more picketed horses. Meanwhile other members of the party rounded up some of the loose herds grazing outside the village.

At any time during this action there was danger that some noise might waken the enemy, or that some sleepless villager might discover the intruders and spread an alarm, which would bring the men pouring out of their tipis, weapons in hand, and ready for use. The raiding party was generally too small to make a stand against an entire village. Their best policy, if the camp was aroused, was to take the horses they had captured or could reach quickly, mount them, and make a dash for home.

In any case, whether the raid was entirely successful or interrupted by the enemy, the raiders started homeward as fast as their horses could take them, for the enemy, unless set entirely afoot by the horse-raid, was almost sure to pursue them in an effort to retake their horses, once they learned of their loss. Generally the raiders rode night and day for several days, stopping neither to sleep nor to eat, munching a handful of meat from their pouches as they rode when they required food. It was a trying ordeal. Inexperienced men sometimes fell asleep and toppled off their horses. Even toughened warriors had the skin worn off their legs and buttocks from the fast, continuous, bareback riding over rough country.

It was not safe for a raiding party to capture too many horses. Driving large horse-herds hundreds of miles homeward was no easy task. The chances of the enemy overtaking such a party were great. Old Indians say that they and their tribesmen seldom were successful in taking more than 60 horses in a single raid.

The ideal horse-raid was one on which a number of fine animals were taken, through careful planning and faultless execution, without bloodshed. However, bloodshed could not be avoided always. Not infrequently a small raiding party on its outward journey met a superior enemy force. Its first reaction then was to take the defensive and to seek cover quickly. If thick timber was near, they ran for it. Plains Indians seldom followed their enemies into wooded areas with dense undergrowth, even though they knew they greatly outnumbered the opposing force. In the timber the defenders could throw up barricades of tree trunks and hold off their opponents until nightfall, when they might escape under cover of darkness. If caught on the open plains, a long distance from timber, the smaller party quickly dug fox-holes two or three feet deep with their knives, strengthening them with piles of stones if obtainable on the ground near the holes. Enemies were usually slow to attack such prepared positions.

The superior force, on the other hand, tried to surround the smaller party and annihilate it before it could become entrenched. Within gunshot Indian fighters on the open plains never stood still. They jumped about, dodging from side to side, making it difficult for the enemy to hit them. Consequently their opponents generally aimed for the waist, and often a little to one side of their target.

When in the midst of the fray users of the old muzzle-loading Northwest trade gun, the most deadly weapon possessed by these Indians prior to 1870, carried the balls in their mouths. They dumped about two fingers of powder down the barrel, dropped a ball into it without any wadding, gave the stock one or two sharp blows to settle the charge, aimed and fired the instant the gun was brought down to the level of the mark. Without wadding the range and velocity of the gun was retarded. Indians were willing to sacrifice these qualities, however, for quickness in firing. One old-time fur-trader said the Indians could discharge four or five shots a minute by this quick-loading method. There was no random shooting. Indians shot to kill individual opponents, but often their aim was poor. They took no prisoners except women and children. They aimed to wipe out the enemy force if possible.

Despite the tendency of some white students to look upon Plains Indian warfare as a sort of game, it was a mighty serious business to the Indians. Casualties were high, considering the small numbers of men involved. Pitched battles between large forces of several hundred on a side were rare. Nevertheless, owing largely to the great number of small parties, there were many years during the 19th century when the Blackfoot lost more than one per cent of their total population in war. This would be equivalent to an annual loss of more than 1,300,000 men for the United States today. White observers in the middle of the 19th century stated that, owing largely to war losses, women among the Blackfoot outnumbered men two or three to one. Were it not for the common custom of polygyny and a very high birthrate, it is doubtful whether the Blackfoot and their enemies could have survived year after year of fighting for more than 130 years.

Present-day military experts acknowledge that old-time Indian warfare embodies many elements of effective tactics. Recently Gen. Douglas MacArthur is reported to have stated: "As a warrior, his [the Indian's] fame is worldwide. Many successful methods of modern warfare are based on what he evolved centuries ago. Individually he exemplified what the line fighter could do by adaptation to the characteristics of the particular countryside in which he fought."

COURSE OF EMPIRE

FREDERIC F. VAN DE WATER

George Armstrong Custer rode over a ridge to his death on Sunday, June 25, 1876; and no one knows just how he died. No white witness survived the annihilation of his immediate command, and the Sioux did not know whom they were fighting and were confused afterward about details of the brief contest. Savage controversy raged as a result of this shocking setback to American arms, though it was not the first which had been administered by the Sioux. This tribe, in the treaty of 1868, was the only enemy which had ever wrung from the United States an admission of defeat in war. The deaths of 264 men of the Seventh cavalry in the Little Bighorn battle were directly traceable to violation by the United States of this treaty, and to the expedition into the Black Hills which Custer led in 1874, and from which he sent back reports of "gold in the grassroots." The treaty was forgotten. It had closed the Bozeman Trail, set aside nearly all of what is now South Dakota as a Sioux reservation, given the Indians the right to hunt north of the Platte, and declared the country north of the North Platte and east of the Big Horn Mountains to be unceded Indian territory, barred to white settlement or even white penetration without the Indians' consent. Apology, dispute, and speculation clutter up accounts of the battle of the Little Bighorn; instead, here is a discussion of the causes of the crisis which reached its roaring climax on that little Montana stream. This is a portion of two chapters from one of the most comprehensive and understanding of the many works on Custer: Frederic F. Van de Water's *Glory Hunter, A Life of General Custer*. It was published in 1934 by Bobbs-Merrill and copyrighted by the author.

SPRING came at last to Dakota and in its train the advance-guard of a fresh host of gold-seekers rolled in upon the Black Hills. The government in general and the army in particular now was to suffer the consequences of the expedition it had so blithely authorized.

War with the plundered Indians would have been a grateful mask for white thievery, but war, which many expected and not a few hoped for, did not come. The Sioux, who had swarmed like hornets under Red Cloud to fight against the Bozeman Road, remained inexplicably patient in the face of greater robbery. The summer of 1875 was the most peaceful that the plains had seen in many years. The wild Indians on the unceded land carried on their century-old war with the neighboring Crows and Shoshones but few whites were molested.

The army, which had caused the government's present plight, went through idiotically comic motions of driving trespassers from Indian land. Troops under Dodge and Crook were sent to clear the Black Hills of interlopers. Even Custer, for a short time that summer, took the field. Miners on French Creek had laid out a town-site and had christened it Custer City. On August fifteenth, Custer marched them solemnly out of Indian territory. Whereupon, most of them turned about and went back. Similar tactics were employed by prospectors whom Dodge and Crook had evicted. By the spring of 1876, there were eleven thousand whites in Custer City alone. And still the Sioux, reservation and "wild" bands kept the peace.

There was to be no war that year, no opportunity for the Glory-Hunter to exchange old laurels for new, and the spirit of Custer fretted and fumed. The sutler, Seip, enflamed an idle and querulous mind into hatred of the whole system whereby he was appointed and of General Belknap, Secretary of War. Rumor fed Custer's resentment, which grew so reckless that, when Belknap on a tour of inspection visited Fort Lincoln, the Commandant deliberately slighted the Secretary. Military courtesy prescribed that Custer should receive the distinguished visitor at the reservation's boundary. Instead, he waited in his office for Belknap to call and when Seip sent in a basket of champagne for the entertainment of the guest, Custer ordered him to take it back.

So the summer passed while men made feeble efforts to avert the rising torrent. The peace had collapsed under larcenous pressure. Nothing could restore it, now. The government attempted to buy from the Sioux the Black Hills country that its citizens already had stolen, and found itself thwarted by a clause of the Laramie treaty.

This provided that no sale of Sioux land could be legal unless three-fourths of the tribe's adult males voted thereon. Not one-eighth the required number gathered for the council the white commissioners held.

The summer waned and the fateful winter of 1875–76 drew in. The climacteric act of the tragedy had opened when Custer was granted two months' leave and fled with his wife and brother, Tom, from the dreary frontier to the gaiety of New York.

There are three main themes in the tragedy that reached catharsis that Sunday of slaughter on the Little Bighorn. They move toward their end even while Custer, elated and relieved, rides with his wife and brother, Tom, away from frontier boredom toward New York. Men and that remoteness called circumstance, or doom, or destiny, guided the triple themes. It is doubtful whether far greater men could have checked their inevitable march. The mortals involved therein had little of greatness.

First in the trinity of motives is the dangerous mental state of white authority, civil and military. The Black Hills have been stolen and those who now tacitly sanction the theft find themselves compelled to justify perfidy by further crime. They must sin further to secure their current loot. Wherefore, army and Indian Bureau alike prepare to break the power of the increasingly indignant Sioux and abolish forever the troublesome frontier.

Second, there is the rekindling desperation of a brutally defrauded people who have distrusted white treaties, with warrant; who had been wheedled, cajoled, bullied into making one more; who now see their last protection, barring their own feeble weapons, more callously violated than all its predecessors. The Sioux did not make this last great war of their race. It was thrust into their faces by men and circumstance.

Circumstance, or doom, is responsible for the third precipitating motive. White men cheat and neglect the reservation Sioux. Impersonal forces are leagued as savagely against the sufferers. An element no more human than the weather hurries on the tragedy.

The forces move, irresistible as triple floods. They meet and blend and wreak immense destruction. They grip the brightest of the trivial figures in their path. They sweep up George Armstrong Custer and whirl him about and suck him under.

He and his wife reached New York early in the fall of 1875. The town offered manifold reliefs to hungers of the body and the spirit—theaters, restaurants, music and the admiring hospitality of town-bred folk for one who had fought the blood-thirsty savages and had hunted buffalo in a land of romance. The editors of *The Galaxy* praised Custer and wanted more articles. Barrett, Custer's intimate, was appearing as Cassius in *Julius Caesar*. Save when some dinner or other social affair interfered, the Glory-Hunter spent each evening in his friend's dressing-room.

Custer was financially embarrassed and it is probable that he confided to Barrett his need of money. His wife relates how her hero laughed when they were compelled to use horse cars instead of cabs or when he had to appear at the houses of the wealthy in a shabby overcoat. Barrett learned also of the manifold sins of Belknap, the Secretary of War. "For some unexplained reason," the actor wrote artlessly later, "General Custer believed the secretary to be his enemy."

There were luncheons and dinners and receptions. There were visits to the theater where Custer and his wife wept together. There were the praise and the adulation of lion hunters. Two months went by. Tom Custer returned at the end of his leave to bleak Fort Lincoln. His brother applied for a three months' extension to Sheridan, who granted it, and Lachesis measured the thread and Clotho raised her shears.

Sheridan indulged his favorite, though on the frontier the flood was rising. It was weather, not men, who struck first against the Sioux. Winter came early and the snows were tremendous. Indian agents reported that hunting would be hampered and that the reservation dwellers would need additional rations before the new year. Congress rose to the emergency by passing the deficiency measure the following spring. Meanwhile, well-disposed Indians starved.

Beyond the reservations, on the unceded land where the parishioners of Sitting Bull still ranged, game was plentiful. Many Indians, with their agents' permission, left the reservations to stave off hunger by hunting there.

On December 6, 1875, the Indian Bureau issued drastic orders to all agents with the Sioux and Northern Cheyennes. The army was already planning to consolidate white occupation of the Black Hills by abolishing the troublesome "wild" Indians living on unceded land. The army had been worried by the exodus of starving Sioux and Cheyennes from the reservations. The Indian Bureau, for once, agreed with the military arm. The order of December sixth informed the agents that all Sioux and Northern Cheyennes who were off their reservations after January 31, 1876, were to be regarded as hostiles.

The order did not reach the agents on their drift-smothered

reservations until December twentieth. The more conscientious immediately sent out runners to find and summon their charges and the "wild" Indians as well. In summer, it was no small task to track down villages scattered over so vast a territory. In a heavy winter, it was almost impossible. The messengers found a few bands of hunters, reservation and wild, in tepees huddled under protecting bluffs by frozen streams. There is no record that even the "hostiles" reached were defiant. There is no record that Sitting Bull, Gall or Crazy Horse ever received the warning at all.

Most of the Indians notified sent word by the runners that they would report in spring, when impassable drifts had vanished and winter-starved ponies could march. The few who were able to plow back to the reservations were disarmed at once, for on January seventeenth, orders commanding this and prohibiting further sale of guns or ammunition had been received. This apparent preliminary to massacre alarmed red hearts further.

Many of the runners themselves could not get back to the reservations until mid-February. On February first, the Indian Commissioner, John Q. Smith, surrendered control of all Sioux and Cheyennes, not then with their agents, to the War Department. On February seventh, Sheridan received authority to proceed against the hostiles.

Disarmed and starving on their reservations, with all promise of succor as vain and mendacious as the now thoroughly pulverized Laramie treaty, the monumental patience of the Indians snapped. Those who were able, fled at once to the far villages of the hostiles. Many more, when spring came, followed them, for by then the purpose of the army had been made plain.

. . .

THE CUSTER BATTLE

SITTING BULL

This is an unusual document. The story appeared July 12, 1878—two years after the battle—in *The Fort Benton Weekly Record*, and the portion given here purports to be a quotation from Sitting Bull, preceded by the words: "As near as Father Genin remembers, Sitting Bull's account of the Custer massacre was about as follows." The story continues, without directly quoting Sitting Bull, that the Indians regarded the fight as "fun" because it was so easy: "they say Reno acted wisely and Custer like a fool." One of the warriors gave Father Genin, who is not identified in the story, a stone war ax or tomahawk bearing twenty-seven horseshoe marks, each supposed to represent a slain Custer cavalryman. Old-timers give Sitting Bull little credit for the victory, however; he was a medicine chief, not a war chief, and others probably directed the battle.

PEOPLE in the United States blame me for having killed Custer and his army. They came to attack me in sufficient numbers to show that they wanted to destroy me and my children. For three days I looked at them coming toward us. Then I assembled the young men, told them to put up the oldest tepees, light fires inside and outside of them, put blankets and other things on sticks and place them around the fires so that they would look like people.

Meanwhile I sent the women and children across the hills to a place of safety. I then turned around two or three bluffs with my soldiers to give Custer time to arrive and commence firing upon the empty tepees. When he did I fell upon him from the rear and in less than two hours destroyed him.

When I saw them coming I called upon God to help me and to liberate me and my children. They must accuse God, for He did the fighting. They think me a very bad man. All I have done in my life has been to try to procure a living for my children and my old parents and save them from the dangers of death.

SOLDIER MUSIC

This came from the Fort Ellis correspondent of *The Bozeman Times*, in which it appeared Dec. 15, 1874.

FROM various sources we gather the following stanzas, adapted to the various drumbeats, bugle calls, etc., in army use. Some of them have nearly crazed us, *but,* the "dinner call"—we hear it yet!

> Officers' wives, get your puddings and pies;
> Soldiers' wives, get your rations;
>> Rations and pies,
>> Rations and pies,
> Officers' wives, etc.

This is the call for orders:

> Come for orders, come for orders,
> Come for orders, come,
> Come for orders, come;
> Come for orders, orderlies all!

The following words apply to that confounded rattle that goes on about 8 P.M.:

> Go to bed, Tom; go to bed, Tom;
> Drunk or sober, go to bed, Tom.

Here is another delightful thing—but we don't know to whom it applies:

> What will you do with the drunken sodger?
> What will you do with the drunken sodger?
>> So early in the morning?
> Put him in the guardhouse till he gets sober,
> Put him in the guardhouse till he gets sober,
>> So early in the morning.
> What will you do with him when he's sober?
> What will you do with him when he's sober?
>> So early in the morning?
> Give him three dozen at the triangles,
> Give him three dozen at the triangles.

This is a beat calling to parade :

> Fifteen minutes to live, to live;
> Fifteen minutes to live.

The following would imply that the sergeants don't know their own call, but who would dare to say so:

> Sergeants all, sergeants all;
> Don't you hear the sergeant's call?

The music (?) of the next call is "beautiful," and is used when parades give way to storms, etc. How happy they look when they hear it!

> There is no parade today;
> There is no parade today;
> There is no parade
> For our brigade,
> For our brigade,
> Today.

But they don't look happy when they hear this:

> Shoulder your shovel, and quick come dig;
> Shoulder your shovel, John Todd;
> Shoulder your shovel, ne'er think of the hod,
> And work with a will, John Todd.

Or this, the working call:

> I called him, I called him—
> He wouldn't come, he wouldn't come;
> I called him, I called him—
> But he wouldn't come at all.

Or this, the stable call:

> Oh, come to your stable—
> Work while you're able—
> Water your horses and give them some corn;
> If you don't do it
> The colonel shall know it,
> And you shall be punished according to law.
> So come to your stable—
> Work while you're able—
> Water your horses and give them some corn!

33

But, when the following sounds, how they jump. And *we;* we end
as we began—with dinner:

> Come; pick them up, pick them up—
>   Hot potatoes; hot potatoes;
>   Pick them up, pick them up;
>   Hot potatoes, hot potatoes—all.

CHIEF JOSEPH'S LAST FIGHT

HELEN ADDISON HOWARD, Assisted by
DAN L. MCGRATH

This account of the tragic finish of the great campaign by Joseph, Chief of the Nez Percé, in 1877, is from *War Chief Joseph*, by Howard and McGrath, published in 1941 by Caxton Printers, Ltd., Caldwell, Idaho. Miss Howard, a former Montanan, now lives in California; McGrath is a member of a Montana family but makes his home in Idaho. Their book has particular value because of its synthesis of materials from various original sources: those which proved of special importance for this portion included Chief Joseph's own story, an interview titled "An Indian's View of Indian Affairs," published in *North American Review*, April, 1879; and Lieutenant Romeyn's account of the battle in the Montana Historical Society *Contributions*, Vol. II. When this battle was fought, Joseph had conducted a masterly retreat of 1,800 miles in 75 days; with never more than 350 fighters he had engaged 2,000 U. S. troops in five pitched battles, of which he had won three, drawn one—and this last one he lost. It was, said General W. T. Sherman, "one of the most extraordinary Indian wars of which there is any record." He paid tribute to the "courage and skill" of the Nez Percé; but he repudiated Miles's promise to them that they would be returned to their own country. He banished them to Indian Territory where they were held for seven years while their numbers declined from 450 to 280. Finally they were allowed to return to the West, but were split up and settled on two reservations. Joseph died Sept. 21, 1904, at Nespilem on the Colville reservation, Washington, and is buried there. (His original home was the Wallowa Valley of Oregon.) It is clear from the account printed here that Joseph believed his surrender to be conditional upon fulfillment of Miles's promise. Because of its historical significance and its intrinsic merit, and for ease in reference, his famous surrender speech has been deleted from the concluding portion of this selection and appears alone immediately following it.

THE country from the valley of the Clarks Fork to the Bearpaw Mountains is rolling plateau land, cut by bluffs and gashed with crooked ravines or coulees. Prickly-pear cactus and sagebrush dot the plains, while cottonwoods cluster along the river bottoms. Although the water is alkaline, bunch grass which nourished the buffalo for centuries grew in abundance and supplied nutritious forage for Indian pony and cavalry charger.

Unaware of another army in the field, the Nez Perces moved along in leisurely fashion after their skirmish at Cow Island. They reached the northern slope of the Bearpaw Mountains within an easy day's march of the Canadian line—and the blessed freedom for the lack of which they had suffered so much and would have to suffer much more. On Snake Creek, a tributary of Milk River, Joseph halted to give his exhausted people and horses a chance to rest, the wounded to recuperate, and to take advantage of the excellent hunting. Here, thirty miles southwest of Fort Belknap, he located his camp in a sheltered valley abounding in game, for he believed himself safe from pursuit.

This belief is evidenced in an interview held in 1900 with Indian Inspector James McLaughlin, in which Joseph said:

I sat down in a fat and beautiful country. I had won my freedom and the freedom of my people. There were many empty places in the lodges and in the council, but we were in the land where we would not be forced to live in a place we did not want. I believed that if I could remain safe at a distance and talk straight to the men that would be sent by the Great Father, I could get back the Wallowa Valley and return in peace. That is why I did not allow my young men to kill and destroy the white settlers after I began to fight. I wanted to leave a clean trail, and if there were dead soldiers in that trail I could not be held to blame. I had sent out runners to find Sitting Bull, to tell him that another band of red men had been forced to run from the soldiers of the Great White Father, and to propose that we join forces if we were attacked.

The last sentence indicates that either Joseph anticipated possible pursuit by American troops into Canada, or his memory was confused as to the *time* when he sent out runners. In any event, he made a fatal pause—the beautiful camping spot in the Bearpaw Mountains, like a siren, lured the little band of Nez Perces to their final downfall. And the chief was big enough to admit his error. McLaughlin reports that Joseph almost wept when he spoke of his fatal blunder.

"I knew that I had made a mistake," he told McLaughlin, "by not crossing into the country of the Red Coats, also in not keeping the country scouted in my rear."

All the while Colonel Miles was secretly approaching the Nez Perces with three troops of the Second Cavalry under command of Captain George Tyler; three of the Seventh commanded by

36

Captain Owen Hale; four companies of the Fifth Infantry, mounted on captured Sioux Indian ponies, Captain Snyder in command; a breech-loading Hotchkiss gun and a 12-pound Napoleon cannon, besides a wagon train guarded by the two unmounted companies of the Fifth Infantry under Captain Brotherton—375 men in all. Miles advanced rapidly and reached the Missouri at the mouth of the Musselshell on September 23.

Upon learning two days later that the Nez Perces had crossed at Cow Island and burned the supply depot on the twenty-third, Miles commandeered the last river steamer for the season and ferried his troops across the Missouri. The colonel then left his wagon train in command of Captain Brotherton, and pushed on with all speed by the northern side of the Little Rockies to intercept the Indians. These mountains are a range fifty miles in extent, running northwest and southeast. About ten miles beyond their northern spurs are the Bearpaw Mountains, with a low divide connecting the two. Miles could make rapid progress because his course led over the foothills and grassy plains.

He kept his Cheyenne scouts on the west side of the Little Rockies to keep him apprised of the Nez Perces' movements. These spies brought him word that the Indians' trail led over the pass between the two ranges. Miles kept the Little Rockies between his command and the Nez Perces' line of march. Thus he continued to approach them from an angle, and managed to keep his presence concealed from the Indians. To guard his movements further, the colonel ordered the soldiers not to hunt or disturb the vast herds of buffalo, deer, antelope, and elk which they frequently encountered.

On reaching the northern end of the Bearpaw Mountains, fifty miles northeast of Fort Benton, the Cheyenne scouts discovered the Nez Perces' camp, eight miles away. Miles reported to the Secretary of War that he broke camp at four o'clock on September 30. The command struck the trail near the head of Snake Creek and followed it to the Indian village, which they reached at 8 A.M. after a forced march of some two hundred miles.

It is thus described by Lieutenant, afterwards Captain, Henry Romeyn, of the Fifth Infantry:

The camp was located on a small stream called Snake Creek, as it proved in an excellent position for defense in a kidney-shaped depression covering about six acres of ground, along the western side of which the stream ran in a tortuous course, while through it, from the steep bluffs forming its eastern and southern sides, ran "coulees" from two to six feet in depth and fringed with enough sage brush to hide the heads of their occupants. Here the Nez Perce chieftain had pitched his camp and here he now made his last stand for battle.

According to the Indians a boy went out to secure his pony about the same hour (eight o'clock), and discovered Miles's Cheyenne scouts. The youth gave the alarm. Part of the warriors had time to hide behind a steep bank, and to take refuge in the entrenchments which it was customary for them to build at each important camp after the Big Hole battle. The Indians, however, had no time for concerted action, and they were unaware of the size of the opposing force.

Meanwhile, Miles's cavalry approached the village at a trot over the rolling, grass-covered prairie. In the crisp air the trot soon quickened to a gallop. As they rode over low ridges, Miles threw his troops into line of battle while in motion. "This gallop forward, preceding the charge, was one of the most brilliant and inspiring sights I ever witnessed on any field," the colonel writes. "It was the crowning glory of our twelve days' forced marching."

"My God!" cried Captain Hale, who commanded the Seventh Cavalry, "have I got to go out and be killed in such cold weather!" He was the personification of the dashing cavalry officer, with slouch hat jauntily perched to one side, and mounted on a mettlesome gray horse.

As they swept over a rise part of the leading battalions of the Seventh Cavalry and Fifth Infantry, preceded by Cheyenne and Sioux scouts, broke into a charge. With a pounding of hoofs over the turf, a creaking of saddles and jingle of bits they struck directly at the village.

The Indians were not completely surprised this time, though, and withheld their fire until the cavalry was within one hundred yards of their rifle pits. Then, instead of breaking and fleeing before the blue-coated soldiers thundering down on them, the Nez Perces stood up to the cavalry charge and poured a cool, deadly volley into the oncoming ranks. They were no ordinary red foe. Soon an empty saddle, and another, and another, appeared among the cavalrymen until the loss became alarming, and the soldiers had to retreat before the withering fire. Within five minutes the

38

Nez Perces had repulsed the first attack at the southwestern end of the camp. They were still fighting for their freedom, for their right to live as free-born human beings, and they must have realized, in desperation, that it would be their last fight.

When part of the cavalry took the bluffs east of the village, the Indians had to abandon a steep butte from which they had first directed their fire against the attacking force. As the mounted Fifth Infantry charged up behind the cavalry, they executed "left front into line" and halted at this crest. They had come up to the valley's edge where the camp was located. Dismounting, the men held their ponies by means of lariats. These troops with their long-range rifles delivered a murderous fire on the village. Their captured Sioux ponies, so accustomed to the firing of guns, stood quietly, and many began nibbling the grass! From the coulees, fifty yards away, the Nez Perces also poured a hot fire, picking off infantrymen and horses.

Captain Hale's K troop had first engaged the Indians, who were ranged on "cut-banks," or bluffs, twenty to thirty feet high. Curiously enough that officer, according to Miles, was the first one killed in the battle! His gray horse fell beside him with a mortal wound. Lieutenant Biddle was the next to fall—a singular coincidence that the only two bachelors at the post should be the first to die! It was the young lieutenant's first battle, too. Hale's ranks were almost decimated.

The battalion of Second Cavalry under Captain Tyler had swung slightly to the left, to attack in the rear and cut off the herds grazing on a high plateau behind the village. In the running fight that followed, Lieutenants Jerome and McClernand succeeded in capturing most of the horses and mules, about eight hundred to a thousand in number. The animals were corralled in a small valley in the rear of the command.

The Seventh Cavalry became separated. Captain Godfrey placed himself between his men and the Indians, and promptly his horse was shot under him. The animal pitched to the ground in a heap, stunning the officer. Trumpeter Herwood ran to his captain and fought off the advancing squad of warriors until Godfrey recovered consciousness and rejoined his troops.

The casualties among the soldiers became fearful. Lieutenant Baird, adjutant of the Fifth Infantry, had his left arm shattered and one ear shot away while he was carrying orders. Captain

Moylan of the Seventh Cavalry received a wound in the thigh. Another officer "had one shot through his belt, another carried away his field glass, while a third took off his hunting knife and cut the skin from an ear," writes Lieutenant Romeyn. "Creeping carefully up to the edge of the bluff to look over, a bullet instantly lifted the hat and a lock of hair for a Sergeant, and another went through the head of a comrade at his side."

So fierce and close was the fighting that the battalion of the Seventh had only one officer unwounded after the first charge. This man, Lieutenant Eckerson, remarked to Colonel Miles, "I am the only damned man of the Seventh Cavalry who wears shoulder straps, alive." That battalion had 53 killed and wounded out of 115, while the loss suffered by Captain Hale's troops amounted to over 60 per cent.

The reason so many officers were killed and wounded was because the warriors deliberately picked them off, for "wherever the Indians heard a voice raised in command there they at once directed their fire. . . ."

Mortality ran high among the Indian leaders also. Yellow Bull reports: "In the first day's fighting were killed Tuhulhutsut. . . . Looking Glass, Alokut [Joseph's beloved brother], and Pile of Clouds."

At the beginning of the attack, according to Romeyn, "a portion of the lodges had been struck and about one hundred ponies packed for the day's march." This band of women and children, defended by fifty or sixty warriors, drove the pack horses and made a bold dash for freedom. They were pursued by G troop of the Second Cavalry under Lieutenant McClernand. After galloping five miles from the village, the warriors halted to fight. The cavalrymen were busy keeping the captured ponies closely herded to prevent them from stampeding back to the Indians. Thus the Nez Perces were able to take the offensive "and forced the soldiers back toward the main body, although they failed in their attempts to retake the stock." Some of the warriors succeeded in reaching the shelter of the Indian camp again, where they aided in its defense. The others escaped, and probably made their way into Canada.

When the first attack began, Joseph was on the opposite side of the creek from the village. This is one of those rare instances in which we have any definite knowledge of his personal activities in battle. It is also unusual for an Indian chief to describe such experiences in his own words. He said:

We had no knowledge of General Miles' army until a short time before he made a charge upon us, cutting our camp in two, and capturing nearly all of our horses. About seventy men, myself among them, were cut off. My little daughter, twelve years of age, was with me. I gave her a rope, and told her to catch a horse and join the others who were cut off from the camp. I have not seen her since, but I have learned that she is alive and well.

I thought of my wife and children, who were now surrounded by soldiers, and I resolved to go to them or die. With a prayer in my mouth to the Great Spirit Chief who rules above, I dashed unarmed through the line of soldiers. It seemed to me that there were guns on every side, before and behind me. My clothes were cut to pieces and my horse was wounded, but I was not hurt. As I reached the door of my lodge, my wife handed me my rifle, saying: "Here's your gun. Fight!"

The soldiers kept up a continuous fire. Six of my men were killed in one spot near me. Ten or twelve soldiers charged into our camp and got possession of two lodges, killing three Nez Perces and losing three of their men, who fell inside our lines. I called my men to drive them back. We fought at close range, not more than twenty steps apart, and drove the soldiers back upon their main line, leaving their dead in our hands. We secured their arms and ammunition. We lost, the first day and night, eighteen men and three women.

At one o'clock in the afternoon Miles ordered a second charge, the object being to cut off the Indians' water supply. Companies A and D of the Fifth Infantry had lost every officer in the first assault, so Lieutenant Henry Romeyn was placed in command and ordered to attack the Indians on the southwest. Part of the Second and Seventh Cavalry closely engaged the Nez Perces in desperate fighting in broken ground intersected by draws on the north and east. While they did so, Captain Carver, Lieutenant Woodruff and the detachment of the Fifth Infantry under Romeyn "charged down the slope, along the open valley of the creek, and reached the west end of the Indian village." But, Miles reports to the Secretary of War, "the deadly fire of the Indians with magazine guns disabled 35 per centum of his [Romeyn's] men, and rendered it impossible for them to take the remainder of the village."

The Nez Perces had too strong a defensive position, Romeyn explained. Because of their withering fire the soldiers could not break through their lines. But fourteen men of Company I under Captain Carter of the Fifth Infantry did succeed in crossing the coulee and reached the lodges. It was these men whom Joseph engaged. His warriors immediately killed five outright—a third of their number—and the others concealed themselves in the draws and gullies until nightfall, when they were able to rejoin their comrades. Lieutenant Romeyn was shot through the lungs in this skirmish, but not mortally wounded.

The troops held their ground until Miles ordered them to withdraw. This proved to the colonel that any more charges would be accomplished at further severe loss to his men.

The soldiers, though, forced the Indians back to the ravines or "coulees" behind their camp. Here the Nez Perces entrenched themselves and easily defended their position against the troops. Indian women assisted in the work of increasing the entrenchments. In many cases they did all the digging by using knives and shovels made of frying pans with sharpened edges. This was accomplished after the first day, according to Yellow Bull. Some of the pits were dug separately and connected by underground passages. These trenches explain why the Indians' casualties were not greater, and why they were able to hold off the superior force of soldiers for five days.

Being unable to dislodge the Indians and suffering fearful losses, Miles withdrew his men at 3 P.M. and laid a siege after throwing a thin line of troops completely around the village. He was considerably worried by the fear that Sitting Bull would come to the Nez Perces' aid and stage another Custer Massacre before Joseph's surrender could be effected.

And, in truth, Joseph did try to establish contact with the Sioux. That very evening he sent six of his most trusted warriors to get re-enforcements from Sitting Bull. The unfortunate messengers, though, stopped at a village of Assiniboines, by whom they were all murdered, probably for their fine guns. It was apparently Joseph's plan to withstand the troops until Sitting Bull could come to his aid. When some of the former's messengers eventually did arrive, however, it was only to discover that the Sioux had learned hearty respect for the U.S. Army. Instead of gallantly joining the beleaguered Nez Perces, Sitting Bull and his people packed up bag and baggage and scampered forty miles farther north from the

Canadian border! Perhaps the timely approach of Howard's brigade may have lent speed to their heels.

Although fighting with their usual grim fearlessness, the Nez Perces did not harm any of the soldiers who fell within their lines, but only relieved them of arms and ammunition. "They even gave some of the wounded water after nightfall when it could be done with safety," writes Lieutenant Romeyn.

The weather turned stormy on the evening of September 30. Snow fell thickly, driven by a high wind that developed into a blizzard. This caused much suffering in both camps, especially among the wounded soldiers who were on higher ground and had no tents or shelters of any kind to protect them from the raw wind, snow, and cold. Nor could they have the comfort of a fire, for every light attracted the marksmanship of Indian sharpshooters. It was not until the next evening of October 1 that Captain Brotherton's wagon train arrived, bringing medical supplies, tents, blankets, and food.

Miles had brought his artillery into action and shelled the Indian camp with disastrous effect. He also sent a dispatch to Howard, saying he had the Nez Perces corralled.

The general had reached Carroll on the Missouri, October 1, and took a boat up the river to Cow Island, leaving Sturgis in command. October 3, Howard dashed on to join Miles, being accompanied by two aides—one, his son, Lieutenant Guy Howard, the other, Lieutenant C. E. S. Wood—and seventeen men, including the two faithful Nez Perce scouts, Old George and Captain John. Arthur Chapman, who had a Nez Perce wife, and was a good friend of Joseph's, also rode with the general in his capacity as official interpreter.

During the evening of October 2, Colonel Sturgis received a note by courier from Miles, informing him of the Bearpaw battle, and asking for re-enforcements. So Sturgis ferried his and Howard's command over the river and started to the relief of Miles with all the troops. Sturgis continued until he was within a two hours' march of the battlefield, when a courier from Howard apprised him of Joseph's surrender. Then he went into camp to await the general's return.

On the morning of October 1 Miles started negotiations for surrender with Joseph and some of his warriors. Joseph sent Yellow

Bull, a subchief, as his representative to meet the messenger of Miles, who entered the Nez Perce camp under a flag of truce. The report of this first interview and subsequent ones we have in Joseph's own words as follows:

Yellow Bull understood the messenger to say that General Miles wished me to consider the situation; that he did not want to kill my people unnecessarily. Yellow Bull understood this to be a demand for me to surrender and save blood. Upon reporting this message to me Yellow Bull said he wondered whether General Miles was in earnest. I sent him back with my answer, that I had not made up my mind, but would think about it and send word soon. A little later he sent some Cheyenne scouts with another message. I went out to meet them. They said they believed General Miles was sincere and really wanted peace. I walked on to General Miles's tent. He met me and we shook hands. He said, "Come let us sit down by the fire and talk this matter over."

Joseph was accompanied by some of his warriors, for Miles stated in his official report to the Secretary of War that at first the Indians seemed willing to surrender and brought along eleven rifles and carbines, but he thought they became suspicious "from some remarks that were made in English in their hearing," and so hesitated to lay down their arms. At any rate, Miles, in his own words, "detained" Joseph in his camp overnight. Meanwhile, he dispatched Lieutenant Jerome of the Second Cavalry to "reconnoiter" the Indian village, which is military parlance for orders to spy on the camp.

When that officer appeared in the village and there was no sign of Joseph, the Indians became distrustful. Yellow Bull himself seized the bridle of Jerome's black horse and pulled the lieutenant out of the saddle. Some of the young men wanted to kill him, but were restrained by Yellow Bull. While Joseph was held as a hostage in Miles's camp, Jerome was likewise "detained" as a prisoner, being confined in a damp, cold, underground passage. His Indian guards had to dance to keep warm in the freezing air. The battle continued intermittently, and they finally left him, saying, "We must fight again pretty soon to get warm."

Just why Miles "detained" Joseph he does not make clear. Perhaps he hoped to speed up the surrender by depriving the Nez Perces of their war chief, or perhaps he feared that Joseph might attempt to slip away, or plot some act of treachery if given his freedom. In any event Yellow Bull came into "Bear Coat's" camp to find out if Joseph was still alive and why he had not returned. Joseph complains:

General Miles would not let me leave the tent to see my friend alone.

Yellow Bull said to me: "They have got you in their power, and I am afraid they will never let you go again. I have an officer in our camp, and I will hold him until they let you go free."

I said: "I do not know what they mean to do with me, but if they kill me you must not kill the officer. It will do no good to avenge my death by killing him."

Yellow Bull was permitted to return to the village where he made good his word about holding Jerome. The next day mutual confidence was restored when Miles showed good faith by releasing Joseph, exchanging him for the lieutenant under a flag of truce midway between the two camps.

In later years Yellow Bull related the affair, from which we can infer that the Indians were almost starving while negotiations were under way:

After we kept Captain [Yellow Bull's mistake; Jerome was a lieutenant] Jerome in our camps for a day and night he wanted something to eat. I and Tom Hill [a half-breed Indian] told him that we had nothing he could eat; that he had better write a note to General Miles and ask him for something to eat. He wrote a note to General Miles, and Red Wolf's son took the message to General Miles, and we made an exchange of prisoners. . . .

Upon Joseph's return to the village he held a council with the surviving chiefs and found them divided about surrendering. "We could have escaped from Bear Paw Mountain," he says, "if we had left our wounded, old women and children behind. We were unwilling to do this. We had never heard of a wounded Indian recovering while in the hands of white men."

Again the battle was resumed.

General Howard approached Miles's camp after dark on a cold, snowy evening of October 4. He could see flashes of rifle fire from the pits of both sides. Miles, bringing his adjutant, Lieutenant Oscar Long, an orderly, and two or three soldiers all mounted, advanced across the prairie to meet the general's command.

Both parties dismounted, and Howard held out his hand, saying heartily, "Hello, Miles! I'm glad to see you. I thought you might have met Gibbon's fate. Why didn't you let me know?"

Instead of answering the question Miles replied with a cold, formal greeting to his superior officer, and asked the general to his tent while another was being prepared for Howard.

With his characteristic kindness and consideration for those beneath him in rank, Howard requested Miles to have the two Nez Perce scouts and Chapman well cared for, and then the others went on to the colonel's tent.

In the presence of his aide-de-camp, Lieutenant Wood, Howard promised to give Miles the credit for capturing the Indians. The colonel, Howard well knew, was ambitious for a brigadier generalship. Miles's wife was a niece of General W. T. Sherman, then General of the Army. Howard further promised not to take over command until after the surrender—a promise which he kept. Then, Wood recounts: "Colonel Miles' entire manner changed; he became cordial, thanked the General for all he had said . . ."

The officers then consulted on the details of bringing about a surrender. The general suggested that his two Nez Perce scouts, Captain John and Old George, who had accompanied him from Idaho and both of whom had daughters in the Indian camp, should be sent as emissaries to Joseph.

In their own tent later that night, Lieutenant Wood reproached Howard for his generous gesture, and reiterated his distrust of Colonel Miles. Again the general expressed implicit faith in Miles, and there the matter rested.

The next day before noon the two Nez Perce scouts parleyed in the village with the war chief and others in council. After much "running to and fro between the camps," Joseph sent his reply, to which White Bird agreed, saying, "What Joseph does is all right; I have nothing to say."

Joseph realized that further resistance was futile and that his hope for aid from Sitting Bull was vain. The terms of surrender as the war chief understood them are best explained in his own words:

I could not bear to see my wounded men and women suffer any longer; we had lost enough already. General Miles had promised that we might return to our country, with what stock we had left. I thought we could start again. I believed General Miles, or I *never would have surrendered*. I have heard that he has been censured for making the promise to return us to Lapwai. He could not have made any other terms with me at that time. I would have held him in check until my friends came to my assistance, and then neither of the generals nor their soldiers would have left Bear Paw Mountain alive.

. . .

True to his word, Joseph made a formal surrender at 2:20 P.M. on October 5, and all firing ceased.

I WILL FIGHT NO MORE

CHIEF JOSEPH

By virtue of its own merit as rhetoric and as literature, as well as the dramatic circumstances of its delivery, this is one of the great speeches in the history of the West. It was given on Bear's Paw Battlefield, south of Chinook, Montana, on Oct. 5, 1877, when Joseph of the Nez Percé at last found himself forced to yield to overwhelmingly superior forces. Probably no surrender was ever given in terms more simple and more moving: note the tangibility of the images of speech —blankets, heart, children, sun; note the reiteration of the elemental factors of defeat—fatigue, cold, hunger, death. Joseph does not say, "I am discouraged"; he says, "My heart is sick." He does not say, "We yield to superior force and guarantee to keep the peace"; he says, "From where the sun now stands I will fight no more, forever." He kept his promise, but the United States repudiated the one made to him. The text of the surrender speech is given here as recorded by James Mooney in "The Ghost Dance Religion and the Sioux Outbreak of 1890," *Fourteenth Annual Report* of the Bureau of Ethnology, Part II, 1892–93.

I AM tired of fighting. Our chiefs are killed. Looking Glass is dead. Toohulhulsate is dead. The old men are all dead. It is the young men who say yes or no. He who led the young men is dead.

It is cold and we have no blankets. The little children are freezing to death. My people, some of them, have run away to the hills and have no blankets, no food. No one knows where they are— perhaps freezing to death.

I want to have time to look for my children and see how many of them I can find. Maybe I shall find them among the dead.

Hear me, my chiefs. I am tired; my heart is sick and sad.

From where the sun now stands I will fight no more, forever.

THE RIVER

"... a prolonged cemetery of
adventurers ..."

THE SONG OF LEWIS AND CLARK

MRS. JOHN BAPTISTE CHARLES LUCAS

Upon the return of the Lewis and Clark expedition to St. Louis Sept. 23, 1806, leaders of the party were entertained at dinner by Mrs. John Baptiste Charles Lucas, who composed a song in Lewis' honor which was sung on that occasion. The first verse is given here, in its original French and in English translation. The incident is described by the hostess's daughter, Mrs. Anne Lucas Hunt, in the Missouri Historical Society's *Glimpses of the Past*, Vol. I, No. 6, May, 1934. Other data on the Lewis and Clark expedition will be found in this book in notes accompanying "The Story of Scammon," Captain Lewis' dog, in the section on animals.

LE Capitaine Louis, pour combler sa gloire,
Aux sources du Missouri s'en est allé boire,
Du mont ou ce fleuve sort,
Il a pris sa course au nord.

Captain Lewis, his glory to crown,
To the springs of the Missouri went to drink down,
From the mount where this river springs forth,
He made his journey to the north.

THE DISCOVERY OF THE THREE FORKS

PATRICK GASS

This account of the arrival of the Lewis and Clark party at the source of the Missouri River is from *Gass's Journal of the Lewis and Clark Expedition,* by Sgt. Patrick Gass, with analytical index and introduction by James K. Hosmer, published by A. C. McClurg. Chicago, 1904.

*S*ATURDAY *27th* [July 1805]. We continued our voyage early, and had a pleasant morning; proceeded on, and at 9 o'clock got through the small mountain. At the entrance of the valley, a branch of the Missouri comes in on the south side, about 60 yards wide; the current rapid but not very deep. Here we took breakfast, and having proceeded on a mile, came to another branch of the same size. There is very little difference in the size of the 3 branches. On the bank of the north branch we found a note Captain Clarke had left informing us, he was ahead and had gone up that branch. We went on to the point, and, as the men were much fatigued, encamped in order to rest a day or two. About 12 o'clock Capt. Clarke and his men came to our encampment, and told us they had been up both branches a considerable distance, but could discover none of the natives. There is a beautiful valley at these forks; and a good deal of timber on the branches, chiefly cottonwood. Also currants, goose and service berries, and choak-cherries on the banks. The deer are plenty too; some of the men went out and killed several today. Capt. Clarke was very unwell and had been so all last night. In the evening the weather became clear and we had a fine night.

Sunday 28th. As this was a fine day, the men were employed in airing the baggage, dressing skins and hunting. Capt. Clarke still continued unwell. Our squaw [Sacajawea] informed us, that it was at this place she had been taken prisoner by the Grossventers [Gros Ventres] 4 or 5 years ago. From this valley we can discover a large mountain with snow on it, towards the southwest; and expect to pass by the northwest end of it. Capt. Lewis had a meridian altitude here, which gave 45 22 34.5 north latitude. We also re-

mained here the 29th, which was a fine day, and the men chiefly
employed in the same way. Capt. Clarke is getting better.

. . .

Friday 9th [August 1805] . . . This morning our commanding
officers thought proper that the Missouri should lose its name at the
confluence of the three branches we had left on the 30th ultimo.
The north branch, which we went up, they called JEFFERSON;
the west or middle branch, MADISON; the south branch, about
2 miles up which a beautiful spring comes in, GALLATIN, and
a small river above the forks they called *Philosophy*. Of the 3
branches we had just left, they called the north *Wisdom,* the south
Philanthropy, and the west or middle fork, which we continued
our voyage along, retained the name of JEFFERSON.* We went
14 miles and encamped on the south side. Our two hunters killed
but one goat.

* The river which they named Wisdom became, on today's maps, the Big Hole,
though the name was retained for the *town* of Wisdom; Philanthropy was too
much for the early prospectors, who renamed it crassly the Stinking-water, but
after another generation it became, and remains, the Ruby. The middle fork for
which the explorers retained the name Jefferson became the Beaverhead; and
Philosophy became Willow Creek. Wisdom, Philosophy, and Philanthropy were
chosen by the explorers in honor of Jefferson, of whom these, they said, were
attributes.

TWELVE DAYS TO ST. LOUIS

This item appeared in *The Fort Benton Weekly Record* June 30, 1881, as the newspaper's reply to an inquiry from "a well known Helena gentleman." Today the flying time by regularly scheduled commercial airline from Great Falls, forty-five miles west of Fort Benton, to St. Louis is twelve *hours*. The story of the *Emily* as told by her skipper, Joseph LaBarge, is to be found in Hiram M. Chittenden's *History of Early Steamboat Navigation on the Missouri River*. The first steamer reached Fort Benton in 1859; the last—after the railroads had come into Montana—docked in 1890. Construction of Fort Peck dam in the 30's probably ended all possibility of river navigation beyond that point.

O N July 20th, 1862, the side wheel steamer, the Emily, left Benton for St. Louis and made the quickest trip ever made by any steamboat to that city. The time was twelve days. No boat has ever even approached this time, which would have been even more remarkably fast had she not been obliged to cut her own wood between Benton and Sioux City, in which operation four to five hours of each day was consumed.

The Emily also claims the honor of the quickest trip from St. Louis to Benton, the return trip being the one on which she scored the time above mentioned. She came up in 31 days and 23 hours, although being obliged to cut her own wood and towing a barge from Dauphin's rapids to Benton. The Emily was built for and owned by Messrs. LaBarge and Harkness, traders at this point, and was named after the daughter of the former. She was one of the fastest boats on the river; and Mr. Jo LaBarge, the present pilot of the Red Cloud, tells us that once he made a trip on her from St. Louis to the mouth of the Yellowstone in 20 days. She was finally sold to the Hannibal and St. Louis railroad and wore herself out in twelve years' service for that company. She was a remarkable boat in her day.

A TRIP TO THE STATES

J. ALLEN HOSMER

A sixteen-year-old boy wrote, printed, bound, and published the book from which this was taken—the second book to be published in Montana. (The first was Dimsdale's *Vigilantes of Montana*.) J. Allen Hosmer was the son of Hezekiah L. Hosmer, appointed by Abraham Lincoln as the first chief justice of Montana Territory, and accompanied his family West when he was fourteen. After the family's eastern trip described in his book, Allen returned to become clerk of his father's court, publish a newspaper for a few months (*Beaverhead News*), and set up and print his book. It was a 94-page volume on newsprint, bound in cardboard; he sold it for a dollar in gold dust. Only five or six copies are now known to exist and they were worth, at last commercial quotation, $1,600 each. One is in the Montana State Historical Society library and one in Montana State University library; the others are held outside of the state. The extracts used here are taken from *Sources of Northwest History*, published by Montana State University, Missoula, which reprinted Allen's story as edited by Edith M. Duncan and published in Vol. XII, No. 2 of *The Frontier*. The full title of his book was *A Trip to the States by Way of the Yellowstone and Missouri, with a Table of Distances*. In 1872 Allen moved with his family to California. There he was admitted to the bar at the age of thirty-five, and shortly before his death in 1907, Miss Duncan reports, he was appointed to the supreme bench of that state.

Introduction

I am about undertaking to write a brief sketch of a trip to the States by way of the Yellowstone and Missouri rivers, which was not only through a beautiful country, but was also very unpleasant.

As I have headed this pamphlet a trip to the States, I will commence at Virginia City in this Territory and finish at Detroit, Michigan.

The story will speak of the camping grounds, the boats, and the beauties of the river.

SEPT. 21, 1865—After a great deal of trouble getting ready, at last a light wagon drawn by two black horses drove up in front of the door and after putting on about half a ton then we all took a farewell glass of wine and got into the wagon. After getting in, one of the neighbors threw an old shoe after us, but the shoe went crooked and we supposed that it meant crooked luck, well, we started at 11 o'clock in the forenoon, and on ascending the divide between the Stinkingwater and Madison rivers, we encountered a storm of snow and rain, and having only a cloth cover to our wagon, we were rather wet when we had got across the divide.

At one o'clock we arrived at the Eight Mile House where some men were a little merry on account of having more liquor on board than they could comfortably carry. . . .

Sept. 22—At about six o'clock we arose and the first thing on the programme was to find our horses, we looked until half past seven, but saw no signs of them, then we got breakfast, and about half past nine we found the horses two miles down the road. . . .

About mid-way in the canyon, in crossing a sideling place in the road, the wheels of our light wagon with its heavy load broke, and the wagon and its contents after turning three times in the air, landed in a ravine thirty four feet from where we started, there were six of us in the wagon and not one of us was hurt, the tongue broke from the wagon and the horses stood still and looked on. Gingerbread, sugar, paper collars, quartz specimens, and divers and sundry other things were found here and there, we gathered them up and we got them to the top of the hill with difficulty on account of the hill being perpendicular. The fire arms landed on the chickens which we were taking to our ranch. . . .

Sept. 24—Left the ranch at about eight o'clock in a lumber wagon, . . . an old man came running up from the East Gallatin and said he had heard some Indians in the water at that place. Then to tell the truth I was frightened, I expected at every turn in the road to be met or pursued by a hostile band of Sioux or Cheyennes, but as good fortune would have it they were not Sioux but Flatheads who were friendly toward the whites but deadly enemies of the Crows who have their hunting grounds in this vicinity. . . .

Sept. 26—We arose very early, and harnessed up the horses and started without breakfast, after driving a few miles we came in

56

sight of the lofty peaks of Immigrant Gulch, and the green trees that border on the Yellowstone, at half past seven we entered the canyon, the rocks on either side rise to the enormous height of almost a mile. . . .

The scenery in this vicinity compares in grandeur with that of the Yo Semite valley in California only the trees are not so high.

We could not start on account of all boats not being built, we spent most of the day in and around the camp, and in the evening formed an assembly and made some rules. One of which was as follows. That they should not fire a gun in the Indian country, (you will see how well this rule was kept), after this was over we retired to our boat.

Sept. 27—Early this morning the boats were finished being thirty six in number and divided into four different fleets No. 1 Knox & Bradbury's fleet of 10 boats, these boats were sharp at the bow thirty two feet long, three feet high, eight feet wide in the centre, and four feet wide at the stern. The names of the boats in this fleet were as follows, No. 1. Jeannie Deans, 2. Montana, 3. (our boat) Antelope, 4. Lady Pike, 5. Helena City, 6. no name, 7. St. Louis, 8. Lady Jane, 9. Otter and 10. Autocrat.

The second fleet was Bivens' of nine boats, these were common flat boats, and were of different length they had small cabins on the stern, they set sail on the 26th and therefore I do not know the names of the boats.

The third, was the German Flats of nineteen boats these were common Flats or mud scows, the family boats had cabins but the others were the plain scow used in the states for hauling mud.

The boats spoken of above were all built of pine lumber. Fleet no. 4. belonging to Van Cleave & Hanson, consisted of four boats, built of Cottonwood lumber, and sharp at each end like the original Mackinaw boat, there were a few other boats which were built for use of private families, one of these was the handsomest boat in the outfit which they called the "Gipsey Nell" it was built similar to Knox's boats only on a smaller scale.

Having described the boats, I will now proceed to describe the trip.

This morning we hurried about and got our things from the wagon into the boat, and at ten o'clock our boat got its crew on board which consisted of the following named persons, Mrs. H. L. Hosmer, Miss S. E. Hosmer, H. L. Hosmer, L. E. Ingersoll of Wis-

57

consin, R. M. Campbell of Detroit, Edward Hosmer of Leaven-
worth, W. M. Buchanan of Sioux City, O. D. Barrett of Washington, D. C. Sheldon Schmidt, a dutchman from eastern Iowa and
myself. . . .

Sept. 28—Having learned that some of the Flat boats that were
to bring families were behind, we agreed to wait for them to come
up, at nine o'clock they arrived and we once more set sail, we ran
into rapids every half mile, just before reaching one of these rapids,
we landed to let the slow boats catch up, in landing, Schmidt (who
was almost always in trouble) attempted to take the rope ashore
by jumping from the bow of the boat, the stove being on the bow,
that set him to stumbling, and next moment he went head foremost into the river and the first thing he grabbed for was the stove,
but he did not hold on to that long, he grabbed an oar and with a
little assistance was saved with but the inconvenience of a good
ducking. O. D. Barrett caught the stove, thus the idea of going on
with uncooked meals soon obviated. Schmidt went back behind
a large boulder and changed his cloths, after that it was a byword
with the folks on our boat that "Schmidt when he went into the
Yellowstone, took the stove along for a life preserver. . . ."

Sept. 29—We arose very early, got breakfast at half past five and
were afloat at six, soon after starting we saw an Elk fight on one
of the distant hills. The river still continues to be full of rapids
and very dangerous ones, the country through which we are now
passing is an open plain, and seemed as if it were filled with
mounds. . . . Twelve miles below Sawyer's camp we passed the
mouth of the Big Rosebud river, which is about half a mile wide
at its mouth, and when we passed it looked rather shallow, we
went on and at half past five we turned a bend in the river, which
runs at the base of a large mountain, it looked as if it might be an
ambush for Indians, the river was not over four hundred yards
wide, notwithstanding the looks of this place our pilot made himself interesting by crossing and camping on the opposite side of
the river which was the worst of the two, I would not speak of this
if there had been any necessity of stopping, but the sun was over
an hour high, and we could get better camping grounds below. . . .

Sept. 30—We arose this morning at half past three, the dew
that fell during the night wet our blankets through a few minutes
after we arose a voice from our boat said a man was in trouble,

we went to see who it was and it turned out to be Schmidt who had gone to get some water to make coffee and fell head foremost down the bank, we got him out and his first exclamation was "Mine Got und Himmel." We set sail at twenty minutes after six, the country now breaks into Yellow sand stone cliffs it is from these rocks that the river receives its name. . . . The rapids still continue to be bad, at half past ten we came to a very bad one, a flat boat got upon a boulder in this rapid and could not be moved, a man started with a rope in a small row boat to be of assistance, but the current was so strong that it upset the boat, and the man floated down a short distance, when somebody threw him a rope which he succeeded in catching and was thus saved from a watery grave. Our boats came along just as this man started out, and our boat was the only one of the Mackinaw's that struck, and we landed on a boulder in the middle of the river, the rest of boats went on and waited for us a mile below, we were almost dipping water when we swung off, we expected every moment to see the bottom of our boat floating on ahead.

Oct. 1— . . . We slept on the bank until midnight, when waking up my ears were assailed with the intermingled cries and howlings of wolves, coyotes, night hawks, and other creatures, whose business it seemed to be to render "night hideous." Among other noises was a peculiar whistle, long, trilling and frequent, which came from different directions. This aroused my suspicions that all was not right, and that the Indians were in reality upon us, and were surrounding us, and signaling each other, to mark their progress. I roused the family and we changed our quarters to the boat, with the intention, as a last resort, to push out into the stream in case of an attack, but just as we had got fairly located in the boat, one of the guards came in, and on making known to him our apprehensions, he, on hearing the marvellous whistle, informed us that it was the call of the male to the female Elk, and was very common, in the rutting season with those animals. . . .

October 3.—We were afloat very early this morning with the rest of the fleet the pilot did not threaten us with hemp, but told us to take our place in the fleet which we accordingly did. During the day we passed a great many red sand stone cliffs described by Lewis & Clarke, and many other things described by them, among which were the Buffalo Shoals, these shoals are six miles in length, and the river is not more than two feet deep, in the deepest place on these shoals, we were two hours crossing these on account of very often running aground, and the moment we would strike bottom all the men would jump overboard and push the boat off, and we would start on again.

The bottom of the river on these shoals is hard yellow sand stone. The fall of three feet, spoken of by Lewis & Clarke as being at the end of these shoals has worn down, and only a rapid marks the spot where sixty years ago there was a waterfall.

About twelve miles below the Buffalo Shoals we passed the mouth of Tongue River which comes in from the south, we passed this river about 2 o'clock in the afternoon. Directly opposite the mouth of Tongue River is old Fort Alexander, which was used as a trading post of the North West Fur Co. from 1825. until 1850., this fort was built by Alexander Culbertson Esq. of Peoria, Ill. This fort is in the same condition as old Fort Sarpee, there being nothing left except two old chimneys.

Late in the afternoon we reached what is called the Bad Lands (proper) the cliffs with veins of coal grow more numerous, the cottonwood groves begin to disappear, and the soil is white sand, rapids are also becoming less frequent.

Our camping ground this night was in the bad lands on a sand bank, when we arrived the men enjoyed themselves by washing for Moss Agates and some very fine ones were found, some of the men went to hunting Elk and Deer, the bullets whizzed around a persons head as if a battle was going on, one Elk and one black tailed deer were all that was killed, we had Elk for supper, and slept in our boats. . . .

October 5.—This morning we arose at half past five, it was a very beautiful morning, and soon after starting we came in sight of blue mountains in the distance, we expected to reach the Missouri by evening, but we were deceived, we passed more of the red hills spoken of by Lewis & Clarke.

At about nine o'clock we passed the mouth of Powder River, which comes from the south. At half past ten we heard a loud roaring ahead, not unlike that of a waterfall, we expected the noise came from a rapid that we had dreaded from our start, which Lewis & Clarke called Wolf Rapid, from the fact of seeing a wolf on a boulder in the rapid, it was what we expected, soon after hearing the noise we came in sight of white surges in the distance, we sail on, the "Jeannie Deans" piloted by Davis entered the rapid first and in trying to avoid the white surges, landed on a rock.

The "Montana," piloted by R. J. Paulison of Haekensack, N.J., followed Davis and got on a rock at the bow, the current then took the boat around and it struck on a boulder at the stern, it was now aground both at the bow and stern, and in a helpless condition. Our boat came next piloted by Edward Hosmer, who made for the white waves, the rest followed us, and all passed through in safety, except No. 6 which received a slight injury at the head of the rapid, Davis' boat got on a rock close to another that stuck out of the water, and one man got out and pushed it off, Paulison as this boat passed threw a rope, which was caught, and they all got off safely. This rapid is almost as wild as those of the Niagara or St. Lawrence rivers.

We camped below and looked at a vein of coal. Wolf Rapid is the last rapid of the Yellowstone, and by far the worst. Today the scenery was large bluffs and high banks. At evening we camped on a sand bank about a quarter of a mile from a small clump of trees, to which place we had to go for wood, some of our men while out after wood, came across an old Indian lodge, and in this lodge they found an old log covered with hyeroglyphics, which were made with some black substance. We drew a sketch of these hyeroglyphics, and I have tried to have them interpreted but as yet have succeeded no further than to find out that they belong to the Blackfeet Indians.

During the evening a very beautiful Aurora Borealis appeared in the north and lit up the whole surrounding country. These lights were so bright, and the night air was so chilly, that we could imagine ourselves in the Polar seas very easily. . . .

October 6.—We left this morning in advance of the other boats, but were passed soon after, and were behind most of the day there being only one or two Flat boats with us. . . .

At about ten o'clock we saw as we supposed, Indians hunting Buffalo, but were not certain whether it was or not, we being behind the others, it was most likely imagination.

We have been looking for the Missouri all day but see no signs as yet, the river is wider and the banks are like the Missouri. In the afternoon we came to a place where the river looked as if it had stopped, one of the men of the flat boat saw this, and said in a forlorn hope sort of a tone "I guess the river's played out," but the river had not played out. . . .

October 7.— . . .

Today we passed a great many curiously formed banks resembling mason work. The banks grow lower and the river wider. We sailed along a little behind the fleet all day. About three o'clock we heard a tremendous firing a little way ahead, we did not know but what the other boats had been attacked by Indians, but it was not so, after going on about a mile, we found the meaning of the firing was that the boats had reached the looked for Missouri.

Where the Yellowstone empties into the Missouri it is about a mile wide, below the mouth the Missouri is the same width as the Yellowstone, but above the mouth it is not much more than wide enough for a good sized steamer to pass through.

We took a farewell look at the Yellowstone and sailed on, after going two miles we passed Ft. William an old ruined fort that was used by the North West Fur Company, some years ago. . . .

After supper (knowing there were no rapids ahead) we started for a nights sail.

At seven o'clock the moon rose just as we were passing the Glass Hills, these hills are on the south side of the river, they receive their name from their smooth appearance, while passing these hills the boys amused themselves by hallooing and hearing the echo, which reminded us of the Hudson Highlands, it being very distinct, they soon got tired of hallooing, after they got through, an Englishman, on No. 6 sang the song "When first I went to sea," he sung it very well, and we felt quite at home during the evening. . . .

October 8.—We landed at half past three for breakfast under a high bank, and were off at five, we sailed through a desolate looking country all day during the day we passed the mouth of the Big Bombese or as it is often called the Big Muddy river, at this river there is a large bend in the Missouri which is about half a mile across, and twelve miles around. . . .

October 9.—This morning we landed on a sand bar at six o'clock for breakfast, after breakfast we started and sailed on with a head wind all day. . . .

October 10.—This morning before daylight we were hailed by some Indians in the following words, "Charley come out cheer," as soon as we heard this all heads were down, and rifles were taken in hand, but as the Indians did not fire at us, we thought we would follow their example.

This day it was very windy and also very cold, at seven o'clock we landed to get wood, and after getting some we started.

The country through which we are now passing belongs to the Assinaboines, which are a very treacherous tribe of Indians, they go on the principle of to-day a friend to-morrow an enemy.

Soon after breakfast we passed the mouth of the Little Missouri River, it is a small stream and comes from the south.

During the morning Schmidt got a little mad and wasn't going to row, and made himself disagreeable generally, finally Major Barrett spoke up and said now you can see the reality of Mr. Lincolns joke the difference between an Amsterdam dutchman, or any other . . . dutchman," this raised a laugh, and succeeded in quieting Schmidt. . . .

At five o'clock we turned a curve in the river, and right in front of us was Fort Berthold, this fort is situated on a very high bank with a vein of coal running through it, this coal is all that they use at the fort for fires. . . .

October 17.—We started this morning before sunrise, and went along "kiting," as the saying is.

After going seventeen miles, we passed Fort Pierre, this is on the west side of the river, and all that remains of it is a number of old chimneys, this place is considered half way from St. Louis to Fort Benton, we did not stop at this place.

At about noon we came in sight of a steamer tied up at the Fort Sully Landing, again the crew were going to desert the boat, we sailed on and found the steamer to be the "Calypso," which in the employ of the Government, for the use of the Indian Commission who had come up to treat with the Sioux Indians.

Major Barrett and our family left the mackinaw for the steamer. . . .

October 19.—This morning we saw a very fine eclipse of the sun. . . .

October 22.—To-day being Sunday we were on the boat most of the day, in the evening the Rev. Mr. Reed delivered a sermon on "Faith," it was a very fine discourse.

October 23.—We are still in quarters and do not know when we will get away. It is raining and snowing, consequently we spent the day in the cabin. The pilot begins to complain, and says, "it will be impossible to get the boat down this season," the river is falling tow or three inches every twenty four hours, and dark

63

prospects of getting down begin to loom up, we have very good meals, and have to enjoy ourselves by sitting in the cabin.

October 25.—Still in quarters and no prospect of departing very soon.

October 25.—A messenger arrived about noon from Col. Pattee, and reported to the Commissioners, that he left the Colonel the night before, one hundred miles back on the Fort Rice road, with fifty Indians belonging to the Ogalala Sans Arc, Minneconjou, Onkpahpah and Blackfeet bands of Sioux, and would be at Fort Sully in four days, and they wanted the Commissioners to wait, and treat with them.

The river is still falling, and the pilot is still complaining.

In the evening the Commissioners held a meeting and passed a resolution, to the effect that, "If the Indians did not arrive on Thursday the boat should start on Friday, after hearing this we retired hoping the Indians would not arrive.

October 26.—It is still very cold, and floating ice appears in the river, the pilot still complains and says he cannot get down. The Indians do not arrive, and the Commission agree that the boat shall start to-morrow, and General Curtis, Governor Edmunds, Judge Guernsey and Mr. Hitt, will remain and receive the Indians, and then go over-land and meet the boat at Sioux City. We were all very glad to hear that the boat was going to start in the morning, and the inmates of the boat spent the evening in playing muggins, euchre, whist, dominoes and backgammon.

October 27.—This morning at ten o'clock the fires were made in the furnaces, the above named gentlemen left the boat, and a company of soldiers commanded by Col. Thornton (commander of the post at Fort Randall) came on board.

At a quarter past eleven they fired a howitzer which meant they were ready to start. At a quarter of twelve, the Calypso with her:
"streamers sailing in the wind,"
was afloat. Soon after starting there was a report that the boat was on fire we went to see where it was, and found the tar covering of the back deck to be in a blaze, but with a few buckets of water we succeeded in extinguishing it without it doing much damage. At two o'clock we stopped to wood, they soon got enough wood, and then they started, after going half a mile they stopped on account of a sand bar, which happened to come in our way, we soon got off, then sailed down five miles and then stopped to wood

again, at four o'clock we again started, we ran very nicely until we reached the foot of Roys Island (eight miles below Fort Sully,) when we again got aground, they began working with the spars, and they worked away until half past nine we got off, when we ran back to last place we took on wood, and camped there for the night.

October 28.—Early this morning the Captain took four men and a yawl and went down and sounded the water on the bar. At ten o'clock the boat again started, and again struck the bar, they then began to work with the spars and nigger, and at two o'clock we got off, and started back to the old wood yard, we took on a good supply of wood, and then started down the river, we had no sooner reached the bar than we struck again, they again went to work and got off at eight in the evening, they were sounding the greater part of the time, and the deepest place on the bar was two feet, and the boat was drawing thirty inches. After getting off the bar we started back to the wood yard for the night.

Captain Morrisson of Keokuk, Iowa (of whom I have heretofore spoken) was playing on a violin in the evening, while the ladies on the boat sung. I was passing behind his chair and accidentally touched his head, and then turned around to excuse myself, when, what should I behold but a wigg on the floor and Captain Morrisson's bald pate exposed to view. He seemed a little embarrassed, but soon got his wig and put it on, amid the laughter of the passengers.

October 29.—This morning we again started, and were again stopped by the bar, at noon we got off. The Captain now began to feel discouraged, and was going to take the boat back to Fort Sully and lay up for the winter, the Commission would not agree to this, but they made an agreement that everything should be taken from the boat and then try it once more, and if they did not succeed they could return to Sully for the winter. So they set sail up stream, and took on a large quantity of wood. They then started back, they landed at the head of the bar and put off all the cargo, except the ladies and children, the passengers and soldiers started on foot for the lower end of the bar, a distance of four miles, and the Calypso put on as much steam as she could without "bustin her biler," and then started for the bar, this time she succeeded in making it. We went down and got on board of her. We could not leave on account of the goods not being on board they had to send to the fort for wagons to take the cargo around the bar, they arrived late in the afternoon, and the goods on board by eight o'clock.

In the evening the Rev. Mr. Reed preached, after which we retired, rejoicing in the great event of the day. . . .

October 31.—Started this morning before daylight, and while we were at breakfast we heard a tremendous thumping on the bottom of the boat, cups of coffee were upset, the table was cleared, and the passengers all hurried to the deck to see what the matter was. It turned out to be a reef of rocks which the boat had run on, they are very bad in low water, but when the river is high they can be passed over without any difficulty. The river at this season was very low, and was also filled with floating ice, and this hindered the pilot's steering. We were on these rocks until three o'clock in the afternoon, they had the spars at work a little while but they didn't seem to do any good, so they stopped them. After they found the spars would do no good, the mate and four men went ashore and made a "dead man." A "dead man" is four sticks planted in the ground, and an anchor or a stout piece of wood is placed between them, (we used an anchor.) a rope was attached to the anchor, and brought on the boat, they then wound the rope around the capstan, which is worked by the nigger engine, we broke four hawsers, and then did not get off, so we tried a fifth one and with it succeeded, after getting off the boat swung, and hit another rock, the jar was so great that it sent a soldier overboard, he had on a heavy blue overcoat and cape, when he fell the cape went over his head, he managed to get this off from his head, and then struck out for shore, but before he got there he landed on a sand bar, and waited for the yawl to come to his rescue. He was brought on board chilled through and his first words were "The boat was too slow for me, and I thought I could reach Fort Thompson before it." Dr. Wood was ready with a hot whisky toddy, the soldier partook of it and then visited a warm fire, at which place he spent the day. . . .

November 10.—We were afloat early. About breakfast time we passed through the Heron's Roost, this is a very narrow place in the river it being not more than a hundred feet wide, and very deep. . . .

. . . After dinner we ventured on deck, and a short distance ahead saw a yellow sand stone bluff, this is the first I remember of seeing since leaving old Fort Clarke. At the foot of this bluff was the mouth of a river, I asked what river it was, and was informed that it was the Big Sioux, which forms the boundary between Dakotah and Iowa, just after passing this, we came in sight of houses, Judge Hubbard told me this was Sioux City. We had really reached the States and our "har" was on our head.

We soon arrived at the landing, got our baggage ashore, and left the boat. We went to the Wauregan House and got rooms, and had made ourselves contented until Sunday night when the stage started for the rail-road. . . .

The Wauregan House, is on the river bank, and is shaded by four or five maple trees. In the evening the enmates of the boat and hotel, had a supper and dance, I being tired went to bed.

November 11.—This morning when we arose, we saw the Calypso winding her way under Floyd's Bluff, this was the last we saw of her she was sunk by a cake of ice, at levee in St. Louis, the following month. . . .

At nine o'clock P.M., the stage drove up in front of the hotel, and only fourteen got on board, besides the baggage and express matter, there were three seats in the coach, and ten occupied them, the other four rode outside with the driver. After going a mile, we all had to get out of the coach, to walk across the bridge over Floyd Creek, because the bridge was full of holes, we took a look at it. In the Middle States, people would hardly trust themselves to walk across such bridges as these, let alone driving a heavily loaded team over. After getting across we all crowded in, and the rattling of the old coach was once more heard.

At twelve o'clock we arrived at American Town, twenty miles from Sioux City, I wanted to see what sort of a town it was, and with difficulty got a peep through the window, and saw the town, this town contains one house and a barn, the people in this country go on the principle of one house a village, two houses a town, and three or more houses a city.

We left this place with a drunken driver named Macklehaney. After going eight miles we came to a bridge, and this fine specimen of a driver, missed the road. The passengers were all asleep, we felt an unusual jar, we woke up and found one side of the coach, five feet higher than the other, the wheels on left hand side had gone off the bridge, we all hurried to the door, and such scrambling was never seen before. Lieut. Rouse, of Poughkeepsie, N.Y., got to the door and was seized with cramps, and it was fun to see them pitch out over him.

A few stayed back and got the coach out of difficulty, while the rest walked on, this was the first night I ever walked on the open prairie, the night was calm, and falling stars could be seen in all parts of the heavens, and we had a very nice tramp "by the beautiful light of the moon," after going two miles the coach overtook us. We jumped in and we were soon in the land of Morpheus.

. . .

Having finished this pamphlet, I must now go to work and make a few apologies. My readers will notice, that in a great many places where there ought to be full stops, nothing appears but comma's, my reason for this is, I had but one small font of type, and scarcely any capitals. One large "W" was all of that letter I had.

Secondly, I must make an apology for the register of the pages, having nothing but a little hand press, and being unable to print more than one page at a time, the register would very seldom print right.

This is my first effort at writing. And having read the printed edition, I find a great many grammatical mistakes, which I must ask you to overlook.

And I also behold more than one typographical error, but they happen in some of the best regulated offices, and besides I don't profess to be a first class typo. Through the kindness of Major Bruce, in lending me a font of type, I am enabled to give a list of the distances on the Missouri River.* . . .

---

* Young Hosmer, a conscientious and painstaking reporter, completed his book with a mile-by-mile log of the Missouri, listing every island, bar, rapid, and fort or landing all the way from Fort Benton to St. Louis.

TWO SONGS OF THE RIVER

Singing was an essential part of the French riverman's life and work. The boat captains usually led the songs, choosing their favorites which had certain rhythms to which they wished the crew to adapt their oar-strokes. The *patron*, or captain, would sing the first verse and his crew would come in on the chorus. The first song given here was one favored by Manuel Lisa in the famous race up the Missouri in 1811 between his boat, the best keelboat ever on the Missouri, and the Astorians, led by Wilson P. Hunt. Hunt's party started out 19 days and 240 miles ahead of Lisa, but the latter, averaging 18 miles daily for 60 days, overtook and passed the Astorians. Accounts of the race by men who were on the boats may be found in Thwaites's *Early Western Travels,* Vols. V and VI. Lisa's song apparently is a very simplified version of an old French air, *"En roulant ma boule."* The other song printed here, "Malbrouck," was a favorite of the French *voyageurs* on the Missouri. Marie Antoinette heard this sung to her baby by the nurse; Napoleon sang it as he started his disastrous Russian campaign in 1812; Beethoven used the theme in 1813; the French of New Orleans and of Montreal brought it to America's rivers—and we are familiar with its melody today, for it is the tune to which we sing "For He's a Jolly Good Fellow." Malbrouck was Marlborough (1650–1722), famous general-statesman ancestor of Winston Churchill; the French sang this song as a derisive funeral dirge for him while he was fighting them. The songs are given here in English translation; the rivermen, of course, sang them in French.

The Three Ducks

BEHIND our house there is a pond,
   Fal lal de ra.
There came three ducks to swim thereon:
All along the river clear,
Lightly, my shepherdess dear,
   Lightly, *fal de ra.*

There came three ducks to swim thereon,
   Fal lal de ra.
The prince to chase them he did run
All along the river clear,
Lightly, my shepherdess dear,
   Lightly, *fal de ra.*

69

The prince to chase them he did run,
  Fal lal de ra.
And he had his great silver gun
All along the river clear,
Lightly, my shepherdess dear,
  Lightly, *fal de ra.*

Malbrouck

Malbrouck has gone a-fighting,
  Mironton, mironton, mirontaine,
Malbrouck has gone a-fighting—
But when will he return?

Perchance he'll come at Easter
Or else at Trinity Term.

But Trinity Term is over
And Malbrouck comes not yet.

My Lady climbs her watch tower
As high as she can get.

She sees her page approaching,
All clad in sable hue:

"Ah page, brave page, what tidings
From my true lord bring you?"

"The news I bring, fair Lady,
Will make your tears run down;

"Put off your rose-red dress so fine,
And doff your satin gown.

"Monsieur Malbrouck is dead, alas!
And buried, too, for aye;

"I saw four officers who bore
His mighty corse away.

"One bore his cuirass, and his friend
His shield of iron wrought;

"The third his mighty saber bore,
And the fourth—he carried nought.

"And at the corners of his tomb
They planted rose-marie;

"And from their tops the nightingale
Rings out her carol free.

"We saw, above the laurels,
His soul fly forth amain;

"And each one fell upon his face
And then rose up again.

"And so we sang the glories
For which great Malbrouck bled;

"And when the whole was ended
Each one went off to bed.

"I say no more, my Lady,
  Mironton, mironton, mirontaine,
I say no more, my Lady,
As nought more can be said."

A JOURNEY IN A BARGE

FATHER NICHOLAS POINT, S.J.

Jesuit Father Point was transferred in 1847, after less than a year in Montana, to Canada, over his protest. He set out by barge from Fort Lewis, boarded a steamer at Fort Union for St. Louis, and went from there to Ontario. He made repeated requests to his superiors to be allowed to return to Montana, but was not permitted to do so—apparently because of his poor health. He died in Quebec in 1868 at the age of seventy. This condensed account of his trip is from A Journey in a Barge on the Missouri from the Fort of the Blackfeet (Lewis) to That of the Assiniboines (Union): Particulars Edifying or Curious, by Father Nicholas Point, S.J. It was reprinted in Mid-America, January, 1931.

I LEFT Fort Lewis on May 19, 1847, which was the day of its funeral or rather of its transference; * for all the transportable materials which had served in its construction were brought down on rafts (*cajeux*) about three miles to a point on the opposite bank, a location preferable to the other one under the three-fold respect of beauty, fertility, and the convenience for trade.

However, on leaving the land in which my heart had struck root so deeply, I could not help sighing while I repeated what a Persian traveler once said in the catacombs of Rome: "So here, as elsewhere, everything changes and all things pass away very quickly." It is true, yes, for the things of this world, but what will not pass away, so I hope, are the riches amassed for heaven during the winter. The denizens of this fort will recall with gratitude Christmas Night, Easter Day, the adult baptisms, the great number of persons brought back to their religious duties, while the Cross which soars aloft in the neighborhood of this cradle of religion will teach travelers coming after us that this land, however desolate it may appear, has been verily a land of benediction, not only for the seven hundred souls there brought forth, but even more so for those who have listened here to the voice of the Lord. . . .

* In 1850, three years after this move, Fort Lewis was renamed Fort Benton, in honor of Thomas Hart Benton, renowned United States Senator from Missouri and friend of the American Fur Company, whose post it was.

(May 29) Today is the Feast of the Holy Trinity. Thanks be to God and to the good disposition of the crew, I have been able to say Holy Mass. Time given to God is never lost. In spite of the threat of a contrary wind, the day was almost what one might wish and the evening charming. The sun, about to finish its course and veiled behind a less transparent sheet of air, had exchanged its fires for the color of ruby. Above its disc, the rotundity of which was plainly visible against an azure background, was suspended a group of clouds shaded with purple, blue and violet in the form of drapery while a row of tall trees casting their shade into the river brought out all that beauty in relief.

What is the crew doing in presence of so rich a landscape? While the men, by the rapidity of their strokes, gave to our barges the appearance of so many chariots competing for a racing-prize, their wives, who were gathered on the platform of the craft, the children being the while under the pilot's eyes, were praying and singing hymns in honor of the Queen of Angels. Never had this desert land heard such hymns. . . .

(May 31) A more than ordinary wind having started up, we had to think of making haste, which gave me occasion to observe how a skillful pilot goes about it to overcome the greatest difficulties of his art, which are to be found in struggling victoriously against perils with a tired-out crew. How did he go about it? Always the first at duty, he (Michel Champagne) gave to the others an example of patience and courage, and as he was equipped with stature, strength and address quite beyond the ordinary, everything contributed to give the rowers an esteem for his person. But what won him together with esteem the hearts of all was the circumstance that he knew how to mingle execution and orders with the gentleness of appeal. Music alone would render all the tones he could employ for his purpose. Here are some of his expressions *recto tono:* "Forward, my dandies! Let us make that point! Courage now! Courage now! Do you see that snag? Don't get stuck on it! Look out for the branches! Make for land! Fine, my good fellows! Here we are on land! It's all over tomorrow! Good appetite, now!"

A mariner never lacks good appetite and so they sup in high spirits. This over, pipes are lit and there is chatting—about what? About the rest which the morrow will bring with it, about the discharge of cannon and the reception that will be given them.

The next day (June 1) a magnificent sun. Its radiant globe stands up under our eyes. Two swans, white as snow, pass tranquilly on our right. A slight contrary wind is blowing but not enough to prevent the barge from going ahead or the cannon from being heard, for scarcely had the first stroke of our oars hit the air than the fort's (Union) flag is run up. Presently the cannon are replying, the walls are sighted, the fort's entire personnel draws near, the barges stop, salutes are given, greetings are exchanged. Finally, comes handshaking and every token of friendship and sign of joy and the whole affair winds up with a banquet which gives pleasure at once to those who give it and those who partake. "For amid the repast the prodigal guests fill up their glasses with coffee as though it were good wine and so banish fatigue."

WHITE CASTLES

STANLEY VESTAL

This appreciation of Montana's most sadly neglected scenic wonderland—the badlands or "breaks" of the Missouri River, which extend from a short distance below Fort Benton all the way to Fort Peck—is from a recent addition to the popular "Rivers of America" series published by Farrar & Rinehart. It is Stanley Vestal's *The Missouri*, published in 1945. Stanley Vestal (Walter Stanley Campbell) has written many books on the West during a career extending over the past twenty years, has edited several others, and is a well-known contributor to magazines. Born in Kansas, he was a Rhodes scholar and a Guggenheim fellow; he has been associated with the University of Oklahoma for thirty years and since 1939 has been professor of English there.

AT intervals above Fort Peck for hundreds of miles the Missouri River affords some of the most extraordinary scenery in North America. All early travelers devote page upon page and plate upon plate to describing and portraying the marvels along the stream. Even the matter-of-fact Lewis and Clark were carried away by what they saw, and the precise and scientific Prince Maximilian compares the scenery with that of parts of Switzerland, remarking that he was reminded "of the Mettenberg and the Eiger, in the Canton of Berne." The curious pinnacles, he says, looked "like the glacier des Bossons in the valley of Chamouny." Continually he refers to the valley of the Rhine.

The names given to landmarks along the stream, such as Citadel Bluff, Cathedral Rock, Eagle Rock, Haystack Butte, Burned Butte, give only a faint idea of the variety of striking formations to be seen there; naming them would exhaust the ingenuity of the most imaginative geographer. Of course, these strange structures must be seen from the river to be fully appreciated, and to-day few travelers pass that way. Throughout the course of its most beautiful and striking scenery, the Missouri is almost without a visitor. The Montana State Guide Book virtually ignores that scenic solitude. Photographers and painters neglect it—a fact as curious and incredible as the country itself.

Moreover, all this region, though now so lonely and neglected, is rich in historic sites—old campgrounds of the earliest explorers, old trading posts and forts, old steamboat landings, and Indian battlefields, such as that where Sitting Bull, singlehanded, killed the Crow chief, or the place where he saved the life of that enemy boy, Little Assiniboin, from his own bloodthirsty warriors, afterward adopting the lad as his "brother." To one who knows the Indian history of the plains, almost every mile along the stream suggests a story.

But now that the Fort Peck Dam has flooded the valley upriver for nearly two hundred miles, some of these historic sites and much fine scenery are under water. Until the dam breaks or the Missouri dries up there will be no more paintings made of that part of the stream.

Fortunately many of the finest things lie above this artificial flood.

One of the strangest and most striking sights along the river, painted by Karl Bodmer and enthusiastically described by his master, Prince Maximilian, stood not far below the mouth of the Musselshell.

One afternoon the prince was in his keelboat speeding upriver before a brisk favoring breeze. He sailed around the bend and saw, to his astonishment, two handsome castles crowning hills on the south bank. Apparently the roofs were of yellowish-red tiles, contrasting agreeably with the snow-white façades, both regularly marked by windows. The middle-aged, untidy little man peered through his spectacles at that amazing vision; he was quite ready to go ashore and pay a visit to those imposing buildings.

It was with some difficulty that his guides persuaded the prince that his "castles" were actually detached sections of a long horizontal stratum of white sandstone, running through the hills on that side. His "windows," they said, were simply perpendicular slits weathered out in the face of the stone and casting shadows, while the "roof" was not of tile but was merely the remnant of an upper, thinner stratum. Nothing daunted, the prince stoutly dubbed his rocks the White Castles, and so they have been called to this day.

But the White Castles are only the beginning of the amazing architectural scenery on the Upper Missouri. Above these it flows through Badlands of a most extraordinary and romantic appearance. Cliffs rise in many places nearly straight up from the water two or three hundred feet, formed of very white sandstone which weathers readily but lies protected under two or three horizontal layers of hard white freestone, covered by the dark, rich loam of the neighboring plain. This plain extends back a mile or so, where rocky cliffs again rise abruptly for perhaps another two hundred feet. Erosion has carved the soft sandstone into a thousand striking figures and majestic shapes. Everywhere one sees what appear to be ranges of large freestone buildings adorned with pale pilasters, long handsome galleries, pinnacles and parapets adorned with statuary, columns with pedestals and capitals entire standing upright or rising pyramidally one above the other until they terminate in a spire or finial.

These are varied by niches, alcoves, grottoes, and have the customary appearance of desolated magnificence.

To complete the illusion, great numbers of martins have hung their nests on every jutty, frieze, buttress, or coign of vantage and hover in flocks about these time-eaten towers. There seems no end to the visionary enchantment which surrounds the traveler—spires, domes, pallid ramparts, ruined balustrades, shrines, palaces, and terraced skyscrapers stand everywhere, buttressed and symmetrical, enriched with monuments and weathered statues thick as upon some old cathedral.

Passing between these silent, natural walls gives one a feeling of visiting the ruins of some ancient city. A man half expects the inhabitants to appear suddenly from shadowy doorways or to look out between the battlements topping some grim old keep. He has the feeling that he is trespassing, intruding. If the climate up there were a little milder, one might expect people to go and chisel out rooms in one of those neat sandstone piles and move right in. Walls and roof are there already. All that is lacking is an interior. There is nothing quite like all this in North America.

In our own time a poet has best celebrated the charms of this part of the river:

"Bad Lands? Rather the Land of Awe! . . .

"Rows of huge colonial mansions with pillared porticoes looked from their dizzy terraces across the stream to where soaring mosques and mystic domes of worship caught the sun. It was all like the visible dream of a master architect gone mad. Gaunt, sinister ruins of mediaeval castles sprawled down the slopes of unassailable summits. Grim brown towers, haughtily crenellated, scowled defiance on the unappearing foe. Titanic stools of stone dotted barren garden slopes, where surely gods had once strolled in that far time when the stars sang and the moon was young. Dark red walls of regularly laid stone—huge as that the Chinese flung before the advance of the Northern hordes—held imaginary empires asunder. Poised on a dizzy peak, Jove's eagle stared into the eye of the sun, and raised his wings for the flight deferred these many centuries. Kneeling face to face upon a lonesome summit, their hands clasped before them, their backs bent as with the burdens of the race, two women prayed the old, old, woman prayer. The snow-white ruins of a vast cathedral lay along the water's edge, and all about it was a hush of worship. And near it, arose the pointed pipes of a colossal organ—with the summer silence for music.

"With a lazy sail we drifted through this place of awe; and for once I had no regrets about that engine. The popping of the exhaust would have seemed sacrilegious in this holy quiet." *

The scene, however, is not always so solemn, for there are many grotesques and weird, amusing figures which suggest all manner of fantastic animal and vegetable creatures. It is a haunt fit for speckled moon-calves. Having shown what order and magnificence can do, it appears that Nature produced these gargoyles in a more lighthearted mood—the timeless jests of Mother Earth. Yet these uninhabited "cities" were not always so. All over the astonishing castles, fortresses, altars, and proud towers mountain sheep cavorted in the good old days. They ran up cliffs like monkeys and marched across the face of steep bluffs like flies. Hunters were fond of their flesh and their skins, and the Indians loved to make spoons of their great curving horns. In fact, in some Indian languages the name given the animal is "spoon-horn." Spoons made of the horns of the rams are often beautiful shapely things, yellow, clouded like jade, or translucent—and quite capacious too, holding a quart or more. They are, in fact, ladles, and serve the purpose of a cup or bowl.

When chasing bighorns over rugged country, the hunter, gasping after his climb, might see the animal apparently leap into space from the edge of the cliff. Hurrying up to look down the dizzy height, he expected to see the ram lying dead at the bottom. But

* See *The River and I*, John G. Neihardt, (New York, 1910), pp. 141–142.

78

no such luck. There it went, safe and sound, bounding away among the ruined temples and stone toadstools. The hunter could only conclude that the animal had dived off and landed squarely on its massive horns; or, if he did not quite believe that himself, he usually tried to make the greenhorns believe it.

But there were animals which did dive off tall cliffs on this part of the Missouri. For in old times, before Indians had acquired guns or steel arrowheads, they knew how to lure or drive buffalo over these precipices so that whole herds crashed to their death in a moment.

This was accomplished by some daring young medicine man, swift of foot, disguised as a buffalo, with skin, horns, and ears complete. Placing himself between the herd and the precipice, he waited until his companions suddenly showed themselves between the herd and the prairie.

Instantly taking alarm, the animals would whirl round, uncertain which way to run. Then, seeing the disguised decoy speeding toward the river, they followed in mad flight, trusting to his leadership.

The buffalo cows quickly outdistanced the heavier bulls, racing after the sprinter at the speed of a fast horse. Only a fleet-footed man could hope to keep in their van, as they steadily gained upon him until they were close on his heels. But he, panting for breath, threw himself into some crevice under the brow of the cliff or into a narrow trench prepared in advance, just as the herd found itself on the brink of the bluff.

Too late the leaders saw the gulf below. Those behind pressed frantically upon them, conscious only of the hunters crowding on their flanks and rear. Those in front were violently shoved over and the others blindly followed—a cascade of living things falling hundreds of feet to the cruel banks of the river below.

Indians waiting along the river butchered the meat at their leisure, leaving what they could not use for the wolves swarming in to share the feast.

Lewis and Clark found the recent wreckage of such a slaughter. In fact they could not have failed to find it, so dreadful was the stench. Wolves, still feasting on the carcasses, were so gorged that a man actually killed one of them with his spontoon. The explorers dubbed the creek where they saw this Slaughter River.

But such bloody scenes are quickly forgotten as travelers mount the stream and reach the narrow gorge above the mouth of Arrow River—the valley of the Stone Walls. There high ramparts of black rock rise from the water's edge. In the midst of the more fantastic forms of sculptured white sandstone, these vast ranges of Babylonian walls seem certainly to be the work of man, so regular are they. They tower up, each varying in thickness from the others, from one to twelve feet, and each evenly laid up, and as broad at the top as at the bottom. The stones are thick, black, and hard, intermixed and cemented with sand and talc.

"These stones are almost invariably regular parallelepipeds of unequal sizes in the wall, but equally deep and laid regularly in ranges over each other like bricks, each breaking and covering the interstice of the two on which it rests; but though the perpendicular interstice be destroyed, the horizontal one extends entirely through the whole work. The stones, too, are proportioned to the thickness of the wall in which they are employed, being largest in the thickest walls. The thinner walls are composed of a single depth of the parallelepiped, while the thicker ones consist of two or more depths.

"These walls pass the river at several places, rising from the water's edge much above the sandstone bluffs which they seem to penetrate; thence they cross in a straight line, on either side of the river, the plains over which they tower to the height of from ten to seventy feet, until they lose themselves in the second range of hills. Sometimes they run parallel in several ranges near to each other, sometimes intersect each other at right angles, and have the appearance of walls of ancient houses or gardens." *

If anyone wishes a walled garden or a fortress readymade, he can find them waiting for him at the Stone Walls. From the top of them a man may see the mountains on a fair day.

. . .

* *History of the Expedition Under the Command of Captains Lewis and Clark,* Nicholas Biddle, editor (New York, 1906), I, 312–314.

THE LAND

"No houses, no highways, no fences, no titles . . . There was a strange clearness to the atmosphere, a bluer tint to the skies."

$\mathcal{M}$ONTANA $\mathcal{N}$IGHT

ELLIOTT C. LINCOLN

This and other poems by Lincoln to be found elsewhere in this book
are from his *Rhymes of a Homesteader*, published in 1920, or from
The Ranch, 1924; both were published by Houghton Mifflin. Lincoln
was unusually successful in communicating in verse a sense of the
"texture" of Montana life. He arrived on a railroad car in 1908 with
$14 in his pocket, homesteaded near Lewistown, later was connected
with the schools there, married Beth Peck, a Lewistown girl, and
moved to California to teach in a private school. He wrote of Montana
in *American Magazine*, January, 1917: "Waking up on a fall morning
in our country is just as near going to heaven as any earthly experience
can be."

MONTANA night. The velvet of the sky
    Is powdered thick with silver dust. Below,
    A realm of half-lights, where black shadows flow
To Stygian lakes, that spread and multiply.
Far to the east the Moccasins rise high
In jagged silhouette. Now, faint and low,
A night bird sounds his call. Soft breezes blow,
Cool with the dampness of a stream hard by.
Dim, ghostly shapes of cattle grazing near
Drift steadily across the ray of light
From a lone cabin; and I think I hear
The barking of a dog. All things unite
To lull the senses of the eye and ear
In one sweet sense of rest; Montana night.

THE LAND THE WOLF MADE

An Indian Story of the Creation

LITTLE FACE

This is "The Creation as Told by Little Face," a portion of the manuscript of Lt. James H. Bradley on Indian traditions. Lieutenant Bradley, an Ohioan who had served with distinction in the Civil War, came to Montana in 1871, and until he died in battle with the Nez Percé at the Battle of the Big Hole, Aug. 9, 1877, spent his free time in historical research. A meticulous reporter and an excellent writer, he left a large quantity of manuscripts which were given to the Historical Society of Montana; they have been printed in several volumes of the *Contributions*. This extract is from Vol. IX, published in Helena in 1923. Little Face, who told this story to Lieutenant Bradley, was a Crow. It had come to him, he said, from his father, who had been told it by the great-grandmother of Little Face. This legend may explain why the Crows, ferocious fighters, were nevertheless usually friendly to the whites and many Crow scouts served with the army—or the finishing touch to the story may have been a diplomatic addition by a later generation.

IN the beginning the earth was covered with water, and the only living things were two spirits of unknown form who floated upon the water, and a large bird resembling a duck. Once as the two spirits floated listlessly here and there, they came together and one said to the other, "This is a bad way to live. I am tired of all this water. Let us make dry land that will be a home for other creatures."

The second spirit assented and they called the duck and ordered him to dive down till he reached the bottom of the deep and bring up from thence a quantity of earth. The duck went down as commanded, but, though he dove a great way, he returned without having reached the bottom. He was sent down a second time and ordered to go deeper, and this time stayed longer, and finally returned with his mouth and feet filled with sand. One of the spirits took the sand and pressed it into a cake and let it dry, after which he took a portion and scattered it around over the water.

No land appeared, however, and then the second spirit cast some of it abroad, when land appeared all around them. A second time he threw the dust, when the land grew larger and they ceased to throw the dust and walked on the land they had made. Then they called aloud and in the West was heard the cry of a wolf and presently he appeared and, coming from the West, joined them.

Then the spirits said to the duck, "Go in that direction and make new land, for it is not yet large enough." And the duck went to the South. In like manner they sent the Wolf to the West to make new land there. Then the spirits waited and after a time the duck returned and said the new land was made. Afterwards the wolf returned and made the same report. Then as the duck had first returned the spirits went first to the South to see what he had done, but they were dissatisfied with the land, for the duck had left too much water in his land, it being full of ponds and lakes, and even the land was low and marshy. Then they went to the West to see what the wolf had done, and they were pleased with that land and told the wolf that he had done well, for there were plains and rivers and mountains forming a country beautiful to behold. Then they told the duck to go and live in the wet country he had made and permitted the wolf to dwell in the finer country made by him.

When all this had been done the spirits took the dust of the earth and rolled it in their fingers and cast it upon the ground and it became a man, who ran a few steps and groped blindly, for though he had eyes he could not open them and saw not. Then the spirits took more dust and formed a woman, who did as the man had done. Then in the same manner they made animals and all creatures that live on land of each, male and female, but all with their eyes closed so that they could not see. Then the spirits told the man to open his eyes but he could not and they opened them for him with their fingers and commanded him to do the same with the woman and all animals. So he opened the eyes of the woman and the animals and all were able to see.

Then the man and woman began to live together, but as they had no house and did not know how to make one they dwelt in the hollow logs and trees. From this time forth men and women and all animals multiplied upon the earth, but all the human beings dwelt in hollow logs. The buffalo made war upon men and women and beat with their hoofs upon the logs in which they dwelt and drove them forth and were very fierce so that men were not able to withstand them. At last the buffalo killed a man and devoured all of him except one arm.

When the spirits saw this they were displeased and one made a bow and another made arrows and gave them to the first man and said to him: "It is not right that the buffalo should kill and eat you, but that you should kill and eat the buffalo, for they were given you for food. Take this bow and arrows and slay them and eat the flesh." So the man took the bow and arrows and shot twice and killed two buffaloes. Then he shot a third time, but this time the buffalo was only wounded, but the herd took flight and the wounded buffalo tossed the arm of the man they had killed and eaten upon his back, and then all ran away. Until then the buffalo had no hump upon the back, but the arm they carried away became a hump, and since then all buffalo have had a hump upon the back.

As the people increased in number upon the earth the spirits divided them into tribes, but as yet all spoke one language. But at last the spirits spoke down from above the earth calling all the people together, and when they had assembled, they gave each tribe a different tongue and none understood the tongue given to the others. The spirits also appointed the place for them to dwell and then commanded all the people to shake hands together. There were people of all colors there, but the white people stood nearest the spirits, and the spirits said so as to be heard by all: "All people are dear to us, but the white people are dearer than all the rest and we command you to live at peace with the white people." Afterwards they commanded them to disperse and the tribes spread themselves over the land.

"I HAVE KNOWN GREEN MOUNTAIN MEADOWS"

JOHN FROHLICHER

John Frohlicher was a member of the creative writing class of Montana State University and one of the editors of *The Frontier* when this verse appeared in that quarterly in the issue of March, 1925, Vol. V, No. 2. After experience in several outdoor occupations including lumbering and mining, he started the study of forestry at the University but later transferred to English. Upon leaving the University he entered the employment of Brown & Bigelow, St. Paul publishers of advertising material, and is now assistant to the president of that company.

YES, I have known
    Green mountain meadows, and swamps where blackbirds
        call,
And pools where stones and water glisten
In the bright hot rays of noontime sun;
And I have travelled newer, longer trails,
Feeling the tug of packstraps on my back,
Hearing the soft slow tread of mountain men—
(My ancestors who knew the Oberland)
Re-echoed on Montana's scarce-known hills.
And I have camped at night by ice-walled lakes
Above the clouds.

I wonder why the pavements hurt my feet.

BEYOND THE MISSOURI IS CLOSE TO HOME

WALLACE STEGNER

Wallace Stegner, a young novelist who first won wide attention with his Little, Brown & Co. prize novelette, *Remembering Laughter,* in 1937, has shown much feeling for the Northern Plains country in his works, especially in *On a Darkling Plain* (1940) and in *Big Rock Candy Mountain* (Duell, Sloan & Pearce, 1944). The scene of much of this last book is in Montana, and it is from this book that the excerpt here reprinted has been taken. Stegner was born in Iowa, attended schools and colleges there and in Utah and California, and for several years taught English in Harvard University. He is now a member of the English Department at Leland Stanford.

LET us sing. Of what? Of man's first disobedience, and the fruit of that forbidden tree whose mortal taste? No. Arms and the man, who first, pursued by Fate and haughty Juno's unrelenting hate? Arma virumque canuts. Let us sing of purple mountain majesties. That's what we've always been best at, the land.

The roadside cabins with Simmons beds, Flush toilets, Private showers,
The barns and cribs and coops and sheds, the houses buried deep in
    flowers,
The towns whose names are Burg and Ville, whose maximum speed is
    Twenty Mi.
Whose signs point in to the business blocks to lure the tourists who
    might shoot by.
"We love our children. Please drive slow." We're also proud of our
    hybrid corn.
"Registered Rest Rooms. Road maps free. Snappy Service—Just toot
    your horn."
Ma's Home Cooking and Herb's Good Eats, Rotary every Thursday
    noon,
Lions Friday. Then straggling streets, the foot on the throttle, the out-
    skirts soon
And the corn again, and the straight flat road, and the roadside split
    with the wedge of speed,
And the wind of a hurrying car ahead blowing the flat green tumble-
    weed.

The kids by the roadside who yell and wave. Texaco. Conoco. Burma-
Shave:

> Blighted romance
> Stated fully.
> She got mad when
> He got woolly.

I'll take it, he said. I love it, whatever good that does. Even if
I don't know where home is, I know when I *feel* at home.

At the next service station where he stopped he felt it even
stronger, the feeling of belonging, of being in a well-worn and
familiar groove. He felt it in the alacrity with which the attendant
shined up his windshield and wiped off his headlights and even
took a dab at the license plates, in the way he moved and looked,
in the quality of his voice and grin. Anything beyond the Missouri
was close to home, at least. He was a westerner, whatever that was.
The moment he crossed the Big Sioux and got into the brown
country where the raw earth showed, the minute the grass got
sparser and the air dryer and the service stations less grandiose
and the towns rattier, the moment he saw his first lonesome shack
on the baking flats with the tipsy windmill creaking away at the
reluctant underground water, he knew approximately where he
belonged. He belonged where the overalls saw the washtub less
often, where the corduroy bagged more sloppily at the knees,
where the ground was bare and sometimes raw and the sand-devils
whirled across the landscape and the barns were innocent of any
paint except that advertising Dr. Pierce's Golden Medical Discovery. The feeling came on him like sun after an overcast day,
and in pure contentment he limbered his knees and slouched
deeper against the Ford's lefthand door.

At sunset he was still wheeling across the plains toward Chamber-
lain, the sun fiery through the dust and the wide wings of the
west going red to saffron to green as he watched, and the horizon
ahead of him vast and empty and beckoning like an open gate. At
ten o'clock he was still driving, and at twelve. As long as the road
ran west he didn't want to stop, because that was where he was
going, west beyond the Dakotas toward home.

HAIL

DALE EUNSON

The elemental savagery of a hailstorm has frightened many Montanans, defeated some, killed others. Dale Eunson writes graphically of such a catastrophe in this portion of a chapter from his novel *Homestead*, published in 1935 by Farrar & Rinehart, the scene of which is central Montana. Born in Wisconsin in 1904, Eunson came to this state six years later when his parents homesteaded near Acton. Later they moved to the Judith Basin and he was graduated from high school in Lewistown. He attended the University of Southern California, for a time was private secretary to Rupert Hughes, and moved to New York. He is now a frequent contributor of fiction to leading magazines.

. . .

SHE had never worked like this; she had never known what it was to work like this, but the joy of the achievement, the beauty of the glistening rows of shocks which huddled so close together was a constant urge for her to hurry.

Several times she looked at the horizon for smoke. She had heard of prairie fires and she knew that if there were one the wheat would go up like tinder. But the sky was crystalline beneath the blazing sun.

At eleven o'clock she saw, far to the southwest, the beginning of a fleecy cloud which hugged the foothills. She knew what time it was because John came around then and she asked him, for she felt that it was almost time to feed the baby again. He pulled his father's old key winder out of his overall pocket and told her. "There're no better watches made nowadays than this one," he said. "Pa carried it fifty years, and it never missed a beat nor a minute one way or another."

She fed the baby and came back to the field for an hour before it was time for dinner. Then she went to the house and sat down while John and Jimmie watered and fed the horses, because she felt that she could not stand on her feet another minute. Pauline was crying, but Anna did not hear. Her senses were numbed. After a while John and Jimmie came into the house and she watched them as they washed their faces and hands in the granite-ware washbasin. Mrs. Thurman bustled ponderously about the room complaining of the heat which penetrated the tar-paper shack and stayed there. But Anna did not feel it or anything but the relaxation of tired muscles.

"You better take it easier this afternoon," John said. "We can't have you getting sick on us."

She tried to smile at him, but even her face was tired. Then for a moment or two she lost consciousness, only to be rudely awakened by Mrs. Thurman's voice with just a touch of acid in it saying: "I said, Anna, that your dinner was ready for you."

She got up listlessly and started to sit down at the table, but she heard John's voice from the porch: "Look here, all of you, what a funny cloud. Come here."

She did not want to go outside to see any cloud. She had seen some strange ones in Wisconsin, clouds which suddenly developed funnels that reached down from a mile overhead, and picked up barns with livestock in them and houses with live people in them and whirled them round and round and crumpled them like soda crackers in a closing fist. No, she had seen plenty of clouds, and she was too tired to look at any more. Besides, it couldn't be a cyclone, for people had told her there were no cyclones in Montana.

So she sat down and stared at the food before her—salt pork and boiled potatoes, boiled cabbage, boiled onions, and radishes. She was so tired that she was not hungry, and only toyed with the portion she piled on her plate. When John came in he said: "Remember that cloud this morning? Well, it's bigger now, piled up white like a snowbank, and the sun's drawing water through it. You ought to see it."

She tried to eat, but she couldn't and pushed back from the table and went out onto the porch. There seemed to be a slight movement in the air, and she beat it into a breeze with a palm-leaf fan. She walked to the corner of the house and looked toward the southwest. John was right—it was a strange cloud. She could not remember ever seeing one just like it. Funny, that the sun should be drawing water in the middle of the day, but there were long slashes of white in the gray curtain which swept earthward from the cloud itself, like strands of white in long, straight gray hair. Over there somewhere, not five miles away, men were

working on the roadbed of the branch line which the Great Northern was putting through between Billings and Great Falls. John
had been told on his last trip to Billings that trains would be running within the next six months.

As she waited there was a rumble like a lonely train heard afar
off. Anna listened to distinguish the sound. But it was like nothing
she had ever heard here before. She said, "John, come here."

He came to her, wiping his mouth with the sleeve of his shirt.
She said, "Do you hear anything?"

He listened carefully and she strained her ears. She could hear
the horses pawing in the stalls, the squawking of the chickens
about them, and the cattle bawling and stamping underneath the
shed which John had built them for protection from the sun near
the well. "No, I don't hear anything unusual," he said. "What did
you think it was?"

She said: "Never mind. It was nothing—just my nerves."

He looked at her as if he did not understand her, and shook his
head. "I guess I'll finish my dinner. Don't you want anything at
all?"

"No. You go back and finish. I'll just sit here a while."

But she could not take her eyes off the cloud which grew aston-
ishingly and swept like a great broom across the prairie. To her left
lay the field of grain, perhaps a sixth of it in bundles, and a small
portion of that piled in shocks. She wondered vaguely if rain
would damage the portion that lay on the ground, but she knew
they could do nothing now. If it rained it would have to rain—
that was all there was to it.

Before John and Jimmie and Mrs. Thurman had finished their
meal she was sure of the noise, but she had no idea what it was.
It seemed to be inside her head, like the roaring of her own blood.
It was all about her, but always growing louder and louder. When
John came back to the stoop she said: "I do hear something now,
no question about it."

He came to her quickly and looked westward. Yes, he could
hear it too. He sniffed the air. "It's going to rain, I guess. Maybe I
better take the canvases off the binder so they won't get wet."

Anna watched him run to the binder which he had left a dozen
rods from the house. It had begun to smell like rain for sure, but
Anna had never heard a rain cloud make a noise like that. It was

now almost like thunder which rolled ceaselessly. She thought that perhaps it had been thunder all along, for at least in the bright daylight she could detect long forks of lightning flickering within the protection of the cloud itself. After each flash the rumble was a little louder, until finally the sun was blanketed from sight, and the cloud commenced to rush faster and faster straight toward the center of the Rim.

John had trouble with the canvases, and before he finished the wind had begun to blow so hard that Anna went into the shack. She was a little afraid of lightning, but she thought if she could not see it she would not mind.

"Is it going to storm, Anna?" Mrs. Thurman asked.

"I'm afraid so."

"Well, thank goodness we didn't wash today."

Unconsciously Mrs. Thurman had raised her voice to be heard above the rumble, and when John came in with Jimmie he shut the door. "We're going to have a jim-dandy," he said. "Listen to that wind!"

But as he said it the wind stopped, as if somebody had suddenly shut off a great fan. "That's funny," he said. "Maybe we're not going to get it after all."

Anna sat in a chair beside the baby's crib, and Jimmie had crawled onto the bed. Mrs. Thurman sat on her cot, because she wanted to get away from the windows and the stove during an electrical storm, while John stood in the center of the room. He started to walk to the door when there came a crash like a stone dropped from a great height.

Anna sat up straight, the blood drained from her face leaving it ashen beneath the sunburn. She said, *"My God—oh, my God,"* stood up, and picked up her baby. She said, "Come here, Jimmie, come to your mother!"

Jimmie ran to her questioningly and, grasping her skirt in his hand, looked up at her face which wore a far-away expression, as if she understood a great many things he did not understand.

Then there was another crash, louder than the first, and another and another, and suddenly it was dark, the gloom in the cabin eerie as the bombardment on the thin roof.

They knew what it was now—hail; but it was hail like none they had ever seen or heard. John opened the door and stood look-

93

ing out at his field, where balls of ice big as hens' eggs were falling. Over his shoulder he said, "What do you suppose this will do to the wheat, Anna?"

She did not answer. The baby in her arms had commenced to cry again, awakened by the thunder on the roof which grew steadily louder. She suddenly realized that she was not hearing the baby, and she looked down at Jimmie who pulled at her skirt but did not open his mouth.

And then came the full fury of the storm. Like a million guns exploding at once and constantly the hail shelled the roof. In all the world there was nothing but sound, stifling, pressing in, beating, pounding, shattering sound. They were all inside a drum and the devil was beating a tattoo. Anna held her breath for a minute and did not realize it, did not know what she was doing. She had taken both hands now and pressed them over the crying baby's ears, for she was afraid the thundering roar might injure the child's sensitive membranes.

She was afraid, too, that the roof would collapse. It did not seem possible that the flimsy boards could withstand such brutal shelling. John came to her, and she saw that tears were running down his face, that his mouth was open wide and round and trembling and that he was crying like a child. He screamed at her, and it was almost funny, because she could not hear him, but his lips formed the words, "The wheat! The wheat!"

She could not think of the wheat now. She could not think at all. She had only one sense, and that was hearing, for her whole being was filled with that blatant, ear-splitting cacophony. No, she could not think about the wheat now. If they lived through it, if the roof did not fall in, that would be enough.

Streams of water poured through the roof, but Anna watched it in dumb contemplation. Then she saw Mrs. Thurman scuttling about, setting milk pans and dishes to catch the streams. She yelled, "Stop it! Never mind!" but Mrs. Thurman could not hear her and went on. The storm broke through new crevices faster than Mrs. Thurman could take care of the old ones.

From the time the first hailstone broke on the roof until the storm began to subside it could not have been more than ten minutes, and from then until the sun again broke through the cloud which still roared eastward it was but another ten minutes. Yet so complete, so ravishing had been its domination that Anna fell weak and depleted into the rocking chair. The cushion was soaked with ice water, but Anna could not rise. Only now did she cry, and she looked up through her tears to see long rays of sunlight streaming through knotholes in the roof. The tar-paper covering was, of course, pulverized and the punishing percussion of the hail had knocked the round pine knots out of the timber. Half a dozen or more of them lay about the floor of the shack in pools of water.

She knew without John's telling her what had happened in the field. He rushed out as soon as the cloud had passed and Jimmie followed him, leaving Anna alone with her baby and Mrs. Thurman. Anna pressed her hands to her temples which throbbed now that the storm had passed as if the blood would crack through. Mrs. Thurman stood in the doorway.

"Poor boy. Poor boy," she sighed. "I'm afraid this will just about finish him."

"Don't—please!" Anna moaned. She did not think she could stand any more, and yet she knew that she must, that she must for one thing go to John now. She got up with Pauline and started to lay her in the crib, but it was wet and soggy, so she handed her silently to Mrs. Thurman and went out through the door.

She had known vaguely the damage the storm must have caused, still the sight shocked her. For something whispered to her that perhaps, after all, the crop would not be utterly ruined, there might be some way in which it could be salvaged. But her first look shattered any faint hope she had harbored. The field, a half-hour earlier a golden fulfillment of their year's toil, was now a tangled mass of wet straw. Here and there a few strands stood pitifully beheaded—like tree trunks after a battle. The binder which had been at the edge of a forest of wheat with its sickle eating into the harvest, now stood desolate in the middle of the plain. And over the whole landscape were the gray hailstones, melting and glistening like sapphires in the sun which shone again as brightly as it had before.

But Anna's eyes were caught and held by the sight of John tramping aimlessly through the field, the boy tagging forlornly at his heels. John's shoulder sagged, he picked his feet up with great effort, and his eyes searched unbelievingly for what had been there only a few minutes before. Anna's throat was suddenly full and she ran toward him, her feet sinking into the mud and dragging through the mat of the fallen wheat. She did not mind so much the devastation of her hopes as the desolation the storm had wreaked upon John.

When she reached him and he looked up at her she could have fallen there in the field and cried. She would never forget the pain and the bitterness that lay in his eyes, the utter dejection of him. His youth seemed to have gone out of him in those short minutes and, since he had always been essentially a simple, trusting man, he was left with no store of worldliness to fall back upon, only a divine acceptance which had suddenly turned to gall and wormwood in his soul.

He tried to laugh now, but his mouth was a pitiful leer, and Anna covered his face with her hand. "Oh, don't, don't, John!" she cried. "It's all right. Who cares about the old wheat. We're safe—and we have each other."

But he was not to be consoled, and he flung her hand away and stood in the middle of the field as if addressing God himself. "I care! I care!" he shouted. "God Almighty! What do you care! What did you do it for? I'm asking you, why did you do it to us?"

Then the tears rolled down his cheeks as the flood of his misery broke over him, and Anna led him stumbling and blinded toward the house. Behind him, plodding along, his small heart bursting with pity for his father who had always been so strong, came the boy. What could he think of to help? What could a little boy do to ease his father's heartbreak?

When they reached the house the idea came to him. Piled high on the ground under the eaves was cold, gleaming ice. Shyly he took his father's hand and said:

"Let's freeze some ice cream."

His mother looked at him as if he had said something wrong, but his father laughed. He laughed and laughed until Jimmie wished that he would stop.

. . .

THE THIRD YEAR

From *Rhymes of a Homesteader* (Houghton Mifflin, 1920).

ELLIOTT C. LINCOLN

THEY say my land will bring eight thousand clear,
    When I make proof, so I am well repaid
    For three long, lonesome years. One month, and then
Back to the busy, friendly world of men:
And yet—I wonder if I am afraid.

The man-talk, clean, fresh clothes, books, music, plays,
Can all be mine again, if I should choose
To sell the claim and purchase old delights—
Things I have dreamed of through the weary nights—
But—can they take the place of things I lose?

The city avenues are throbbing now,
An endless stream of rushing motor-cars;
Wet pavements glimmer in the warm spring dark.
Will street lamps, shining through the city park,
Replace the glory of the prairie stars?

Shall I be welcomed by the old-time friends,
Or must I learn new faces, other ways?
Can office buildings, forty stories high,
Thrill like far mountains, white against the sky?
Can I forget the sun-drenched, careless days?

Three years ago the city held for me
All that I loved. I feared this empty view
Of sagebrush scrawled upon a baking plain.
These three long years, can they have forged a chain
Too strong to break? Have old gods changed for new?

THE ORIGIN OF THE BAD LANDS

RED BIRD

This story, reprinted in the *Sun River Sun* of Nov. 27, 1884, was obtained by a reporter of the Mandan, N.D., *Pioneer* when he interviewed Red Bird, an old chief of the Mandan Indians. Bad lands and "breaks" are a spectacular feature of the Montana landscape in several sections, particularly on the Missouri in the central part of the state, and in eastern Montana along the Yellowstone.

MANY hundred years ago what is now the bad lands was a high plain or tableland, covered with rich pastures and forests abounding in all kinds of game. They were the favorite hunting grounds of all the tribes who annually came to participate in the chase, and procure their winter supply of meat —the calumet grounds where all could meet in common, and the bloody hatchet was buried, as in the famed Pipestone valley in Minnesota, where all nations of red men could meet with no enemy to molest or make them afraid.

But finally a fierce mountain tribe of many thousands took possession of these famed hunting grounds, driving and keeping all other people out. Many futile attempts were made to dislodge them without avail. Many lives being lost in the numerous battles for their recovery, a great council of all the tribes of the plains was called, and their medicine men ordered to invoke the Great Spirit in their behalf. After fasting many days and suffering self-tortures, applying acts of their medicine men, the Great Spirit heard their cry and shook the earth with his wrath.

The earth became darkened, smoke and fire belched forth from the ground, the vivid lightning flashed and the thunder rolled, and the mountains sank and the valleys upheaved to the sky. The earth rose and fell like the waves of a storm-tossed ocean, burying all in one common grave. Towering buttes and desolation marked the spot where once stood the fertile plains. Not one man, woman or child was left to tell the tale of the haughty tribe of the mountains who had incurred the anger of the Great Spirit, leaving these Bad Lands as a monument to his wrath.

A FOREST FIRE EXPLOSION

H. T. GISBORNE

Hailstorms and blizzards, bad as they are, can't approach the forest fire in destructiveness, for it destroys a resource which has been a century or more in the building; and now that the great areas of grass which fed the prairie fires are gone, the woods blaze is the most terrifying spectacle Montanans are ever apt to see. This story of one has special interest on several counts. First, it describes the natural counterpart of the man-made atomic bomb: readers may find the account strangely reminiscent of newspaper stories about that frightful weapon. Second, the fire described—man-caused but accidental —was one of the worst in the known history of Montana. And finally, its author is a veteran Forest Service official, who is now silviculturist in charge of the division of forest protection, Region No. 1, with headquarters in Missoula. He wrote this for Vol. X of *The Frontier*, November, 1929. The fire occurred that summer.

NEWSPAPER accounts of large forest fires in the northern Rocky Mountain region frequently refer to "runs," "blowups," and occasionally to "explosions" of the fire. Many Federal, State, and private timber protective organization officers, and some unfortunate homesteaders, have seen these fires "blow up" and "explode," but either because the incident was attended by so much grief and worry, or because the spectacular features were obscured by the necessity of being somewhere else, few of these men have attempted to describe the event.

When Montana's largest man-caused fire, the 90,000-acre Half-Moon conflagration, ran this summer from Teakettle Mountain to Belton and Glacier Park Headquarters in one afternoon it left a trail of desolation which will ruin that twelve-mile auto drive for thousands of autoists for many, many years. No visitor to Glacier Park can escape that blot on one of Montana's beauty spots. Homesteads, ranches, and small sawmills were reduced, not to heaps of ashes, but to mere traces of light and dark ashes, small patches of fused china and glassware, twisted metal bedsteads, bent drive shafts, and cracked engines and saws. Several families lost all that they had struggled throughout life to acquire. The region lost the soft green forest that made it beautiful, and that supplied the materials and the chance for labor which made life possible.

At the Dessert Mountain forest-fire lookout station, four miles south of Belton and 3,000 feet above it, the man on duty made fast time down the nine-mile trail to Coram Ranger Station when the head of this fire came roaring toward his mountain. But the natural wind channel, formed by the gorge of the Middle Fork of the Flathead river, drew the center of devastation past him temporarily. Two days later, on August 23, 1929, we went back to the top of Dessert to obtain measurements of atmospheric temperature, humidity, and wind, and to note for comparison the behavior of the fire in different timber types on different slopes and exposures according to the prevailing weather. Forest protective organizations ought to know at all times for all parts of their properties what fire behavior to expect according to their current weather measurements. With such knowledge it should be possible to give the utmost protection when the danger is greatest, and to spend the least money when the danger is least.

We arrived at the lookout station about noon and after making a first series of weather measurements I went north the half mile along the ridge top to Belton Point, a secondary observation station. From this point the north face of the mountain drops two thousand feet in one mile, the contours running east and west, to the gently rolling and flat topography meandering four miles away by the Middle fork of the Flathead river.

At this time the southern flank of the fire was still over a mile from the base of the steep north end of the mountain. Perhaps six miles of "front" were visible, the rest hidden by soft swirls of big columns of smoke. I knew no attack was being made along this line at that time, all available men and equipment being concentrated around the town of Belton and around Park headquarters, with fire on all sides of them, trying first to save these most valuable properties. Although the front below me was beginning to boil actively in the green timber, as a result of the rising temperature and wind and decreasing afternoon humidity, it was not yet crowning extensively. And with the light wind coming from the southwest, diagonally opposing the advance toward the south, I thought it was safe to go down to the spring, some 800 feet in elevation and thirteen switchbacks by trail, below Belton Point and on its eastern slope.

The trip to the spring and back to the lookout station, with a five gallon backpack, was completed just in time for the four o'clock weather measurements. It seemed preferable, however, to make these on Belton Point, closer to the fire and where the front, which was now very active, could be seen more extensively than from the main station. This was a sad decision, because it resulted in no measurements whatever.

The lookout, Mr. Tunnell, who had been cleaning up the cabin while I went for water, decided to go with me to Belton Point. As we walked toward it smoke was boiling up from the north end of the mountain in a tremendous pillar towering thousands of feet above our 7,400-foot station. Just as when one looks up from the sidewalk at the base of a skyscraper the top is out of view, so the top of this column of smoke was hidden by its sides even though we were over half a mile from its base. For some unknown reason the customary roar of such rapidly rising masses of smoke, gas, and flame was not present in this case, nor did I notice it later when the mile wide whirling "explosion" developed and swept in under us. It was obvious, nevertheless, that the fire front which had been over a mile from the base of the mountain an hour ago was now going to reach Belton Point before we could, or at least before we would.

Like all truly massive movements the great pillar of smoke belching from the north face of the mountain seemed to move slowly. Black bodies of unburned gases would push their fungoid heads to the surface of the column, change to the orange of flame as they reached oxygen, and then to the dusty gray of smoke. Huge bulges would grow slowly on the sides of the column obliterating other protuberances and being in turn engulfed. We could see beautifully, as the atmosphere between the fire and us was kept clear by the light southwesterly wind. There seemed to be no danger as the mountain of smoke leaned appreciably with this breeze, and leaned away from us. We went forward about two hundred yards.

Such a spectacle, even as it enlarged one's heart enough to interfere with normal breathing, made us wish for the presence of others to enjoy the thrill. We stopped to take two pictures, one of the soft and apparently slowly boiling smoke column to the north, and one to the northeast out across the two-mile-wide canyon that slashes north and south between Dessert Mountain and the range tipped by Pyramid Peak. Down there lay the valley in the shadow of death, but although even the poor photograph portrays it, we did not realize what was to happen in the next few minutes.

Drifting across the north and open end of this canyon, dark, dirty, sinister curtains of smoke kept out the clean sunlight and reduced all objects to a dull gray-brown color. From the northwest shoulder of the mountain across the trough, belches of flame would rip through the smoke surface with a light of a hideous color never used by Maxfield Parrish. The high cirque forming the head of Kootenai Creek on the eastern slope, across the divide from us, was burning out in one brief instant. All the colorful beauty of the Alpine flora surrounding two lovely little lakes nestled high up in the home of the ptarmigan was being turned to deathly ashes. For perhaps half a minute the flames leaped hundreds of feet above the rocky ridge top, followed by billows of dull, funereal smoke as a mountaineer's paradise became a Hell's Half Section.

Even as I snapped these two photographs we noticed that the wind velocity was increasing. One glance at the boiling inferno north of us and we saw the reason. The southwest wind, sweeping gently as it was around the northwest shoulder of Dessert Mountain, was striking the periphery of a rising mass of hot gas and smoke. The result was the beginning of a whirling, clockwise motion, with the deep canyon east of us acting to draw the center of suction into it.

Suddenly—yet it seemed slowly, the movement was so massive —the curtain of smoke across the mouth of the canyon bulged at about our level, perhaps two thousand feet above the creek bottom. The bulge moved south, up the canyon, and as it moved it dipped deeper and deeper until it touched the creek, turned toward the southwest and up the slope toward us, turned west, then northwest, and then north away from us and toward the northern tip of our mountain and the center of great heat. The map shows that this revolving mass was more than a mile in diameter.

Most of this we saw over our shoulders as we sprinted south along the open ridge-top trail to the lookout cabin. As we dashed in the door to snatch our packsacks with what clothes we had not unpacked from them, we saw a second whirl developing. As we came out the door, hurriedly adjusting our shoulder straps, the new revolution swept majestically up the creek, up the slope under the lookout cabin—but a full quarter of a mile below us—turned west, northwest, and north, and obliterated the spot from which we had taken our pictures.

Then came the finale, the explosion, the display that should terminate any really spectacular show. The suction of this rising mass of heat drew the air across our ridge with a velocity that bounced me up against the lookout house as I stood there gaping. This clean, cold, and therefore heavy air literally tore across the ridge and down the eastern slope to remedy the vacuum and to ignite the waiting torches. Like a mile wide and crystal clear wedge, it drove in under the solid whirl of superlatively hot smoke and lifted it fifty or sixty feet, so that we could again see the entire slope from ridge top to creek bottom. As the oxygen in this fresh air reached the trees, brush, windfalls, and grass which had been super-heated by the big whirls, everything burst into flame at once. According to the map about two square miles of surface area, over 1,300 acres, were devastated by these two whirls in a period of possibly one or two minutes.

Ordinarily the front of a forest fire advances like troops in skirmish formation, pushing ahead faster here, slower there, according to the timber type and fuels, but maintaining a practically unbroken front. Even when topography, fuels, and weather result in a crown fire, the sheet of flame leaps from one tree crown to the next, changing green forest to black ruin at a relatively slow rate, from one-half to one mile an hour, according to two measured runs on the Sullivan creek fire. "Blow-ups" begin when such "runs" commence to throw spots of fire ahead of the advancing front, the spots burning back to swell the main front and thereby adding appreciably to the momentum of the rising mass of heat. Men have been able to race out to safety from in front of many ordinary runs and crown fires. Some men have escaped and some have been trapped by blow-ups. But when square miles of forest, in the course of a few seconds, are blanketed by a smothering, blistering whirl of heat so great that the temperature of all animal and vegetable material is raised far above the ignition point yet cannot burn for lack of sufficient oxygen, then, when the oxygen comes, a true explosion results.

Two days later, entering the canyon east of Dessert Mountain from its northern end, to blaze a trail in to the now slowly burning front and to select a safe site for a fire camp, I found the body of a young grouse. Sitting erect where it had been actually scared stiff by the terrifying whirl of death sweeping into its canyon home, it was facing toward the direction from which the great heat had come. Undoubtedly too frightened to fly, the little bird's muscles had hardened in paralysis. Even the neck and head were still alertly erect in fear and wonder. The beak, feathers, and feet were seared away. The perfectly balanced body still sits there, one of thousands of such monuments to man's carelessness.

About eight feet farther up the blackened slope a pine squirrel, sometimes called "Happy Jack," lay stretched out at full length. The burned off stubs of his two little hands were reaching out as far ahead as possible, the back legs were extended to the full in one final hopeless push, trying, like any human, to crawl just one painful inch farther to escape this unnecessary death.

THE OLD FREIGHTER COMES BACK
IN A FORD

GRACE STONE COATES

This is from *Portulacas in the Wheat*, a book of Mrs. Coates's verse published by Caxton, of Caldwell, Idaho, in 1932. Mrs. Coates, wife of a Martinsdale rancher, was assistant editor of *The Frontier* at that time, a frequent contributor to it and to other publications. She is also the author of *Black Cherries*, a novel, and *Mead and Mangel-wurzel*, another volume of poetry.

WITH drum of motor and droning tire,
Rattle of bridges, and culvert's jar,
An old man is headed for Heart's Desire
(His son at the wheel of a new Ford car)—
A man who loyally held apart
The way of his feet from the way of his heart.

I

Missouri's a good state—I'm no traitor;
 Anna loved it, and I love Anna.
She couldn't bear to have me a freighter,
 And that's how it was I left Montana.
But it came to seem I couldn't die
Till I'd been back once to say good-bye.

People caution me there'll be changes—
 Antelope gone from the plowed-up prairies;
Maybe! . . . God hasn't moved the ranges;
 I'll take a chance on old St. Mary's!
Spanish Peaks will smile in the sun,
Telling me things that are never done.

I know Sun River still comes hurrying
 Out of its canyons, spinning and prancing
Over the shallows. I'm not worrying
 About government projects and roadhouse dancing!

105

Some of the rollickers do not dream
How much like earlier folks they seem.

II

We're having fun at the tourist camps—
    Humanest people, just like the rest,
Some of them honest, and some of them scamps,
    But half of them sighing, "It's not the West,
Montana isn't the West, any more!"
I smile—at something I've heard before.

My father was one of the forty-niners,
    Down by the Isthmus, and back by the Horn;
But when he landed, part of the miners
    Were getting restless, and saying forlorn:
"Too many pilgrims here for me;
It isn't the West like it used to be!"

The West! The dusty pine scent spills
    Its memories. August snows remote
Look down. The fervor of blue hills
    Stings in my eyes and stabs my throat.
I wonder if to find the West
A man must carry it in his breast.

III

I've been studying changes—great
    Enough to set a man's heart on fire!
A motor pulling a mile-long freight
    By just one finger touching the wire!
Where I lurched and swung with a ten-mule team
Men have seen a vision and dreamed a dream.

Such a miracle is a star
    That sets the whole sky right for me.
The East says: *This is the way things are;*
    But the West is singing of things to be;
And that is what holds her children true
To her timeless will, that of old was new.

Doubts recede in the faith that rises.
　Power carriers, striding the hill,
Quicken our hearts with far surmises
　Of what shall be when our hearts are still.

. . .

We're going back, now, just as we planned it;
Missouri's a good state—I can stand it.

MULLEIN

MARY BRENNAN CLAPP

Mrs. Mary Brennan Clapp is a resident of Missoula and teaches in the English department of Montana State University. She is the widow of C. H. Clapp, formerly president of the University. This poem is from her book of verse, *And Then Re-Mold It*, published in 1929 by Harold G. Merriam, Missoula.

THERE is nothing lovely in mullein.
It is lanky and weedy and rough.
And its yellow blossoms soon burn out
To brown, untidy stuff.

And yet, it is like candles
Each summer sets anew,
Lighting my memory back to days
I rode the hills with you.

MY COUNTRY

ARAPOOISH, CHIEF OF THE CROWS

"Crow country" is approximately that drained by the Yellowstone, Powder River, Wind River, Little Missouri, and the Nebraska. Something of the Indian's great feeling for the land he knows can be sensed in this emphatic statement. Arapooish made it to Robert Campbell, a fur trader; the interview is reported by Lt. James H. Bradley. It is in Vol. IX of the *Contributions to the Historical Society of Montana*.

THE Crow country is a good country. The Great Spirit has put it exactly in the right place; while you are in it you fare well; whenever you go out of it, whichever way you travel, you fare worse. If you go to the south, you have to wander over great barren plains; the water is warm and bad and you meet with fever and ague. To the north it is cold; the winters are long and bitter and there is no grass; you can not keep horses there but must travel with dogs. What is a country without horses?

On the Columbia they are poor and dirty, paddle about in canoes and eat fish. Their teeth are worn out; they are always taking fish bones out of their mouths; fish is poor food.

To the east they dwell in villages; they live well, but they drink the muddy waters of the Missouri—that is bad. A Crow's dog would not drink such water.

About the forks of the Missouri is a fine country; good water, good grass, plenty of buffalo. In summer it is almost as good as Crow country, but in winter it is cold; the grass is gone and there is no salt weed for the horses.

The Crow country is exactly in the right place. It has snowy mountains and sunny plains, all kinds of climates and good things for every season. When the summer heats scorch the prairies, you can draw up under the mountains, where the air is sweet and cool, the grass fresh, and the bright streams come tumbling out of the snowbanks. There you can hunt the elk, the deer and the antelope when their skins are fit for dressing; there you will find plenty of white bears [grizzlies] and mountain sheep.

In the autumn when your horses are fat and strong from the mountain pastures you can go down into the plains and hunt the buffalo, or trap beaver on the streams. And when winter comes on, you can take shelter in the woody bottoms along the rivers; there you will find buffalo meat for yourselves and cottonwood bark for your horses, or you may winter in the Wind River valley, where there is salt weed in abundance.

The Crow country is exactly in the right place. Everything good is to be found there.

There is no country like the Crow country.

BEYOND LAW

There was "tragedy, which was short, sharp,
and decisive."

THE HANGING OF "CAPTAIN" SLADE

THOMAS J. DIMSDALE

This is a chapter from Montana's first book, *Vigilantes of Montana, or Popular Justice in the Rocky Mountains*, by Thomas J. Dimsdale, schoolmaster and newspaper man of Virginia City. Dimsdale ran the first installment of his book in *The Montana Post*, of which he was editor, on Aug. 26, 1865, and published the work in book form in Virginia City; the Library of Congress catalogue lists the date of the book as 1866, with D. W. Tilton & Co., owners of *The Post*, as publishers. J. A. Slade, subject of this chapter, was one of the most fascinating characters in Montana history and his execution by the Vigilantes caused much controversy, for he alone among the Vigilantes' victims was never accused of murder or highway robbery in the Territory. For these crimes twenty-two others, according to Dimsdale's list, were hanged and scores more fled or were banished. Though the execution of Henry Plummer, sheriff and leader of the road agents (it is described in Chapter XIX of Dimsdale's book), was perhaps more significant historically, Slade's story has particular interest because of the picture it gives of the lawless community and the character of its citizens. Slade, according to Dimsdale, may himself have been a Vigilante and was not a member of Plummer's bloodthirsty gang of road agents; but like many a better man since, he talked too much. The story attracted the interest of Mark Twain, who tells it in Chapters IX, X, and XI, Book I, of *Roughing It*, drawing heavily upon Dimsdale's account.

J. A. SLADE, or, as he was often called, Captain Slade, was raised in Clinton County, Ill., and was a member of a highly respectable family. He bore a good character for several years in that place. The acts which have given so wide a celebrity to his name were performed especially on the Overland Line, of which he was for years an official. Reference to these matters will be made in a subsequent part of this chapter.

Captain J. A. Slade came to Virginia City in the spring of 1863. He was a man gifted with the power of making money, and when free from the influence of alcoholic stimulants, which seemed to reverse his nature, and to change a kind-hearted and intelligent gentleman into a reckless demon, no man in the Territory had a greater faculty of attracting the favorable notice of even strangers, and in spite of the wild lawlessness which characterized his frequent spells of intoxication, he had many, very many friends whom no commission of crime itself could detach from his personal companionship. Another and less desirable class of friends were attracted by his very recklessness. There are probably a thousand individuals in the West possessing a correct knowledge of the leading incidents of a career that terminated at the gallows, who still speak of Slade as a perfect gentleman, and who not only lament his death, but talk in the highest terms of his character, and pronounce his execution a murder. One way of accounting for the diversity of opinion regarding Slade is sufficiently obvious. Those who saw him in his natural state only would pronounce him to be a kind husband, a most hospitable host and courteous gentleman. On the contrary, those who met him when maddened with liquor and surrounded by a gang of armed roughs, would pronounce him a fiend incarnate.

During the summer of 1863 he went to Milk River as a freighter. For this business he was eminently qualified, and he made a great deal of money. Unfortunately his habit of profuse expenditure was uncontrollable, and at the time of his execution he was deeply in debt almost everywhere.

After the execution of the five men on the 14th of January the Vigilantes considered that their work was nearly ended. They had freed the country from highwaymen and murderers to a great extent, and they determined that in the absence of the regular civil authority they would establish a People's Court, where all offenders should be tried by a judge and jury. This was the nearest approach to social order that the circumstances permitted, and though strict legal authority was wanting, yet the people were firmly determined to maintain its efficiency and to enforce its decrees. It may here be mentioned that the overt act which was the last round on the fatal ladder leading to the scaffold on which Slade perished, was the tearing in pieces and stamping upon a writ of this court, followed by the arrest of the judge, Alex Davis, by authority of a presented derringer and with his own hands.

J. A. Slade was himself, we have been informed, a Vigilanter; he openly boasted of it, and said he knew all that they knew. He was never accused or even suspected of either murder or robbery committed in this Territory (the latter crimes were never laid to his charge in any place); but that he had killed several men in other localities was notorious, and his bad reputation in this respect was a most powerful argument in determining his fate, when he was finally arrested for the offense above mentioned. On returning from Milk River he became more and more addicted to drinking; until at last it was a common feat for him and his friends to "take the town." He and a couple of his dependents might often be seen on one horse, galloping through the streets, shouting and yelling, firing revolvers, etc. On many occasions he would ride his horse into stores; break up bars, toss the scales out of doors, and use most insulting language to parties present. Just previous to the day of his arrest he had given a fearful beating to one of his followers; but such was his influence over them that the man wept bitterly at the gallows, and begged for his life with all his power. It had become quite common when Slade was on a spree for the shopkeepers and citizens to close the stores and put out all the lights; being fearful of some outrage at his hands. One store in Nevada he never ventured to enter—that of the Lott brothers —as they had taken care to let him know that any attempt of the kind would be followed by his sudden death, and though he often rode down there, threatening to break in and raise ——, yet, he never attempted to carry his threat into execution. For his wanton destruction of goods and furniture he was always ready to pay when sober if he had the money; but there were not a few who regarded payment as small satisfaction for the outrage, and these men were his personal enemies.

From time to time, Slade received warnings from men that he well knew would not deceive him, of the certain end of his conduct. There was not a moment, for two weeks previous to his arrest, in which the public did not expect to hear of some bloody outrage. The dread of his very name, and the presence of the armed band of hangers-on who followed him, alone prevented a resistance which must certainly have ended in the instant murder or mutilation of the opposing party.

Slade was frequently arrested by order of the court whose organization we have described, and had treated it with respect by paying one or two fines, and promising to pay the rest when he had money; but in the transaction that occurred at this crisis, he forgot even this caution, and goaded by passion and the hatred of restraint, he sprang into the embrace of death.

Slade had been drunk and "cutting up" all night. He and his

companions had made the town a perfect hell. In the morning,
J. M. Fox, the sheriff, met him, arrested him, took him into court,
and commenced reading a warrant that he had for his arrest, by
way of arraignment. He became uncontrollably furious, and seiz-
ing the writ, he tore it up, threw it on the ground, and stamped on
it. The clicking of the locks of his companions' revolvers was instantly heard and a crisis was expected. The sheriff did not attempt his capture; but being at least as prudent as he was valiant,
he succumbed, leaving Slade the master of the situation, and the
conqueror and ruler of the courts, law and law-makers. This was
a declaration of war, and was so accepted. The Vigilance Committee now felt that the question of social order and the preponder-
ance of the law-abiding citizens had then and there to be decided.
They knew the character of Slade, and they were well aware that
they must submit to his rule without murmur, or else that he must
be dealt with in such fashion as would prevent his being able to
wreak his vengeance on the Committee, who could never have
hoped to live in the Territory secure from outrage and death, and
who could never leave it without encountering his friends, whom
his victory would have emboldened and stimulated to a pitch that
would have rendered them reckless of consequences. The day
previous, he had ridden into Dorris's store, and on being requested
to leave, he drew his revolver and threatened to kill the gentlemen
who spoke to him. Another saloon he had led his horse into, and
buying a bottle of wine, he tried to make the animal drink it.
This was not considered an uncommon performance, as he had
often entered saloons, and commenced firing at the lamps, causing
a wild stampede.

A leading member of the Committee met Slade, and informed
him in the quiet, earnest manner of one who feels the importance
of what he is saying, "Slade, get your horse at once, and go home,
or there will be —— to pay." Slade started and took a long look
with his dark and piercing eyes, at the gentleman—"What do you
mean?" said he. "You have no right to ask me what I mean," was
the quiet reply, "get your horse at once, and remember what I tell
you." After a short pause he promised to do so, and actually got
into the saddle; but, being still intoxicated, he began calling aloud
to one after another of his friends, and at last seemed to have forgotten the warning he had received and became again uproarious,
shouting the name of a well-known prostitute in company with

those of two men whom he considered heads of the Committee, as a sort of challenge, perhaps, however, as a single act of bravado. It seems probable that the intimation of personal danger he had received had not been forgotten entirely; though, fatally for him, he took a foolish way of showing his remembrance of it. He sought out Alexander Davis, the Judge of the Court, and drawing a cocked derringer, he presented it at his head, and told him that he should hold him as a hostage for his own safety. As the Judge stood perfectly quiet, and offered no resistance to his captor, no further outrage followed on this score. Previous to this, on account of the critical state of affairs, the Committee had met, and at last resolved to arrest him. His execution had not been agreed upon, and, at that time, would have been negatived, most assuredly. A messenger rode down to Nevada to inform the leading men of what was on hand, as it was desirable to show that there was a feeling of unanimity on the subject, all along the Gulch.

The miners turned out almost en masse, leaving their work and forming in solid column, about six hundred strong, armed to the teeth, they marched up to Virginia. The leader of the body well knew the temper of his men on the subject. He spurred on ahead of them, and hastily calling a meeting of the Executive, he told them plainly that the miners meant "business," and that, if they came up, they would not stand in the street to be shot down by Slade's friends; but that they would take him and hang him. The meeting was small, as the Virginia men were loath to act at all. This momentous announcement of the feeling of the Lower Town was made to a cluster of men, who were deliberating behind a wagon, at the rear of a store on Main street, where the Ohling-house stone building now stands.

The Committee was most unwilling to proceed to extremities. All the duty they had ever performed seemed as nothing to the task before them; but they had to decide, and that quickly. It was finally agreed that if the whole body of the miners were of the opinion that he should be hanged, the Committee left it in their hands to deal with him. Off, at hot speed, rode the leader of the Nevada men to join his command.

Slade had found out what was intended, and the news sobered him instantly. He went into P. S. Pfouts' store, where Davis was, and apologized for his conduct, saying that he would take it all back.

The head of the column now wheeled into Wallace street and marched up at quick time. Halting in front of the store, the executive officer of the Committee stepped forward and arrested Slade, who was at once informed of his doom, and inquiry was made as to whether he had any business to settle. Several parties spoke to him on the subject; but to all such inquiries he turned a deaf ear, being entirely absorbed in the terrifying reflections on his own awful position. He never ceased his entreaties for life, and to see his dear wife. The unfortunate lady referred to, between whom and Slade there existed a warm affection, was at this time living at their ranch on the Madison. She was possessed of considerable personal attractions; tall, well-formed, of graceful carriage, pleasing manners, and was, withal, an accomplished horsewoman.

A messenger from Slade rode at full speed to inform her of her husband's arrest. In an instant she was in the saddle, and with all the energy that love and despair could lend to an ardent temperament and a strong physique, she urged her fleet charger over the twelve miles of rough and rocky ground that intervened between her and the object of her passionate devotion.

Meanwhile a party of volunteers had made the necessary preparations for the execution, in the valley traversed by the branch. Beneath the site of Pfouts' and Russell's stone building there was a corral, the gate-posts of which were strong and high. Across the top was laid a beam, to which the rope was fastened, and a dry-goods box served for the platform. To this place Slade was marched, surrounded by a guard, composing the best-armed and most numerous force that has ever appeared in Montana Territory.

The doomed man had so exhausted himself by tears, prayers, and lamentations, that he had scarcely strength left to stand under the fatal beam. He repeatedly exclaimed, "My God! my God! Must I die? Oh, my dear wife!"

On the return of the fatigue party, they encountered some friends of Slade, staunch and reliable citizens and members of the Committee, but who were personally attached to the condemned. On hearing of his sentence, one of them, a stout-hearted man, pulled out his handkerchief and walked away, weeping like a child. Slade still begged to see his wife most piteously, and it seemed hard to deny his request; but the bloody consequences that were sure to follow the inevitable attempt at a rescue, that her presence and entreaties would have certainly incited, forbade the granting of his request. Several gentlemen were sent for to see him in his last moments, one of whom (Judge Davis) made a short address to the people; but in such low tones as to be inaudible, save to a few in his immediate vicinity. One of his friends, after exhausting his powers of entreaty, threw off his coat and declared that the prisoner could not be hanged until he himself was killed. A hundred guns were instantly leveled at him; whereupon he turned and fled; but, being brought back, he was compelled to resume his coat, and to give a promise of future peaceable demeanor.

Scarcely a leading man in Virginia could be found, though numbers of the citizens joined the ranks of the guard when the arrest was made. All lamented the stern necessity which dictated the execution.

Everything being ready, the command was given, "Men, do your duty," and the box being instantly slipped from beneath his feet, he died almost instantaneously.

The body was cut down and carried to the Virginia Hotel, where, in a darkened room, it was scarcely laid out, when the unfortunate and bereaved companion of the deceased arrived, at headlong speed, to find that all was over, and that she was a widow. Her grief and heart-piercing cries were terrible evidences of the depth of her attachment for her lost husband, and a considerable period elapsed before she could regain the command of her excited feelings.

J. A. Slade was, during his connection with the Overland Stage Company, frequently involved in quarrels which terminated fatally for his antagonists. The first and most memorable of these was his encounter with Jules, a station-keeper at Julesburg, on the Platte River. Between the inhabitants, the emigrants and the stage people, there was a constant feud, arising from quarrels about missing stock, alleged to have been stolen by the settlers, which constantly resulted in personal difficulties, such as beating, shooting, stabbing, etc., and it was from this cause that Slade became involved in a transaction which had become inseparably associated with his name, and which has given a coloring and tone to all descriptions of him, from the date of the occurrence to the present day.

There have been so many versions of the affair, all of them differing more or less in important particulars, that it has seemed impossible to get at the exact truth; but the following account may be relied on as substantially correct:

From overlanders and dwellers on the road we learn that Jules was himself a lawless and tyrannical man, taking such liberties with the coach stock and carrying matters with so high a hand that the company determined on giving the agency of the division to J. A. Slade. In a business point of view, they were correct in their selection. The coach went through at all hazards. It is not to be supposed that Jules would submit to the authority of a newcomer, or, indeed, to any man that he could intimidate; and a very limited intercourse was sufficient to increase the mutual dislike of the parties, so far as to occasion an open rupture and bloodshed. Slade, it is said, had employed a man discharged by Jules, which irritated the latter considerably; but the overt act that brought matters to a crisis was the recovery by Slade of a team "sequestrated" by Jules. Some state that there had been a previous altercation between the two; but, whether this be true or not, it appears certain that on the arrival of the coach, with Slade as a passenger, Jules determined to arrest the team, then and there; and that, finding Slade was equally determined on putting them through, a few expletives were exchanged, and Jules fired his gun, loaded with buckshot, at Slade, who was unarmed at the time, wounding him severely. At his death, Slade carried several of these shots in his body. Slade went down the road, till he recovered of his wound. Jules left the place, and in his travels never failed to let everybody know that he would kill Slade, who, on his part, was not backward in reciprocating such promises. At last, Slade got well; and, shortly after, was informed that his enemy had been "corralled by the boys," whereupon he went to the place designated, and tying him fast, shot him to death by degrees. He also cut off his ears, and carried them in his vest pocket for a long time.

One man declares that Slade went up to the ranch where he had heard that Jules was and, "getting the drop on him," that is to say, covering him with his pistol before he was ready to defend himself, he said, "Jules, I am going to kill you"; to which the other replied, "Well, I suppose I am gone up; you've got me now"; and that Slade immediately opened fire and killed him with his revolver.

The first story is the one almost universally believed in the West, and the act is considered entirely justifiable by the wild Indian fighters of the frontier. Had he simply killed Jules, he would have been justified by the accepted Western law of retaliation. The prolonged agony and mutilation of his enemy, however, admit of no excuse.

While on the road, Slade ruled supreme. He would ride down to a station, get into a quarrel, turn the house out of windows, and maltreat the occupants most cruelly. The unfortunates had no means of redress, and were compelled to recuperate as best they could. On one of these occasions, it is said, he killed the father of the fine little half-breed boy, Jemmy, whom he adopted, and who lived with his widow after his execution. He was a gentle, well-behaved child, remarkable for his beautiful, soft, black eyes, and for his polite address.

Sometimes Slade acted as a lyncher. On one occasion, some emigrants had their stock either lost or stolen and told Slade, who happened to visit their camp. He rode, with a single companion, to a ranch, the owner of which he suspected, and opening the door, commenced firing at them, killing three and wounding the fourth.

As for minor quarrels and shooting, it is absolutely certain that a minute history of Slade's life would be one long record of such practices. He was feared a great deal more, generally, than the Almighty, from Kearney, west. There was, it seems, something in his bold recklessness, lavish generosity, and firm attachment to his friends, whose quarrel he would back, everywhere and at any time, that endeared him to the wild denizens of the prairie, and this personal attachment it is that has cast a veil over his faults, so dark that his friends could never see his real character, or believe their idol to be a blood-stained desperado.

Stories of his hanging men, and of innumerable assaults, shootings, stabbings and beatings, in which he was a principal actor, form part of the legends of the stage line; nevertheless, such is the veneration still cherished for him by many of the old stagers, that any insult offered to his memory would be fearfully and quickly avenged. Whatever he did to others, he was their friend, they say; and so they will say and feel till the tomb closes over the last of his old friends and comrades of the Overland.

It should be stated that Slade was, at the time of his coming West, a fugitive from justice in Illinois, where he killed a man with whom he had been quarreling. Finding his antagonist to be more than his match, he ran away from him, and, in his flight, picking up a stone, he threw it with such deadly aim and violence that it penetrated the skull of his pursuer, over the eye, and killed him. Johnson, the sheriff, who pursued him for nearly four hundred miles, was in Virginia City not long since, as we have been informed by persons who knew him well.

Such was Captain J. A. Slade, the idol of his followers, the terror of his enemies and of all that were not within the charmed circle of his dependents. In him, generosity and destructiveness, brutal lawlessness and courteous kindness, firm friendship and volcanic outbreaks of fury, were so mingled that he seems like one born out of date. He should have lived in feudal times, and have been the comrade of the Front de Boeufs, De Lacys, and Bois Guilberts, of days almost forgotten. In modern times, he stands nearly alone.

The execution of Slade had a most wonderful effect upon society. Henceforth, all knew that no one man could domineer or rule over the community. Reason and civilization then drove brute force from Montana.

One of his principal friends wisely absconded, and so escaped sharing his fate, which would have been a thing almost certain had he remained.

It has often been asked, why Slade's friends were permitted to go scot free, seeing that they accompanied him in all his "raids," and both shared and defended his wild and lawless exploits. The answer is very simple. The Vigilantes deplored the sad but imperative necessity for the making of one example. That, they knew, would be sufficient. They were right in their judgment, and immovable in their purpose. Could it but be made known how many lives were at their mercy, society would wonder at the moderation that ruled in their counsels. Necessity was the arbiter of these men's fate. When the stern Goddess spoke not, the doom was unpronounced, and the criminal remained at large. They acted for the public good, and when examples were made, it was because the safety of the community demanded a warning to the lawless and the desperate, that might neither be despised nor soon forgotten.

The execution of the road agents of Plummer's gang was the result of the popular verdict and judgment against robbers and murderers. The death of Slade was the protest of society on behalf of social order and the rights of man.

BALLAD OF LONG GEORGE

As Sung by Calamity Jane of the Good Old Days

MARION LeMOYNE LEEPER

"Long George" Francis, six-feet-six and 190 pounds, 45 years old, convicted rustler, came to a spectacular end on Christmas Eve, 1920. On his way to spend Christmas Eve with a schoolteacher friend and with his car filled with gifts for her, he accidentally drove over a bank onto frozen Milk River. His leg was broken; he tried to make a splint for it and crawled three miles on the ice. Then, realizing that he was doomed to freeze, he cut his throat. At the time he was under sentence for grand larceny and was due back in Havre within a week to be escorted to prison. This poem appeared in *The Frontier*, Vol. XVIII, No. 2, Winter, 1937. The author was a member of the English faculty of Northern Montana College at Havre. In addition to magazine verse, she had a book of poems, *Once Heaven Was Music*, which was published by Dorrance in 1939. She died two years later in Lewiston, Idaho.

LONG GEORGE was a cowboy bold
Rope 'em, boys, and throw 'em down
The weather it was desperate cold
Ice and snow on the lone prairee

Long George cut into a herd
Rope 'em, boys, and throw 'em down
Stole ten cows without a word
Ice and snow on the lone prairee

Jury said they'd hang him high
Rope 'em, boys, and throw 'em down
Long George heaved a heavy sigh
Ice and snow on the lone prairee

Asked if he could see his girl
Rope 'em, boys, and throw 'em down
Teachin' out to Sandy Pearl
Ice and snow on the lone prairee

123

Old judge said he'd let him go
Rope 'em, boys, and throw 'em down
If he'd turn up for the show
Ice and snow on the lone prairee

George he promised he'd be there
Rope 'em, boys, and throw 'em down
Hangin' his heels down in the air
Ice and snow on the lone prairee

After seven days went past
Rope 'em, boys, and throw 'em down
All the boys was plain downcast
Ice and snow on the lone prairee

They knowed he wouldn't let 'em down
Rope 'em, boys, and throw 'em down
Judge went cussin' round the town
Ice and snow on the lone prairee

The boys went searchin' for a week
Rope 'em, boys, and throw 'em down
They found Long George near Sandy Creek
Ice and snow on the lone prairee

He was frozen to the bone
Rope 'em, boys, and throw 'em down
But, by gosh, he was headin' home!
Ice and snow on the lone prairee

They knowed he'd been to see his girl
Rope 'em, boys, and throw 'em down
Because in his mitten was a soft brown curl
Ice and snow on the lone prairee

The boys all drunk till they was tight
Rope 'em, boys, and throw 'em down
They packed him home and buried him right
Ice and snow on the lone prairee

HOLIDAY IN YELLOWSTONE PARK

EMMA CARPENTER COWAN

This is the story, condensed from the complete account in Vol. IV of the *Contributions to the Historical Society of Montana,* of one of the most remarkable human experiences on the Montana frontier or any other frontier. George F. Cowan, the writer's husband, was an attorney in Radersburg, then the county seat of Jefferson County. Born in Columbus, Ohio, in 1842, he arrived in Helena in 1865 and married Emma Carpenter ten years later. Two years after their marriage they took the holiday trip described herein, to Yellowstone Park, which had been established in 1872 as our first national playground. On the way home they encountered the Nez Percé. Cowan was shot three times—once in the head. He crawled for four days and nights without food, then was almost burned to death by a runaway campfire. Rescued, he was put into a carriage which rolled off a cliff and dumped him on the hillside. He was finally brought to a bed in a hotel; a man who was dressing his wounds sat on the bed, it collapsed, and Cowan was hurled to the floor. That almost finished him, but not quite. He recovered, enjoyed a long and successful career in Montana, moved to Spokane in 1901, and died there in 1926 at the age of eighty-four. Mrs. Cowan died in the same city in 1938. Not all the men of the frontier were as tough as George Cowan, but the thirty-five-year-old lawyer might well be regarded as epitomizing the courage and durability required of Montanans of his time.

THE summer of 1877 was exceedingly hot and dry. This, together with a grasshopper raid, which was not the least of the trials of the pioneer, made the necessity of closing up the house to keep out the pests almost unbearable. My brother Frank, visiting us from Helena, told us of his intention to visit the Park, and asked us to be of the party. It required but little effort on his part to enthuse us, and we soon began preparations for the trip. Several people from our town, Radersburg, talked also of going, but by the time we were ready, one acquaintance only, Mr. Charles Mann, joined our party from that town. I induced my mother to allow my young sister, a child of a little more than a dozen years, to accompany me, as I was to be the only woman of the party and she would be so much company for me.

The party consisted all told of the following persons: A. J. Arnold, J. A. Oldham and a Mr. Dingee, all of Helena, Mr. Charles

Mann, my brother, Frank Carpenter, Mr. Cowan, my sister, self and cook named Myers. We were nicely outfitted with an easy double-seated carriage, baggage wagon and four saddle horses, one of them my own pony, a birthday gift from my father years before, which I named Bird because she was trim and fleet. That I was fond of her goes without saying. We were well equipped in the way of provisions, tents, guns and last, but not least, musical instruments. With J. A. Oldham as violinist, my brother's guitar, and two or three fair voices, we anticipated no end of pleasure.

We left Radersburg the 6th of August, camping the first night at Three Forks. Our way lay up the Madison via Henry Lake, a road having been built to the Lower Geyser Basin from that direction. Although some parts of this would scarcely pass as a road, we traveled it without mishap. The second day's ride brought us to Sterling, a small town in Madison county, and it was a pleasant one. But as night approached, we were still some miles from town. Leaving our slower baggage wagon, we pushed on, reaching town after dark. As we could not camp until the wagon came, we went to the hotel for supper, and made camp later. Several of the townspeople joined us there, and we heard for the first time rumors of Indian trouble. Some advised us not to go farther, but we did not think it more than an old time Indian scare, and when morning came, bright and beautiful, we decided to go on our way. Often, with night, I would feel somewhat timid, but with the daylight my fears would be dispelled. . . .

. . .

Thursday, the 23d of August, found us all at the home camp, as we termed it, ready to retrace our steps towards civilization. We had had a delightful time, but were ready for home. This day we encountered the first and only party of tourists we had seen, General Sherman and party. They had come into the Park by way of the Mammoth Hot Springs. Of them we learned of the Nez Perce raid and the Big Hole fight. We also received the very unpleasant impression that we might meet the Indians before we reached home. No one seemed to know just where they were going. The scout who was with the General's party assured us we would be perfectly safe if we would remain in the Basin, as the Indians would never come into the Park. I observed, however, that his party preferred being elsewhere, as they left the Basin that same night.

That afternoon another visitor called at camp, an old man by the name of Shively, who was traveling from the Black Hills and was camped half a mile down the valley. Home seemed a very desirable place just at this particular time, and we decided with one accord to break camp in the morning, with a view of reaching it as soon as possible. Naturally we felt somewhat depressed and worried over the news received. My brother Frank and Al Oldham, in order to enliven us somewhat, sang songs, told jokes, and finally dressed up as brigands, with pistols, knives and guns strapped on them. Al Oldham, with his swart complexion, wearing a broad sombrero, looked a typical one, showing off to good advantage before the glaring camp fire. They made the woods ring with their nonsense and merriment for some time.

We probably would not have been so serene, had we known that the larger part of the audience consisted of the Indians, who were lurking out in the darkness, watching and probably enjoying the fun. Such was really the fact, as they informed us later, designating Oldham as Big Chief. The advance party of Indians had come into the Basin early in the evening. Before morning the entire Indian encampment was within a mile of us, and we had not heard an unusual sound, though I for one slept lightly.

I was already awake when the men began building the camp fire, and I heard the first guttural tones of the two or three Indians who suddenly stood by the fire. I peeped out through the flap of the tent, although I was sure they were Indians before I looked. I immediately aroused my husband, who was soon out. They pretended to be friendly, but talked little. After some consultation the men decided to break camp at once and attempt to move out as though nothing unusual was at hand. No one cared for breakfast save the Indians, who quickly devoured everything that was prepared. By this time twenty or thirty Indians were about the camp, and more coming. The woods seemed full of them. A line of timber was between us and the main camp. Some little time was required to pull down tents, load the wagons, harness and saddle the horses, and make ready for travel. While Mr. Cowan was engaged elsewhere one of the men—Mr. Arnold, I think—began dealing out sugar and flour to the Indians on their demand. My husband soon observed this and peremptorily ordered the Indians away, not very mildly either. Naturally they resented it, and I think this materially lessened his chances of escape.

So much ammunition had been used on the trip, especially at Henry lake, that the supply was practically exhausted. Mr. Cowan had five cartridges only, about ten all told in the party. It was a fortunate thing probably that we had no more, for had the men been well armed, they would have attempted a defense, which could only have ended disastrously to us. Six men arrayed against several hundred Indians splendidly armed would not have survived long.

We drove out finally on the home trail, escorted by forty or fifty Indians. In fact, they all seemed to be going our way except the squaw camp, which we met and passed as they were traveling up the Firehole towards Mary's lake. A mile or more was traveled in this way, when the Indians for some reason called a halt. We were then a few hundred yards from where the road enters the timber and ascends the hillside. One of the Indians seated on a horse near Mr. Cowan, who was also on horseback, raised his hand and voice, apparently giving some commands, for immediately forty or fifty Indians came out of the line of timber, where they had evidently been in ambush for our benefit. Another Indian, addressing Mr. Cowan and pointing to the Indian who had given the command, said in good English, "Him Joseph." And this was our introduction to that chief. Every Indian carried splendid guns, with belts full of cartridges. As the morning sunshine glinted on the polished surface of the gun barrels a regiment of soldiers could not have looked more formidable. We were told to backtrack, which we did, not without some protest, realizing however the utter futility. The Indians pretended all this while to be our very good friends, saying that if they should let us go, bad Indians, as they termed them, would kill us.

Passing and leaving our morning camp to the right, we traversed the trail towards Mary's lake for two miles. We could go no farther with the wagons on account of fallen timber. Here we unhitched, mounted the horses, taking from the wagon the few things in the way of wraps that we could carry conveniently, and moved on. It gave us no pleasure to see our wagons overhauled, ransacked and destroyed. Spokes were cut from the buggy wheels and used as whip handles. We did not appreciate the fact that the Indians seemed to enjoy the confiscated property. One young chap dashed past us with several yards of pink mosquito bar tied to his horse's tail. A fine strip of swansdown, a trophy from Henry lake, which an ugly old Indian had wrapped around his head turban fashion, did not please me either.

Regardless of the fact that they had been harassed and hard pressed and expected battle any moment—not from Howard's command, whom they termed for some reason "squaw soldiers,"— but from the Bannack Indians, eighty of whom were the advance scouts for General Howard—the majority of the Nez Perces were light-hearted and seemed not to worry over the outcome of their campaign. Perhaps to worry is a prerogative of the white race. The Bannack scouts referred to were following closely at the heels of the Nez Perces and could have attacked them several times had they so desired, but for some reason they did not.

After traveling some ten miles, a noon camp was made, fires lighted and dinner prepared. Poker Joe (we did not learn the Indian name) acted as interpreter. He talked good English, as could all of them when they desired. Through him we were told that if we would give up our horses and saddles for others that would be good enough to take us home, they would release us and we would be allowed to return to the settlement without harm. Many of their horses were worn out from the long, hurried march. Under the circumstances we acquiesced, and an exchange began. I was seated on my pony, watching proceedings, when I observed that two or three Indians were gathering around me, apparently admiring my horse, also gently leading her away from the rest of my party. They evidently wanted the animal and I immediately slipped out of the saddle to the ground, knowing I should never see my pony again, and went over to where Mr. Cowan was being persuaded that an old rackabone gray horse was a fair exchange for his fine mount. He was persuaded.

It occurs to me at this writing that the above mode of trading is a fair reflection of the lesson taught by the whites. For instance, a tribe of Indians are located on a reservation. Gold is discovered thereon by some prospector. A stampede follows. The strong arm of the government alone prevents the avaricious pale face from possessing himself of the land forthwith. Soon negotiations are pending with as little delay as a few yards of red tape will admit. A treaty is signed, the strip ceded to the government and opened to settlers, and "Lo, the poor Indian" finds himself on a tract a few degrees more arid, a little less desirable than his former home. The Indian has few rights the average white settler feels bound to respect.

In a measure I had gotten over my first fright. The Indians seemed friendly and the prospect of release probable. Poker Joe, mounted on my husband's horse, made the circle of the camp, shouting in a sonorous voice some commands relative to the march apparently, as the squaws soon began moving. He came to us finally and told us we could go. We lost no time in obeying the order. Two of our party, Dingee and Arnold, escaped into the timber at this time, though they were not missed by Mr. Cowan or me until later. All went well with us for half a mile or so. Then to our dismay we discovered Indians following us. They soon came up and said the chief wanted to see us again. Back we turned, passed the noon camp, now deserted, and up and on to higher timbered ground. My side saddle had been placed on a poor old horse and given to me, but the others were without saddles. We rode along the trail, my husband and I in advance, followed by my sister and brother and others of our party, Indians on every side, twenty or thirty of them. Their gaiety of the morning was lacking, the silence seemed ominous. The pallor of my husband's face told me he thought our danger great. I hoped we would soon overtake the squaw camp, for I fancied we would be safer. They seemed the same old dirty Indians familiar to all Western people.

Suddenly, without warning, shots rang out. Two Indians came dashing down the trail in front of us. My husband was getting off his horse. I wondered for what reason. I soon knew, for he fell as soon as he reached the ground—fell headlong down the hill. Shots followed and Indian yells, and all was confusion. In less time than it takes me to tell it, I was off my horse and by my husband's side, where he lay against a fallen pine tree. I heard my sister's screams and called to her. She came and crouched by me, as I knelt by his side. I saw he was wounded in the leg above the knee, and by the way the blood spurted out I feared an artery had been severed. He asked for water. I dared not leave him to get it, even had it been near. I think we both glanced up the hill at the same moment, for he said, "Keep quiet. It won't last long." That thought had flashed through my mind also. Every gun of the whole party of Indians was leveled on us three. I shall never forget the picture, which left an impress that years cannot efface. The holes in those gun barrels looked as big as saucers.

I gave it only a glance, for my attention was drawn to something near at hand. A pressure on my shoulder was drawing me away from my husband. Looking back and up over my shoulder, I saw an Indian with an immense navy pistol trying to get a shot at my husband's head. Wrenching my arm from his grasp, I leaned over my husband, only to be roughly drawn aside. Another Indian stepped up, a pistol shot rang out, my husband's head fell back, and a red stream trickled down his face from beneath his hat. The warm sunshine, the smell of blood, the horror of it all, a faint remembrance of seeing rocks thrown at his head, my sister's screams, a sick faint feeling, and all was blank.

Of the others of the party, all had run for the brush, including my brother. An Indian followed him and was about to fire, when Frank for a reason best known to himself, made the sign of the cross. The Indian immediately lowered his gun and told my brother to follow him. No other attempt was made on his life. He saw me ahead of him several times, fastened with a strap behind an Indian. He did not dare to make a point of getting near enough to speak. He was helping to drive the horses. We had overtaken the squaw camp. We afterwards learned that the chiefs, suspecting mischief from a few lawless Indians, had sent back Poker Joe to prevent further trouble.

After coming to my senses my first recollection was of a great variety of noises—hooting, yelling, neighing of horses—all jumbled together. For a while it seemed afar off. I became conscious finally that someone was calling my name, and tried to answer. Presently my brother rode close beside me. He told me later that I looked years older and that I was ghastly white. He tried to comfort me and said the Indians had told him no further harm should befall us. It seemed to me the assurance had come too late. I could see nothing but my husband's dead face with the blood upon it. I remember Frank's telling me my sister was safe, but it seemed not to impress me much at the time.

The Indians soon learned that my brother was familiar with the trail, and he was sent forward. Over this mountain range, almost impassable because of the dense timber, several hundred head of loose horses, pack horses, camp accoutrements, and the five or six

131

hundred Indians were trying to force a passage. A narrow trail had sufficed for tourists. It was a feat few white people could have accomplished without axe or implements of some sort to cut the way. It required constant watching to prevent the loose horses from straying away. As it was, many were lost and recovered by the Bannack Indians later. The pack animals also caused trouble, often getting wedged in between trees. An old squaw would pound them on the head until they backed out. And such yelling! Their lungs seemed in excellent condition.

The wearisome up-hill travel was at length accomplished. Beyond the summit the timber was less dense, with open glades and parks. Finally, at dusk we came to quite a valley, which had already begun to glow with campfires, though many were not lighted until some time later. The Indian who was leading my horse—for I had been allowed to ride alone after recovering consciousness, the Indian retaining a grip on the bridle—threaded his way past numerous campfires and finally stopped near one. As if by a pre-arranged plan someone came to the horse, enveloped in a blanket. Until he spoke I thought it to be an Indian, and I was clasped in the arms of my brother. Tears then, the first in all these dreary hours, came to my relief. He led me to the fire and spoke to an Indian seated there, who, I was told, was Chief Joseph. He did not speak, but motioned me to sit down. Frank spread a blanket on the ground, and I sank down on it, thoroughly exhausted. A number of squaws about the fire were getting supper. My first question had been for my sister. I was told she was at Poker Joe's camp, some little distance away, together with the old man Shively, who was captured the evening before we were. I was told I could see her in the morning, and with this assurance I had to be satisfied. Food was offered me, but I could not eat.

My brother tried to converse with Chief Joseph, but without avail. The chief sat by the fire, sombre and silent, forseeing in his gloomy meditations possibly the unhappy ending of his campaign. The "noble red man" we read of was more nearly impersonated in this Indian than in any I have ever met. Grave and dignified, he looked a chief.

A squaw sat down near me with a babe in her arms. My brother wishing to conciliate them, I suppose, lifted it up and placed it on my lap. I glanced at the chief and saw the glimmer of a smile on his face, showing that he had heart beneath the stony exterior.

The squaw was all smiles, showing her white teeth. Seeing that I was crying, the squaw seemed troubled and said to my brother, "Why cry?" He told her my husband had been killed that day. She replied, "She heartsick." I was indeed.

The Indians were without tepees, which had been abandoned in their flight from the Big Hole fight, but pieces of canvas were stretched over a pole or bush, thus affording some protection from the cold night air. My brother and I sat out a weary vigil by the dying embers of the campfire, sadly wondering what the coming day would bring forth. The Indian who had befriended him told him we should be liberated and sent home. But they had assured us a safe retreat the day previous and had not kept faith. Near morning, rain began falling. A squaw arose, replenished the fire, and then came and spread a piece of canvas over my shoulders to keep off the dampness.

. . .

Only a short distance away, which I would have walked gladly the night before, I found my sister. Such a forlorn looking child I trust I may never again see. She threw herself into my arms in a very paroxysm of joy. She seemed not to be quite certain that I was alive, even though she had been told. Mr. Shively, the old man before referred to, was at this camp, and I was as glad to see him as though I had known him always. He gave us much encouragement. The Indians had talked more freely with him and he had tried to impress upon them the wisdom of releasing us, telling them we had lived many years in the West and had many friends and that it would be to their advantage to let us go.

Poker Joe again made the circle of the camp, giving orders for the day's march. We were furnished with horses and my brother came up leading them. The four of us rode together that morning. We reached the crossing of the Yellowstone near the mud geysers at noon. The Indians plunged into the stream without paying much regard to the regular ford, and camped on the opposite shore. At this point a few days later, the Bannack Indians, scouting for Howard, came to this camp and found a poor old wounded Nez Perce squaw, who, too sick to travel, had been left here with bread and water within reach. They proceeded to kill and scalp her without delay, celebrating this great achievement with a war dance when the General's command arrived.

We watched the fording for some time, and finally crossed, finding the water deep enough near the farther bank to swim the horses, thus getting ourselves uncomfortably wet. Fortunately, one seldom takes cold in camp life, however great the exposure. During the forenoon the Indians had captured a soldier, a deserter evidently. He told them of the Helena tourists camped near the Falls, the number of the men and horses. In fording, we observed that five warriors were with the party. It was composed chiefly of the squaw camp, and we concluded the warriors had retraced their steps to attack the Helena party. Why they were not attacked until the next noon we could only conjecture.

At the squaw camp, dinner was being prepared. I had begun to feel faint from lack of food. I forced down a little bread, but nothing more. Fish was offered me, but I declined with thanks. I had watched the squaw prepare them something after this wise: From a great string of fish the largest were selected, cut in two, dumped into an immense camp-kettle filled with water, and boiled to a pulp. The formality of cleaning had not entered into the formula. While I admit that tastes differ, I prefer having them dressed.

A council was being held. We were seated in the shade of some trees watching proceedings. Six or seven Indians—the only ones who seemed to be in camp at the time—sat in a circle and passed a long pipe one to another. Each took a few whiffs of smoke, and then one by one they arose and spoke. Poker Joe interpreted for us. Presently he said the Indians had decided to let my sister and me go, together with the soldier who had been captured that morning, but would hold my brother and Shively for guides. I had not been favorably impressed with the soldier. Intuition told me he was not trustworthy, and I refused to go unless my brother was also released. This caused another discussion, but they agreed to it, and preparations were made for our departure. A search was made for my side saddle, but without avail. It was found later by some of Howard's soldiers near where Mr. Cowan was shot.

Some of our own bedding, a waterproof wrap, a jacket for my sister, bread and matches, and two old wornout horses were brought, and we were ready. We clasped hands sadly with our good friend Shively, promising to deliver some messages to friends in Philipsburg should we escape. His eyes were dim with tears. In reality, I considered his chances of escape better than our own, and so told him. The Indians needed him for a guide. "We may be intercepted by the warriors out of camp," I said. "No," he replied, "something tells me you will get out safely."

We crossed the river again, my brother riding behind Poker Joe, who went with us a half mile or more, showing us presently a well defined trail down the river. He told us we must ride *"All Night, All Day, No Sleep*—we would reach Bozeman on second day." He reiterated again and again that we must ride all night. We shook hands and set out, not very rapidly. My brother walked and the horses we rode were worn out. It seemed folly to think we could escape. Furthermore, we placed no confidence in the Indian. I regret to say that as soon as he was out of sight we left the river trail and skirted along in the timber.

. . .

About noon the signs of some one ahead of us were apparent. In crossing streams, pony tracks in the wet sand were plainly seen, and the marks of a rope or lasso that had been dragged in the dust of the trail indicated Indians. They often drag the rope thus, I am told. We passed Lower creek and stopped a very short time to rest the horses. A few hours later, in rounding a point of timber, we saw in a little meadow not far beyond, a number of horses and men. At the first glance we thought them Indians. Frank drew our horses back into the timber and went forward to investigate. He returned in a very few minutes and declared them soldiers. Oh, such a feeling of relief!

Imagine their surprise when we rode into the camp and my brother told them we were fleeing from the Indians, the only survivors of our party, as he believed then. The soldier we had left in the Nez Perce camp the day before was a deserter from this company. Retribution closely followed transgression in this case. Mr. Shively escaped after being with the Indians ten days, but the fate of the soldier we did not learn.

This company of soldiers was a detachment from Fort Ellis, with Lieutenant Schofield in command. They were sent out to ascertain the whereabouts of the Nez Perces, and were returning in the belief that the Indians were not in that vicinity. Of them we learned that General Howard was closely following the Indians. Many of their actions were thus accounted for. The soldiers kindly prepared supper for us. I remember being nearly famished. Camp had been made for the night, but was quickly abandoned, and arrangements made for quick travel. We were mounted on good horses, and the poor old ones, that had done us good service notwithstanding their condition, were turned out to graze to their hearts' content.

As we were about to move off, a man came hurrying down the trail. He proved to be one of the Helena party and believed himself the only one alive of that party. He said they were attacked at noon. Frank and I concluded that Poker Joe knew what he was talking about when he told us to travel all night. A horse was provided for this man, hurry orders given, and we set out for the Springs, some seventeen miles distant. This night, unlike the previous one, was dark and cloudy. We passed over some of the roughest mountain trails near Gardiner that I ever remember traveling. Many of the soldiers walked and led their horses. Near midnight we reached the Mammoth Hot Springs, tired out and stiff from long riding, but truly thankful for our escape.

. . .

On Monday, Mr. Calfee, a photographer, invited us to go to Bozeman with him. He said he had a pair of wild mules and a big wagon, but if we wished, he would take us. We were anxious to get home and very glad of so good an opportunity. The Englishmen and their guide also decided to return to Bozeman. Wonderland had lost its attractions for the nonce.

. . .

We drove to Bozeman next day. A few miles from the town we met seventy or eighty Crows, escorted by Lieutenant Doane on their way to intercept the Nez Perces. They looked rather more dangerous than any we had yet met. After reaching Bozeman, my brother eventually went with this party nearly to the Mammoth Hot Springs in his endeavor to reach the point where Mr. Cowan was shot, but was compelled to return again to Bozeman without accomplishing that result.

In the meantime I had reached my father's home. Kind friends and neighbors had kept the news of our capture from my people until the day we reached home, then prepared them for our coming, thus sparing them much of the suspense. I reached there worn out with excitement and sorrow. Years seemed to have passed over my head since I had left my home a month previous.

From the time I learned of the close proximity of General Howard's command to the Nez Perces at the time Mr. Cowan was shot, I could not but entertain a faint hope that the soldiers might have found my husband alive. Yet, in reviewing all of the circumstances, I could find little to base such a hope upon. Still, as one after another of the party were accounted for, all living, the thought would come. I believed I should know to a certainty when my brother returned from his quest.

I had been at home a week, when one afternoon two acquaintances drove to the house. My father not being in, I went to the door. They would not come in, but talked a few minutes on ordinary subjects. Then one of them handed me a paper and said news had been received of Mr. Cowan, that he was alive.

In the "Independent" extra I found this account:

COWAN ALIVE. He is with General Howard's Command. Whereabouts of Howard.
(Special to the Independent), Bozeman, September 5.
Two scouts just in from Howard's command say that Cowan is with Howard and is doing well and will recover.
He is shot through the thigh and in the side and wounded in the head.
Howard was fourteen miles this side of Yellowstone lake. This news is reliable.   LANGHORNE.

Some way the doorstep seemed conveniently near as a resting place just at that particular time. Presently they told me the particulars. He was badly wounded, but would live; was with Howard's command, and would either be sent back to Virginia City or brought the other way to Bozeman. For the time being, this news was all sufficient. A day or two passed. I learned nothing more. My brother Frank came, but had the same news only that had been given me. The hours began to drag. I decided to go to Helena with my brother, as from that point telegraphic news could reach me much sooner. After arriving at Helena, however, a whole week passed before a telegram came to me, stating that my husband would be in Bozeman the following day.

I lost no time in going. At Bozeman, however, I found he had given out at the Bottler ranch on the Yellowstone. A double-seated carriage was procured for the trip, and once again I found myself traversing the familiar and oft traveled road. But this day the sun shone. My husband had notice of my coming and was expecting

137

me. I found him much better than I dared anticipate, and insistent on setting out for home without delay.

We arranged robes and blankets in the bed of the carriage. With his back propped up against the back seat, he was made quite comfortable. I occupied the back seat, Mr. Arnold and the driver the front. Mr. Arnold, whose escape is elsewhere noted, reached the Howard command and was among the first to aid Mr. Cowan when that command found him, and he had remained with and cared for him like a brother ever since.

We stopped for a hand shake and congratulations at the Ferril home on Trail creek. We had rather a spirited team and made fair progress. Late in the afternoon we were at a point seven miles from Bozeman in Rocky canyon. The road bed was graded around a steep hillside for some distance. We could look down and see the tops of trees that grew on the stream far below. Presently we experienced the novel and very peculiar sensation of seeing our carriage resting on those self same trees, wheels uppermost, ourselves a huddled mass on the roadside. Merely a broken pole strap, a lunge forward of the horses as the carriage ran up against them. The buggy tongue caught, snapped and threw the carriage completely over. Fortunately the seats were not fastened and we were left, a bundle of seats, robes, blankets and people on the hillside, shaken but not much hurt. The carriage, from which the horses had freed themselves, made one more revolution as it went over and landed as described. We were thankful to have left it at the first tip.

Mr. Cowan was lifted to a more comfortable position by the roadside. Not long after, a horseman leading a pack animal came along. Our driver borrowed the horse, making the trip to Fort Ellis and back in the shortest possible time and returning with an ambulance. The seven miles seemed long ones, and before we reached Bozeman Mr. Cowan was almost exhausted, his wounds bleeding and needing attention. He was carried by careful hands to a room in the hotel as soon as the crowd had thinned somewhat. Mr. Arnold arranged to dress the wounds, and in order to do so seated himself on the side of the bed, when lo, the additional weight caused the whole inside of the bed to drop out and down on the floor. This sudden and unexpected fall, in his enfeebled state, nearly finished him. A collapse followed, from which he did not rally for some time.

A week passed before we were able to travel further. I think the anxiety for my husband alone sustained me during this trying time. As it was, my nerves were all awry. Had I been morbidly inclined, I might have conceived the idea that some avenging Nemesis was following in his foot-steps, which nothing but the forfeit of his life would satisfy.

By the time we reached home Mr. Cowan was able to hobble about on crutches. The winter passed however before he was entirely well. A severe gunshot wound through the hip, a bullet hole in the thigh, a ball flattened on the forehead, and the head badly cut with rocks—few, indeed, are the men who could have survived so severe an ordeal. Our month of out-door life and a fine constitution, coupled with a strong will power, worked a miracle almost.

After receiving the pistol shot in the head, some time must have passed before he regained consciousness, as the sun was just tipping the tree tops, proving that the afternoon was far advanced. At the time of receiving the shot in the thigh he supposed the bone broken, as he was unable to stand. By this time, however, the numbness was gone, the blood had begun to circulate, and he could move his foot.

The intolerable thirst that follows gunshot wounds impelled him to try to reach water. Absolute quiet reigned. Yet, as he raised himself by the branch of a fallen tree, an Indian who had evidently been waiting for other Indians observed the movement and immediately fired at him. The ball passed through the point of the left hip, and he fell, fully expecting the Indian to come up and complete the work. Presently several Indians passed along the trail, and again all was silence.

Some time passed before he again began the quest for water, crawling on hands and knees, as he could not now stand. He would go until exhausted and then rest in the branches of some fallen pine tree. Not before noon of the next day did he finally reach a stream of water, though he had crawled parallel with it some miles without being aware of the fact on account of the timber and dense undergrowth. He fairly lay in the water, quenching his thirst. Then with hands and teeth he tore his underwear into bandages and dressed his wounds as best he could.

Even though the month was August the nights were cold in

this altitude, so that this was added to his other discomforts. He continued crawling, getting up on the hillside that he might better watch the trail. Several times he heard and saw Indians passing, and one night nearly came upon two who were sleeping.

His idea was to reach the home camp in the Lower Basin, believing he might be found more readily in that vicinity, also that he would possibly find food and matches there. He was four days and nights crawling the ten miles. Tuesday he reached the camp and found a few matches, but nothing to eat. A double handful of coffee was picked up, which he contrived to pound up in a cloth, and an empty syrup can answered very well to boil it in. Nearly half was lost by the can's falling into the fire. Still, enough remained to strengthen him considerably.

In the afternoon of the next day two of Howard's scouts found him and gave him food and blankets, placing him where Howard's command would find him. The scouts were taking rations to the Bannack Indians, who, with Fisher, were scouting for Howard. They had passed Mr. Cowan the day before and been seen by him, but of course he supposed them Nez Perces. The scouts left him after building a fire which came near being his undoing. A heavy wind in the night caused it to get beyond his control, and a timber fire resulted from which he had great difficulty in escaping. As it was, hands and knees were burned in trying to crawl away.

Thursday brought to him Howard's command, also Arnold and Oldham, of our party, the latter slightly wounded in the face, and he was assured of the safety of his wife, her brother and sister. His wounds were dressed, the bullet that had flattened on his skull removed, and he was made as comfortable as circumstances would permit.

And then began the hard, wearisome travel. Over rough new made roads he was carried by the command where oftentimes the wagon was let down the mountain side with ropes. Over stumps and rocks and fallen timber they made their way. From fever and the sloughing of the wounds, he had become so emaciated that Arnold, though himself a small man, could easily lift him out of the wagon. The trip was indeed a hard one. It would seem that the determination to live, come what would, alone brought him out alive, where others with less will power would have succumbed.

Many years have passed since the events herein narrated occurred, yet retrospection is all that is needed to bring them to mind clear and distinct as events of yesterday—many years, since which life has glided on and on, with scarce a ripple beyond the every day sunshine and shadow that falls to the lot of each and all of God's people.

CATTLE RUSTLERS AND VIGILANTES

GRANVILLE STUART

This excerpt from Stuart's *Forty Years on the Frontier* describes the opening engagements in Montana's most spectacular "wild west" episode—the cleanup of the Missouri rustlers by "Stuart's Stranglers." The book, published in 1925 by Arthur H. Clark Company, Glendale, Calif., is a collection of Stuart's journals edited by Paul C. Phillips, professor of history at Montana State University. Stuart's arguments helped to save the Stockmen's association from the inevitable disgrace attached to extra-legal action—then he took his own men and went out and did the job himself. The cleanup reached its climax in a pitched battle with a large group of rustlers in a coulee in the secret Missouri River "breaks"; this battle is also described in the book. Stuart, born in Clarksburg, then in Virginia, in 1834, accompanied his family to California in 1852 and came to Montana in 1857 with his brother James. They did the first major gold prospecting in the Territory at Gold Creek in 1858. He was subsequently a merchant in Alder Gulch, member of the Territorial council, and initiated large-scale cattle ranching in central Montana in the early '80's. In 1891 he became state land agent and personally chose the 600,000 acres of school lands given Montana by the Federal Government. In 1894 he was named minister to Uruguay and Paraguay and spent five years there; in 1904 became public librarian in Butte, and died in 1918, soon after his appointment as state historian. His first wife was an Indian, to whom, unlike some others, he was a thoughtful and affectionate husband as long as she lived. His home on the famous DHS or "D-S" ranch at Giltedge was a cultural center, with a large library and school for his own and neighbors' children. His daughter, Mrs. E. C. ("Teddy Blue") Abbott, is living in Lewistown, and a son, Charley, now a very old man, lives near the Missouri badlands south of Malta.

AT the close of the fall roundup (1883) our tallies showed that we had suffered at least a three per cent loss from "rustling." These thieves were splendidly organized and had established headquarters and had enough friends among the ranchers to enable them to carry on their work with perfect safety.

Near our home ranch we discovered one rancher whose cows invariably had twin calves and frequently triplets, while the range cows in that vicinity were nearly all barren and would persist in hanging around this man's corral, envying his cows their numerous children and bawling and lamenting their own childless fate. This state of affairs continued until we were obliged to call around that way and threaten to hang the man if his cows had any more twins.

The "rustlers" were particularly active along the Missouri and Yellowstone rivers and our neighbors in the Dakota bad lands were great sufferers. A meeting of stockmen was called at Helena on October 16 to consider what best to do. The first thing necessary was to discover the leaders and to locate their rendezvous. It was then decided to bring the matter before the Stock Growers' Association at the regular spring meeting.

The second annual meeting of the Montana Stock Growers' Association convened at Miles City on April 20, 1884. There were four hundred and twenty-nine stockmen present. The citizens' welcome was as cordial as it had been the previous year and the same splendid entertainment offered, but the meeting itself was not the harmonious gathering that the previous meeting had been. Everybody seemed to have a grievance. The members of the association that had been members of the legislature the previous year came in for their full share of censure. We were blamed for everything that had happened but the good weather.

The matters for consideration were overstocking the ranges, the dread pleuro-pneumonia, or Texas fever, that was claiming such a heavy toll in Kansas and Nebraska, and how to put a stop to "rustling."

The civil laws and courts had been tried and found wanting. The Montana cattlemen were as peaceable and law-abiding a body of men as could be found anywhere but they had $35,000,000 worth of property scattered over seventy-five thousand square miles of practically uninhabited country and it must be protected from thieves. The only way to do it was to make the penalty for stealing so severe that it would lose its attractions. When the subject was brought up some of the members were for raising a small army of cowboys and raiding the country: but the older and more conservative men knew that that would never do.

I openly opposed any such move and pointed out to them that the "rustlers" were strongly fortified, each of their cabins being a miniature fortress. They were all armed with the most modern weapons and had an abundance of ammunition, and every man of them was a desperado and a dead shot. If we had a scrap with them the law was on the side of the "rustlers." A fight with them would result in the loss of many lives and those that were not killed would have to stand trial for murder in case they killed any of the "rustlers." My talk did not have the conciliatory effect that I expected and seemed only to add fuel to the fire. The younger men felt that they had suffered enough at the hands of thieves and were for "cleaning them out" no matter what the cost.

The Marquis de Mores, who was a warm personal friend of mine and with whom I had had some previous talks on the subject, was strongly in favor of a "rustlers' war" and openly accused me of "backing water." The Marquis was strongly supported by Theodore Roosevelt, who was also a member of the Montana Stock Growers' Association from Dakota.* In the end the conservative members of the association carried the day and it was voted that the association would take no action against the "rustlers." In some way the "rustlers" got information about what was done at the meeting and were jubilant. They returned to their favorite haunts and settled down to what promised to be an era of undisturbed and successful operations.

While we were absent on the roundup, a party came to the ranch, stole a valuable stallion and a number of other good horses. Another party collected twenty-four head of beef steers from the Moccasin range and attempted to drive them north of the line into Canada; but when they found they could not evade the range riders, drove the cattle into a coulee and killed them, leaving the carcasses to spoil.

At the close of the roundup there was a meeting of a few stockmen at the "D-S" ranch. They and some men employed by the Stock Growers' Association had been watching the operations of the rustlers. The captain of this band of outlaws was John Stringer who answered to the sobriquet of "Stringer Jack." He was a tall handsome young fellow, well educated, and of a pleasing personality. His distinguishing features were his piercing gray eyes, white even teeth, and pleasant smile. He came to Montana in 1876 and hunted buffalo along the Missouri and Yellowstone rivers and was a conspicuous figure around the wood yards, trading posts, and military cantonments. He did not drink to excess but was an inveterate gambler. When the buffalo were gone he turned his attention to rustling cattle and stealing horses and estab-

* The Marquis had a packing plant at Medora, N. D. Roosevelt operated a ranch near the Montana–North Dakota boundary.

lished his headquarters on the Missouri river at the mouth of the Pouchette.

There were rustlers' rendezvous at the mouth of the Mussel-shell, at Rocky Point and at Wolf Point. J. A. Wells had a herd of cattle on the Judith river in charge of a herder who had eight saddle horses. On the twenty-fifth of June, Narciss Lavardure and Joe Vardner came up the river and camped opposite the Wells camp. Next day the herder crossed the river to look for some stray stock and as soon as he was out of sight Vardner and Lavardure crossed the river and drove off the seven saddle horses. They were going up Eagle Creek on the run when they accidentally met William Thompson, who knew the horses and ordered them to stop. Lavardure answered by turning and firing at Thompson but his horse plunged and he missed his mark. Thompson, who was well armed and riding a good horse, gave chase. He shot and fatally wounded Vardner and after a race of six miles, captured Lavardure and brought him and the horses back to the Wells camp. Thompson and his prisoner were taken across the river in a skiff and the latter placed in a stable under guard. At 2 A.M. on the morning of the twenty-seventh the guard was overpowered by an armed posse and Lavardure was taken out and hanged.

Sam McKenzie, a Scotch half-breed, had spent two years around old Fort Hawley on the Missouri river under pretense of being a wolfer but in reality was one of the most active horse thieves. He stole horses in Montana, drove them across the line into Canada, sold them, then stole horses up there and brought them back and sold them around Benton. He had been very successful in dodging the authorities on both sides of the line because of his many friends among the Cree half-breeds in Canada and in the Judith basin. On July 3, McKenzie was caught in a canyon a few miles above Fort Maginnis with two stolen horses in his possession and that night he was hanged from the limb of a cottonwood tree, two miles below the fort.

Early in June two suspicious characters came into the Judith basin with a small band of horses with a variety of brands on them and among them two fairly good "scrub" race horses. Word of their suspicious appearance and actions came to us and we telegraphed to several places to try to find out who the men were and whence they came.

I first met them on July 3, while out range riding, when I

accidentally came on their camp at a spring just above Nelson's ranch (the old overland post office). The men were as tough looking characters as I have ever met, especially Owen who had long unkept black hair, small, shifty, greenish gray eyes and a cruel mouth. "Rattle Snake Jake," despite his bad sounding sobriquet, was not quite so evil looking as his pal, though he was far from having a prepossessing appearance. Both men were armed, each wearing two forty-four Colt revolvers and a hunting knife. When I rode into their camp, Fallon was sitting on a roll of blankets cleaning a Winchester rifle. Owen was reclining against a stump smoking and another Winchester lay on a coat within easy reach. Owen was self-possessed, almost insolent, "Rattle Snake Jake" was civil but nervously tinkered with the gun and kept his eyes on me all the time I was in their camp. I knew that they were a bad lot, but had nothing to cause their arrest at that time, but decided to keep an eye on them while they were on the range.

On the morning of July 4 Ben Cline came along the road with a race horse on his way to Lewistown. "Rattle Snake Jake" saw the horse and challenged Cline for a race. Cline did not want to race, giving as his reason that he had his horse matched against a gray mare to run at the races in Lewistown and wanted to get his horse over there in good condition. After a little bantering on the part of Fallon a race was arranged between one of his horses and Cline's for fifty dollars a side, and a level stretch of road almost in front of Nelson's house selected for the race course. Owen bet ten dollars on the Fallon horse with one of Cline's companions. The Cline horse won the race and Cline and his companions resumed their interrupted journey to Lewistown.

Shortly after Cline and his friends left, Owen and Fallon packed up their belongings and set out for Lewistown. At this time Lewistown was just a small village, but they were having a Fourth of July celebration and people from a hundred miles in every direction had flocked to town, to take part in the festivities.

Owen and "Rattle Snake Jake" arrived in town about one P.M., rode up to Crowley's saloon, dismounted, went in and had several drinks and then rode on to the race track. Here they joined the throng around the track but took no part in the betting until almost the last race when they bet quite heavily and lost their money. This, together with a few drinks of bad whiskey, put them in an ugly mood.

146

A young man by the name of Bob Jackson, dressed in costume, representing Uncle Sam, rode in the parade and afterwards was at the race track, still wearing the grotesque costume. For some unaccountable reason his presence near Owen gave that gentleman offense and he struck Jackson over the head with the butt of his revolver, felling him to the ground; then placing a cocked revolver to Jackson's head, compelled him to crawl in the dust like a snake. Owen then turned to "Rattle Snake Jake" and said, "Well I guess we will clean out this town" and at that shot at random into the crowd, but fortunately did not hit anybody.

The desperadoes mounted their horses and rode back to the saloon where they each had more drinks; then flourishing their revolvers in a threatening way and cursing and swearing, declaring that they intended to clean up the town, swaggered out into the street.

Quite a number of men who had been at the race track, sensing trouble hurried back to town, went to Power's store and armed themselves with Winchesters and took up positions in the buildings on either side of the street. Out in the street "Rattle Snake Jake" mounted his horse and Owen started to mount his, when he spied Joe Doney standing in front of Power's store. Revolver in hand he started to cross the street. When within a few feet of the walk Doney pulled a twenty-two caliber revolver and shot him in the stomach. A second shot struck Owen's hand, causing him to drop his revolver.

Doney ran into the store. Owen quickly recovered his revolver and fired at Doney just as he disappeared inside the door. The men in the store answered the shot with their Winchesters and Owen retreated up the street toward a tent occupied by a photographer. "Rattle Snake Jake," revolver in hand, started to ride up the street in the opposite direction, when a shot fired by someone in the saloon struck him in the side. He kept on for a short distance when his cartridge belt fell to the ground and he drew up to recover it. Looking back he saw that Owen was not following him but was wounded and could not get away, and turning his horse he rode back to his comrade through a perfect shower of lead coming from both sides of the street and together the two men made their last stand in front of the tent.

The citizens in the store and saloons and from behind buildings kept up their firing, while the two desperadoes standing exposed to their merciless fire, coolly and deliberately answered shot for shot, emptied and reloaded their guns and emptied them again until they could no longer pull a trigger.

Two young men, Benjamin Smith and Joseph Jackson, were crossing an open space a short distance from the tent when "Rattle Snake Jake" caught sight of them, and dropping down on one knee took careful aim and fired on them. The first shot grazed Jackson's cheek and the second pierced his hat and took a lock of his hair. The third one lodged in Smith's brain, killing him instantly.

A few minutes later Owen reached for his rifle, pitched forward and fell to the ground, and almost at the same moment a bullet struck "Rattle Snake Jake" in the breast and he dropped. As soon as both men were down the citizens ceased firing but the bandits continued with their revolvers so long as consciousness remained. When the smoke of battle cleared away examination of the bodies showed that "Rattle Snake Jake" had received nine wounds and Owen eleven, any one of which would have proved fatal.

In the evening Judge Toombs held an inquest over the bodies, the photographer, in front of whose tent they were killed, took their pictures, and then they were given burial on a little knoll on the Pichette ranch.

On the afternoon of July 4, a telegram came to me from Buffalo, Wyoming, stating that Charles Fallon, alias "Rattle Snake Jake," and Edward Owen, were desperate characters and were wanted at several places. The two men had spent the winter on Powder river at the mouth of Crazy Woman, gambling, horse racing, and carousing. On their way north they had stolen some good horses from John R. Smith's ranch near Trabing, Wyoming, and traded them to the Crow Indians. Later on we learned that Owen was from Shreveport, Louisiana, and was wanted there for killing a negro. Charles Fallon hailed from Laredo on the Texas border and was wanted in New Mexico for shooting up a ranch and burning buildings and hay stacks.

. . .

A FIGHT AT GROGAN'S

CLYDE F. MURPHY

Butte's development as a mining camp came comparatively late, and unlike Bannack and Virginia City, it always had law—of a sort. But in the roaring days of the "wars of the copper kings" the law was discreet, especially in the neighborhood of lusty Dublin Gulch. This account of a fatal fight is a portion of a chapter in the novel *Glittering Hill* by Clyde F. Murphy, published in 1944 by E. P. Dutton. The book, scene of which is Butte, won the first Lewis and Clark Northwest prize, a Dutton award for the best manuscript submitted that year by a Northwest writer. Murphy was born in Great Falls in 1899, served in the First World War, lived in Butte, attended Montana State University and was admitted to the bar in 1923. He became a successful Los Angeles attorney but gave up his practice to write, and was planning another novel with a Montana scene when death unexpectedly ended his career June 5, 1946.

TOM felt much better as he walked along the narrow sidewalk of the Gulch. The early September air had a bite to it, not cold enough for an overcoat but nippy and invigorating just the same. Tom stretched his legs in long strides and breathed deeply. When he entered Grogan's, a few minutes later, he observed that the crowd which had collected extended almost to the street door. Tom whistled in surprise. A Dublin Gulch saloon packed to the gills with customers was something new.

Tom reached the door and stood in the fringe of the crowd, sensing that all about him was oddly still. Peering over the heads of those between him and the bar, Tom suddenly saw that which impelled him to elbow forward through the crowd. Passing between Cassidy and Hogan, he tapped Derg Finley on the shoulder who stood aside to let him by. Pushing onward he was soon abreast of Phelim Keane and Gribbin and Stubby Cavanaugh, standing tense and fearful, and at last stepped into the open space where Bruiser Gowdy had Denny O'Shea backed against the bar, with the lapels of Denny's coat gripped tightly in his fist. Just as Tom stepped free of the first rank of quiet men, Bruiser's voice sounded:

"You're the one I been lookin' for."

The tone of Gowdy's voice was angry. His grip tightened, nearly lifting Denny from his feet. Pasty white, Denny seemed unable to speak a word. Tom had never seen him so scared. Something in the air, in the tenseness of the room, perhaps the threat of instant violence, caused Tom to move quickly. He laid his hand on Gowdy's shoulder.

"He's all right," Tom said easily. "I'll take him home if he's bothering. . . ."

The Bruiser, without turning his head, threw his left arm. It struck Tom in the face, glanced upward, knocking Tom's hat from his head to the wet drain below the rail.

Tom's anger flared with the sting of Gowdy's blow but, intent only upon getting Denny out of trouble, he did no more than seize Gowdy by the shoulder and swing him free of Denny. Tom's grip had been strong; the force of his action threw Gowdy backward so violently he nearly fell into the crowd. Then Tom said sharply,

"Get going, Denny."

Denny darted into the crowd toward the door. As Tom reached in the drain for his hat, he heard a scream of warning. Then something thudded heavily in his groin. Tom had heard, more than felt, Gowdy's kick. Had it been lower Tom would never have known what had struck him. A quick spasm tightened his stomach but he was still aware of things. Only a weakness, a numbness told him he'd been hurt. Then a sudden pain stabbed him fiercely. Doubling over, he clutched his groin and settled to his knees.

Then came a blinding crash. The Bruiser had kicked him again, this time squarely in the face. Tom heard the bridge of his nose crackle and collapse; the metal hooks on Gowdy's shoes dug his flesh below the eyes. Before him spread a brush of small exploding stars. The pain began like a hot needle at his eyes, shot back through his brain and struck the inner shell of skull. He heard, as from a distance, a strange unearthly shriek and when it ceased he knew it had been his own involuntary cry of pain and fear. His eyes went red and he felt himself thrown at fearful speed until the back of his head struck a solid object. Hearing a dull clang, like the crash of a cymbal, he landed between two card tables which, as they tumbled, sent liquor glasses crashing on the wall. His breath knocked from him, Tom was inert a few seconds, barely conscious, with blood pouring from his nose, in a thick stream, staining his best gray suit. He lay weak and helpless and terribly sick at his stomach. Everything now had turned strangely, fearfully quiet.

In his pain and confusion it seemed to Tom that he was lying prone on the bottom of a pool, translucent, green, the area near him brightly iridescent. Voices were muffled and objects in his vision, darkly monstrous, resembled dreary shapeless ghosts. Noises of an outside world began, suddenly, to invade his own. The voices, once a mere hum, had grown to a roar. White faces crowded at him, and though shaky and sick, he fought for sight, strength and sense.

The familiar things were coming: small lights at the top of the back bar, a tall red man before a wide gray glass—Chaunce of Grogan's bar. An open avenue, flanked by rows of frightened, pitying men. And, squarely in the middle, a big beast named Gowdy, the man who had taken him off guard, the man who had kicked him to his knees and then, while he was kneeling, kicked him in the face. Gowdy was waiting, ready.

All was clear to Tom, all except what had happened to Denny. When Tom tried to say "Denny," no sound came out of his throat and the effort sent a blinding, tearing pain through his nose and face. Trying to get breath through his nose, he failed; the nose was crushed, both nostrils were shut. Tom was thinking fast, making up for time lost while he lay stunned upon the floor. He knew that when he came out of the tangle of tables and chairs, Gowdy would be on him in a flash. If he went down this time, he would not get up again.

Tom rolled and wriggled along the floor until he was below a standing table. Hugging the supporting center post of the table with one arm, he slowly lifted to his knees. Crouching there, like a crippled animal, he peered out from under the table at the circle of frightened men in the center of the saloon, hearing only the sucking of his breath and a steady buzzing in his head. Blood was coming from his nose down his face, dropping off his chin to splatter on the floor.

There was no sound, except his rasping breath. The men about him watched him; horror in their eyes. Clearly, they thought him mad. He was relieved. If only the man who had kicked him thought him mad, and waited, Tom would have time to gather strength.

Staying where he was, under the table, Tom slowly drew his feet forward until he squatted like an Indian at a fire. A sudden weakness came when he was off his knees. It dulled his eyes; the ranks of men about him merged into one great hideous animal, formless in body and possessed of many blenched faces and wide staring eyes. Tom shook his head to clear it and blew through his lips, sending sprinkles of blood on the floor. Then the weakness passed. His head was sound and clear.

When Tom saw Gowdy the second time, his blood began to pound. The blood pulsed stronger and stronger through his body; it made him warm all over. The warmth and the pounding were in his fingertips, pressed hard upon the floor.

Tom tested his legs by springing slightly and exulted to find that he was firm. The warmness of his body remained; his blood was bounding. Just as he was ready to get out from under the table, Gowdy leaped toward him, resolved to end the fight.

Tom hurled the table into Gowdy's path. When it crashed in the center of the floor, it blocked Gowdy's rush an instant, just enough to let Tom clamber to his feet.

As Gowdy charged he swung his right fist. Tom dodged under it. When Gowdy's beefy arm went over his neck, Tom was partly crouched below it; he spun about, pinioned Gowdy's arm to his right shoulder and then, with a fierce upthrust, he drove his free shoulder into Gowdy's armpit. That trick was one Tom had learned from fighting in the woods. When Tom heard a quick snapping sound and then a scream of pain, he knew that Gowdy's arm was out of joint. Hanging to the injured arm, Tom bent low and pulled Gowdy over his head, hurtling him through the air to land, with his breath knocked from him, in a sprawled heap near the bar. His right arm extended grotesquely from his body.

Gowdy was stunned an instant but soon recovered and, apparently fearing Tom's feet, he jumped up, his face white and sweaty from his pain. Again he charged Tom, this time holding his left arm straight before him, with the right dangling loosely at his side.

Tom leaped and struck. How many times he struck, no one could have told; his crashing fists sent the Bruiser's head flipping back with sudden jerks until he reeled against the bar, a thick stream of blood flowing from his nose, now flattened on his face. Tom's next blow, a glancing one on the mouth, snapped three of Gowdy's teeth at the roots and sent them rattling on the floor.

152

The mouth dribbled foamy blood and Gowdy's eyes, rolling upward, showed only half circles of the whites. When his arms dropped uselessly at his sides and Tom's fist landed on his chin, Gowdy's knees buckled and his body dropped. But Tom did not let the body fall; as it sagged downward, he pressed it, with his shoulder, against the bar, beating the head and face until they were spongy with blood. Slowly the Bruiser's body settled, his feet sliding outward, his body sprawling until he lay, open-mouthed, with a wide black gap where the knocked-out teeth had been.

Tom crouched and seized the hair. The crowd, standing back and hardly breathing, watched Tom, holding to the stringy mop of hair, lift the head and crash it on the rail. About to crash the head again, the hair, now smeared with blood, slipped between Tom's fingers. The head struck against the marble of the drain. The neck seemed free, the head loose, like that of a broken doll. Tom stared briefly at the face, convulsed and blue beneath the blood. A frightful, stricken hush had settled on the bar.

No one moved and no one spoke as Tom got slowly to his feet. Walking toward the door, dazed and aimless, he wavered from his weakness. He passed between gravely silent Gulchers who stared not at him but at Gowdy on the floor. Halfway across the sidewalk, Tom wilted, then stumbled weakly to the horse trough and stood clutching it as the lights of Dublin Gulch spun in a great wheel of fire which faded quickly and was lost in darkness. Tom had pitched, face downward, in the mud below the trough.

MEN . . .

". . . so varied, so versatile, so virile . . . unique characters with strange and sometimes unknown history and weird experiences . . ."

A MONTH IN THE LIFE OF A TRADER

JAMES H. CHAMBERS

This is an extract from *Original Journal of James H. Chambers, Fort Sarpy*, contained in Vol. X, 1940, of the *Contributions to the Historical Society of Montana,* published in Helena by the Society. Fort Sarpy was built in 1850 on the north bank of the Yellowstone a short distance below the mouth of the Rosebud; it was named for J. B. Sarpy, a partner in the Chouteau fur company. Chambers is reported in the notes of Vol. X to be "the mystery man of the fur trade in Montana" and he did little in his journal to dispel any of the mystery. He was born in 1820, probably was in the Yellowstone country before 1850, and is believed to have died about 1860 or a few years thereafter, perhaps killed by Indians. From his journal there emerges a fascinating picture of life on the fur-trade frontier, the hardships, the viciousness, and the brutality of post life, and the jealousies and personality conflicts of tough men isolated from the normal associations of a civilized community.

June 1856

Sat. 1—Started early & came on the big Muddy 1 p.m. crossed Mr. Wray's goods safely & camp'd on the opposite side caught some forty or fifty fine fish killed several ducks commenced raining about nine P.m. & continued to rain or rather pour to daylight—made 28 miles

Mon. 2—dried off Started about 10 a.m. commenced raining about 2 p.m. & rained constantly during the night kill'd one deer—Camp'd where they kill'd the Frenchman—15 miles

Tues. 3—Some difficulty in finding our horses found them in the hills—laid by all day Still raining hard kill'd 1 Elk & 2 deer

Wed. 4—Made an early start left Mr Wray & his waggon travelled hard came on to Wolf Point examined the tracks of our lost horses followed them on to the Porcupine Seen tracks of men with the horses but the last rain has washed the sign that it is impossible to follow the trail—gave up the pursuit & returned to Govt Camp got in there late in the night Kill'd an Elk & eat Chouquette & myself had our horses hobbled brot them in about ten

157

or eleven O clock & picketed them then laid down & in a few minutes our horses got frightened & stampeded we followed them in the dark but could not find them— I am afraid they are stolen

Thurs. 5—got up before day   Chouquette & myself took different directions hunted all day without success came back to camp hid our saddles &c. packed our blankets, provisions &c. & took it on foot. Camp'd on River Au Trembe— made 20 miles

Fri. 6—Very sore this morning   my right hand severely poisoned noon'd at Frenchmans came on to Big Muddy found it very high   kill'd a deer took the skin & tied up our clothes guns & blankets   Started across the Muddy—had got but a few feet when the cramp took me in my left arm—being an expert swimmer I paid but little attention to it— I told Chouquette to keep on with the pack & I would make the shore   Some way when he got in the middle of the stream the cramp took me in the legs   I went down twice   on coming up I laid my left arm on the pack & it turned over & fill'd   I told C— to keep on with the pack & I would manage to get over—he became frightened & let go of the pack which sunk to the bottom—I came near drowning but thank Providence I got out safe but perfectly naked & barefooted   forty seven miles of hard travelling before me the country full of Prickly Pears & Enemies nothing to protect my feet nor even a knife to defend myself—Choquette dive & brot up a shirt & pr of pants—he got satisfied & left   Mosquitoes & horse flies very bad—I started at a trot & kept on untill ten O clock —the night very cool   Chouquette gave out—we laid down in the prairie—not to sleep but to shiver with the cold—made sixty five miles

Sat. 7—got up at day break very cold & stiff   Started C's teeth chattering like castanets   he begged of me to stop untill the sun would get up   I consented knowing well what I would suffer from the sun as I was entirely naked & he had shoes—pants & shirt   started when the sun got up & came slow—got to little muddy about 10½ a.m. laid down in the willows for a couple of hours could not stand the mosquitoes   Started C ahead to the Fort to send clothing

to me   kept on & met Mr R Denig with a my horse & a
suit of clothes one mile from the fort   arrived at 1 p.m.
horribly sun burnt—made 17 miles

Sun. 8—hobbling around feet sore & body awfully Blistered

Mon. 9—the Pain excruciating

Tues. 10—Still suffering

Wed. 11—Some little better

Thurs. 12—opened the Blisters about 1½ galls of water came from
them

Fri. 13—Commenced to feel something like myself

Sat. 14—the skin commencing to pull of me

Sun. 15—took a short ride

Mon. 16—peeled like an onion

Tues. 17—doing nothing of consequence   Bouchie & Chouquette
returned from the Big Muddy   bring my rifle &c that I
lost on the sixth ult—all right that accounts for the stains
in this book being as it was one of drowned articles

I have not wrote up my journal on account of my being
buisy in the meantime   ten Assynaboins have been kill'd
by the Sioux—Sir Geo Gore arrived from a two years
hunt   both company's boats arrived—A Missionary Doct
Macky & Lady came to convert the Indians

. . .

OLD BATEESE

FRANK B. LINDERMAN

Affectionately, Frank B. Linderman comments on the passing of a riverman, in the French-English *patois* (usually it contained also some Chippewa or Cree) which was brought to Montana by the *voyageurs,* the hunters and trappers. Linderman contributed this poem to *The Frontier,* Vol. VIII, No. 3, May, 1928. It is reminiscent of the work of William Henry Drummond, author of *The Voyageur, The Habitant* and other books of verse about the French-Canadian people. For a biographical note on Linderman see p. 489.

OUI, she's pass, Bateese La Forge
  Today 'bout ha'-pas' ten.
  W'en she's stop firs' tam our place?
 Monsieur, HI'm small boy den.
My fadder sit beside de fire,
  An' me, HI'm play hon floor—
She's col' houtside lak anyt'ing—
  Some person rap hon door.
"Bienvenue," my Fadder call;
  My Modder say, "De pries'!"
De cabban door is open, slow,
  An' dere she is—Bateese!
Mushrat cap, an' mackinaw
  W'ite wid snow an' sleet,
Beeg w'isker, too—an' blanket pant,
  Botte sauvage * hon feet.
She's spick no word; jest stop hon fire
  Wid blue eye straight hon me.
"Mus' be yo're 'ongry," Modder say,
  An' hol' Bateese say, "Oui."
De win' is 'owl, garou, also;
  Come tam to sleep pour me—
My Fadder ask, "Yo're sleepy, too?"
  An' hol' Bateese say, "Oui."
Dat's mos' she's spick, jes' "oui" two tam.

* Heavy woodsmen's boots.

No good pour make de talk,
But hon de reevaire, Sacre Bleu!
　She's premier hon de bark canoe!
Sam lak de Hinjin hon de woods;
　Know everyt'ing is dere;
'Ow Madame doe is 'ide de fawn,
　'Ow bes' to trap de bear,
Blow call an' fool hol' Monsieur Moose,
　Ketch bevaire hon de slide,
Trap mushrat, too, an' chop de wood,
　Mak moccasin beside.
She's tak me by de han', Bateese,
　An' me, HI'm learn som-e-t'ing,
'Ow modder duck is mak believe
　He's got de busted wing,
'Ow Madame goose is place de hegg
　In sof' roun', leetle nes',
An' mak dem warm wid fedder, w'ite,
　He's scratchin' hoff hees breas';
'Ow pheasant drum, w'ere trout is bite,
　W'ere beegest berry grow;
Ever-t'ing is mos' wort'while,
　Mongee! hol' Bateese know.
She's come our place so quiet, lak,
　An' now she's go, sam way.
Saint Peter say, "You lak come in?"
　An' hol' Bateese say, "Oui."

OTTO MAERDIAN

This is one of the most charming and refreshing memoirs of the Montana ranching frontier ever printed. Otto was a dry goods clerk in Alton, Ill. At the age of twenty-two he set out with his cousin, Ed Adam, and their dog, Don, to seek his fortune in Montana. He saw central Montana, just coming into its own in 1882 as a great ranching country, through the eyes of a town-bred boy: everything was new and exciting—and expensive. He was hard up for girls, pants, fishing flies, cake, an almanac, slippers, blotters, and writing paper. And he didn't want any of the requested items sent collect. This is a condensation of an edition of his letters prepared by Lucia B. Mirrielees of the Montana State University English faculty under the title "Pioneer Ranching in Central Montana." First published in March, 1930, in Vol. X, No. 3 of *The Frontier*, it was reprinted in the University's *Sources of Northwest History*, No. 10 (general editor, Paul C. Phillips). Otto Maerdian died a few years after the publication of his letters. His widow is living in Big Timber, Mont.

St. Paul, May 28, 1882.

Dear Sister

We just arrived about ten minutes ago, 9:15 P.M. We had a splendid day. The weather was fine and as warm as could be. Everything is O.K. Don looks kind a dirty just now. Will take him to the river tomorrow and clean him.

By the Letter head you will see we are stopping at the Merchants Hotel. We have a Room together. It is very nicely furnished. I guess if we would be in one that is furnished one quarters as nice out there, we might call it a Palace. We met a fellow on board that is going out to the same place we are.

Tell all the girls to write two or three sheets of fools cap so I will have something to read when I get there. I know I will be kind-a lonesome.

Hope you have forwarded the tent because we want to cut down all expense possible. Have got a Cook Book.

Will write when I get to Miles City and tell you how we passed the time and how near we came to being Recked.

Hoping this will reach you and the rest all well. I will close by sending my love to all.

From your true brother and strayed Sheep—

Otto.

Miles City   June 1/82

Dear Sister

We arrived yesterday evening about nine o'clock; had a long and tiresome ride. The train went rather slow and we lay on a side track all night. Tuesday we passed over some very nice country and the scenery was grand. Can see prairie for five hundred miles. You can look over fifty miles of prairie in some places and not a tree to be seen. Every thing looks green and every here and there it is dotted with an old buffalo scull that some body has killed, and the wolves have made a feast of what was left on it. I saw lots of prairie dogs; some places there are regular villages of them. They dig up the ground and it looks as though it had been plowed. Saw thousands of ducks going through Minnesota a few snipe and chickens. Saw about twenty antelope and one white tailed deer, one Jack rabbit and some plover.

In the western part of Dakota we passed through what is called the bad lands; it is the roughest country ever I saw, and the hills are straight up and down. No body could ever get up there, they are high, and all this gray colored ground looks like tile but makes the scenery grand. The hills are covered with grass on top and the sides are bare. We passed some places where for miles we could see nothing but sage plants. I don't like the land right around Miles City. We are going farther west in a day or two.

Every thing costs about two prices. I went in a dry goods store this morning. They sell calico that we used to sell for 8 cts at 12. Lonsdale muslin is .17. Washington oil calico 3/4 wide we sold for 12c is 25c. We wanted to go to Ft. Keogh and they wanted five dollars for a horse & buggy. It is three miles; guess we will walk it. Have not seen any Indians since we left St. Paul; saw two Indian Squaws. I have enclosed samples of flowers I got on the prairie while walking around this morning.

Guess I will have to quit writing or it will cost me six cents if I get too much paper in it. Direct all mail same as before until farther notice and write soon. Ed got two letters this morning from home. Give my regards to all.

Your Brother,

Otto.

Excuse bad writing done in haste. It is as hot as it can be, 75 in shade. How is that for high?

Miles City June 9/82

Dear Sister

We have moved our headquarters from the hotel to a tent. We bought a mans outfit team wagon harness and cooking utensils. We moved yesterday afternoon slept in the tent last night and have done our own cooking.

It is awful hot here. I have been putting our tools together and put handles on all of them. We are waiting for my tent and Ed is waiting for a draft from Home. We bought our team with out money from a man in Wisconsin. He left yesterday and is trusting us with them they are two fine horses big and strong. One is Black and the other sorrel. Give my regards to all the Boys & Girls and write soon. Excuse scribbling, for it was written on wagon seat in camp.

from your brother

Otto.

I was going to have a tintype taken of myself but the price was too high, $1.00 a piece.

Hot Springs   June 25/82

Dear Sister

We are now about fifty miles from Bozeman. We would have been there last night but we were off of the road one whole day, and last Thursday we camped on White Beaver creek all day to look at the land in the valley. . . .

Yesterday was my birthday; did not celebrate, am celebrating it today. It being Sunday, we concluded not to travel. One of horses is sick. I am afraid we will lose her. I cut the cake this morning the one that had been cut but I gave Ed a big piece about twice as large as I used to cut at home. After he eat it he said, "Golly, that is good; lets have some more," and he cut another piece. We see how it is. We have been living high here lately. Everything costs pretty much. I have eat bread that cost twenty-five cts a loaf, and it is not one half as good as the worst bread ever you baked. It looks dark and tough as old beef. The loaves are small like those long loaves you get at the store. Although the bread is poor, I am getting fat, I believe. I tried on my stiff hat this morning, the first time I had it on since we left Miles City. It looked natural only I am sunburnt like the dickens. Look like a nigger.

We expect to get to Bozeman tomorrow eve or Tuesday. Will not stay there any longer than we can help. We saw lots of land that suits us, but the ranch men tell us that it is all taken up; so I guess it will be hard for us to get land worth much. The land up here is very good but you can't raise anything on it unless you irrigate it, which will take quite a lot of work. We are going to try and get a place in Sweet Grass Valley if we can. . . .

This is the greatest place for saloons and restaurants ever seen. We passed one place called Youngs Point. There were 4 houses in the place and 3 of them were saloons and the other a restaurant.

I think I will go down to the hot springs this afternoon and get a drink of the hot water. The folks around here say it is just like that in Arkansas.

Sending my love to all I will close from

> Your Brother,
> Otto.

Bozeman July 1/82

Dear Sister

I was very glad I heard from you for we are going to leave Bozeman tomorrow morning. Are going back to Sweet Grass. We are going up the valley in search of ground for our ranch. They say it is all taken up, but if we can't find land there we are going up on the Musselshell river, about 50 or 75 miles north of the Yellowstone river, where we think we can get a place. We met a man at Hot Springs that was going up there. He seems to be a very nice man. He gave us lots of information, told us several men from whom we could learn more about sheep and the land. He wanted us to go with him, but we had to come here for our mail and provisions so we could not go. He said he would show us around the country and help us lay out our ranch and give us all we needed at Bozeman, for flour was $12.00 a hundred lbs, and here it is $3.50; so you see we will save $8.50 if we buy it here. He seemed to take a lot of interest in us and told us all we asked of him.

I think we will like the Musselshell valley all but one thing. The Indians are not as much civilized as they are around here. If we find a place up there we will be Booked in this country for five years; then if we want to we can stay or leave. We will have what land we are on and do with it what ever we want to.

We have been having plenty of fresh meat. On the way I killed an antelope, and this man gave us a big piece of Elk meat it was fine. He was a lawyer and lived in Colorado for 2 years; then came here and opened a ranch on the Musselshell.

We arrived here Thursday eve at six o'clock. It is a very nice place, the nicest place I have seen since I left St. Paul. It looks like a civilized town a long side of the rest. There are 2 Churches, Court house, fine large brick school and the nicest lot of small dwelling houses all painted white with green lawns and level as a floor. There are lots of brick store buildings here. That is something you don't see the whole length of the Yellowstone river. We only saw one brick house on our trip from Miles City, and that was at Stillwater. . . .

Give my regards to all and write soon and often for there is nothing like news from home. Tell Rude if he wants to come out here he will have to quit smoking. Cigars cost 25c each. I have not drunk a drop since I left St. Paul. It costs too much. Beer is 15c a glass and I can't stand that when there is good water with in ten minutes walk.

I am your loving Brother,

Otto.

Marion   July 10/82

Dear Sister

We are now on the Musselshell river and don't like the country as well as we thought we would. It is a very nice Valley, but there is no timber nearer than fifteen miles; so we are going back on Sweet Grass creek. I think we can find some good land there, but it will be a job to irrigate it. It is a very nice valley. The water in the creek is clear as crystal. You can see the bottom of it any place. There are lots of trout in it. I caught one last Saturday evening that was sixteen and one half inches long, and I tell you it was fine eating. That same day I killed a Grouse; so we lived high that day. Today we baked, or rather fried, our first batch of bread.

You ought to have seen it. My dog would not eat it. We had fried potatoes, tea and bread for supper. The bread we laid on the cloth and every time we looked at it we would laugh so tears would come in our eyes. Some fellow showed us how to bake this fine bread. It took the cake. We satisfied our appetite by laughing. Ed broke the loaf open and smelled it. He said the smell reminded him of how he used to steal hot biscuits at home when his mother baked them. He blamed the poor bread on the flour like all women do. When they don't have good bread they always say the yeast did not rise or the flour was poor. We have been living on pan cakes in place of bread. We like them and have them twice a day. We have not eaten any bacon for two weeks, are tired of it. . . .

Say, will you go to the store and buy me about six yds of cottonade or mole skin for two pair of pants, make them and send them by mail? I would like the mole skin if you can get it. They had a piece of slate color with a narrow white stripe very dark and a brown stripe they were both striped alike and were about 30c or 40c a yard. Don't send anything good, for I will not have any use for it. Have worn out one pair of those light pants. Line the mole skin pants with some of papa's old pants so they will be warm. Send me a pair of buckskin gloves with them; have it registered so it will come safe. Send by mail, and if I ever get rich enough to pay you I will send the money.

I am your loving brother

T. O. M.

Puetts Ranch July 28, 1882

Dear Sister

I am now on the land where I intend to settle. We have found a place that suits us and are waiting for Mr. Puett to get back from Ft. Benton to survey it for us. We had his compass the other day and tried to survey it, but some of the cornerstones were gone so we could not do it. I am awful tired. I was up in the mountains yesterday cutting timber for our house. I tell you it was a hard job, but I stuck to it and brought a load with me. It is nine miles from here, and it is a very lonesome place; there is no sound to be heard but your ax and the wind blowing in the pine trees. There is one place about five hundred yds from where I chop where you go down in a hollow about one hundred and fifty feet and there you find a creek of the finest and coldest water ever I drank. I make ice tea every time I go up to chop. It is boss.* I put Ed on to it. He thinks it is quite a treat to have ice tea. The creek goes down into the rocks and you ought to see how fast it runs; don't know whether it ever comes out any place or not, but it is in a very lonely place. There are lots of tracks of wild animals. I guess that is about all there is that ever goes around it. I don't feel safe when I go there, and yesterday I forgot my revolver and I felt "kinder weak in the knee."

I have to go and see how the bread is now. Wait a minute and I will finish.

By the way did you send those pants? If you have not, send them by mail. I think I forgot to tell you how to send them. When you send my things, always send it by mail. If it is too heavy to send in one package make two of it. It will cost twice as much either by express or freight. There are no railroads or boats here so it cost a great deal to have any thing sent here.

I think I will go to Bozeman next week to get the mail; hope there will be a sack full for me. It seems as though I haven't heard from any body for six months. . . .

. . . What do you think I have struck? An old † lady. She is a widow, and she said she wanted to be my mother while I am out here. She came from St. Louis out here seventeen years ago. She is about forty in years. It is Mrs. Peuet. She is a fine lady, and she gave us several pies and told us to come and see her often. The pie struck me natural right where I live. We ran out of lard so she gave us as much as we got at Miles City for $1.00. She has no daughter or I would think there was something at the back of it. Her nephew is with her; he is an Illinois boy. He is about twenty five. He is quite a nice young fellow. He watches her sheep. They have nine hundred and some over, I have forgotten just how many. They sheered five hundred and thirteen sheep and got over four thousand lbs of wool. How is that for high? Sheep sheared 13 lbs of wool, and they had an old ram that sheared 17 lbs. If we can only get a flock that will do that well, we will be all O. K. The general average of wool to a sheep is six lbs and their average eight. Oh I am bound to be a stock raiser for the next five or six years!

Say, send me a box of this kind of writing paper. I am very

* "It is boss": it is good; "swell."
† See the third sentence following!

nearly out and we are over 150 miles from a place to buy it so I wish you would. You can buy it cheaper there and send by mail. I wish you would keep an account of what you buy for me and if I ever get the money, I will pay it back.

I have done all kinds of work already: have sewed my clothes, shoed one of our horses, mended the wagon, tended Peuets sheep, doctored our horse, cut wood, and am going to help build our house—and lots of things I have done.

Fishing is fine. I went out every day last week and caught a fish for dinner. Caught one trout that measured nineteen and three-quarter inches. He was a monster; broke my pole at the joint, but I fixed it again and I caught eight or ten that measured over 15 inches. They are the prettiest fish to catch ever I saw. You see them swimming along the bottom of the creek, drop in your fly, and it hardly touches the water when he has it. In your next letter send me some light green zephyr split, some medium red, some blue, and a spool of button hole silk, orange color. Take it off of the spool so you can put it in an envelope.

Tell Rude to shoot a red bird and send me the feathers. Tell him not to muss them any more than he can help. I want to make some flies to fish with. Send three or four yards of the Zephyr or German town wool. I think I can make the flies. They are fifty cts a piece, and if you get them snaged it comes off. You don't use any bait, nothing but the feather. The fish think they are bugs and bite like good fellows. The La-da-das ought to come up here. If they wouldn't open their mouths when they caught one of those salmon colored trout about fifteen inches long I don't want a cent! They are pretty fish, salmon color with dark blue back and spotted all over on the sides and top. They have teeth three row of teeth on the lower jaw and three on the upper; the teeth are very small and sharp as a needle. The first one I caught I put my finger in his mouth and he closed on it. It felt kind a queer a long side of the fish at home; so I took it out in a hurry.

We are going to change our Post Office Box to Big Timber after I go to Bozeman. It is about 18 miles and Bozeman over 150. That will be our Sunday ride.

It takes all the spare time I get to write to you at present. After we get our house built I think I will have more time.

Hoping this will find you all well and wish to receive an abundant supply of mail when I get to Bozeman, I will close.

Sending my love and regards to the girls and boys. I am your loving

Brother,
OTTO.

All seems to be going on well. The work is awful hard but I am going to nuckle down to it and put it through. Hope the Lord will reward me in the end.

Extra Suppliment

We have been living like Chinese for the last week on boiled rice. It went fine. Today we will have antelope. A man by the name of Andrew brought us a half of one last night so we will have saratoga potatoes and antelope stake for dinner. Sometimes I go out along the creek and pick wild goose berries. They are splendid; just like tame ones only not so large. Beans are pretty good when you can't get anything else. Mrs. Peuet says she will make butter in a few weeks and then we can have all the buttermilk we want.

Will write the balance some other time. I have to go about a mile and a half to mail this and see a man about his mower to cut our hay. Write often and tell the girls to write. I will have more time after I get the house built.

Your Brother.

Puetts, Aug. 11/82.

Dear Sister:

I received your letters dated June 27th and July 9th. Was very glad to find you all well and am very thankful for the money you sent me. I was really in need of it when I got it. I left here for Bozeman Friday A.M. with seven dollars in my pocket, and with that I had to get the horse shoed and buy some nails, an ax handle, and my lunch besides. I did not know how in the world I would get any lunch out of that amount after having paid for them; so I thought I would have to live on hopes of getting some thing when I got to camp. Thought I would have to take Dr. Tanner's method of living on water, but when I opened the letter & found the P. O. Order I was all O. K. and began to feel fat. Every thing is so high out here and you have to have a pocket full of money to get any thing.

I have sent to H. Filley to send me some sole leather. My boots are played out, and there are quite a lot of snake in this country; so I don't trust shoes much. Ed killed a big rattle snake about fifty yds from our camp while I was gone. It had seven rattles and a button. I have the dinamite yet and if any should get over my shoe tops I will use it to blow it down. As yet I have not pulled the cork. You seem to worry a good deal about me going too near the Indians. Why I have not seen any since I left Miles City & I saw but six or eight there. There are two families of half breeds about a half mile from us, but they are civilized and are better neighbors than most white people. Folks call people "neighbors" if they live within ten miles from them. We have ten families with in five miles of us. Two old Batchelors are about as far as from our house to Levises from where we are; so we aint out of calling distance. One of them, Mr. Andrews, was here this A.M. All the people around here are real nice folk; you ask them any thing and they give you all the information they can, and if you want any thing they lend it to you in a minute. We are going to help Puetts make hay today and to morrow, and they are going to let us have there mower; so it won't cost us any thing to cut our hay.

The Indians don't come through only in the fall and spring, and the settlers watch them so close that they don't get a chance to do any thing. Last year some went through that did not do just as the settlers wanted them, and they were driving off there horses; so the settlers made for them and took the scalp of one. He is in the sod near the mountains. The settlers make them walk chalk when they come around here.

Ed did not do any thing on the house while I was gone so it is not done yet. When I got back I found him fast asleep.

I think we have a pretty honest lot of people out here. We have left the tent several times and have been gone all day and not a thing has been touched.

I almost forgot there is going to be a young lady and her brother out here in the spring. They have taken up some land near us. She is rather nice looking, too. I had an introduction to her mother; she seems to be a nice lady. I have been clubbing myself because it was not her daughter instead of her, but I will get around that. I will go and see her brother and perhaps I may get a chance to know her. I made a big mash on Di Hunter's daughter. I took dinner there on my way to Bozeman and she set down near by and waited on me. After dinner we had quite a long talk and she told me to come & see her some time. She just came out here last fall and is a fine looking girl. Her father has the Hot Springs & is putting up a hotel there. . . .

I got eleven letters when I got to Bozeman, seven from home and four elsewhere. Was glad it panned out so well, and you don't know how much good it does to hear from home.

I am not particular when Pa sends the money now but I would like about $35 to enter my land with. I think we have got a good lot of hay ground. I am going to try and get some of this rail road land; it is fine. The rail road will pass Sweet Grass this fall about 18 miles south of us.

We are on the Sweet Grass Creek on what is called Cayouse flat. There is a spring runs through our land of nice clear water full of fish but too small to catch.

Tell Bob to save the brass wire that comes around white shirt linen and send it to me. It is very fine and braided, or to send me some of this gold colored trimming they use for masquerade suits. I want it for flies; also send a small piece of guta percha. Get it at the drug store. I want to make me some flies to fish with. Guta percha about the size of a walnut, hammer fine, and put in an envelope.

Brother,

Write often. OTTO.

Aug. 22, 1882

Dear Sister:

Ed has gone to Big Timber today to get the mail. Hope I don't get left. We have not got our house done yet. It seems as though we never will. We have been helping Mr. Puett make hay for the last seven days; so I have got some hay seed in my hair already. . . .

We have found a good substitute for eggs. When we make corn cake we use yellow corn meal and it look as though it was filled with eggs. Eggs are 8 1-3c apiece, pretty cheap.

I am your loving brother,

OTTO.

Puetts, Sept. 20, 82

Dear Sister:

I was down to Big Timber Sunday and got a letter from you dated July 30th. I cant imagine what kept it so long on the road. I also got the pantaloons. I like them very much; think I will be in style when I wear them. They are the first Old Gold pantaloons I ever saw. I am sure that is not the style now out east is it?

I suppose you learned through Pa that we lost one of our horses. Well, we have bought two, not near as big as our other one was, and we are going to use our first one for a third one should we have a big load. We have not paid for them yet. Wish you would tell Pa to send my money so we can pay for them, and we will have to get some blankets for cold weather. We have not got a cent left; all the money we have is five dollars & eighty five cents, and that is the balance I have left from the spending money you sent me. . . .

We have about got our house done. We put poles on top today & tomorrow we will plaster the roof with mud & then we will chovel dirt on it. That is the way they put roofs on houses out here where shingles are scarce. We will finish it this week if we can keep at it.

Your loving Bro
OTTO.

Sept. 28, 1882

Dear Sister:

I received your letter and would have answered it before but thought I would wait until Ed went to Big Timber so he could take it down.

I have written a pretty stiff letter to the Post Master at Bozeman about the other Hdkfs and that letter of yours and Lulu's. I think a little talk will bring him to time. Your letter was there over a month and a half.

About the money, we are rather hard up at present. Have bought two horses but have not paid for them. The man ticked us for them. They are two brothers and are nice men. We owe them 175 dollars yet. This is a hard country on a poor man. They all are independent and wont sell any thing unless they can get a price for it, and us poor chaps have to stand it. If we ever get fixed, we will do just the same. The horse we got goes all right in harness. I tried him the other day and he did not make much fuss.

I have not worn the pants yet. I have made one mash on Mrs. Puett's niece. She is an Illinois girl from Lexington. She came on a visit and bought a round trip ticket, but she liked it so well that she sent her ticket home and her father left Sunday for home so she is going to stay. The old lady says she is going to buy a piano for her. Wont we have a jolly time when the 'pianner' gets here?

She called on us instead of us calling on her, and invited us down to see her. She sent for us to come down last Friday and spend the evening with her pa before he left. Ed went but I stayed at home and watched the children. You want to know how far it is to Puetts? Only two miles. I used to think it was far, but when I got to getting milk for nothing it seemed only half so far. They are not the nearest neighbors. There are two others but they are bachelors. There is another family about 1½ miles west, Mrs. Roberts. She is a fine lady about 25 years old and a very nice girl, but Puetts is on the road and we leave our mail there so it is the handiest.

I wish we had half even one eighth of the fruit you put up, for I have not tasted a bite so far.

Our house has three rooms. One we live in the other we cook in and one the length of the house but narrow at the back of the house we use for a work shop. You ask what we do for windows. Puetts gave us one window sash and we bought six lights and put it in the door. We have 4 more lights; so we will make a sash for them. Will send a plan some day of our palace.

You must think people out here live awful queer, asking if they have stoves. You can get stoves by paying for them. We intend to send east for ours; we save from 10 to 20 dollars on it, but houses are not furnished very nice. The country is too new yet; can't get them. We cook in our fire place so far. It is a poor way. We are not in our house yet. I am kind afraid of it. We have a dirt roof & it is pretty heavy; am afraid it will cave in on us.

From your loving Brother,
OTTO.

Tell Rude to send me a pound of walnuts in a cigar box by mail. I want to plant them to see if they will grow.*

Puetts, Dec. 13, 82.

Dear Sister:

I received your letter quite a while back and would have an-

* They won't.

swered them, but we have been camping in the mountains the past 3 week getting out timber for sheep sheds before the snow got too deep. We got about 400 trees out & about 300 pulled out & hauled where the snow wont bother them. The rest we will have to leave. The snow is so deep that we could not do any thing; so we moved down Monday and I started to haul the timber home today.

You ask where I put up for the nights when I go to Bozeman. Why I sleep in the wagon & take chuck enough to last me on the way. It is quite a tiresome job, I should remark. It is riding for 10 days. If it was not for the scenery I think I should die on the road. You want to know what kind of a place Big Timber is. It is a fine town 3 buildings built of logs one is a store & saloon, one a dwelling & the other a feed stable the Marble fronts are so numerous I wont stop to mention them. That horse you think we ought not to have bought goes fine & I am going to try & ride him some day. We just saved about $50 dollar buying him unbroke. I got the cake you sent by mail. It was kind of dry. It would have tasted better if we had had some wine with it. We did not make it look sick at all. All there was left of it was the box & string; came very near eating them.

I have not cut my other fruit cake yet, will sample it Christmas. Ed could not wait so cut his some months ago. I will have a picnic on it.

You say our old cat died. I wish there was a way to send a cat by mail, for the mice are awful bad out here. They spoilt one of Ed's woolen shirts & a pair of socks for me & carried off about a bushel of oats for us. They are thick as flees on a dogs Back. . . .

I sent for some strychnine for wolves; hope you have sent it. I saw four yesterday morning. I can buy it out here, but they ask $8.00 an ounce & you can get it for $1.60, want the crystalized. I would like to have it before I go on that hunt if I can get it. Their fur makes nice robes & I want an overcoat out of them. They are pretty thick around here you can hear them every morning & evening. Most of the rabbits out here are white. There are few other kind. I have not killed much game, have no time to hunt. I have killed quite a number of chicken; I would kill them on my way to Puetts.

The rail road has been at Big Timber for some time & is about 40 miles beyond toward Bozeman.

Ed was going up on the Musselshell this morning to see what we could do in the way of buying sheep, but the weather was so bad he gave it up. I hope Pa has sent the balance of my money. If not, tell him a St. Louis draft will be best. Money orders can not be sent in larger than fifty dollar sums & I would have to go to Bozeman to get them cashed.

Send me one of my Cabinet photos if there are any of them at home. I want one of them. Also have Rude & Pa get some taken I would like one of theirs & yours send them together so they will not be so likely to get damaged. Dont wait six months to send them. . . .

Wishing you all a Merry Christmas & a Happy New Year with love & regards to all I remain your loving Bro,

OTTO.

P.S.—Send me a pair of common slippers, some Almanacs, & ink blotters. I did not get to mail this today. Ed left for the Mussel-shell river this afternoon, will be gone 4 or 5 days; so I am all alone in my glory. Send a pair of heel plates for my skates.

Puetts, Jan. 7, 83.

Dear Sister:

Your letter was received all O. K. but not when you expected in the New Year. I got it a few days after Christmas. I also got the cake; got it New Years eve. It was fine, beats the one I had all hollow.

I spent my Christmas going to the Party. Had an immense time. There were about seventy ladies there and you ought to see how they dress. I was perfectly surprised when I entered the hall to see women in this country dress so fine. Nearly every one had on a silk or satin Dress & they were made real neat. They come from all parts of the Country and cold as it was, every body seemed satisfied for going. We left home at daylight and got there at about Eight o'clock. We stopped about 2 hours at Big Timber to feed the team and get some thing ourselves.

New Years I put in at Big Timber. We bought a stove so we had to stay there all day. I helped the P. Master get out his quarterly report. I did all the writing for him. He called off the numbers & I filled the blanks. After we were done he said I would make a good Post Master. It is the queerest Job I ever saw. They have to

176

keep an account of all the stamps they sell—cancel—& buy and every 3 months send it to Washington. They came out $42.00 behind last quarter; so it aint very profitable.

I got on to our colt today, the one we broke to harness. He did not want me there so he thought he would dump me off, which he did. I had no saddle so I put on a blanket and it came off, I with it. I don't think I would have slid off if it had not come loose. I held on to the bridle & got Ed to help me up on to him again, & he went all right then. I am going to Big Timber tomorrow; so I got a saddle today & I will try him again tomorrow.

I tapped the Dynamite Christmas eve. It is pretty slick. There is more in a tablespoon full of it than there is in a whole bottle of what you get out here.

We are having quite a little winter, plenty of snow. Ed is making a sleigh & we have some sheep bells so we will have some music & a ride day after tomorrow. I made a pair of heel plates yesterday. The creek in front of our house has overflowed & is frozen & slick as glass; so I am going to try my skates some day when the wind don't blow. It has been blowing awful hard the last few days, and the snow has drifted in some places about 5 ft. deep in other places the ground is as clear of snow as can be.

Wishing to hear from you soon, I am your loving brother,

OTTO.

Puetts, Jan. 28/83.

Dear Sister:

. . . Our place or neighborhood is to be called Melville. We have a post office & will have a service next spring. Send my mail to Big Timber as usual, and when we have a service I will change it.

So hoping to hear from you soon I will close remaining your loving brother,

OTTO.

April 11/83

Dear Sister:

. . . I don't think I told you that I went to Livingston & had a lady go with me. It was a picnic, had a high old time. It was Cora Marshal, one of our neighbors and a little daisy too. We stopped two days at Hunters Hot Springs and, while there, there were two young ladies visiting Hunters. Mrs. Hunter took me up in the parlor and knocked me down to them. It was a grand treat. Old Dr. he was there and he gave us some history of Montana, and she set em up to hot water and after that we played a few games and adjourned next day. We left about 4 P.M. for this young lady's sister's about six miles from the Springs. Got there just before dark and in time for supper. I did not eat. Just imagine me eating. I have forgotten how to eat. We had a time after supper. I have never had so much fun since I left home as I did that night. They have a parlor organ and singing and dancing till noon. It was a picnic for this country. The young lady stayed up there and is not coming home until May 1st. I felt sorry when I left there for home and had to go alone. She has been out here but a short time, came last fall from Iowa.

Hoping this will find you all well and wishing to hear from you soon I am your loving bro

OTTO.

Melville, April 30/83

Dear Sister:

. . . Say I believe I would like to have you send my light suit out for I have nothing to wear this summer only my black suit & Montana broadcloth (overalls). Also send my watch. Make me a few chamois skin bags to carry it in. I need a watch bad, for when I go any place half the time I can't find what time it is, and while out at work I can't tell when noon comes and we lose more time than a little by it. When you send it, send it by Express and have the agt give you a receipt for it. Put the clothes in a box and put the watch inside of the clothes where it won't slip to the side or corners of the box. Have pa bind the box around the edge with hoop iron and to take a good strong box. Please pay Express charges on it.

Have it send Via Chicago to St. Paul care N. P. railroad Exp. Have this put on one corner of the box; then I will get it in a short time. Otherwise it may go by way of Utah and N. and nobody will know when it will get here.

Your loving Brother,

OTTO.

Melville, May 13/83

Dear Sister:

We have a regular mail service through here now three times a week so you can direct my mail to Melville, M. T. (Via Big Timber). We are getting quite civilized here lately. After a while we won't know ourselves.

Tell Mrs. Johnson I think if her Nephew was out here, he could get work but he would find it a very rough place and in regards to Christianity, it makes no dif. He would have to do as the rest of the fellows out here. It is all day and Sunday too. He would find the cowboys a hard set to work with. Stock raising out here is so different from what he is used to that experience in that country would do no good out here. All the experience he wants, to know how to throw a rope and ride. They turn there cattle out and in spring and fall they round them up and brand them and turn them out again. Sheep is different. He might find his experience in raising them to help him, but winter herding would be hard on him; it is so cold. I advise her not to let him come to this country unless he goes into business for himself, for they don't have any mercy on any body. The cow boys are all right if you get acquainted with them and treat them all right, but otherwise they are not; and if you bother them it is better if you look a 'letle oud.'

You ask about Mrs. Puett. I tell you about her and leave the girl out. This time she is quite well and goes out horseback every day. She is riding the range now seeing to her horses. She has two bands of horses and they keep her busy. . . .

If you get this before you send the box with my suit, have Pa send me a sack of shot 25 lbs of No. 8. I can't get it out here. If not too late, how is cake: Put in my Christmas cake and candy. It will come all O. K. but pack it so it won't get on the clothes, and fix the shot so it won't fall from one end of the box to the other when they move or roll it.

Give my regards to Kate and all the girls and love to Pa and Rude and write soon.

Your loving brother,
OTTO.

179

THE STORY OF THE COWPUNCHER

CHARLES M. RUSSELL

Charley Russell, who was one of them, describes the Montana cow-puncher in this story from *Trails Plowed Under*, published in 1937 by Doubleday, Doran. The book is a Montana classic, in fact probably *the* Montana classic. Other excerpts will be found elsewhere in this volume.

SPEAKIN' of cowpunchers," says Rawhide Rawlins, "I'm glad to see in the last few years that them that know the business have been writin' about 'em. It begin to look like they'd be wiped out without a history. Up to a few years ago there's mighty little known about cows and cow people. It was sure amusin' to read some of them old stories about cowpunchin'. You'd think a puncher growed horns an' was haired over.

"It put me in mind of the eastern girl that asks her mother: 'Ma,' says she, 'do cowboys eat grass?' 'No, dear,' says the old lady, 'they're part human,' an' I don't know but the old gal had 'em sized up right. If they are human, they're a separate species. I'm talkin' about the old-time ones, before the country's strung with wire an' nesters had grabbed all the water, an' a cowpunch-er's home was big. It wasn't where he took his hat off, but where he spread his blankets. He ranged from Mexico to the Big Bow River of the north, an' from where the trees get scarce in the east to the old Pacific. He don't need no iron hoss, but covers his country on one that eats grass an' wears hair. All the tools he needed was saddle, bridle, quirt, hackamore, an' rawhide riatta or seagrass rope; that covered his hoss.

"The puncher himself was rigged, startin' at the top, with a good hat—not one of the floppy kind you see in pictures, with the rim turned up in front.* The top-cover he wears holds its shape an' was made to protect his face from the weather; maybe to hold it on, he wore a buckskin string under the chin or back of the head. Round his neck a big silk handkerchief, tied loose, an' in the drag of a trail herd it was drawn over the face to the eyes, hold-up

* The original cowboy hat was low-crowned.

fashion, to protect the nose an' throat from dust. In old times, a leather blab or mask was used the same. Coat, vest, an' shirt suits his own taste. Maybe he'd wear California pants, light buckskin in color, with large brown plaid, sometimes foxed, or what you'd call reinforced with buck or antelope skin. Over these came his chaparejos or leggin's. His feet were covered with good high-heeled boots, finished off with steel spurs of Spanish pattern. His weapon's usually a forty-five Colt's six-gun, which is packed in a belt, swingin' a little below his right hip. Sometimes a Winchester in a scabbard, slung to his saddle under his stirrup-leather, either right or left side, but generally left, stock forward, lock down, as his rope hangs at his saddle-fork on the right.

"By all I can find out from old, gray-headed punchers, the cow business started in California, an' the Spaniards were the first to burn marks on their cattle an' hosses, an' use the rope. Then men from the States drifted west to Texas, pickin' up the brandin' iron an' lass-rope, an' the business spread north, east, an' west, till the spotted long-horns walked in every trail marked out by their brown cousins, the buffalo.

"Texas an' California, bein' the startin' places, made two species of cowpunchers; those west of the Rockies rangin' north, usin' centerfire or single-cinch saddles, with high fork an' cantle; packed a sixty or sixty-five foot rawhide rope, an' swung a big loop. These cow people were generally strong on pretty, usin' plenty of hoss jewelry, silver-mounted spurs, bits, an' conchas; instead of a quirt, used a romal, or quirt braided to the end of the reins. Their saddles were full stamped,* with from twenty-four to twenty-eight-inch eagle-bill tapaderos.† Their chaparejos ‡ were made of fur or hair, either bear, angora goat, or hair sealskin. These fellows were sure fancy, an' called themselves buccaroos, coming from the Spanish word, *vaquero*.

"The cowpuncher east of the Rockies originated in Texas and ranged north to the Big Bow. He wasn't so much for pretty; his saddle was low horn, rimfire,§ or double-cinch; sometimes 'ma-cheer.' ‖ Their rope was seldom over forty feet, for being a good

* Tooled leather; ornamented with floral or geometric designs.
† Stirrup-hoods to avoid tangling in brush and prevent foot slipping through.
‡ Hip-length protective leggings.
§ "Full double cinch."
‖ An extra leather covering over the whole saddle, named probably for an early maker.

deal in a brush country, they were forced to swing a small loop. These men generally tied, instead of taking their dallie-welts, or wrapping their rope around the saddle horn. Their chaparejos were made of heavy bullhide, to protect the leg from brush an' thorns, with hog-snout tapaderos.

"Cowpunchers were mighty particular about their rig, an' in all the camps you'd find a fashion leader. From a cowpuncher's idea, these fellers was sure good to look at, an' I tell you right now, there ain't no prettier sight for my eyes than one of those goodlookin', long-backed cowpunchers, sittin' up on a high-forked, full-stamped California saddle with a live hoss between his legs.

"Of course a good many of these fancy men were more ornamental than useful, but one of the best cow-hands I ever knew belonged to this class. Down on the Gray Bull, he went under the name of Mason, but most punchers called him Pretty Shadow. This sounds like an Injun name, but it ain't. It comes from a habit some punchers has of ridin' along, lookin' at their shadows. Lookin' glasses are scarce in cow outfits, so the only chance for these pretty boys to admire themselves is on bright, sunshiny days. Mason's one of these kind that doesn't get much pleasure out of life in cloudy weather. His hat was the best; his boots was made to order, with extra long heels. He rode a center-fire,* full-stamped saddle, with twenty-eight-inch. tapaderos; bearskin ancaroes, or saddle pockets; his chaparejos were of the same skin. He packed a sixty-five-foot rawhide. His spurs an' bit were silver inlaid, the last bein' a Spanish spade. But the gaudiest part of his regalia was his gun. It's a forty-five Colt's, silverplated an' chased with gold. Her handle is pearl, with a bull's head carved on.

"When the sun hits Mason with all this silver on, he blazes up like some big piece of jewelry. You could see him for miles when he's ridin' high country. Barrin' Mexicans, he's the fanciest cow boy I ever see, an' don't think he don't savvy the cow. He knows what she says to her calf. Of course there wasn't many of his stripe. All punchers liked good rigs, but plainer; an' as most punchers 're fond of gamblin' an' spend their spare time at stud poker or monte, they can't tell what kind of a rig they'll be ridin' the next day. I've seen many a good rig lost over a blanket. It depends how lucky the cards fall what kind of a rig a man's ridin'.

"I'm talkin' about old times, when cowmen were in their glory.

* Single-cinch.

They lived different, talked different, an' had different ways. No matter where you met him, or how he's rigged, if you'd watch him close he'd do something that would tip his hand. I had a little experience back in '83 that'll show what I'm gettin' at.

"I was winterin' in Cheyenne. One night a stranger stakes me to buck the bank. I got off lucky an' cash in fifteen hundred dollars. Of course I cut the money in two with my friend, but it leaves me with the biggest roll I ever packed. All this wealth makes Cheyenne look small, an' I begin longin' for bigger camps, so I drift for Chicago. The minute I hit the burg, I shed my cow garments an' get into white man's harness. A hard hat, boiled shirt, laced shoes—all the gearin' known to civilized man. When I put on all this rig, I sure look human; that is, I think so. But them shorthorns know me, an' by the way they trim that roll, it looks like somebody's pinned a card on my back with the word 'EASY' in big letters. I ain't been there a week till my roll don't need no string around it, an' I start thinkin' about home. One evenin' I throw in with the friendliest feller I ever met. It was at the bar of the hotel where I'm camped. I don't just remember how we got acquainted, but after about fifteen drinks we start holdin' hands an' seein' who could buy the most and fastest. I remember him tellin' the barslave not to take my money, 'cause I'm his friend. Afterwards, I find out the reason for this goodheartedness; he wants it all an' hates to see me waste it. Finally, he starts to show me the town an' says it won't cost me a cent. Maybe he did, but I was unconscious, an' wasn't in shape to remember. Next day, when I come to, my hair's sore an' I didn't know the days of the week, month, or what year it was.

"The first thing I do when I open my eyes is to look at the winders. There's no bars on 'em, an' I feel easier. I'm in a small room with two bunks. The one opposite me holds a feller that's smokin' a cigarette an' sizin' me up between whiffs while I'm dressin'. I go through myself but I'm too late. Somebody beat me to it. I'm lacin' my shoes an' thinkin' hard, when the stranger speaks:

" 'Neighbor, you're a long way from your range.'

" 'You call the turn,' says I, 'but how did you read my iron?' *

" 'I didn't see a burn † on you,' says he, 'an' from looks, you'll

---

* "Read my iron"; recognize my brand, know my origin.
† Brand.

go as a slick-ear.* It's your ways, while I'm layin' here, watchin' you get into your garments. Now, humans dress up an' punchers dress down. When you raised, the first thing you put on is your hat. Another thing that shows you up is you don't shed your shirt when you bed down. So next comes your vest an' coat, keepin' your hindquarters covered till you slide into your pants, an' now you're lacin' your shoes. I notice you done all of it without quittin' the blankets, like the ground's cold. I don't know what state or territory you hail from, but you've smelt sagebrush an' drank alkali. I heap savvy you. You've slept a whole lot with nothin' but sky over your head, an' there's times when that old roof leaks, but judgin' from appearances, you wouldn't mind a little open air right now.'

"This feller's my kind, an' he stakes me with enough to get back to the cow country."

* "Slick-ear": maverick, unbranded calf (an innocent person).

THE HOMESTEADER

ELLIOTT C. LINCOLN

From *Rhymes of a Homesteader* (Houghton Mifflin, 1920).

BURIED up to his ears in debt,
Fighting the heat, and cold, and wet,
His chances worse than an even bet—
You'll find the homesteader.

Eyes burned out in the summer sun,
Skin like a beefsteak underdone;
You'd think him fifty—he's thirty-one—
But then, he's a homesteader.

Winter comes, and his note is due
(Summer was dry, and nothing grew),
So he sells his gun, and a cow or two,
And hopes, does the homesteader.

Rough and broken his acres lie,
Half of them white with alkali;
But they mean that thing he couldn't buy—
A home—to the homesteader.

One part hero, and three parts fool,
All of him bulldog grit, as a rule.
He's slow to learn, but he stays in school.
"Here's How," Mister Homesteader.

LAST YEAR OF DROUGHT

IRA STEPHENS NELSON

Here, in a glance into the mind of an aging and beaten man, is an unusually moving study of the bewilderment and despair born of relentless drought. It is a fragment from Ira Stephens Nelson's novel, *On Sarpy Creek,* published in 1938 by Little, Brown. Nelson, born in Oklahoma in 1912, was brought to Montana by his parents when he was five and the family settled on a ranch on Sarpy Creek in the southeastern section of the state. This was his first novel. Nelson attended Billings Polytechnic Institute and tried many jobs—even that of night nurse in an insane asylum in Iowa—before writing the book. At the time of its publication he was a resident of California.

OLD JIM was saddened, and within himself he would be glad when the time came for him to die. He had passed his sixty-ninth year. Even at best, he knew he would not see so very many more years. He did not want to live much longer. He had no money, and more and more in these last few winters and summers he had seen that he could not be so heft with work; he could not bear up under hot sun; he could not wade snow, and shoulder into cold winter wind; even now if he gathered up every last thing he owned and sold it for money, he could not garner enough to pay the debts he owed in this world. Old as he was, poor as he was, uneducated old-time Westerner as he was, what good was there in his staying on here many more years, he thought? He had not felt this way as long as Ellen was with him. He'd stay, though, till the Lord knowed his time was up, and let him go. But all his life he had worked hard and done his poor best; now an old man, he had less than nothing, the fields all around his house were bare of any growth; he soon would have nothing to feed the cattle and horses he had raised and already mortgaged for money to buy grain which he had already fed them. And the rich and verdant land he had first loved nearly half a century ago, loved so that he had brought his young wife here with bright plans and high hopes—this land was changing. It was crumbling, moving, dying, before his very eyes. He felt in his heart that this was no ordinary drought. No! Let the newspapers and supposed-to-be wise men talk what they would over drought cycles and rainy cycles and spots on the sun. This land was changing; and unless the Government stepped in with all its money and power to do with, this land in a few score years would surely be scant with neighbors. He would not live to see what happened. But in these last few years a feeling had grown upon him—with the deep power of a prophecy. This change in these vast Western dryland regions had come and would continue to come, with a deadly creeping. You could feel it; you could go out in the hills at night and feel a loneliness different than ever before, dead loneliness akin to that of a vast tomb, and hot wind whined through the dark laden with dust powder that settled to bury even fences, so that poor dumb hungry beasts would walk right over them in pitiful search for grass and water. The dust billowed and rolled, from the ground you stood on to high aloft in the sky, so that there were no stars, no moon; and no sun by day. On such a day, it was like long hours of too dusky, unnatural twilight—yellow, brownish twilight when you could see nothing; by day and even more so by night it was awesome; if a man be alone in the hills in that wind and deep dark that was full of sting and force and feel of all these things unexplained, it struck fear in his heart. Even the wild beasts, more knowing to nature than we are, were stricken with the fear of this unknown force. They crouched behind low, slowly dying bushes, and worried in their own way, maybe, even as men worried. Was not the whole world in a turmoil? Oh, there were a few folks, no doubt, to whom this was all only a rumor. A few moneyed or simple ones, who found life very solid, very credulous. A few folks who did not think very deeply, and laughed at the thought that any civilization could crash. Yet what of these stories of the fall of Babylon, and of these things you read of great cities buried, one on the other, centuries apart, each a separate civilization? Lord! how long ago men and women and growing children had lived proudly on the streets of those cities! How was a man to figure this world out, anyhow, old Jim thought? How was a man to know what to think, when it was all summed up? The more you think and read and study and learn the more flabbergasted and in doubt you be. On one side, half of the world repeats: "Turn to the Lord, your God. He gives you life, and He takes it away. Live believing in Him, and when you die, you shall not die, but shall have everlasting life. You shall go to heaven, or you shall go to hell. You will go some place, anyhow." On the other side, the other half of the world says: "Why man, you are not created by God. You are the natural development of evolution. See, we have proven it, haven't we? In the beginning, life was like a tub of jelly floating in the sea, and the sea covered the whole earth. In a few million years, or thereabouts, the jelly had evolved to things that crawled, or swam; then to things that walked and climbed trees; finally to monkeys. See how the ape man and cave man came into life? You are but a man evolved from them, having developed— at last!—that most glorious result of all the mysteries of evolution, a *mind;* when you could think and plan, you became truly the master of all you surveyed. Now you—all of you!—are wonderful! wonderful! But when you die your very flesh will rot swiftly as any flesh will rot when it is dead. And for you—that is the end!"

Now which, and what, was a man to believe, old Jim pondered. Both could not be right. And could both be wrong? He did not know. He only knew that surely we must all die in our time, and we are on this earth no more.

And surely we are all wonderful in our own creation, however it came to be. With the mind to think and feel, to be happy, or unhappy, to love and hate . . . you and you and you!

In old Jim it was significant that no more did he argue or rail out his opinions of the Government, or ways of the world, or religion. He was hushed. In his own mind he had admitted some vague and weary defeat. Soon he would not be able to make a living for his own self. He was poor in money and things that stood for money. He knew he was ignorant. He admitted to himself how little he really knew. Take God Almighty, for example. Maybe there was a God, holding out His hand to offer everlasting life. Maybe there was not. How was a trivial man to know? After all, did it matter much? Many a man worked hard all his life, doing the best he knew how, and when he grew old and was broke, his grown sons and daughters marrying off, his wife gone, he was glad to lay down and die in peace, whether or not he had any thought of living again.

Discouraged as he was, old Jim could not help but say, as everyone else said: "This will be the last year of drought and hard times, most likely. It cain't last much longer."

THE BAD ACTOR

MAX MILLER

Max Miller was born in Michigan and his present home is in California, but part of his childhood was spent on a ranch eighteen miles southeast of Conrad, Mont. His experiences there are recounted in *The Beginning of a Mortal*, published by E. P. Dutton in 1933; the selection given here is a chapter of that book. Miller started as a reporter in Everett, Wash., and in 1932 published his first book, *I Cover the Waterfront*, which was widely read. He was a naval lieutenant during World War II and his most recent books are *Daybreak for Our Carrier*, *The Far Shore*, and *It's Tomorrow Out Here*, all written while he was in service. His first literary product was a school exercise describing the experience of a boy with a horse and scraper trying to save the dam on a dryland ranch during a spring flash flood while his father was absent. Remnants of the dam are still visible on the old Miller place near Conrad.

WE must have been riding in the wagon for an hour before we saw our next team. It was coming towards us, and my father drove partly off the road to give the other team one of the ruts.

Each time we had passed another team while we were driving out from town, the other drivers and my father would exchange a wave of the hand. And the further we drove, and the fewer teams we saw, a wave of the hand was followed by: "Howdy," or "Cold, isn't it," or "Hope you beat the storm."

This last driver turned off the road to give my father as much room as my father had given him. The driver waved his hand and said: "Quite a load you got there, mister. Good luck."

My father had started to wave back, but stopped his hand in midair. And whatever he was going to say to the other driver, he did not say. He stared instead, and the other team joggled on by them towards town.

When our wagon was back in the road and when nothing at all was ahead of us now, my mother remarked: "You weren't very civil to him, it seems to me."

My father answered: "I was too surprised for one thing, and I had my reasons for another."

My mother did not comment on this right then, and I settled deeper down into the old buffalo robe, for we were driving straight into the wind. On the bottom of the wagon were three hot stones wrapped in a gunny-sack. My father had put them there a few minutes before our train had reached the station. The wagon was so deep that my feet hardly could reach the stones from the high wagon-seat. But their warmth could be imagined, anyway.

The ground was so frozen that the wagon wheels seemed to be bumping over rocks. Nearer town we had passed through some fields of stubble. It had appeared just like brown grass to me, and now the brown grass appeared just like stubble. My father had tried to tell me which was which, and then had given up trying after I had made too many mistakes.

Each time we had crossed a hill and I had seen a shack way ahead I had asked: "Is that our shack?" And my father had answered: "No, not yet. I'll tell you when we come to it. We've only fifteen miles yet. That's all."

But when the miles came down to twelve and I was still asking, he replied: "No. For goodness sake, no. You'd better try talking about something else."

So I tried, but nothing else would come to my mind except the word painted in gold on the wagon. The word was "Racine." I began humming it out loud as we jogged along, but the word did not make sense. The "g" had been left off the end, so I put it there myself. "Racing, racing, racing," I hummed over and over, trying to keep time with the horses. But this was hard, as the horses would not walk or trot in step.

"Why don't you try taking a nap?" my mother suggested. Then she turned to my father: "What was the trouble with that man?"

This referred to the man we had passed a while back, and my father answered: "He shot his partner through the liver."

"No! When?"

"Three months ago. He's a bad actor."

"He certainly must be." My mother's words sounded like pop-corn popping. "Why isn't he in jail?"

"The law's lax," my father said. Both my mother and father became silent after this. But the words "The law's lax" were better words than "Racing, racing," so I changed them for "The law's lax, the law's lax," and the new words fitted in more easily with the horses' hoofs.

"What else has he done?" my mother asked.

"Isn't that about enough, I should think."

"But you said that he was a bad actor. I thought maybe he'd done something else. Why did he shoot him?"

"That's just it. Nobody knows except what he said himself when he brought the body into town. He said the usual thing. Self-defense. But no witnesses to check up, of course."

"My, my, my. Come to think of it, he did have a cold-blooded eye when he drove by."

"A cold-blooded eye when he drove by," I hummed.

"Be quiet a minute, will you." This came from my mother. The sky had been gray when we left town, but now the sky was almost black. On The Coast the sky did not become so black unless it was raining. But here nothing fell from the sky at all, and so much vacant ground was everywhere that I could not understand why we had to go so far to find room to build a house. I wanted to ask my father but he was too busy talking with my mother.

"I suppose we shouldn't judge too hastily," she said. "But where these people out here have to depend on their neighbors so much, it's a shame, isn't it?" She answered her own question. "Yes, it's a shame."

A flake of snow fell upon the buffalo robe. I saw the flake first.

"Look," I called. "Look. We're going to have snow." The flake did not melt, although on The Coast the first flakes usually always melted. Snow always made us fellows glad back there. But here nobody seemed glad but me.

My father flapped the reins upon the horses: "Come on, Ruby, come on. You're lagging."

Two more flakes fell, then two more, then three fell all at once. I began to lose count.

My father flapped the reins again. "Come on. Stop lagging." The horses changed their walk to a trot. But we heard another team coming up behind us. This other team was going faster than we were, and my father drove his horses off the road to give this other team more room. My mother turned around to see who would be driving so fast.

"It's him," she said.

"Who?" my father asked.

"Him. That man again. I think he's just trying to show off."

But when the other wagon came alongside of us, the driver

stopped his horses, then called to my father. The man had a water bucket in his hand, and he reached the water bucket over to my father.

"This must've dropped off your wagon a couple miles or so back," the man said.

My father took the bucket and examined it. "Why so it is. So it is." The snap was still on the handle, but the part above the snap was broken off. The bucket had been hanging to our hind axle.

The man wheeled his wagon around towards town again.

My father called over to him through the wind: "What! You don't mean you're not making back for home in such weather."

"Nope. I'm still making for town," the man answered.

"And you drove clear out of your way with this?"

"Why not?" The man started his horses, then waved his hand. "Well, good luck. And quite a load you got there."

"Yes, quite a load," my father agreed as he waved back. He started our horses, and once more we were on our way into the wind.

"How far now?" I asked.

"Ten'r'leven miles."

and we rode fast the last ten miles for the sun was coming up and we wanted to get under cover.

The banks of the coulee at Sand Creek were not very high, but they were very steep, and we could not see what was at the foot of the bank until we got right to the edge of the coulee.

We rode up at a gallop and stopped at the edge of the coulee and I looked down.

There, lined up close under the bank, was a row of thirty Blackfeet Braves, each one armed and standing beside his horse, and all grinning.

An Indian enjoys a joke on someone else. And they certainly had the laugh on us. They had seen us coming for miles and had waited for us as we galloped right into their trap.

If our horses had been fresh we could have taken chances on getting shot and made a race for it, but the last ten miles had taken the heart out of our nags and we knew it. The Indian horses were fresh and then it was easily 100 miles back to the nearest body of whites.

I looked at Broadwater. At that time Miss Chumiseero must have seemed far away. His complexion turned an ugly green. I do not know how I looked, but I felt green.

"We're caught," said Broadwater. "What'll we do?"

It did not take long to decide it. I said, "Let's pretend we think they are friendly and ride right into them."

He nodded his head and we spurred our horses down the bank and right into the bunch. They were very friendly and very hilarious—all except the leader, who was very solemn.

He stepped up and slapped each of us on the leg and motioned each of us to dismount. We obeyed. As we left the saddle we each lifted our holsters from the pommel, with two pistols, and each had his rifle in his right hand.

They gathered around close, laughing and commenting, but offered us no violence. They led our horses to one side and stripped off the saddles and bridles.

"What are they going to do?" Broadwater asked.

I had a hunch from the start what they would do and they did it. They put our saddles, bridles and hackamores on two of the worst looking old skates we had ever seen. Then the leader made signs for us to mount and go on our way.

The horse they had given me was a little, scrawny runt, but he still had a little life left. But the mare they gave to Broadwater was a fat, lazy old thing that had rheumatism and had been used by the squaws as a travois animal to haul wood. She was slower than an ox.

As soon as we got away from the grinning bunch of bucks we tried to get up a little speed. My horse finally managed to trot and in no time I was a hundred feet ahead of Broadwater.

"Wait, Alex, wait for me," Broadwater would yell. He would dig in the spurs but the nag simply could not trot. I finally dropped behind and pounded the old mare over the back with my heavy lariat, but we could not make more than two miles an hour.

As I laid on with all my might, I would say, "Get up! Get up, there. There's a young lady up the trail that's worried about us." And Broadwater would grit his teeth and swear.

We tried walking and leading the horses. They soon wore us out with their pulling back. Then we tried walking and driving them, but that did not get us along any faster, so we finally settled down to riding a two-mile gait, with me pounding the old mare on the back with my lariat.

We travelled all day and slept that night and the next day at noon came poking into Fort Benton.

There we told our story to the Indian agent and turned over the ponies to him. He at once ordered out a lieutenant and thirty cavalrymen to go in pursuit of the Indians.

We hired fresh horses of Carl & Steele and went on to Helena, making it in two days. We found Miss Chumiseero radiant and happy and glad to see us.

We stayed in Helena a few days, then rode back to Fort Benton in time to meet the ox trains.

The first thing the Indian agent said to us was, "I've got your Indians. Come and see them."

It seems that the detachment of cavalry had picked up the trail and had soon overtaken them. They were making for the Canadian line. Being better mounted, they captured the bunch, a man at a time. As each brave found himself being overtaken by Uncle Sam's riders he halted and threw up his hands.

Only two got away—and they were mounted on our horses.

We went out to look at the prisoners. The grin had been wiped off their faces. They were a pretty sulky lot. It was our turn to

laugh and we did. They gave us some black looks. The agent held a council with them and there was a good deal of speech making and finally they were turned loose.

When we got back from Fort Union on our third trip the Indian agent had recovered our two horses. It seems that the head men of the tribe voted that our horses were "hoodoos" to the tribe and must be returned, so the fellows who made the trade with us had to bring them back to Fort Benton.

In 1898,* some twenty-three years later, when I was mining on the Salmon River, Colonel Broadwater wrote, asking me to visit him in Butte. I went over and he entertained me at the famous Silver Bow Club.

He had made a lot of money on government contracts, building Fort Belnap [Belknap] and Fort Assinaboine [Assiniboine] on Milk River and also in mining. I told the story of the horse trade to the members of the Commercial Club of Butte and when I got to the account of Broadwater riding the old travois mare with me beating her up with a rawhide rope, he began ordering champagne and kept it up until he had spent several hundred dollars.

* Date in error; it was six years after Broadwater's death. The visit probably occurred in 1888.

OUTCAST

GWENDOLEN HASTE

This poem and others by Gwendolen Haste quoted later are from her book, *Young Land*, published in 1930 by Coward-McCann, which in this editor's opinion contains some of the best verse ever published about Montana. Miss Haste was a resident of Montana from 1915 to 1918 and again from 1920 to 1924. She majored in history and English at the University of Chicago and won *The Nation's* poetry prize in 1922. She helped her father edit *The Scientific Farmer*, first in Lincoln, Neb., and later in Billings. After moving to New York she joined the staff of *The Survey*, went from there to the consumer service department of a large food processing corporation, then married.

OLD Man Carver
Came from the East.
He never sat
At their thundering feast.

He never knew
Their whiskeyed nights.
He was farming stones
While they hunted fights.

When they told of bloody
Barroom rows,
Carver could only
Speak of cows.

His words of seed corn
Were nothing beside
The story of Jed
And the grey wolf's bride.

OUTCAST

So he sat dumb
In the crossroad store
While they spun shattering
Tales of gore.

They granted Carver
Could farm like hell,
But he had no beautiful
Lies to tell.

...AND WOMEN

"... love and loyalty and courage immeasurable in speech ..."

LITTLE BROWN GINGERBREAD MAN

EDWARD H. COONEY

This gently affectionate tribute to the frontier mother who made Christmas a memorable experience though she lacked access to toy shops, confectioneries, or department stores, appeared in *The Great Falls Leader* on Christmas Eve, 1929, and has been reprinted annually by that newspaper since. Edward H. Cooney, veteran Montana newspaperman, was *The Leader's* editor for many years. When he wrote this poem he had just been stricken by illness which brought his death on Easter Sunday, April 20, 1930. Cooney was born in Iowa in 1865 and arrived in Alder Gulch the same year—his mother brought him, an infant in arms, in a covered wagon to join her husband, already established in Montana Territory. Edward H. Cooney worked for *The Rocky Mountain Husbandman,* one of the first Montana papers, and *The Anaconda Standard* before joining *The Leader* in 1899. In 1923 the editor of this book went to work for him as a cub reporter; as news editor he copy-read this poem for its first appearance, and a few months later he sadly wrote the story of its author's death. Music subsequently was written for the poem by Dr. Robert Stevens, a Great Falls organist and pianist.

THE little wool stockings hung plump on the nails
    By the side of the chimney of rocks;
    And the little wood dollies, with painted pigtails
Looked prim in their calico frocks—
'Twas the morn of a Christmas, in time long ago,
After Santy had called with his van—
And from each little stocking, with face all aglow,
Peeped a little brown Gingerbread Man.

He was not much for shape and his mouth, all agape,
Was made from a large pitted prune;
And his tight little eyes made of currants—like flies—
Shone warm as the sunlight of June.
His wide little belly was flat as a hake;
His head was spread out like a fan—
For his baker baked love, more than art, in the make
Of the little brown Gingerbread Man.

In each stocking was sugar, like candy, pulled white;
With doughnuts all sprinkled like snow;
And a weazened red apple for each little tike,
On the morn of a time long ago.
It was cold—as the snow sifted in on the floor
And, in tiny drifts, twisted and ran—
But not cold, ice, or snow, could bring chill to the glow
On the face of the Gingerbread Man.

L'ENVOI

The joy bells of Santy ring sweetly today,
As he calls in his aeroplane van—
But memory drifts back to the old wooden shack
And the little brown Gingerbread Man!

HOMECOMING—THE WATER MAN

JESSIE TREICHLER

This is an excerpt from "Homecoming," in the *Antioch Review*, Vol. II, No. 2, Summer, 1942, published at Yellow Springs, Ohio. The *Review* says it is part of a novel, *Cora Gray*. Dated "Cottonwood, Montana, 1909," it presents vividly the experience of a young mother uprooted from the Middle West and brought to a raw Montana homestead town. The author, formerly Jessie Cambron, came to Montana State University from Harlowton and was graduated, an English major, in 1931. She married Paul Treichler, who also was a student there and who obtained A.B. and M.A. degrees at the Missoula school. They went on to Yale, where he studied drama, and thence to Antioch College, where he is director of dramatics and she is a member of the administrative staff.

. . .

THE first breakfast was over in the new home. Emptying into the teakettle the last of the bucket of water which Will had brought in just before bedtime, she turned to him.

"Now, Will, you show me where the well is, and I'll carry my own water after this."

"There ain't no well, Cora. Not in the whole town of Cottonwood. Ever'body buys their water at fifty cents a barrel. I borrowed that pailful from Labrees over there."

Cora looked at him for a full minute, letting the fact sink in. It was so startling that there was no well any place in the whole town that at first she almost laughed at the oddity of it. But as the words seeped fully into her housekeeping and maternal consciousness, she realized that it was no laughing matter. She thought of the children's clothes that needed to be washed, and the tubfuls which she had planned to use in scrubbing the house. She looked at him hard, hoping he was joking. As she saw he was speaking the truth, dismay deepened in her face. She mustn't let Will see the extent of her consternation. Forcing a dismal smile, she held out the bucket to him.

"Well, borrow another pailful for me, will you? Then we'll get three or four barrels of water to start with. How do we do that?"

"The water man comes around three times a week. He's due to come t' this part of town today. Rose Labree said she'd make him come here. But you're gonna be disappointed, Cora; he only lets each family have one barrel at a time—and you only get three barrels a week—it keeps him workin' overtime as it is t' keep the town in water. He hauls it from the river about three miles away."

Cora looked at Will unhappily. He patted her shoulder roughly, half-sympathetic, half-amused.

"My poor little scrubber. You just gotta read a book in place a scrubbin' all the time."

Cora pushed out her chin. "Don't you worry about me. The rest of these people seem to have lived through it. But how they keep clean, I don't know."

When Will came back with a bucket of water, he set it down carefully on a rough table beside the stove. "We gotta remember to return this, Cora. It's about as bad as horse-stealin' not to pay back water in these parts." He laughed and shrugged. "Well, I'm off. I'll eat dinner at the beanery this noon—then you can just git the kids a bite, and won't have to bother about me."

"You'll do no such thing," Cora said briskly. "Think I came all the way out here to have you eating downtown? People'd think you had a fine wife! You can bring home some meat for dinner, and Joe and I can go down this afternoon and lay in a store of things. You can put up some shelves in the kitchen for me, and build me a bread box. I'll make biscuits today; then I'll get some yeast and bake tomorrow."

"Pancakes for breakfast?" Will wanted to know.

"Pancakes for breakfast."

Although barrels of unpacked household goods still stood in the middle of the floor and the house was in complete disorder, Cora already saw in her mind's eye a clean and spotless home where activities ran on schedule: Monday, washing; Tuesday, ironing; Wednesday, baking; Thursday, mending; Friday, cleaning; Saturday, more baking; Sunday, church and a roast for dinner. White pancakes for fall and spring; buckwheat pancakes for winter. She smiled happily at Will.

Turning briskly to Barbie she said, "Barbie, you take Jeff out in the yard. The two of you can start carrying the little chunks of wood around to the back—I'll show you where. Joe can take the big chunks and stack it later. Joe, you can chop down sagebrush;

and Barbie and Jeff can pile it at the back, and we'll burn it. We've all got to work."

"The sagebrush'll make a terrible smudge, Cora—" Will began. He broke off abruptly. "Never mind, honey," he said. "When the water man comes, you'll find a new barrel around on the shady side of the house." He picked up Jeff and carried him down the steps. "Yes, sir, my boy, we've all got t' step lively when your mother's around. She'll make great men of us yet." He smiled at Cora to show that there was no malice in his remark.

In the middle of the morning, Cora heard a team drive up to the door. Barbie shouted from the yard, "The water man's here! The water man's here!"

Joe came to the door and said politely, "Here's the water man, Mom. You'd better come talk to him. Barbie's making an awful racket."

Cora went outside to find a strange contraption resembling a hayrack drawn up to her door by two powerful horses. The vehicle was filled with many barrels covered with wet gunny sacks, held in place by staves. At the front of it, seated on a kitchen chair which was fastened to the frame, was a small man in neat blue overalls, with an oversize straw hat on his head. Through gold-rimmed spectacles, he peered benignly at her.

"Howdy, Mrs. Gray," he said with great dignity. "I'm the water man. Rose Labree said you needed water, and I come right over."

He climbed down from his chair. "You kin hold the reins," he said to Joe, as though he were conferring a great honor on him.

Joe took them carefully and stood at rigid attention, with the reins clenched tightly between tense fingers. Seeing Barbie's look of disappointment, the water man said to her, "I'll need you to hold the gunny sack off'n the bar'l."

"Our barrel's around here on the shady side of the house." Cora led him around to it.

He looked it over with the eye of a connoisseur. "Good. Good. A good tight bar'l that'll last you fer many a day. But it oughta be sunk in the ground, Mrs. Gray. Yes, it really oughta. It'll stay cooler in summer that way, and be handier t' git at any time. I never could git these other folks that lived here to berry their water, but you git Mr. Gray t' sink this bar'l jist as soon as it gits empty."

"But the children might fall in," Cora objected.

He began deliberately to fill the barrel from one on the wagon, a bucketful at a time. "No, you kiver it with a tub. An' the children mustn't never go near the water bar'l. Not never! It's a sin that oughta be punished by death er worse."

He uttered these words in the most soft and gentle voice imaginable. Barbie dropped the wet gunny sack she was holding and backed slowly away from the barrel, looking at it with horror.

Cora saw he wasn't joking. "Is there no way I can get more than a barrel at a time, Mr.—?" she asked.

"My name is of no importance, Mrs. Gray," he said rather pompously. "What I bring you is the important thing. I am the water man."

After giving Cora a moment to absorb this thought, he answered her question firmly. "The water man don't know of no way you kin get more'n a bar'l at a time, Mrs. Gray. Everybody does without all he wants so's everybody kin have. It seems awful hard at first, but you'll be glad later, becuz it'd soon run up inta more money'n you c'd afford. There ain't no family in town oughta be so spendin' with water they have to pay more'n a dollar 'n a half a week fer it. That's whut three bar'ls come to. Now I know about whut Bill Gray makes; an' he cain't afford t' have me sell you more'n three bar'ls a week, not even if you beg fer it on bended knees."

Cora felt both irritated and apologetic. "I'm not spendthrift with water! I simply need some immediately for a lot of washing and scrubbing I have to do."

He smiled at her soothingly. "You newcomers gotta learn, Mrs. Gray. Now what you do, Mrs. Gray—you make all the kids wash in the same water. Be fair to them. Let the little boy wash first one day, the big boy the next, the little girl the next. That way nobuddy's cheated, and all's equally clean. An' tell 'em not t' drink so much. An' use about a third as much fer cookin' an' dishwashin' as you're used to. Peel your potatoes without no water. When you wash clothes, jist wash 'em outa one tubful and rench 'em outa one more. Then you save your rench water from one week to use for your wash water the next."

He delivered all this in a rapid singsong, as though it was something he had repeated many times. Finished with his task of filling the barrel, he turned back to the wagon.

Cora said, "Just a minute; I'll get your money."

"No, Mrs. Gray. Not fer the first bar'l. It comes easier t' pay fer the second. An' life's tough enough these days even when you git the first bar'l a water free."

He took the reins from Joe and climbed back up on his seat. From this height he smiled down at Cora in a kindly fashion. "Don't let it knock yer props from under yuh, Mrs. Gray. You'll git along better'n you think fer."

He paused, then fixed the children with a mild eye, and said slowly and impressively, "An' don't never, never, never let me hear of you little Grays havin' water fights. When you wanta throw water, you go t' the river. You hear me!"

A cluck to his team, and the makeshift water wagon went lumbering off. Though his seat jiggled furiously beneath him, the little man sat very erect. About a block away he turned around and called out something.

"What?" cried Cora.

"Boil it!" shouted the water man. His voice came back on the wind. "Boil—it!" The wagon creaked off.

"Well, I never!" Cora said with a helpless laugh at Joe. "I think we're in a country of crazy people. But he's right about one thing —you children stay away from that water barrel, or I'll give you good spankings."

"I'll never go near it, Mama—never! He'd kill us all!" Barbie spoke with great intensity, enjoying the quivering fear which sounded in her voice.

"I guess I'd have something to say about that," Cora said. "But just the same—and I mean it—you remember not to go near that barrel."

Cora stood for a moment looking at the barrel. A gust of wind whipped around the corner of the house, and it seemed to her that she could see the film of dust deposited on the water. She got a washtub from the kitchen and put it over the top of the barrel.

Her eyes searched the countryside. A narrow road, with deep ruts, wound across the plain behind their house, disappearing between two small brown hills. No tree was to be seen, but in places the sagebrush grew almost as high as lilac bushes. The air was fresh and heady, drenched with the fragrance of the sage; but to Cora the country was as ugly as anything she had ever seen, and she turned to go inside without reluctance. Out here she could do little, but inside she could do much. Sagebrush could be pulled up

209

from the yard, only to expose an expanse of brown dirt. She looked at the barrel angrily. There could be no question of flowers or grass or trees with water selling at fifty cents a barrel.

As she entered her house, she felt an excitement which was always hers when she came within her own four walls. Inside these four walls, she could control the wild shiftlessness of the West. Inside these walls she could bathe her children and scrub their ears and see that they were clothed in clean garments. Inside these walls she could bake bread and apple pie and fry chicken as she had been taught to do back home in Iowa. She hung some pans on nails sticking out from the kitchen walls, and vowed that Will should make her shelves before the week was out.

That evening Cora looked about her again, this time with a feeling of great contentment. She had taken the water man's advice, and had used her wash water for scrubbing her floors and wood work; but even so, she thought ruefully, the barrel of water was already more than half gone. The house now had a steamed, soapy smell about it; and depressions in the uneven floor still showed damp spots from the recent scrubbing. The children's clothes were hung on nails in the tiny closet, or were sorted into neat piles on kitchen chairs which Cora had ranged along one side of the wall. White lace curtains, still creased from their packing, covered the shining windows. White cotton bedspreads covered the beds, even Barbie's cot; and Barbie had been cautioned that there was to be no more jumping up and down on it. A huge pile of sagebrush was stacked at one side of the yard, and at least one tiny patch of ground directly at the front of the house was completely cleared.

The mood of close identification of herself with her family was still upon Cora. When the dishes were done, she brought some darning into the circle of light cast by the oil lamp. So sharp was her perception of Will and each of the children that it seemed to her they sat within a charmed circle. Joe was hunched over the table reading a book. Barbie, who was curled up on her father's lap, put her finger on his throat now and then in an attempt to feel the rumble of his voice as he talked to her mother.

"It's time for you to go to bed, Barbie," Cora said, smiling quietly at her daughter.

"Papa used to sing to me before I went to bed," Barbie objected.

"That's right, I did," said Will. "I used to sing to you. And I'm glad t' have the chance t' be singing to you again. What'll it be?"

Barbie wrinkled her forehead in an attempt to remember the songs her father had sung to her before he went to Montana.

Joe said, "Sing that one about the old man who's going up North to freeze to death, Papa. It used to make Barbie cry, but it's pretty; and she's got to grow up some time and quit crying."

Will gathered Barbie more closely to him. She watched his mouth and throat intently as he started to sing.

> I'm goin' from the cotton fields,
> I'm goin' from the cane,
> I'm goin' t' leave the old log hut
> That stands down in the lane.
>
> When the sun goes down tonight—
> Oh, it makes me sigh—
> When the sun goes down tonight,
> I'm goin' t' say goodbye.

Will's voice, singing the plaintive, sentimental white man's version of the Negro's thoughts, rose full and rich in the quiet autumn air. A patch of moonlight, brighter than the glow from the oil lamp, shone on the floor. The evening was chilly, and no fire was built. Somewhere in the distance Cora heard the great clearness of hoofs of a plodding horse and the turning wheels of a wagon. She looked about her at these people she loved most of all those on earth, and felt a lonesome peace in accepting as home this strange land in which she found herself. She could almost feel the miles and miles of silent prairie stretching out away from her, and she could hear the wind, rushing through space, with never a treetop to stop its breathless speed. She pulled her rolled-up sleeves down over her cold arms.

> Now Dinah she don't want t' go,
> She says she's gettin' old
> An' she's afeared she'll freeze t' death,
> That country am so cold.

A long, shuddering sob from Barbie interrupted the song. "Oh, Papa, I can't stand it. Truly I can't. It's too sad."

"No, Barbie, you gotta hear it all. You can't just say you can't stand things and not listen when a body wants t' sing a song. You let me finish, and then I'll sing a funny one for you."

Barbie put her hand over her mouth, and cowered down against her father's chest. He stroked her hair gently as he finished the song for Joe, and wiped the tears from his own eyes when he had finished. Then he picked Barbie up in his arms and started waltzing gaily about the floor with her as he began to sing his next song:

> Now McManus loaned a dress suit
> For the ball the other night.
> The coat was much too large for him,
> The pants they was too tight—

FRONTIER HOME-MAKER

NANNIE TIFFANY ALDERSON AND
HELENA HUNTINGTON SMITH

Helena Huntington Smith, a young Eastern writer, has produced in collaboration with two Montana pioneers two of the best books on frontier life published in recent years—*We Pointed Them North*, written with the late "Teddy Blue" Abbott, and *A Bride Goes West*, in which she collaborated with Mrs. Nannie T. Alderson of Birney. Here are a few of the delightful observations on men, music, motherhood, and a full life, as recorded by Miss Smith from the musings of Mrs. Alderson, who was eighty-two years old when *A Bride Goes West* was published by Farrar & Rinehart in 1942. She had spent sixty years in Montana up to that time. Few came to the frontier with so little preparation: she had been carefully reared on a slaveholding West Virginia plantation and waited on at every turn. Her father was reported to have been the first Confederate officer slain in the War between the States. Her husband brought her to the Birney country in southeastern Montana, still the section which most nearly approximates the open range frontier.

O NE of my first lessons as a western wife was that location in that almost uninhabited country was not a matter of cities and roads, but of rivers and divides. Rivers, like women, were few, and they gained in importance proportionally, while the location of every tiny creek might be a matter of life-and-death importance to men and animals alike.

≫≪

I HAD little voice, but my listeners were hungry for music and no prima donna ever enjoyed so heart-warming a triumph as I did that night. . . .

Mr. Brown's choice was a very teary song about a little child who was left alone by his parents. The house caught fire and flames crackled around him; each verse ended with the sad refrain, "Lost in the fire"—but in the final stanza rescue came, and the last line of all was "Saved from the fire." Particularly touching was the part where his baby voice lisped: "God told me you would come." I sang a good deal for cowboys afterwards, and that song was always their favorite.

≫≪

215

BACK home in West Virginia I had thought myself quite a house-wife. Mother was ill a great deal and I carried the keys, feeling very proud as I went about with her key basket, unlocking closets and giving things out. But out here I found that I didn't know, as they say, straight up. On the ranch we had meat without end, milk, and butter (if I made it), and later a few vegetables. Every single other necessity of life came from Miles City. Once a year when the men went in to ship their cattle they laid in supplies—hundred-pound sacks of flour and sugar, huge tins of Arbuckle coffee, sides of bacon, evaporated fruits and canned goods by the case. What you forgot you did without. I don't know how many times in those first months I thought: "Oh, if we'd only remembered" this or that.

⇒⇒ ⇐⇐

THE West was very tolerant toward the lesser faults of human conduct. It was even willing to overlook the greater if they were not repeated. A man's past was not questioned, nor a woman's either; the present was what counted. A man could even be known as wanted by the law elsewhere, yet this was not held against him here so long as he showed a willingness to walk the straight path. Half the charm of the country for me was its broad-mindedness. I loved it from the first.

⇒⇒ ⇐⇐

THE experience taught me something I never forgot. I saw that I was beginning to feel sorry for myself—the lowest state to which a woman's mind can fall. And I made up my mind to stop it. Many times in the years that followed I forgot this worthy resolve, but I always came back to it sooner or later. I still think it the most important lesson that any wife can learn, whether she lives in a house of cottonwood logs or in a palace.

⇒⇒ ⇐⇐

THERE is nothing a woman left alone on a ranch can't imagine when she is afraid.

⇒⇒ ⇐⇐

WHILE living on Tongue River I saw living disproof of the old belief that while no house was big enough for two women, any house was big enough for two men. There were a number of bachelor households around us, within hailing distance, so to speak. It was a common arrangement out here for the young man who didn't have money to take in a partner who did, and the two of them would live together and divide the work. I noticed that they fell out just about as often as two women would have done, and for reasons that weren't any better. Each one would think he was doing more than his share, or they would get on each other's nerves in the long winter months, and would disagree over little things just the way women do.

—»» «««—

I NEVER had chloroform with any of my children except the one born in West Virginia. The old Kentucky doctor in Miles City didn't give it—I know no reason why. Long after I had had all my own children, I was told that in Birney the women kept chloroform on hand and learned to use it. Once, by means of it, they even saved a life.

They had sent for the agency doctor when this woman was expecting her baby; not the doctor I knew, but another, for this was several years later. They said he boasted of having nine diplomas, and was considered first rate, but when she had been in labor for a night and a day, uselessly, and they saw she would die like this, he confessed that he had never had a baby case before, and he fell on his knees and begged for forgiveness.

They sent a cowboy riding to Sheridan then, sixty miles away, for a doctor they knew to be competent; and during the fifteen hours that it took the cowboy to get there and the doctor to get back, those women kept her under and kept her pains stopped with chloroform. Without it she would have been dead before he arrived. The man they sent rode at a gallop without stopping, except to change horses; he rode into ranches and simply took what he found in the corral. No one would have refused a horse in such a case, but had anyone done so the horse would have been taken, at the point of a gun if necessary. On his way in he arranged relays of fresh horses for the doctor. He made the ride in six hours; the doctor, coming out, took eight or nine. Cousin Peachey Cox, who tells of all this, says that she never forgot the sight of the doctor's buggy coming over the hill, against the sunrise.

The baby was dead, but the mother lived and had four children.

—»» «««—

No MODERN, civilized person can possibly comprehend what the roads of those days were like—even the good ones. They were washed-out, narrow and full of rocks that jolted the teeth out of our heads; they hung over the edge of precipices; they were so steep that you almost fell backwards out of the wagon going up-hill, and almost fell over on the horses' rumps going down. One time we were going on a visit to the Browns', over the well-travelled Tongue River road, and when we were crossing a wash at the bottom of a gully, the bump catapulted Patty out of the wagon—hurling her head *through* the spokes of the wheel! Mabel with great presence of mind jumped down and pulled her out. Luckily the team was gentle and we could hold them. . . . To have been packed into a wagon and started out in the middle of the night, into an unknown, almost trackless part of the country, with two small children, heaven knew what horses and perhaps a strange driver—well, I'd rather have faced the Indians.

>>> <<<

I HAVE often noticed that it is the little things that trouble a woman, while only the big ones trouble a man. Some of these men had table manners which got on my nerves. We had one guest for a season who always licked the spout of the syrup jug, after pouring the syrup on his hot cakes every morning. I can't tell you how it affected me, to see this happen at my table every day. I begged Mr. Alderson to speak to the man, but of course he never would.

>>> <<<

WE had a little piano which was played at all our parties, and at all the parties in the Tongue River country. It was a miniature Steinway, two octaves short, that had belonged to some friends of ours in Miles City. They had brought it out from New York for their little girl, and when they left and went east we bought it from them for twenty-five dollars. I believe it was made originally for some kind of exhibition, but I never really knew its earlier history. I only knew that when the family came west to live on a ranch, the piano was sent out by freight, on the Northern Pacific; that it was unloaded at Rosebud station, on the Yellowstone, a few miles west of Miles City, in the midst of those bleak, sagebrush-covered hills. It was fall then, and the river was running full, so for several weeks the little piano sat on the open station platform, protected only by its crate, while they waited for the river to freeze over so they could take it across. The experience

218

didn't seem to hurt it any—though some of its sweetness of tone may have dwelt in the uncritical ears of those who listened to it.

At any rate, I am sure that no other Steinway ever gave half the pleasure that little piano did. For years it was the only piano in the Birney country—until Captain Brown bought one for the Three Circle. Whenever my children went to a dance, the boys would load it in a wagon, throw a tarp over it in case of snow or rain, and off it would go. It was borrowed for parties by neighbors from miles around, and everyone loved it as though it were something alive. From time to time the cowboys talked of sending to Sheridan and getting somebody to come up and tune it. But for some reason this was never done, and the only time it was ever tuned was once when my daughter Mabel and a friend of hers took a monkey wrench and tightened up the strings.

So THE last twenty years have been serene ones. Before that, my friends tell me, I led a hard life. Perhaps—but I don't think an easy one is ever half so full.

MRS. SENATOR JONES

ELLIOTT C. LINCOLN

From *Rhymes of a Homesteader* (Houghton Mifflin, 1920).

"The —— Bridge Club met at the home of Mrs. —— on Wednesday last. Mrs. Senator Tom Jones, a pioneer of —— County, made high score, the prize being a pair of silk stockings." (Item from the society column of any Sunday paper in the Northwest.)

WOULD you tell an old pal, Mrs. Senator Jones,
If the stuff that he's readin' is true?
Was there somethin' wrong with the dealer's box
That the bank paid nothin' but four-bit sox
To her that was Boston Lou?

Now, honestly, didn't you grin at yourself
Sittin' at that ladylike game?
Did you think of the days when chips was few?
Did a full house look the same?

Remember the night, down at Timothy's place,
When you emptied your poke on the black,
An' the wheel spun round, an' it left you broke,
An' you laughed as if it was all a joke,
An' you slapped old Tim on the back?

Remember the smoke, an' the dealer's drone,
An' the click of the ivory ball?
The Big Game was runnin' on day an' night,
With twenty thousand, gold, in sight,
An' the hush when a man would call?

Ain't there plenty of times, Mrs. Senator Jones,
When the lookin'-glass shows you're—well—plump,
That somethin' pulls at you from the past,
Till you have to talk pretty loud an' fast
To keep down the risin' lump?

Say, Lou, when you feel it's a mighty big job
Livin' up to that "Senator" stuff,
Jest remember the old gang's kind of proud
To have Lou one of the top-notch crowd;
Set your teeth, keep a-fightin'! jest bluff!

THE FIRST SCHOOL IN MONTANA

LUCIA DARLING

Lucia Darling was Mrs. S. W. Park of Warren, Ohio, when she wrote this account of her pioneer teaching experience for Vol. V of the *Contributions to the Historical Society of Montana,* published in 1904. She was the niece of Sidney Edgerton, first governor of Montana Territory, and reached Bannack with the Edgerton and Sanders families Sept. 17, 1863. In the following month, she indicates in this report, she started the school. It may not have been actually the *first;* letters in the same volume of *Contributions* from A. B. Davis and Mrs. Frank E. Curtis report respectively that Miss Kate Dunlap taught a subscription school at Nevada (near Virginia City) in the summer of 1863, and that Mrs. Henry Zoller had a private school that summer in Bannack for primary scholars, the effort lasting only two months. Mrs. Sarah Raymond Herndon writes in the same volume that the first *public* school district was organized at Virginia City and classes were held, beginning March 5, 1866, in a church; next year a schoolhouse was built. Mrs. Herndon was principal and was paid $125 a month for the six-month term. Pupils wrote and edited a school paper, *The School Dispatch,* which, she says, was "read every other Friday afternoon" in the school. On the alternate Fridays they had spelling matches. These Friday afternoon affairs, she writes, always drew a good crowd of townspeople.

. . .

THERE are unwritten chapters in the history of every new settlement, which no pen will ever write, but could they be written, they would tell of many heroines as well as heroes, women as brave and deserving of credit as those who landed from the Mayflower. They have had much to do in "winning the west," and a higher civilization has always followed closely in the footsteps of the woman pioneer. It is the pioneer homemaker and the pioneer teacher who have paved the way for the permanent church and Sunday-school, and have often exerted a more lasting influence than was realized at the time. Bannack was tumultuous and rough, the headquarters of a band of highwaymen, and lawlessness and misrule seemed to be the prevailing spirit of the place. But into this little town had drifted many worthy people who unbendingly held firmly to their principles of right.

222

There were few families there and the parents were anxious to have their children in school, and it never was known when there came a cry from the children that some school-ma'am did not rise up in response. I was requested to take charge of such an institution, and the question of finding room in which to teach was a matter of some difficulty. We learned of a man in town who owned some houses which it was thought might answer the purpose, and Chief Justice Sidney Edgerton, who was my uncle, went with me to interview him. With some difficulty, we found his humble residence and rapped loudly at the door. For some time, no one responded, but finally a man's voice called "Come in." Pushing open the door, we saw in the dim light a man lying on buffalo robes on the floor. He did not rise to meet us, for he had not fully recovered from the results of imbibing too freely from the favorite and profuse beverage then so plenty, and his voice was still too thick to be easily understood. My uncle stated to him our errand. "Yes, glad of it," he said. "D—d shame; children running around the streets; ought to be in school. I will do anything I can to help her; she can have this room." He kept on telling us how much a school was needed, and how willing he was to assist in establishing it, till my uncle interrupted him by asking what rent he would charge for the room. "Well, I will do anything I can; I will give it to her cheap. She shall have it for fifty dollars a month. I won't ask her a cent more. It is dirt cheap." And he continued dilating upon his interest in educational institutions, with many profane expletives. We left him still telling of his wish to be generous; but we decided that a rude habitation of that quality, plastered inside and outside with mud, with a mud roof and dirt floor was not dirt cheap, even with the exorbitant prices at that time prevailing in Bannack, and that the room was not suitable for my purpose. It was some time in October, 1863, I think, that the school was opened in a room in our own house, on the banks of the Grasshopper creek near where the ford and foot bridge were located, and in hearing of the murmur of its waters as they swept down from this mountain country through unknown streams and lands to the distant sea. Some difficulty was encountered in improvising seats and desks for the pupils, and in securing school and other books appropriate for our purpose.

At first we had only morning sessions. There was no discussion nor was there any difference of opinion as to what system of school books should be used, for the scholars were obliged to use such books as they had brought with them, or as could be secured from their neighbors, for there was no book store in the country, and the American Book Company had not then been invented. It was a somewhat strange gathering of school books for they came from Maine and Missouri, and many other states were represented. There was a vacation in the term, superinduced by the approach of the holidays, and rendered imperious by a very severe spell of cold weather. All who were there will remember it as being one of the coldest winter seasons known in that region. The exciting time when the Vigilance Committee effectually rid the Territory of the band of highwaymen occurred during this period, and the gallows tree up "Hangman's Gulch" many times bore fruit "for the healing of the nation." School was opened again on the approach of warm weather, but was discontinued for a summer vacation. The next term of my school was taught in a cabin built on the banks of the stream opposite our house by Charles Sackett and Richard Fenn of Tallmadge, Ohio. Later, they sold it to the government to be used as a Senate Committee room, while the First Legislature was in session.

. . .

The houses in which this school was taught did not approach in architectural beauty the "Little Red School House" and it is gratifying to learn that the mud covered, mud plastered and mud lined house, with its wooden benches and improvised desks, has given place to finely equipped school houses and that our somewhat incongruous method of study compelled by the diversities of our school books has yielded to courses of study which meet the approval of the best teachers in the land. Since that remote time, I have been identified for a period with one of the historic schools of the country of great repute, usefulness and promise; but I look back to the days I spent striving to help the little children in Bannack with a profound gratification. The school was not pretentious, but it was in response to the yearning for education, and it was the first. Those of us who have lived in Montana in the early days feel the greatest interest and pride in the advancement of the new State. To us she is "our" Montana, and our great hope for her is that she may improve her facilities for education, purify her politics, strengthen her morals, increase her wealth, and enlighten her government till she shall stand as a beacon light in the West fulfilling the grand mission it is given her to fulfill.

THE KISKIS

MAY VONTVER

May Vontver, a teacher, attended summer sessions at Montana State University and worked in the creative writing classes of H. G. Merriam. When this story appeared in *The Frontier*, Vol. IX, No. 3, March, 1929, she was superintendent of schools in Petroleum County. She is now living in Wyoming. This moving story of hardship on the homestead frontier probably grew out of her own experiences; it illustrates quite effectively the great influence of the conscientious rural teacher in developing the social personality of her group.

H ADN'T you better eat in the house today? It is cold outside," the teacher suggested.

Pretending not to hear her the three Kiskis slipped silently through the door with their double-handled Bull Durham tin can. They stood in a knot on the south side of the school-house and ate from the one tin. From her desk Miss Smith observed that they now and then put one bare foot over the other to warm it. This was the second time they had disregarded her invitation to eat in the house with the others. The rest of the children had drawn their seats into a circle about the stove and begun to eat.

Teddy Kirk at last decided to enlighten the teacher: "They have only bread in their lunch-pail. That's why they won't eat with us."

Miss Smith made no reply. She suspected that the lunches of the group around the stove weren't very sumptuous either. She knew hers wasn't. The people with whom she boarded were homesteaders, too.

"What about these Kiskis? Who are they?" she asked Mr. Clark that evening at supper.

"The Kiskis?—Oh, they took up their claim here last fall. They are pretty hard up. They have only one horse. Kiski hauled out all the lumber for his shack and barn with it. Thirty miles it is to Hilger. I was hauling wheat then and I used to pass him on the road walking beside the load and pushing when it was uphill."

Miss Smith smiled crookedly. One horse in a country where four- or six-horse teams were the rule was somewhat ludicrous. It was pathetic, too.

"Now, now! you needn't look that way! Kiski broke ten acres with that horse of his last spring. Got the ground in shape and got it seeded, too. The horse pulled and the old man pushed and, by golly, they got it in." There was respect, even admiration, in his voice.

"They have eight children, though," Mrs. Clark broke in. "The two oldest girls are doing housework in Lewistown."

Eight children. That meant three at home younger than the ones at school.

"Have they any cows?"

"One, but she's dry now. It's pretty hard for them."

Miss Smith decided not to urge the Kiskis again to eat in the schoolhouse.

The Kiskis in school were painfully shy. Rudolph, the oldest, going on eleven, hid his timidity under a sullen demeanor. Once in a while, however, he could be beguiled to join in a game of "Pum-Pum-Pull-Away" or horse-shoe pitching. He was a good pitcher. Margaret, next in age, expressed her shyness in wistfulness. Johnny, barely six, refused to speak. Never would he answer a question in class. Never a word did he utter to the children on the playground. He might, now and then, have made remarks to his sister and brother in Bohemian, but, if so, he wasn't ever caught making them. Yet, he was by nature a happy child. When anything comical happened in school or something funny was said he would laugh out loud with an especially merry infectious laugh. It was plain that he observed and understood more than his usual behavior indicated. The teacher, mindful of her psychology texts, tried vainly again and again to utilize these occasions of self-forgetfulness by surprising him into speech.

At the beginning of the term in September every child had come to school barefoot. As the season advanced the other pupils, family by family, donned their footwear, but the Kiskis continued to arrive barefoot, although it was now late in October and getting cold.

"Why don't you wear your shoes?" "Aren't your feet cold?" "Haven't you got any shoes?"

With their bare goose-fleshed feet Rudolph, Margaret, and Johnny picked their way between the prickly pear cactus without answering. But it was plainly to be seen that more and more the continued questioning and the curious staring at their bare legs and feet embarrassed them.

Gradually the weather grew colder. The cracked gumbo froze to cement. Still the Kiskis came barefoot to school.

Then the first snow fell. It was but a thin film. Disks of cactus and tufts of bunch grass stuck through. Yet it was heavy enough to show plainly the tracks of the Kiski children's naked feet.

One day when John and Margaret had planned to reach school just as the bell rang, to escape the inevitable and dreaded comments of the others, they miscalculated the time. All the children were on the porch watching as the Kiskis walked, heads down, toward the schoolhouse.

"I don't see how you can stand it!"

It was the irrepressible Teddy Kirk speaking. The others left their remarks unspoken, for this time Margaret answered and there was defiance in her indistinct mumble.

"We like to go to school barefooted. We get there quicker that way."

She did not tell them that they had not come barefoot all the way; that at the hill nearest the school house they had stopped and undone the gunnysacks wrapped about their feet and legs and hidden them under a rock. When they went home they would put them on again, for no one else went their way.

But little Johnny wasn't so good at keeping his mouth shut at home as he was at school. He didn't know any better than to tell that none of them had worn the gunnysacks *all* the day. Fortunately or unfortunately for the children, a little Old World discipline was exercised upon them. The next day they wore the gunnysacks *all* the way to school. They wore them all day, too.

Their schoolmates and their teacher after a while grew used to seeing the coarse string-bound sacks, but the Kiskis never became used to wearing them. No longer did Rudolph take part in the games. Margaret grew sullen and unapproachable like him. On pleasant days when the girls strolled by two's and three's with their arms about each other Margaret stood alone in a corner against the wall. Sometimes they invited her to come with them; but she never answered. All recess she would stand there just looking at the ground. At last the girls quit asking her. Margaret made believe that she did not notice either them or their neglect. No longer did Johnny's laughter ring out in unexpected places. All three were creeping farther and farther into their shells of silence. Finally Rudolph ran away. After two days his father located him in a barn, where he had been hiding in the hayloft. Unless he had milked the cows in that barn he had had nothing to eat during his absence. He was brought home and made to go back to school.

In November the threshers came to Kiski's place. Because the field there was so small, they made that threshing their last job before pulling out of the country. Mr. Kiski hauled the wheat to Hilger and bought shoes and stockings for the children who attended school.

Other school children, the smaller ones especially, always proudly displayed their new shoes at school the first day they wore them. Several times that fall the teacher had been asked to admire the pretty perforations on the toes, the shiny buttons, or the colored tassels on the strings. But the Kiskis were almost as painfully conscious of their new foot wear as they had been of the gunnysacks. They arrived with faces darkly flushed, sat down immediately, and pushed their feet far back under their seats. The teacher had hoped that to be shod like others would gradually restore their former morale. She was mistaken.

Kiski's cow had come fresh. The children had butter on their bread now. Miss Smith heard about it. She had occasion to pass by the children as they stood eating and she saw that it was really true about the butter. Yet the Kiskis would not eat with the others. They continued to go out at noon time. If the weather was severely cold or stormy they ate in the hall, quickly. Then they would come in, without looking at anyone, and go to their seats.

As the four-month term drew to a close Miss Smith's heart ached for the Kiskis. They had not learned a great deal from their books; she had been unable to supply them with the many bare necessities they lacked; and their own keen realization of being different had made their attendance a torture. They were so unapproachable, too, that she had found little opportunity to show them her love and sympathy. She had had but one chance that she knew of to do so, and she was grateful for that one occasion, though it had not affected the Kiskis' silence nor changed in the least their subsequent conduct.

It came about in this way. Miss Smith had been late to school. There had been a heavy snowfall in the night and she had not had previous experience in breaking trail. If she had not been new in the country she would have known that wading three miles through knee-deep snow takes considerable time. When at length she reached the school house the Kiskis were there standing about the cold stove. All were crying—even Rudolph! They had been too miserably cold and numb to attempt building a fire for themselves. As soon as Miss Smith had the fire crackling merrily she took Johnny in her lap, undid the new shoes and stockings, and began to chafe the cold little feet. And when his crying still persisted she began telling "The Tarbaby." She had noticed early in the term that he particularly relished this tale. And sure enough, at the very first "Bim" of Brother Rabbit's paw on the tarbaby's cheek Johnny laughed through his tears right out loud—something he had not done for a month. Miss Smith decided to tell stories all day.

She felt justified in entertaining the Kiskis this way, for they were the only pupils who braved the roads that day. She had a great fund of fairy tales and folk tales and a gift for telling them; also she had that day an audience whom professional entertainers might well have envied her. Johnny leaned against her knee. She put one arm about Margaret, who stood on one side, and would have put the other about Rudolph on the opposite side had she dared. He was a boy and eleven. With shining eyes and open mouths they drank in "Cinderella," "Hansel and Gretel," "Snow-White," "The Hag and the Bag," "Jack and the Beanstalk," "Colter's Race for His Life" and "Mowgli."

Only to replenish the fire and melt snow for drinking water did Miss Smith stop. Her audience was too timid and self-effacing to make any spoken requests, but after each happy ending their eyes clamored, "More, more!"

At noon the water on the top of the stove was boiling. Miss Smith put condensed milk and a little sugar in it and brought the hot drink to the Kiskis in the hall. For out there they had gone as soon as she announced that it was dinner time. They accepted with smiles and drank every drop, but without a word. Miss Smith, too, stayed in the hall to drink her tea with them. Then the story-telling went on again, until three o'clock in the afternoon, when the teacher bundled them up in some of her own wraps and sent them home.

Going back to her boarding-place, stepping carefully in the tracks she had made in the morning, Miss Smith reflected that should the county superintendent ever learn of her program for the day she would be in for a reprimand. In such a case, she thought, she would defend herself on the grounds that since formalized education had failed noticeably to benefit the Kiskis, it was not altogether unreasonable to try a little informality. Anyhow, she was fiercely glad that the Kiskis' school-term would include one happy day.

It was with sorrow and regret that Miss Smith made her way to the school-house on the last day of the session. With the other pupils she had accomplished something in the way of progress, but the Kiskis she would leave embittered, shyer, and more isolated than she had found them.

She had just reached the shack and barely had time to pile the kindling into the stove when she was aware of subdued noises in the hall. She thought absently that it was unusually early for the children to be arriving. When the door opened a crack to allow some one to peer in, she began to wonder what was going on. Then with a rush the three Kiskis were at the stove.

With her unmittened purple hands Margaret was thrusting something towards her. It was a small square candy-box of pristine whiteness. A wide pink silk ribbon ran obliquely across the top and was looped into a generous bow in the center.

"We brought you a present, Teacher," Margaret began breathlessly.

This time, however, Rudolph did not want his sister to be the chief spokesman. "There are fourteen pieces, Teacher. Two have something shiny around them. We looked."

And before Miss Smith had time to recover from this surprise a miracle came to pass. Johnny spoke, and he spoke in English!

"It is to eat, Teacher. It is candy."

Miss Smith said, "Thank you, children. It was very good of you to give me this."

She shook the stove-grate vigorously. The ashes flew into her eyes. She had to wipe them.

"Open it, Teacher. Open it now."

The teacher took the box to her desk. The Kiskis followed and stood about her watching. There really were fourteen pieces. Johnny pointed out the two with tinfoil. Each of the fourteen reposed daintily in a little cup of pleated paper. It was a wonderful box and Miss Smith was lavish with praises of it.

She held the opened box out to them. "Take one," she invited; and as they made no motion, "Please, do."

The three black heads shook vigorously. Johnny's hands flew behind him.

"They are for you, Teacher," they protested. "You eat."

But Miss Smith couldn't eat just then. More than anything else she wanted to see the Kiskis enjoy the contents of that box themselves. She felt small and unworthy to accept their astounding offering. But again, how could she refuse to accept it and kill cruelly their joy in giving? It was a gift not to be lightly disposed of. An inspiration came.

"Would you care if I shared it? There is enough so that every child in school can have a piece. Johnny could pass it around when they all get here. Would you like that?"

"Yes, yes, yes." Their black eyes shone.

Johnny carried the box to his seat and sat down with it. Rudolph and Margaret hovered about the teacher, happy, eager, excited. Rudolph explained how it all came about.

"Anna came home from Lewistown last night. Margaret and I wrote her a letter once and told her to buy us a present for you. We were afraid she'd forget, but she didn't."

Teddy Kirk was coming. Rudolph and Margaret saw him and ran out on the porch.

"We brought candy for teacher. You are going to get some, too. Johnny has it. Come and see!"

Teddy was too taken aback to say anything. They led him in easily. The pieces were counted again.

Other children came. Rudolph and Margaret met each new arrival before he got to the door. To each in turn Johnny exhibited the box and its contents. He did not mind being the center of attraction now. He made use of his new-found speech, too.

"I am going to pass it around," he told them. "When the bell rings I am going to pass it."

Rudolph and Margaret talked. They chattered. The other children kept still. They had to get used to these new Kiskis.

When the bell rang, a few minutes before time, everybody was in his seat. Johnny got up and passed the candy. Teacher saw to it that he got one of the shiny pieces.

Candy—candy of any kind—was a rare treat to everybody. These chocolates were very fresh. They had softy creamy centers. Some had cherries in them. The children had not known that sweets like these existed.

They took their time about the licking and nibbling. Delights such as these had to be given their just dues. There was no needless or premature swallowing. And to think that the Kiskis had provided it! The Kiskis were assuming importance.

The Kiskis ate candy, too. They beamed on everybody. They had had something to give and everybody thought their gift wonderful.

The sun shone. At recess the girls again walked about by two's and three's. Margaret walked with them. Teddy presented Rudolph with one of his horse-shoes, and Rudolph began to pitch it. Edward, the other first-grader, found a string in his overall pocket and promptly invited Johnny to be his horse. Johnny accepted.

He trotted; he paced; he neighed surprisingly like a horse. Then he kicked at the traces a while.

"You should say 'Cut it out,'" he instructed his driver.

That noon the Kiskis ate lunch in the school-house.

WAITING

ELLIOTT C. LINCOLN

From *The Ranch* (Houghton Mifflin, 1924). A phrase in another selection in this book, "Frontier Home-maker," is pertinent: "There is nothing a woman left alone on a ranch can't imagine when she is afraid."

THAT steak'll be like leather in a minute.
    I wish he'd come: he said he'd sure be home
    In time for supper, but it's half-past six
An' no Jim yet. Oh well, I might 'a' known it.
Killin' myself to get his meals on time,
An' not a once—except, o' course, for breakfast—
But everythin' got cold before he et.
Just fix a little piece of fence, he said,
Down by the spring. The short way home from there
Is up the crick trail. Guess I'll go an' look.

There's nothin' this side of the bridge, that's sure,
An' nothin' to the hay corral. The bend?
There's somethin' white there, an' it's movin', too—
I put his gray shirt in the wash this mornin'—
It must be him! I'll get the glasses—

                         No,
Oh no, it ain't. It's just a white-face calf
Goin' to water. Guess I'd better eat.
I wish he'd get a dog.

            'Most half-past eight—
I'm glad the moon's up.

            Listen! seems to me
The gate squeaked. Yes, an' there's old Randy's nicker!
He don't forget he's got a home, but Jim,
A lot Jim cares. Suppose he'll want his supper.

233

Well, all the supper that he'll get tonight
He'll rustle up himself. He's got to learn.

That's funny, Randy's nickerin' again.
Wonder what keeps 'em. Sounded like they'd stopped
Down at the gate. Maybe I'd better go—
Perhaps they're bringin' home a calf or somethin'.
Where's my coat?

        'Tis Randy. Jim! oh Jim!
I wonder—why—why—*why!* This stirrup's smashed
And Randy's mud clean up the side! *Where's* Jim?
One rein broke, too. He must be hurt! Oh Lord
Why don't he get a horse a girl can ride!
He's maybe—

        Steady Randy,—whoa there now—
I've got to do it!—Who there, whoa, you beast!
Damn you—oh damn you!

          No use, he won't stand.
I'd start an' walk, but out there in the hills
I'd never find him, not in fifty years.
An' then if Jim came home an' found me gone
He'd worry. Seems to me I'd better go
Back to the house.

        There's that clock strikin' ten!
Just one more look, an' then I'll go to bed.
Wish I could sleep.

        No, nothin' comin' yet.
How bright it is! Hear the fool coyotes!
It's always cold here nights, even in summer.

Listen! What's that? Somethin'—or some one's—comin'
On the old road down by the chicken house.
There 'tis again! He wouldn't come that way—
Why should he?

WAITING

Look! I see it now! I see him!
Limpin'—he's hurt—but—

Jim! I'm comin'! Jim!

Wait there!

Oh sweet, good, dear, kind God, it's Jim!

INDUSTRY

"... a tumultuous struggle ... we were profligate of our lives, our labors, and our sacrifices ..."

THE LAST PISKAN

JAMES WILLARD SCHULTZ AND JESSIE LOUISE DONALDSON

James Willard Schultz, Montana's most prolific and perhaps best-known writer, lived among the Blackfeet most of his life. Born in the East in 1859, he came to Montana to hunt buffalo in 1877, married Fine Shield Woman, a Blackfeet, and later became a trader. Their son, Hart Merriam Schultz (Lone Wolf), born in 1884, became a painter and sculptor. Many years after Fine Shield Woman's death, Schultz married, in 1932, Jessie Louise Donaldson, a teacher with whom he had collaborated on *The Sun God's Children* (Houghton Mifflin, 1930). An extract from that book is given here, describing the change —spurred by white greed—of the Blackfeet economy from communal industry as represented by the *piskan* which required the services of the whole tribe, to modern "rugged individualism," which wiped out their means of subsistence. The dream of Many Tail Feathers was not unique: similar visions were reported by leaders of several Plains tribes as having occurred to them at about the same time. Of Schultz's scores of books and stories, his best known are probably those he wrote for children and he was long one of America's most popular writers for boys. Mrs. Schultz is a leader in the Indian crafts movement and they moved from the Blackfeet country to Wind River, Wyo., where she helped to develop crafts projects. His name in the tribe is Far-Off White Robe; hers is Ermine Woman.

I HAVE given "corral" as the translation of the Blackfeet *pis-kan*. It is not that; for some days, Guardipe, Many Tail Feathers, and I have been discussing the real meaning of the word, and we have decided that the nearest we can come to it, in English, is "remaining place."

The Blackfeet tribes had *piskans* in all parts of their country, from the Saskatchewan south to the Yellowstone, and they were all of like character: the fall was a cliff, at the foot of which was a stout, half-circle corral, made of tree-trunks and branches and rocks. Directly above the corral was the apex of the great V of rock-piles, which extended out upon the plain for several miles, the outer ends of the two lines about a half-mile to three fourths of a mile apart.

The *ahwawakiks* (callers-in), of whom there were several in each tribe of the Blackfeet, were looked upon as very sacred men, to whom Sun had given power to entice the buffalo into the great V of rock-piles, so that the people concealed at the piles could frighten and drive them on to the cliff edge and to quick death in the corral at its base. The callers-in or decoyers of the buffalo always disguised themselves with buffalo robes and buffalo head masks, and went out to bring in a herd either on foot or on horseback. This could not be accomplished, however, and was never attempted, when the wind was from the *piskan* toward the herd.

A *piskan* that can be easily visited by Glacier National Park tourists is at a cliff on the north side of the Two Medicine (Lodges) River, about a mile above Holy Family Mission, and a mile below the Park-to-Park Highway. Where the corral or holding place stood are from three to five feet of decomposed remains of buffalo, and, strange to say, great quantities of maggot shells, which endure long after the bones and horns of the animals upon which the flies fed and deposited their eggs have turned into dust. Arrowheads and other flint implements are plentiful in and around this ancient *piskan*.

The very last *piskan* that the Pikû'ni tribe of the Blackfeet used was one that they had several miles above the present town of Choteau, Teton County. On a day in the 1850's, as near as we can determine it, a very large herd of buffalo was successfully decoyed there, a brown river of the animals falling from the cliff edge down into the *piskan*. That night, a man of the tribe, Many Tail Feathers, had a vision, as the Blackfeet call a dream.

A buffalo bull came to him and said: "My son, you are doing my children great wrong: you Pikû'ni are killing so many of them that they are fast decreasing in number, and, unless you cease decoying them into your *piskans,* they must soon all perish. Now, this I ask of you: destroy your *piskan* that you have here, and cease using your other ones. If you will do so, I will give you some of my sacred power, my medicine. It is so very powerful that it will keep you safe from the bullets and the arrows of your enemies. So shall you become a great warrior and a chief of your people. Now, then, your answer."

"I shall do as you request. I will destroy this *piskan,* and urge my people to cease using our others," Many Tail Feathers replied.

The buffalo bulls' chief then told him just what articles he should procure and keep, as the insignia of the buffalo bull chief medicine, and taught him, also, the songs of the medicine. The bull chief then vanished.

Many Tail Feathers awoke, and was almost overcome when he realized what a very powerful vision it was that he had experienced. Soon after daylight, he went out and set fire to the fence of the *piskan*, and, returning to camp, told the people that he had burned it, and for what reason. Later on, the chiefs of the tribe invited him to their council, and, having heard him relate his vision, they decided that the buffalo bull chief was right about the *piskans*, for by decoying herds of buffalo to them, it often happened that many more of the animals were killed than the people could use; they therefore ordered that, from that day, the *piskans* should remain forever idle. And as the buffalo bull chief promised Many Tail Feathers, so did he prosper. He had many battles with the enemies of the Pikû'ni, killed many of them, and always came out of a fight without so much as a scratch upon his body. Because of his bravery and his kindness and generosity to all of his people who needed help, he became a very great chief and lived to extreme old age.

Such is the reason the Pikû'ni give for abandonment of the *piskan* as a means of procuring meat. The real reason, however, was that, with its own steamboat transportation on the Missouri River, the American Fur Company, at its Fort Union and Fort Benton posts, would buy all the buffalo robes that the Blackfeet tribe could tan. That meant the end of community (*piskan*) killings of the animals. Each man of them now was eager to hunt for himself and his family; the more robes that his women could tan, the richer he would be in the coveted useful and ornamental goods of the white men. Incidentally, this was a severe blow to the Hudson's Bay Company. Transportation was so difficult and expensive between its Saskatchewan posts and deep water, at York Factory, Hudson's Bay, that it could not afford to buy bulky buffalo robes, a few bales of which would fill a large canoe or batteau. Therefore, it lost the trade for beaver and other fur skins that it had had with the Blackfeet and their allies, the Gros Ventres and Saksi.

BUTTE LIGHTS

JASON BOLLES

"Butte Lights" is from *Magpies' Nest*, the collected poems of Jason Bolles, published in Bozeman in 1943 by Martha Bolles. Other poems from this book and notes on Bolles will be found elsewhere in this volume.

THERE is a glory in the mountain night,
A splendor underneath the last wild crest
Of a new world. The horned elk on the height
Looks down where lately he was dispossessed.
The eagle gravely watches from her nest
Close to the upland's uttermost last spire.
The wolf beholds and howls his fierce unrest,
The coyote's grin is crooked a little wryer,
To see the night bespangled with bright fire
Where snows are older than the name of man—
The lights of Butte outflung across the dire
Reaches of granite in triumphant span.
Where the bear lurches, where the brown deer stamps,
Mankind has hung the wilderness with lamps.

NIGHT SHIFT

J. F. R. HAVARD

J. F. R. Havard, who wrote this story for *The Frontier,* in which it appeared in November, 1930, Vol. XI, was a member of the class of 1933 at the Montana School of Mines. He became manager of the United States Gypsum Company plant at Heath, Mont., and is now manager of that company's operations at Midland, Calif. This is a straightforward account of an ordinary night in a mine—"not unusual in any respect." Yet there is a sense of immanent drama and imminent peril. Note the caution with which the blasts are counted, lest the next shift drill into an unexploded shot—one of the most frequent causes of mine disasters; that is the peril. For the drama, see the hope based upon the "lifter" which "drilled black," the dream of a bonanza. We are indebted to Dr. Francis A. Thomson, president of the School of Mines, for an explanation of the "black lifter." A "lifter" is a hole drilled into the face of a heading near the bottom and it is blasted last, usually by using a longer fuse, in order to lift and throw back the material blasted out of the face by explosions in the drill holes above it. As the drill steel penetrates the face of the working, it explores rock or ground which has not been seen and the experienced miner watches the color of the "drillings" which are constantly being washed back from the point of the drill by a stream of water forced through the hollow drill steel. Tourmaline, except in gem form, is usually a black worthless silicate which drains out of the drill hole as black mud; but the valuable sulphide minerals such as copper, lead, and zinc, though not black themselves, yield a black streak or powder. Thus the miner, seeing black mud oozing from the drill hole, hopes the steel has encountered a vein or ore body, but fears it may be only tourmaline which he would consider worthless.

I

MOUNTAIN Consolidated Mining Company was driving a three-thousand-foot development tunnel deep into the granite base of that bare-topped, forest-skirted mammoth of the northern Rockies known as Red Mountain.

This is the story of one February night shift, not unusual in any respect and without the sharp excitement that marked other shifts —for instance, the night when the miners reeled out into the open from a gassy tunnel and one husky fellow collapsed with purple

243

face and ballooned chest, or the New Year's morning when the water ran blood-red after the blast and everyone thought that the Big Strike had been made.

The mercury on this particular night was stagnant at twenty below and the sky was clear and without moon. A distant offshoot of the Continental Divide stood in jagged silhouette against the haze of the Northern Lights. The canyon, the sides of the mountains, the pines, the ice on the creek, the winding road—all things —were snow-covered. But the snow was thin atop the warm, tar-papered engine-house. A barren circle of roof on the log blacksmith shop surrounded the forge's sooty stack. And the end of the dump, which crowded Ten Mile creek against the far bank, was smeared with the day shift's muck.

II

The night crew of six men was going on shift. The miners were in the small dry-room behind the engine-house, changing to their digging clothes in the yellow glow of their carbide lamps and the warmth of an old box-heater, while Slim, the young engineer, started his semi-Diesel-engine-driven air compressor. This was Mountain Consolidated's first winter and operations were as yet crude. The only means of ventilation in the tunnel, then past the thousand-foot mark, was an ancient compressed-air sucker, salvaged from a deserted mine, and many battered lengths of second-hand tin pipe.

Since the miners were not expected to enter the tunnel until the compressor was operating and the sucker drawing bad air from the face, Slim was making his starting preparations rapidly. The thin, long flame of his carbide lamp, which was hooked miner-style to his cap, hissed and gurgled as he stepped quickly around the engine with an oil can or a chunk of waste. In a corner of the engine-house a blow torch, enveloped in a greasy pile of flame, tossed wavering shadows on the rafters of the low roof. Parts of gleaming gray paint and polished brass reflected the firelight, and the pride of the engineers in the company's newest and finest piece of machinery.

Slim turned on the blow torch and placed a roaring blue flame on the hot tube in the engine's liner head. A miner opened the dry-room door, looked at the torch, and turning to the men, warned them, "She'll be running in a few minutes." The "hard-rockers" tightened the laces of white rubber boots, donned black slickers, rammed southwesters on their heads and selected dry gloves from the assortment under the stove.

The tube cherry red, Slim inspected the engine for the last time, squinted at an air gauge, opened a valve and quickly jerked and released the starting lever. It was difficult work with only a carbide lamp to dimly outline the machine. The engine turned over slowly, sluggish with cold, was hit by another charge of starting air and still another, fired, missed, fired again, and with increasing cadence of explosions began to gather speed. A little generator was belt-driven from one of the fly-wheels and a light gradually glowed into brilliance on the switchboard. Slim made rapid adjustments here and there, and, stepping to the switches, snapped on the electricity. Lights flashed in the dry-room and engine-house, up in the blacksmith shop, out on the end of the dump, at the tunnel mouth. The compressor cut out, and idling, the engine rumbled softly with only twenty pounds' pressure on the air piston.

The miners walked through the engine-house, climbed the steps to the blacksmith shop, recharged their lamps, and then, illuminated for a brief second under the light on the portal timbers, one by one stepped into the square blackness of the tunnel.

III

The shivering trammer, Dave, out in the icy air to dump a steaming carload of muck, rapped on the air line. In response to the signal, Slim appeared in the engine-house doorway.

"Give 'em the air," Dave shouted.

Slim waved answer, slammed the door, stepped to the engine and threw the unloader lever. The swishing of air through idle valves ceased and became a sharp clicking; the gentle throbbing of the exhaust gave way to a staccato pounding that tossed rings of smoke high into the air and told ranchers seven miles down the canyon that young Bill's men were drilling another round. The gauge on the receiver quivered up the scale and, pound by pound, gained pressure toward the unloading point of ninety-five, with sucker turned off and miners ready to drill.

245

IV

At the face of the tunnel, mounted on a horizontal jack bar, a high-speed rock drill hammered a churning length of steel into the granite. A wild terror of sound roared from the machine, clamored and echoed against the ragged walls, surged into the deafened ears of miners and muckers, and crashed for hundreds of feet down the tunnel before losing its terrific energy. The whole place seemed to vibrate until the walls must collapse, and the big drops of water that spattered men, muck and slippery rails were as if shaken from the roof. Compressed air fog spouted from the drill's exhaust port and enveloped the entire scene, softened the hard walls, shrouded the figures of the men, dimmed the carbide lamps into yellowness, and, permeated with oily odor, drifted back into the darkness.

Gaunt, hook-nosed, taciturn John knelt on the muck pile, turning the crank at the end of the machine and expertly forcing the steel ahead. Indian-faced and patient as the drill vibrated forward, he made only two motions, the rotary twist of his right arm on the crank and the slow turn of his head to squirt tobacco juice over his shoulder. When a length of steel was driven to its shank, he jerked a little control, threw the machine into part speed and cranked it back while it chugged evenly. Sam, his partner, plump, pink, white-haired and lazy, stood between bar and face, ready to change steel in the instant between the backward and forward motions of the drill. If the machine stuck, Sam pounded the steel with his wrench. Except to fill the water tank, he seldom moved from his position, where he changed steels and contemplated the slime that oozed from the holes. But sometimes the drillers had trouble.

The muckers sweated. Perspiration rolled down their faces, their wet shirts clung to their thick chests, their damp trouser knees were worn smooth by the shovel handles. When Scotty, the canny Highlander, bought his annual pair of working pants, he promptly sewed three patches on the left knee, where the shovel rubs, and two patches on the right knee and the seat. The patches came from the overalls that were to be retired from active service. He and his stocky partner, Ed, worked side by side, scraped their shovels on the turn sheet, plunged the "square-points" under the muck, lifted the rock over brawny shoulders, and crashed their

246

loads into the car behind, working tirelessly and with perfect timing. Car after car was pushed empty to the muck sheets, and car after car disappeared loaded down the track to the trammer. When one mucker rode a car to Dave's switch, the other cleaned the sheets of spilled rock and picked down the pile. The two muckers were convinced that they were the best pair of shovelers in all the camps of the county.

Suddenly, with a silence that crashed like sound, the drill ceased roaring. Something was wrong; a length of steel refused to fit into place. Sam inspected the chuck. He exploded into profanity. He raved and sputtered and somehow conveyed the information that the water needle was smashed. John mumbled one blasphemous sentence and bit off a corner of plug.

Sam glanced at the muckers and noticed that they had a car nearly full. "Oh, Scotty!" he shouted, and when the Scotchman heard him above the noise of shovels and the hiss of escaping air, "Say, will you tell Dave to get a water needle? And, let's see, about the powder"—Sam conferred a moment with his partner—"twelve primers, all double—it's damn wet—and a box of powder."

"You bet, Sam." Scotty and Ed threw a few final shovelfuls on the loaded car and pulled out the wedge from under the wheels. Scotty pushed off, jumped on the little platform at the rear of the truck, slung his light on the side and went coasting downgrade towards the portal. At the switch ahead a light glowed. It swung up and down, clear-track signal from Dave. The car gathered momentum. A few feet from the switch Scotty grabbed his light and dropped off. Dave swung on, throwing his weight so as to gain even more precious speed. "Water needle—dozen primers, double—box-a-powder," yelled Scotty above the racket of the car. "All r-i-g-h-t," came the fading answer from the trammer as he careened down the crooked track, clicked over joints, flashed past timbers, swayed close to buttresses of rock, ducked his head under sprags, clanked over switches, and hoping that no treacherous roof-fragments had fallen on the rails, sped recklessly towards the looming, dull-gray portal with rickety car and ton of muck.

V

It was three in the morning. The miners had drilled the top holes, eaten lunch and, returning to the face, had just completed putting in the lifters. The muckers had shoveled the last car off the rough and had laid and weighted the sheets. Dave, the trammer, who worked split shifts, was already home and asleep.

It was nearly time to spit, time to light the fuses that set off the round. Scotty, who hated to be in the tunnel when the shots went off, was nervously loading a car with dulled steel. Sam was handing sticks of powder to John, who drove and tamped them into the holes. Ed was waiting for the spare powder.

John carefully pushed the last primer, with its long fuses, into place, and shoved the final two sticks of powder after it. Sam handed the box to Ed, who flung it into Scotty's car.

"Let's go," said Scotty, climbing in with the powder. Ed pushed off, jumped on the foothold, and the car sped down the track. Lights buzzing, wheels rattling, steel clanking, Scotty and Ed and the left-over dynamite coasted wildly towards the portal.

With speed and precision, the miners spitted their holes. Sam cut the fuses and John touched them off with his carbide lamp. No time was wasted. Sam's lamp hung within easy reach in case his partner's should fail. Each newly lighted fuse contributed to a thickening haze of heavy, white smoke. The cut, breast and back holes were spitted in order, and the important lifters last of all. With the smoke choking them and the fuses sizzling ever closer to the caps, the miners turned and walked, almost trotted, down the tunnel.

The concussion of the first shot to go off struck them a dull blow and snuffed out their lights when they were still several hundred feet from the portal. In the darkness they kept walking, while a series of reverberating blasts followed, eight explosions in all. "One short, on top," grunted Sam. After a pause, the tunnel was shaken by three muffled thuds in quick succession, the heavily loaded lifters breaking clean the bottom of the advance and throwing the muck back upon the sheets. The miners stopped only at the portal to hang up the "one short" board,* and then emerged into the bitter sting of open air, where clouds of vapor rose from their wet, crinkling slickers and shiny southwesters.

Slim, his face thrown into deep shadow by his cap lamp, stood at the tunnel mouth to meet them. The lights of the homeward-

* Warning the next shift that one charge did not explode.

bound muckers glimmered between the trees that lined the mile-long road to camp.

"Oh, Slim," said Sam, "that righthand lifter drilled black. May be only tourmaline. Well, the boys'll know in the morning; no use us worrying."

"We're supposed to be pretty close to that Netty May vein," replied Slim as he preceded the two men to the engine-house. "Sam, if we stay here long enough we may see trains of ore running out of this tunnel and a big mill on the hillside there and tractors hauling concentrates down to the N.P. and . . ."

"Yeh—if we stay long enough," sneered John.

After he had cut in the load on the compressor to give the sucker more power, Slim stepped into the room where Sam and John were changing clothes and washing.

"I hope she'll warm up, I'm sick of thawing out everything all the time," complained Slim, who was not used to the long, severe cold spells of the mountains.

"Didn't I tell you it'd go forty below?" asked Slim, and without waiting for an answer, "I spent two years up in the middle of Alaska. Say, talk about cold, sixty below it was and we sunk our shaft through a hundred feet of frozen ground."

"This is a hell of a country," grumbled big John from deep in his throat as he leaned over to lace his boots. He was unconvinced that any place could be worse.

Sam wrestled with a red mackinaw. John's comment amused him; he chuckled and his blue eyes, pale Montana blue, were almost buried between fat cheek and gray brows. "Say, you shoulda been around here back in the eighties, that first winter when me and another lad come into the eastern part of the state. We got caught late in the fall out in the cattle country with winter on the way fast, so we had to get to work and throw us up a cabin. Didn't have nothin' to chink it with except lots of cow dung. Got it built just in time. It smelled to beat hell, but when she got fifty below we was OK. After that blizzard the cattle was lyin' dead for many a mile around. October of eighty-eight, I think."

John gnawed off a corner of plug. Slim grinned at the yarn. Sam spattered tobacco juice on the floor. Lunch buckets under arm, lamps in hand, collars turned up, the two miners headed for the door.

"Good night," said Slim. John made no response. "Tap 'er light, kid!" sang out Sam, and then turned grinning: "About that lifter and the Netty May, remember what the old prospector said—'Where ore is ore is, and where ore ain't there I be.' So long."

VI

At four in the morning, Slim, his shift in, strode through the little mining village. He walked past the deserted saloons—with false fronts and sagging roofs—where the hob-nailed and rubber-booted gentry had gathered forty years before, to make this one of the "roaring camps." It was a phantasy of Slim's, especially when passing the skeleton of the old mill on a dark winter night, that the shades of those "single-jackers" * were watching with jealous and skeptical eyes this crew of men drive the Red Mountain tunnel, far under the snow-covered scars of forgotten prospect holes. He thought of Sam's black lifter and the expectations for the next round—always the next round. He thought of the old prospector's saying, humorous, but grim, "Where ore ain't there I be." Still that right-hand lifter had drilled black.

Come on, bonanza!

* Miners who drilled by hand, with a hand drill and sledgehammer.

THREE MINERS' SONGS

Though Butte is rich with songs, some of them adaptations from folk ballads from all over the world, few have ever been published. Here are three from the famous mining camp. The first is an obvious variant of one of the many versions of "The Cowboy's Lament." The other two are reprinted from *Copper Camp* (Hastings House, 1943), the book of Butte stories compiled by the WPA Writers' Project and sponsored by the Montana department of agriculture, labor, and industry. The first of these *Copper Camp* reports is an "old miner's ballad"; the other it attributes to Matty Kiely, Butte miner and minstrel. Jim Brennan, mentioned unflatteringly in two of the songs given here, was the tough shift boss of the Mountain Con mine. In "Matty Kiely's Song" the "b-r-r-r" was his vocal representation of the air drill used by the miners, called a "buzzy." The term "rustling" in this song means he was looking for a job.

I Came to Butte City

'TWAS once in the saddle I used to go dashing,
'Twas once as a cowboy I used to be brave;
But ain't it a pity I came to Butte City
To work for Jim Brennan—and now to my grave!

My Sweetheart's a Mule

My sweetheart's a mule in the mine.
I drive her with only one line.
On the dashboard I sit
And tobacco I spit
All over my sweetheart's behind.

Matty Kiely's Song

B-r-r-r-r-r-r-r-r-r-r-r-r
I rustled at the Diamond—I rustled at the Bell;
I rustled all summer—and I rustled like hell.
B-r-r-r-r-r-r-r-r-r-r-r-r!

B-r-r-r-r-r-r-r-r-r-r-r-r!
I rustled at the Gagnon and I rustled at the 'Sweat,'

251

The Stewart and the Greyrock—and I'm rustlin' yet.
B-r-r-r-r-r-r-r-r-r-r-r-r!

I'm a buzzy miner—indeed I am;
Old Jim Brennan just gave me the can.

DISASTERS

For drama, nothing in the history of Montana—and little in that of the whole country—can equal the spectacular disasters of Butte, "biggest mining camp in the world." Here is a story about them, their horrors and their heroism, from *Copper Camp*. There is no author's name on *Copper Camp*, but the introduction says: "If regulations of the Montana Writers' Project did not prevent, the cover of this book would bear the name of William A. Burke as author." The book is based largely upon the observations, memories, and research of Burke, publicity man and news writer and native of Butte. It contains a host of good stories about the famed camp and its "richest hill on earth." It was published by Hastings House in 1943.

A T its safest, mining is a dangerous occupation, and the average miner accepts its dangers with a fatalistic attitude. Like most men engaged in dangerous work, he is apt to scoff at it, although the nearness of death is always foreboding.

It is not known what early-day humorist christened loose, hanging slabs of ground with the name of the camp's leading undertaker; but for years, "Bar down the 'Larry Duggan'!" was a common expression for a dangerous slab or rock hanging over a miner's head. Larry Duggan's mortuary on North Main Street was a landmark for years. The old-timer will add that when the safety campaign began to make the mines safer, Larry had himself elected sheriff.

When the cantankerous "Buzzy" air drills first came into operation with their clouds of deadly silicosis-breeding dust the miners promptly labeled them "Widow-makers."

In referring to "missed-holes," or dynamite charges that have failed to explode, it was not uncommon to hear a shift boss tell a miner, "There's a couple of 'requiem high masses' in that stope. Better keep an eye for them." Anything for a laugh.

But joke though he might, the experienced miner early adopted his own safety measures designed to keep accidents at a minimum.

Not counting the unavoidable major disasters the copper camp's average of fatal accidents throughout the years of operation probably created fifty to a hundred widows annually. That's why the cemetery population exceeds the 1940 census. The camp remembers best the big accidents that can't be laughed off.

Butte's first major mining calamity occurred on November 23, 1889. A fire broke out in the shaft of the Anaconda Mine, sending smoke and gas through the workings. Fortunately, the fire occurred between shifts with most of the miners out of the workings. Only six were killed and two badly injured.

It was the custom that when a fire broke out in any mine for every mine on the hill to blow its whistles, setting up a piercing wail that usually scared the town out of its wits, causing understandable fear to those having friends or relatives underground.

"When the mine whistles blew in chorus," says a veteran of the period, "every woman in Butte, whose old man was down in the holes, would throw her shawl over her head, grab a couple of kids, and hit out lickety-split for the mine he was workin' in—dead certain that he was being burned alive."

A fire broke out in the Silver Bow Mine in the spring of 1893, causing the miners to scurry for safety. All but nine escaped. A public funeral was held for the victims with the entire town in mourning, and a large sum was collected for the dependents of the victims. Since then Butte has dug deep into its pockets on many similar occasions.

The next big mine fire, while not claiming lives, was the cause of considerable inconvenience. It was in August, 1900, when the hoist and entire surface workings of the Parrot Mine were destroyed by flames. The miners' change dry was among the buildings burned down, and with it, the clothing of the miners. Considerable money and valuables belonging to the miners working in the mine at the time were reduced to ashes.

John Harrington of Centerville, a veteran of that blaze who lost his roll and a "new tailor-made suit" in the conflagration, tells of his experience.

"I had been workin' day-shift at the Parrot and the night before the fire, I had just paid for a new tailor-made suit, and I put it on and went for a stroll around town. I had a piece of change in me pockets, and it wasn't long before I was sittin' in a faro game.

"Well, sir," continued John, "I never had such luck in me life. I couldn't lose, and long about six o'clock in the mornin', I was winners, a thousand dollars.

"I says to meself, this is one time in your life you won't be a damn fool. You'll save this money and make a trip to the old country. So

I has it changed into a thousand-dollar bill and puts it in the inside pocket of me new tailor-made suit.

"It was gettin' late in the mornin' and I didn't have time to change me clothes, so I grabbed me bucket at the boardin' house and hurried up the hill to the Parrot.

"I changed into me diggin' clothes in the dry and left the tailor-made suit and the thousand-dollar bill in the mine locker, went down into the mine, and put in a tough shift, what with me not havin' a wink of sleep.

"To make a long story short," ended Mr. Harrington, "when I come up out of the mine that even', the dry was burned to the ground and with it me thousand dollars and the new tailor-made suit. It was the first and only money I ever saved in Butte," he added sadly, "and I never did get to make the trip to the old country."

Evidently 1911 was a jonah year for mine accidents. On April 24 the engine at the Leonard Mine, while lowering the shift, got out of control. This caused the mine cage with its burden of fourteen men, nine on the upper deck and five on the lower deck, to fall from the surface to the sump, some fifteen hundred feet. The five men on the lower deck were killed outright. The nine on the upper deck were more fortunate, but all received injuries that kept them in the hospital for many months.

Again that year disaster struck the camp. This time at the Black Rock Mine on September 3, and sadly, the victims all were little more than boys.

Before the introduction of child-labor laws, it had been the custom in the Butte mines to hire boys of school age as "nippers" or toolboys. It was their job to go from place to place in the workings of the mines and pick up dull or damaged tools, including drilling steel, and to replace them with tools that had been sharpened and repaired. Each level in the mine had its own nipper.

The nippers carried the damaged tools to the stations on the various levels where they were pulled to the surface, usually about a quarter of an hour before the men were hoisted at the end of the shift. At that time, and before the introduction of "safety-boats" (a container to prevent drills from falling through the grating on the floor of the cage), the collected steel was piled none too carefully on the decks of the mine cages.

Although it was strictly against safety rules, it long had been the custom of the nippers to ride to the surface on the same cage with the dull tools and steel, thus gaining a fifteen-minute advantage over the rest of the miners. It was to gain this fifteen minutes that eight Black Rock nippers, not one of whom had reached his twentieth birthday, piled aboard the tool cage on that fatal Sunday morning.

On its trip to the surface, in some unexplained manner, the steel became loosened from the bottom of the cage, and one or more pieces of the heavy, sharp metal forced its way through apertures and protruded into the shaft. The cage rising to the surface at express train speed, became a grinding, tearing juggernaut, pulling the shaft's timbers and wall-plates from their moorings in its wild ascent. The eight nippers were literally ground to pieces. But two were alive when the twisted and battered cage reached the surface. Both were horribly mutilated.

The years 1915–16–17 in turn witnessed the three most devastating disasters in the camp's history, climaxing with the Speculator fire of 1917 that remains to date the most disastrous in the annals of all quartz mining.

On October 19, 1915, sixteen shift bosses and assistant foremen on surface for their lunch hour were grouped around the shaft of the Granite Mountain Mine awaiting the 12:30 whistle to announce the time for lowering the mine cage to take them down below to their work. Beside them on the surface turn-sheets a small hand-truck with twelve cases of forty-per cent dynamite also was waiting to be lowered.

At the first blast of the whistle, from a cause that has never been determined, the twelve boxes of powder exploded with a roar that could be heard for miles. The sixteen men standing around the shaft were blown to atoms. Fingers with rings attached were found a mile from the scene. Undertakers scoured the surrounding hills for days, seeking portions of bodies. What they found was sealed in caskets and a combined public funeral was held.

Shortly after the explosion, several undertakers were engaged in searching for fragments of the victims' bodies. As small parts were found they were placed in one large basket. A well-known character, drawn to the scene with thousands of others, watched with morbid fascination.

"Hm-m-m," he commented to a bystander. "Puttin' 'em all together in one basket—Corkmen, **Far-do**wns, Cousin Jacks, Democrats, Republicans, Masons, and Knights of Columbus. There's goin' to be a helluva mix-up there on Resurrection Day!"

Early the following year fire broke out in the workings of the Pennsylvania Mine. Fortunately, it was undergoing repairs at the time and no great number of men were working. Twenty of the forty or so in the mine at the time fell victims to the deadly gas. Once again Butte mourned and combined funeral services were held with the entire city in attendance.

The United States had been at war over two months on the night of June 8, 1917. War industries were clamoring for copper. Every mine in Butte was working to capacity. Among them was the big Speculator, with close to two thousand miners employed on the two shifts.

Oddly, it was at the Speculator where the "Safety First" campaign had been most stressed. A crew of safety engineers was employed. All modern safety improvements and practices had been installed, and motion pictures showing safety methods were periodically shown to the employees. Attendance was compulsory. The "Company" was desirous of keeping accidents at a minimum and did not tolerate the slightest infraction of safety rules.

But on that June evening, the night shift of some nine hundred men had been lowered and were at work. During the late afternoon and evening, ropemen and shaftmen had been lowering a huge, insulated electric cable to operate the ventilating fans on the lower levels. The heavy cable had somehow become fouled and was hanging suspended in the shaft. For some time the workers had been vainly trying to free it. The assistant foreman on the night shift had descended to aid in the difficulty. The cable was an old one, with the insulation in some places frayed and worn. Sallau, the assistant foreman, his carbide light in hand, was examining it in an endeavor to find some way of breaking the tangle and getting it started down the shaft once more. In some inexplicable manner, his carbide light came in contact with the frayed edge of the insulation.

Like a lighted match dropped in gasoline, the insulation burst into flame. Acting as a chimney, the draft in the up-cast shaft pulled the flames toward the surface, and in an instant the entire length of the cable was ablaze. As the dry shaft timber caught fire, it was but a moment before the entire three thousand feet of shaft had been turned into an inferno.

At the first flash, Sallau and his assistants hurriedly descended out of danger, below the path of the flames. But now the damage was done. Any effort on their part to prevent the spread of the fire was hopeless and would undoubtedly have led to their cremation. It was but a few moments before the flames were shooting out of the mouth of the shaft on surface, consuming with incalculable speed the dry timbers, and forcing the deadly smoke and gas onto every level in the mine.

An instant before the cable was ignited the mine cage with two station-tenders aboard had been lowered into the mine. Hardly had it disappeared from surface before flames bellowed forth from the mouth of the shaft. The hapless men had been lowered into a flaming furnace. Too late, the engineer on duty discovered their peril. It was some time later that the white-hot cage was brought back to the surface. A few charred bones and metal overall buttons were all that remained on its scorched deck.

Underground, on every level, the scene was the same. Many of the miners, smelling the first whiff of smoke, had made a run for it and escaped through the levels of other mines adjoining the Speculator. Fortunately there were connections to neighboring mines on almost every level. These men were quickly hoisted to surface.

On the eighteen-hundred-foot level of the Speculator, two hundred men escaped into the Badger State Mine by battering their way through a fifteen-inch concrete bulkhead with sledge hammers and heavy timbers.

On surface at the mouth of the blazing shaft, any rescue work until the fire had burned itself out, was impossible. Word was sent to all other mines in the camp for rescue crews.

In answer to the call came ambulances, trucks and other vehicles carrying first-aid and fire-fighting equipment. The presence of "dead wagons" and hearses offered a grim foreboding. News had spread rapidly in the city, and thousands came to the mineyards. Scenes were pathetic as those having loved ones below gazed with frantic appeal at the smoking shaft.

Statements gathered from the rescued as they arrived from the other mines were practically all the same. Miners had been compelled to feel their way in the darkness of the drifts and cross-cuts. One of their number who knew the way advanced ahead of the others. Those behind formed a human chain, each holding to the one ahead of him, and staggered blindly through the gases that were becoming stronger minute by minute. The rescued told harrowing tales of hundreds of their fellow-workers lying dead throughout the mine where they had fallen.

Without number were the stories of heroism of the miners. If feats of bravery could have saved the scores of entombed men there would have been but few fatalities, for never were more heroic sacrifices made in any mining catastrophe. Many in the copper camp are alive today because of the deeds of their fellow workers.

Gas from the Speculator had swept into the Diamond Mine almost immediately. Luckily, however, most of the miners employed in this mine had time to reach the safety of the mine cages and were hoisted to the surface. Not all were so fortunate. Con O'Neil, foreman of the mine, and three miners were trapped by the onrushing gas and died gasping in their tracks.

Hours later, as the fire in the Speculator burned itself out, an attempt was made to enter. Over a dozen volunteers were loaded on the mine cage, among them, the assistant foreman, Sallau, whose carbide light had inadvertently caused the blaze. As the cage reached its destination and the rescuers stepped off, they were met by a blast of the deadly gas and all perished on the turnsheets of the station. Further attempts at rescue were abandoned until fresh air had been pumped into the mine.

Butte was stunned and shocked. A rapid check of the survivors indicated that over two hundred miners had been trapped below. Barring a miracle, all had perished, for survivors had reported seeing the drifts and stations strewn with dead. Scenes in the mine yard were heartrending. The hospitals were crowded with the injured. Thousands crowded frantically seeking word of some loved one. Regular army soldiers, stationed on guard duty in Butte at the time, were pressed into service and endeavored to keep some semblance of order.

Two days and a night had passed since the first flames had swept up the shaft. Fresh air was being pumped into the mine, and safety engineers decided that at last it was safe for rescue squads to descend to bring up the bodies of the victims. All hope of anyone being alive in the mine had long been abandoned. It was then that a small miracle happened. Sitting in his chair in the engine room, the engineer of the Speculator was astonished to hear a signal flash from the depths where a moment before he had been positive there was no living person.

Somewhere below, someone had escaped the deadly gas.

Again the signal flashed. Startled into instant action, he threw the various levers and throttles. The giant engine hummed, the cable unwound from the whirling drums, and the cage descended to the level the engine-room indicator showed the signal had come from.

A brief pause—and again a signal—this time to hoist.

Up came the cage. Before the astonished eyes of the hundreds who had crowded around the shaft, nine men—blackened—haggard—stepped from the cage, blinking in the sudden sunlight but bringing the joyous news that sixteen more of their fellows were alive below and waiting to be hoisted.

Down the shaft and up again traveled the cage, until in all, twenty-five miners had been brought back from the dead into the sunlight of the mineyard.

It was a startling tale these survivors told—a story of the heroism and sacrifices of one man who died that others might live—the story of Manus Duggan, a common miner; a simple tale of heroism, but twenty-five Butte miners owed their lives to Duggan's act.

Within an hour after the fire started, the twenty-five-year-old miner marshalled a group of twenty-nine men and gathered them together in a cross-cut into which the deadly gas had not yet penetrated. Hastily erecting a makeshift bulkhead of timber, canvas, clothing and dirt, he took charge of the little group of men in the small, cramped cross-cut, keeping up their morale and preventing them from making the break for a supposed safety that would certainly have meant their end. As tiny apertures appeared in the bulkhead, Duggan forced them to strip their clothing from their bodies to plug the gaps and keep out the gas.

As the long hours passed, breathing became more and more difficult. When Duggan saw at last that it was only a matter of minutes before they would all succumb, he decided to seek a path of safety for his charges. Taking three of the men, he set out to find a safe path into some other mine, intending, if successful, to come back and guide those left behind. Manus Duggan and his three followers never returned. Days later their blackened bodies were found in a drift where they had fallen.

The remainder of the little band, after waiting a reasonable time for Duggan's return, decided to chance everything in a rush for the station. Any risk was better than slow death in the cross-cut. Desperately they set out in a group. To their joy and surprise on reaching the station they found pure air. The air pumps had done their work well. Frantically, delirious with joy, they gave the station signal and rang for the cage.

Butte received news of their rescue with elation. Houses of sorrow were changed into homes of rejoicing as the rescued men returned. On all sides were words of praise for the hero, Manus Duggan. His wife and three small children were offered the sympathy of the city.

For weeks the copper camp mourned. Both private and public funerals were held. Identification of the one hundred and sixty-three bodies recovered was difficult, and many were never identified. The North Butte Mining Company estimated damage to the mine at a million dollars. Compensation to dependents of the victims totaled $800,000; about $400 for the life of each miner. To date it is the camp's greatest disaster. There has not been a major accident since, but the town knocks on wood—the miners are never too safe and anything can happen underground.

JOE BOWERS' SONG

This famous frontier song was not, of course, of Montana origin.
However, its popularity with the miners and the fact that it figured
uniquely in the early history of Butte should make it of particular
interest. The Summit Valley camp, subsequently Butte, heard it sung
so often by one of its citizens that he was nicknamed Joe Bowers and
few, apparently, knew his real name, Joseph Townsend. His name
appears in the records of the community as early as 1864, so he was
one of the first settlers. He constructed a ditch for mine operations,
taking water from Silver Bow Creek near the present suburb of
Meaderville, and diverting the stream through Buffalo Gulch and
Hungry Hollow. The ditch was called "Joe Bowers' Ditch" and was
sold by Townsend in 1867. The story is contained in a manuscript
history of Butte by Mrs. Kate Hammond Fogarty of that city's public
library. A copy is in the library of the Historical Society of Montana.
The version of the song printed here is that used by Mrs. Fogarty.

MY name is Joe Bowers
And I've got a brother Ike;
I come from Old Missouri,
All the way from Pike.
I'll tell you why I left there,
And why I came to roam
And leave my poor old mammy
So far away from home.

I used to court a girl there,
Her name was Sally Black,
I axed her if she'd marry me,
She said it was a whack.
Says she to me, "Joe Bowers,
Before we hitch for life,
You ought to get a little home
To keep your little wife."

O Sally! Dearest Sally!
O Sally! For your sake
I'll go to California
And try to make a stake.

Says she to me, "Joe Bowers,
You are the man to win;
Here's a kiss to bind the bargain."
And she hove a dozen in.

When I got to that country
I hadn't nary red;
I had such wolfish feelings
I wished myself 'most dead;
But the thought of my dear Sally
Soon made those feelings git,
And whispered hopes to Bowers—
I wish I had them yet!

At length I went to mining,
Put in my biggest licks,
Went down upon the boulders
Just like a thousand bricks.
I worked both late and early
In rain, in sun, in snow;
I was working for my Sally—
'Twas all the same to Joe.

At length I got a letter
From my dear brother Ike;
It came from Old Missouri,
All the way from Pike;
It brought to me the darndest news
That ever you did hear,
My heart is almost bustin',
So please excuse this tear.

It said that Sal was false to me,
Her love for me had fled;
She'd got married to a butcher—
The butcher's hair was red;
And more than that the letter said
(It's enough to make me swear)
That Sally has a baby;
And the baby has red hair!

263

THE FRUIT TRAMPS

DOROTHY MARIE JOHNSON

Though operations on the scale indicated in this story are perhaps more characteristic of northern Washington, Montana knows the "fruit tramps," and during the season their "home"—in so far as they have any—is briefly in the northwestern and extreme south-western part of this state. Dorothy Marie Johnson, whose home was in Whitefish, wrote this story for Vol. X of The Frontier, *January, 1930; an English student at Montana State University, she was a frequent contributor to the magazine. After graduation she went East, and is now managing editor of* The Woman *and a well-known writer of fiction for the* Saturday Evening Post.

THE great fruit harvest of the West. Truckloads of boxes of loose packed apples rolling in from the orchards, men jumping to platforms to receive them, piling boxes in walls six feet high, with aisles between. Men emptying apples into bins, rollers pulling them up under wiping cloths to flap off the dust and insecticides. The steady growl of machinery filling the sheds.

Women on stools under brilliant lights, white gloved hands sorting swiftly, endlessly—Extra Fancy, Fancy, C grade, Culls, into carriers that dump them again into more bins. Men and girls wrapping shining apples with unerring swiftness, packing them into boxes. Men wasting no motions, slapping on lids with swift hammer blows.

Packed boxes stacked high, trucked away to storage or to cars. Endless fruit trains congesting railroad traffic. And all through the vast sheds, the clean odor of new lumber where the shook is stacked, and the keen, sweet scent of the fruit.

Hurry, hurry! Ten hour days—twelve hour days, the crop is good this year. Work Sundays, extra pay. Hurry, hurry! Schools closed down for the harvest, stores closed if a frost comes to loosen the fruit on the trees; students and clerks and housewives and children swarming through the weeds of the orchards, picking, trucking, sorting, receiving, packing, lidding, box-making.

Money, money! The towns go crazy Saturday nights. Pay checks every week, spent before next pay day. Women in overalls critically examining fur trimmed coats, trying on smart hats in the late-open stores. The pickers, the packers, the box makers all getting money. And after a while, the men who raised the apples get some money too.

That's the rub. Helen's father was an orchardist. All the year around money was going out, winter pruners to be paid, a new spray outfit to buy, irrigation rights to wrangle over and pay for, pickers to pay, truckers to pay. Going on credit the whole year, skimping, worrying—and then, when the fruit was sold, money all at once. Too many things to pay for—a new car, new clothes for the kids, old grocery bills, new furniture. Money gone; more credit.

Even when she was a half-grown girl, Helen wasn't going to follow the fruit. The orchards smelled of rotten eggs and scorched rubber from the insecticide spray. You learned to worry about the hail, and the wind limb-bruised the fruit or knocked it clear off. No, she was going to be a stenographer.

But she picked apples during harvest, tangling her feet in the weeds, scratching her face and arms up in the trees, covered with stinging dust. She fell off a ladder now and then. Dad was short-handed again, with such a big crop, and she'd have to help. He'd pay her same as the pickers. Maybe he would.

When she was sixteen, she was big enough to sort in the sheds. Then she got her pay regularly and Dad found other pickers.

Long hours under the brilliant lights, with rollers bouncing the apples softly past you, jumping them up and around and over. You learned to tell the grade at a glance. When the whistle blew that you had been waiting for, you slid off your stool, tired clear through. If you had let any bad ones go through, maybe you could get back early and sneak them out of the bins before the inspector caught them there.

Women don't dress to look pretty when they work in the fruit. Old kitchen dresses and comfortable shoes; knickers or overalls. If you can still look attractive when you quit after ten hours, with two more coming if the sheds work at night, if you can still walk with some energy, so the lidders and receivers notice you when the gang runs for the row of Fords outside—then you're pretty. They looked at Helen.

She worked three years sorting, while she was in high school.

"I'm saving it," she told her folks haughtily. "Maybe I'll go to college."

"Why, that's just fine!" her mother praised. "Billy, that's too much butter for that slice."

Her father wiped his sleeve across his mouth. "Sure, kid; save your money and you'll be rich some day. But not in the fruit business."

There were new clothes she could buy with that twenty-five or so a week. She hadn't saved much, by the time she was out of high school.

"Guess I won't go to college this year," she announced. "I'll work in the fruit this fall and go to business college. Then after I work a while I'll go to college. I don't know just what I want to take up, anyway."

"That's just fine, dear," her mother agreed.

"Yep. Save your money," her father grinned.

New crowd at the shed when the season opened. Always a new crowd, with a sprinkling of town people, regulars. New men up from California, expert lidders and box-makers.

But Helen saw only one new man up from California.

Tall and dark and smiling, Jim was. Always smiling, even with twelve hours of continuous hammering behind him: one, two, three, four. One, two, three, four. Another row of nails from the stripper. Always pounding, flipping the boxes over onto the rollers; always smiling to himself, white teeth showing, as he piled up a record for that day, for that week. Piece work, making money.

"Get in, kid. Take you home in Lizzy."

"Think I want to walk back?"

"Oh, I'm not so bad."

"Your car is, though."

But she rode. She went to supper with him at a restaurant full of tired, chattering people, frantic hashers running from table to kitchen. Clatter of dishes, smoke. People crowding, eating, talking. All she saw was Jim's smile.

"By gosh, kid, first girl I ever saw looked good in bib overalls. Been in the fruit long?"

"Since I was a kid. Those were Dad's apples we packed today."

"Good crop he had. Graded high. Going to the Argentine, weren't they? Gee, that pounding gets a guy's arm. I use a bottle of

liniment a week during the season. You get old quick in this business. Guess I'll quit it."

"You're good, though. You must make good money. You had the
record of the sheds last week."

"Hundred and twenty-one dollars in last week's pay check, kid.
But the apples were coming through good, not many culls. Can't
lid boxes unless you get the fruit through the graders."

"Some of 'em can't lid boxes anyhow. Gee! And I get forty-five
cents an hour!"

"You ought to learn to pack, kid. Packers make money."

"But it takes a couple of seasons to learn, and I'm going away to
business college. That is, I think I am."

"Sure, get out of the game. You get old too soon."

"Sure. I'm going to business college."

"Take you to the dance Saturday?"

"Well, I was going out home Saturday night. Would you bring
me home early?"

"Sure—early Sunday morning."

"Say, Dad will yell!"

"I'll talk to him. Shall we take some other kids?"

"Oh, sure."

"Let's not. Just you and me."

"Well, all right."

The towns go wild on Saturday night. Money to burn, things to
buy, stores all open, service stations rushed. Open air dance floor
crowded with people from other towns, people past weariness,
crazy with money and freedom. All day Sunday to sleep.

She never went to business college. They were married when
apple harvest closed.

"Wish I'd saved my money now, kid. Wish I could get you
things."

"I've got a little, Jimmy. I don't want things—just to keep house
and take care of you."

"That takes money. Well, I won't follow the fruit any more. By
gosh, I'll work. I'll do pruning this winter if I can't get a steady job
in the mills. Save my money."

"Maybe I could get a job somewhere for this winter and help
out."

"Kid, I hate to have you work. I want to take care of you."

267

"But it'll be so nice to have some money coming in, when you might not have work, or something."

"Gee, you're a good little kid! I might go back to California for the oranges. Haven't missed a season for eight years."

"No, Jimmy! Don't you leave me! You said you'd quit the fruit. We'll settle down like other folks. Apple knockers are just tramps, my dad says."

"Well, if you think I'm a tramp—"

"No, honey; that's only what my dad says. But we want to settle down. Light green voile curtains, and the kitchen table yellow."

"Have your curtains dark green, and I'll think I'm in an orange grove, kid."

"We'll get along. We'll be awful happy."

She got work in a bakery. There wasn't much winter pruning to do; not much of anything.

"Gee, this country closes up tight when the season's over. Heard about a job from a guy at the pool hall, but it's gone now."

"We'll make out."

She dyed her mother's old curtains pale green, and the table was yellow. She worked all day at the bakery, and took care of her house after work. It was hard, but lots of women do that during harvest, and work ten hours.

Jimmy's earnings paid for gas and tires. Her pay was regular, so she took care of the rent and groceries.

The next fruit harvest came. Soft fruit went fast, and apples began to roll in. The warehouse bosses telephoned from house to house: Be at work in the morning; opening up.

Women made their plans. "Get your own lunch, you kids. Have the spuds on when I get home for supper. Get your dad to help you; he'll be home from the store before I get here."

The tang of apples filling the vast sheds, odor of box shook fresh and keen. Loose apples in boxes piling up in walls. The harvest!

Jimmy lidded for two graders, smiling at his work. Another row of nails from the stripper; his old stripper. Never need that again after this season. Helen massaged his swift right arm every night; a bottle of liniment a week.

She was head sorter at her machine; responsible, swift. Jimmy used to wave at her from far down the machine, sneaking out when the boxes weren't coming along. She waved back with a white gloved hand. Their last season!

One of the women said, "Let's swamp the lidder. Keep him crazy."

"By gosh, let's try it!"

They told the packers down the row. They told the veteran dumper to keep 'em coming. Told the receivers and the flunkies to keep 'em coming. They'd swamp Jimmy.

The shining fruit rolled. Backs ached, hands were weary. Sorters were dizzy, relentless. Swamping Jimmy! The packers, doing piece work, made a record. The veteran dumper gave out and a new man jumped to help.

Workers at the other graders were laughing now, watching. Swamping Jim, the crack lidder from California!

After an hour they were exhausted. Helen sighed and bent over the jumping apples on the belt. They went on and on.

Jimmy sauntered out, smoking a cigaret, against the rules. He cupped a hand to his mouth and shouted through the din, "Why the hell don't you send down some apples? Here I am loafing for ten minutes!"

No, they never swamped Jimmy!

But Jimmy didn't save any money. His and Helen's, it all went as it came. There was only a hundred dollars when the harvest was over. A hundred dollars for a stake.

The day the sheds closed down they all worked in heavy sweaters. No heat; it spoils the fruit. They worked quietly at all the machines. A comradeship was ending, a harvest was over. Friendships were ending, work was ending. At three in the afternoon the apples were gone. Pay checks in the morning.

"Kid, let's go to California for the oranges. You could learn the oranges just as well."

"Oh, but Jimmy—"

"Kid, there's nothing doing here."

"I couldn't get on at the bakery now—"

"I got a new idea for a stripper; nails stick in these boughten ones."

"Oh, I don't know. Maybe I could learn to pack."

"That's the idea, kid. Learn to pack. Takes a year or two, but that's where the money is in the fruit for women."

Washington to Oregon to California, from season to season, from apple harvest to orange harvest, they follow the fruit. Homeless, despised, from rich to penniless. Living in tourist parks, or paying high rent for a bare room. Buying a cot, eating off a packing box. No green curtains, no yellow table. A suit case and a nail stripper, roll of blankets and some tin plates jolting in the back seat. Working and wandering.

They follow a luscious harvest.

THOSE MINING CASES

BERTON BRALEY

Hundreds of involved complaints and countercomplaints in mine litigation tied up the courts of Butte and the Supreme Court of Montana during the famous "copper wars" of the Amalgamated (subsequently Anaconda Copper Mining Company) and F. A. Heinze, young engineer, early in this century. Braley, then a reporter for the Butte *Evening News,* commented upon the legal lunacy in verses printed Nov. 9, 1905. In March, 1906, after Amalgamated had bought Heinze out for $10,500,000, a total of 110 suits involving claims of more than 70 million dollars were dismissed in Butte district court. For additional notes on the Montana career of the well-known author of this verse, see page 349.

THE plaintiff, who is not himself
  But quite another man,
  Desires to clear the atmosphere
Upon a legal plan.
The party of the second part,
  Who also owns a third,
Desires to mine along a line—
  Or so it is averred.

Defendant prays to quash the case,
  Alleging forcefully
That since the plaint
  Might be but ain't,
The answer cannot be.
  The witnesses all testify
It might exist, because
  Cross-questioning is not the thing
To prove she never was.

And now the co-respondent asks
  The right to file a bill,
Alleging that his name is Pat
  And Chauncey's name is Will.

271

The plaintiff asks for forty years
   In which he can amend;
Defendant claims that Jesse James
   Is plaintiff's only friend.

In short, to make the matter clear,
   The common law will show
That rain and sleet are not complete
   Unless they're mixed with snow.
The lawyers all explain the suit
   And yet, I'm still in doubt;
This legal knot—say, tell me what
   The deuce it's all about!

"ONE DARK HARD WINTER"

MILDRED WALKER

Mildred Walker is Mrs. F. R. Schemm of Great Falls, where she has lived for about twelve years. Two of her seven books, *Unless the Wind Turns* and *Winter Wheat,* use the Montana scene. She was born in Philadelphia, was graduated from Wells College, and married Dr. Schemm while he was working as a physician and surgeon in the Michigan woods. Later, while he taught and worked in the University of Michigan Medical School, she obtained an M.A. there and won the Avery and Jules Hopwood award with her first novel, *Fireweed.* The selection here reprinted consists of the first two chapters of *Winter Wheat,* published in 1944 by Harcourt, Brace. In this book the author projects with unusual effectiveness the "rich secret feeling . . . of treasure in the ground" and in the hearts of the rancher, his tough-fibered Russian wife and their daughter, who are the central characters. *Winter Wheat* and another of Mildred Walker's novels, *Dr. Norton's Wife,* were Literary Guild selections. A seventh novel, *The Quarry,* was scheduled for publication in the fall of 1946.

I

SEPTEMBER is like a quiet day after a whole week of wind. I mean real wind that blows dirt into your eyes and hair and between your teeth and roars in your ears after you've gone inside. The harvesting is done and the wheat stored away and you're through worrying about hail or drought or grasshoppers. The fields have a tired peaceful look, the way I imagine a mother feels when she's had her baby and is just lying there thinking about it and feeling pleased.

It was hot, though, like a flash-back to July. I was glad we weren't cooking for harvest hands. There wasn't any fire in the stove and everything was spick-and-span because I had just washed the dinner dishes. Mom was out having another look for the turkeys that were always wandering off. Dad was lying on the couch in the other room waiting for the noon broadcast of wheat prices to come on. We had to sell our wheat this month and not hold it over; that is, we did if I was going to the university that fall. It might go higher along toward Christmas, but we couldn't wait for that.

The house was so quiet I could hear Mom calling the turkeys down by the barn. Dad told Mom not to bother, they'd come back by themselves, but Mom worried if anything was lost or left unlocked.

"When I've got something, I take care of it," she always said.

I washed some cucumbers while I was waiting. They were bright-green and shiny in the water. I used to play they were alligators when I was a child. Then I fenced them in with my hand and poured off the water into the kettle on the stove. When you have to carry every drop of water you use half a mile, you don't throw away any.

And then it began. I knew before Dad turned it up. The voice of the man who announces the wheat prices is as familiar to me as Dad's. It's different from anybody's voice around Gotham—more like one of those city voices that broadcasts the war news. That voice touches us here, and all the ranches spread out over the prairies between the Rockies and the Mississippi. It touches all the people in Clark City, thirty miles from here, who live on the ranchers, even though they try to forget it.

"Here is your Grain Market Broadcast for today: Spring and Winter . . . up two."

I could add two to yesterday's price, so I didn't have to hear any more, but I listened out of habit and because I love to hear it.

"One heavy dark Northern Spring . . . fifty-two." The words came so fast they seemed to roll downhill. Nobody ever calls it all that; it's just spring wheat, but I like the words. They heap up and make a picture of a spring that's slow to come, when the ground stays frozen late into March and the air is raw, and the skies are sulky and dark. The "Northern" makes me feel how close we are to the Rockies and how high up on the map, almost to Canada.

"One dark hard Winter . . . fifty-three."

It's just winter wheat to the people who raise it, only to me it means more than that. It means all the winter and all the cold and the tight feeling of the house in winter, but the rich secret feeling I have, too, of treasure in the ground, growing there for us, waiting for the cold to be over to push up strong and green. They sound like grim words without any comfort to them, but they have a kind of strength all their own.

"Durum, Flax, and Rye . . . up one." The broadcast ran on. Mom came in while I was standing there listening.

274

"Wheat's up," I told her.

Mom nodded. She stood there untying her bandanna and I watched her as though I didn't know her face better than my own. Mom's is a quiet face with a broader forehead than mine and dark brows and eyes and a wide mouth. She doesn't show in her face what she thinks or feels—that's why people in Gotham think she's hard to know—but when she laughs, the laughter goes deeper down in her eyes than anybody's I know.

I look more like Dad. He is tall and thin and has light hair and blue eyes and his face shows what he thinks or feels. Mom is square and stocky with broad shoulders and hips. It's just as well that I am more like Dad in my body. I like being slender and straight. I am strong like Mom, though, and I like working in the fields better than in the house.

Dad clicked off the radio and came out to the kitchen. "Well, we'll go over and tell Bailey we're going to sell. Fifty-three is good enough. Come on, Ellen, you can drive me over."

I took off my apron and was running across to the barn for the pickup before Dad had taken his hat from behind the door. I felt so excited I couldn't walk soberly.

Glory, it was hot! I had the doors of the truck tied open with a piece of rope so the air could rush through, but it felt hot enough to scorch my bare ankles, and the heat of the engine came up through the rubber soles of my sneakers.

You can't see the elevator till you get past our place. There's only one in Gotham, but it stands up from the crossroads like a monument. That and the railroad station are the only things to let people know Gotham's a town.

"I feel I'm going for sure, Dad," I told him.

"You bet you're going," Dad answered. "The war spoiled college for me, all but one year. Nothing's going to spoil it for you. Might's well drive way in. It'll keep the car from burning up."

So I drove the truck up the ramp inside the high shelter of the elevator. That's fun. Dad says that's the way covered bridges feel back East where he comes from.

"Hi!" I called out to Bailey. He's the one who runs the elevator. Mr. Mathews was with him. Mathews is the inspector from the Excelsior Milling Company. Dad leaned against the wall of the office, talking to Mathews and Bailey about the heat. It seemed a long time to me before he said:

275

"Well, I thought I might as well sell. It isn't going much higher."

"Nope, it ain't," Bailey said. "Mathews and I were just sayin'."

"I doubt it," Mr. Mathews said kind of carefully.

"This girl's going to college on that wheat money, so I guess I'll take it now," Dad said. "It's up to you, Bailey, to keep the price of wheat up so's she can stay there."

I sat down on the running board of the truck while the men were talking, because it was cooler. All of a sudden, a swallow flew out of the shadowy corners way up in the roof. It made a quick shadow on my face as it swooped past. A swallow flying always makes me feel cool. Then I felt Mr. Mathews looking at me and that made me hot again. I had on my oldest pair of jeans rolled up almost to my knees and a white polo shirt that was maybe a little tight. I snapped my fingers at Bailey's big tiger cat so he'd look at her instead of me. The cat's too lazy to move usually, but this time she yawned and stretched and came over to me. Dad was talking. He loves to talk, and I suppose it's hard on him that Mom says so little. Dad isn't a rancher naturally. He'd be happier, I think, if he had done something else.

"No, sir, most folks are changing over to winter wheat, but I'm going to stick to raising both. I had a hundred acres in spring and it gave twenty-five bushels, but of course you take more of a risk. Year before last, I only got ten bushels to the acre. Winter wheat you plant in the fall and you don't have to worry so much about moisture, but my wife's the one that holds out for planting some spring too."

I stood up, spilling the cat off my lap. I'd heard all that so many times before. But I like hearing him say "my wife" that way, as though he was proud of Mom's judgment. The people in Gotham, Dad too sometimes, act as though Mom weren't quite . . . quite equal to Dad. It hurts me. I stood leaning against the wall idly reading the calendars and notices posted there: "No Smoking." "This Elevator Does Not Sell Clean Seed"—that means the seed you buy there for planting may have weeds in it and you can't come back and blame them for it. There was an advertisement of Karmont wheat that Dad says was developed especially for me because it has Russian and American parents, too—from Kharkov and Montana. He calls me Karmont, sometimes, to tease me. A big fly-specked placard read "Heavy Northern Spring . . . Dark Hard Winter"—the words are like something you know by heart, something you know without learning. They have a deep solemn sound . . . I couldn't explain it to anybody. Suddenly, it seemed to me as though those words I had always known—"Heavy Dark Northern Spring . . . Dark Hard Winter"—held in them all my living here.

"Ellen, you go ahead. I'm going to stay and have a game," Dad said. He and Bailey and Mr. Mathews went inside the little office.

"Okay. I'll leave the pickup for you. I'll walk back," I told him.

I stepped out of the shadow of the elevator and the sun seemed to wrap around me and press down on my bare head. Mom says that's the way you get sunstrokes, but I like it on my head. I like my hair brushing hot against my neck, too.

In two weeks, I thought, I'll be far away from here—and I'd never been more than three hundred miles before. I looked at the corrugated tin sheds below the elevator where they store salt and oil and feed and thought how I used to slide down them. I'd just as soon right now, only the tin would be so hot it would blister my seat. I looked at the store. It didn't do much of a business, because most people sent away for big mail orders. There was the cellar hole they dug one time for a community church, but folks didn't agree and they didn't have a crop that year, so they never finished it. I felt as separated from Gotham as though I didn't even know it. I was so excited I could have run in spite of the hot day. Then I discovered something funny: my hands were ice-cold. I pushed them down into the tight pockets of my jeans. I had known I was going and yet, with deciding to sell the wheat today, I could feel it more.

II

Unless there is company, and there seldom is, Dad and Mom and I sit in the kitchen in the evening. In the summertime, if one of the boys from Gotham comes to see me we sit out in the pickup.

That night Dad was reading the morning paper that gets to Gotham in the evening. Mom was ironing. I sat at the table with the plate and knife and fork pushed back so I had room for my tablet. I was figuring up my expenses again.

It was bright in the kitchen. Mom had a hundred-watt bulb on the one cord that hung down from the ceiling. It was so bright you couldn't look at it, but Mom liked lots of light. We hadn't had electricity at the ranch so very long. Mom said all her life in Russia

she had cooked and ironed and mended by the light of a wick in a
bottle of kerosene, and she liked the feeling of being able to turn
on the light the minute it got dark and have it shine on everything.
She didn't like the shades pulled, either. Our house was like a light-
house for people coming up past the coulee.

"If I get the job in the cafeteria," I figured out loud, "that'll leave
only my room and books and railroad fare, besides my tuition."

"And if you don't like working in the cafeteria, you needn't,"
Dad said, almost angrily, putting down his paper.

"That wouldn't be much to do," Mom said. They're often like
that. And then I try to turn them both the same way.

"Oh, no, I won't mind that," I said. "That'll be fun."

I drew a line under the figures. At the top stood "railroad fare"
and just seeing it there made it hard to keep my mind on anything
but going. Tomorrow . . . tomorrow night at this time I'd be on
the train.

"You go ahead and do what you want, Ellen, and if you want
to join a sorority you do it. Have yourself a good time. If we should
have a bad year and not be able to send you the whole four years,
you'll have had your year, anyway. I remember how I felt when I
was in college."

He meant to make me feel good and free; he couldn't see that
he put fear in my mind at the same time. If they did have a bad
year! It was like a drop of temperature in the middle of a summer's
day; you begin to worry about hail striking. I looked over at Mom.
She was folding a shirt on the ironing board, buttoning the little
buttons down the front. But I could see by her lips she didn't like
Dad to talk that way.

"You'd always rather eat to bursting one meal than spread it out
over two," she told Dad. "If she take care, her money'll go longer."

I made little marks on the page. I felt pulled two ways again. I
have since I was a child. I love Dad's way of talking that makes him
seem different from other ranchers. He's lived here twenty-three
years, but he still says "back East where I come from." He's the one
who gets excited when I do about spring coming or a serial running
in the magazine we're both reading, but it's what Mom says that I
depend on. When Mom used to say "Don't worry" about my pet
chicken or dog or new calf, it always got well. Dad is always talking
of going some place, not now, but next year, maybe. Mom seems to

278

think of nothing farther away than today or perhaps yesterday or tomorrow morning.

Mom folded the ironing board and put it inside their bedroom that was just off the kitchen. She carried in the freshly ironed clothes. Dad went back to his paper. When Mom came back she took beans from the cupboard to soak for tomorrow. Dad always said Mom could make all the dishes he'd had back in Vermont as well as though she were a New Englander herself, instead of a Russian. All of a sudden, I realized that tomorrow when those beans would be ready to eat I'd be going away. It gave me a funny feeling.

"I'll be taking the train tomorrow night," I said aloud, more to hear it myself.

"We can drive you into town in the afternoon," Dad said, dropping his paper on the floor.

"There's no need to go to town; she can catch the train at Gotham just as well. We haven't nothing to take us into town for," Mom said.

"Well, we don't have to decide tonight," Dad said, but I knew he wanted to go into Clark City. It wouldn't be so flat as just seeing me go off on the train from Gotham. My going away was hard on both of them; they were so different—and I was part of them both. It made me uncomfortable to think of leaving them.

While I was getting ready for bed in my room that's off the front room, I saw how it would be if I left from town. We'd go in right after dinner and go around to the stores, Dad going one way and Mom and I another. Dad would probably have his hair cut at the barbershop and stop in the bank and meet someone he knew to talk to. Then we'd meet at the big store on the corner and go to the cafeteria for supper. The train stops ten minutes or so at the station in town and there are other people and excitement and you have time to wave from the platform and then again from your window by your seat. We went to the station in Clark City to see the Goodals off when they went back to Iowa.

If I left from Gotham, we'd just drive down in the truck and wait till the train came. It only stops long enough for you to get on and you hardly have time to taste the flavor of going away.

I sat on the bed in my pyjamas with my arms around my knees. I couldn't keep from thinking of that time Dad went back East. I tried to, and then I just sat still and looked straight at it. Sometimes that's better than working so hard to keep from looking at what's in your mind.

Dad went all the way back to Vermont when his mother died. It was in November and it was already dark when the train came through Gotham. Even now, I could feel how cold and dark it was. I held Mom's hand. Dad was so dressed-up he seemed strange. He had gone to town and bought a new dark suit and a hat and gloves, not work gloves or warm gloves, but soft gray ones that made you feel gentle to touch them. Mom didn't like it. We stood there without saying anything until Dad told Mom to remember to call Mr. Bardich, our neighbor, if the cow didn't calve tomorrow.

"I'll manage," Mom snapped back.

"I wish you could go, Anna," Dad said to Mom, "and we could take Ellen."

"I don't want to go," Mom said, and the tone of her voice hurt to hear. I could feel more than the night coldness around us; I could feel Mom and Dad drawing away from each other. I wanted to say something to bring them together. Dad mustn't go this way, but I couldn't say anything.

Then I heard the train and the big round beam of light cut through the darkness like a harrow turning the dark earth. It shone hard on our faces, making them look queer and unreal.

Dad was going.

"Dad!" I screamed, jumping up and down. Dad lifted me off the ground to kiss me and held me so tight I could feel how he loved me. Suddenly, all of me rushed out to him and I loved him so much I forgot all about Mom and the sharp, hard sound of their voices a few minutes ago. I felt then, at eight, how much Dad and I are alike.

The train was rushing toward us. Over Dad's shoulder I watched it come. It was going to take him away.

"Dad, please take me with you," I sobbed in his ear.

I felt his soft gloved hand on my cheek.

"I won't go away without you next time," he whispered, and set me down. He picked up his bag. I wanted him to kiss Mom; I had never seen him kiss her. But he didn't.

"Good-by, Anna Petrovna," he said, looking at Mom. I had never heard him call her by two names before.

"Good-by," Mom said, standing still, without smiling.

Then he was gone and the crossroads were darker than ever. The train light shone on the high window in the top of the grain elevator for a moment and then that too was dark. We got into our old Ford and Mom drove back to the house. My throat ached all the way. The name Dad had called Mom kept saying itself in my ears: "Anna Petrovna, Anna Petrovna." I wanted to ask Mom about it, but it was tied up somehow with that bitter cold sound of their voices.

Our house seemed lonely when we came back to it. It seemed to be hiding under the coulee. I went with Mom to put the truck in the barn that was bigger than the house. I think Mom was prouder of our barn than the house, anyway. We walked back to look at the cow that was going to calve. She was just a big light blob in the dark, waiting. I had thought she was exciting this morning, but now she seemed sad, too.

The wind blew when we walked across the open space to the house and I couldn't help shivering with the cold. Inside the house it was warm, but empty.

"Bring your nightgown in here and I heat you some milk," Mom said.

I drank the milk sitting on a stool in front of the stove. It tasted good, but the lonely ache in my throat was still there. I picked up my clothes and hung them neatly behind the stove and put my cup on the sink board. Mom was fixing oatmeal for tomorrow morning.

"Good night, Mom," I said almost timidly, standing beside her. She seemed wrapped around in a kind of strangeness. Then she turned around and drew me to her. The front of her dress was warm from the stove. I felt the comfortable heat through my gown. She laid her hand against my face and it felt rough and hard but firm. I dared ask her something I wanted to know.

"Mom, was that really your name—what Dad called you?"

Her voice sounded surprised. "Why, Yeléna, you know that; Anna Petrovna. You know I am born in Russia, in Seletskoe."

"Yes, but I didn't know your other name," I said.

"Anna Petrovna Webb." She pronounced it slowly. "Once I think what a funny name Ben Webb is!" She laughed. Her laugh was warm and low like our kitchen, and comfortable. The house seemed natural and right again.

"Mom, can I sleep in your bed with you while Dad's gone?"

"Yes, *Yólochka moya.*" Mom called me her pet name for me, and I was comforted. It meant small pine tree. "Pine trees are strong trees, Yeléna. You should see the great black forests in Russia," she used to say.

But now that I am grown I feel the wall of strangeness between them, more than when I was a child. I wondered how they would get along without me.

Dad went past my window and I could smell his pipe. Mom was in the kitchen still.

"Anna, come outside and get a breath of air," Dad called to her. I heard the screen door close sharply.

"The windbreak's stirring like it rain tomorrow." Mom's accent makes what she says sound final.

I slipped my feet into my sheepskin slippers and went out as I was, in my pyjamas, my hair loose around my face.

"What are you doing out here?" Dad asked gruffly but as though he was glad I had come.

"It's hot inside," I told him. It was good to be outside. The heat seemed to bring the sky down close. It was not dark even at ten o'clock. The stars were faint. Over against the house the shoulder of the coulee was darker than the sky, cutting the air from the earth. I followed the sharp line a long distance. That was the way tomorrow would cut my living here from the rest of my life, I thought unhappily, but with a kind of prickling of excitement in me. I lifted my eyes to the sky, where the lighter darkness was all of one piece. The sky drew me as it always had, making me feel light and airy. I left Mom and Dad there and ran in my slippers up the side of the coulee.

The top of the tree that makes shade by our kitchen door comes even with the ridge of the coulee. In the daytime I can see far off to the mountains. I have the whole sky to myself. I did what I used to do. I lay down flat on the ground where I could smell the sagebrush close to my face and see every star in the sky. The earth was warm and hard under me. I rolled over on my side and looked down at our house. Mom and Dad were sitting there on the bench. Somehow, I felt sad looking at them down there. I almost didn't want to go away and leave them. I ran back down the hill to them, like a child.

"Well," Dad said, "young lady, if you're going to leave us to-morrow . . ."

"Yeléna, go get to bed," Mom said shortly; she pronounced the "Ellen" differently, the Russian way, Yeléna.

A SONG OF THE WIRE FENCE

ELLIOTT C. LINCOLN

From *Rhymes of a Homesteader* (Houghton Mifflin, 1920).

MILLIONS of miles of shining metal threads
    Cutting the plain in geometric lines,
    Climbing aloft among the mountain pines,
I show the way wherever Progress treads.

I bound the cultivated fields of man,
  Divide his cattle from the masterless,
  I form a barrier to the wilderness;
I end that which has been since time began.

My barbed and twisted strands have marked the change
  That comes when Nature pays the debt she owes.
  I whisper to each heedless wind that blows
The last low dirges of the open range.

PIONEER LUMBERING

ANTON M. HOLTER

The pioneer Montana industrialist had to contend not only with cut-throat competition, but also with highway robbers; business hazards included a dearth of mechanics, a two-year interval between the order of new equipment and its arrival, and "trade dust"—gold dust which was adulterated with sand. And there was the personal hazard of freezing to death. Anton M. Holter, a Norwegian carpenter, came to Iowa in 1854 and to Montana in 1863, to establish himself as one of this state's notable pioneers. He was thirty-two when he arrived in the Territory; he died in Helena in 1921 at the age of ninety. This account of his experiences was edited by Miss Margaret E. Parsons, assistant librarian at Montana State University, and appeared in *The Frontier*, Vol. VIII, No. 3, May, 1928.

AFTER three years' residence at Pike's Peak (in what is now Colorado), I returned to my former home in Iowa and in the spring of 1863 started with a team of oxen back to Colorado, where I stopped about six weeks. During this time a company of 200 men was organized to go to what was then called Stinking Water, Idaho, but is now known as Ruby River, in Madison County, Montana.

This company left Colorado on September 16, 1863. It was well organized, having a captain and other officers, and was governed by a formal set of rules and regulations. The weather was pleasant and food for the stock was excellent. Hunting and fishing were especially fine—too much so in fact for so much time was spent in sport that we made slow progress, and finally a Mr. Evenson, with whom I had formed a partnership, and afterwards did business with under the firm name of Holter and Evenson, and myself, became fearful that we would be unable to reach our destination before winter, and decided it was best for us to leave the train and strike out for ourselves at a greater rate of speed.

We had purchased a second-hand sawmill outfit, intending to go into the lumbering business on reaching our destination. There was yet at least a thousand miles to cover, so one morning we yoked up our oxen and struck out alone. During the night a few more teams overtook us (having also become alive to the necessity for haste if we were to reach our destination before severe cold weather set in), and every night for some time thereafter other teams caught up with us until we were about forty souls in all.

We had some heavy snow storms and cold weather during November, but finally reached Bevin's Gulch, our temporary destination, about ten miles from Virginia City. The remainder of the company, however, got snowed in, and so far as I ever learned, none of them reached Montana.

Mr. Evenson and I finally selected a location for our sawmill, and after considerable hardship we reached the top of the divide between Bevin's and Ramshorn Gulches on December 7, where we went into temporary camp, with no shelter beyond that afforded by a large spruce tree. As the snow was getting deep and there was no feed for stock I started the next morning for Virginia City (18 miles distant) with the cattle, hoping to sell them; but finding no buyer, I started to take them out to the ranch of an acquaintance twenty-five miles down the Stinking Water. On the way I was held up and robbed by the notorious George Ives and his companion, Irvin[g]. After I had complied with Mr. Ives' command to hand him my purse, I was ordered to drive on. He still held his revolver in his hand, which looked suspicious to me, so in speaking to my team I quickly turned my head and found that he had his revolver leveled at me, taking sight at my head. Instantly I dodged as the shot went, receiving the full force of the unexploded powder in my face—the bullet passing through my hat and hair. It stunned me for an instant, and I staggered against the near leader, accidentally getting my arm over his neck, which prevented me from falling. Almost at once I regained my senses and faced Ives, who had his pistol lowered, but raised it with a jerk, pointing it at my breast. I heard the click of the hammer, but it missed fire. I ran around the oxen, which became very much excited, and my coming in a rush on the other side scared them still more and they rushed against Ives' horse, which in turn got in a tangle with Irvin[g]'s horse, and during the confusion I struck out for some beaver dams which I noticed close by; but the men soon got control of their horses, and to my agreeable surprise they started off in the opposite direction. What had apparently changed their purpose was the sight which also now met my eyes, that of a man driving a horse team who had just appeared over the hill and was now near us. I learned afterwards that Ives and Irvin[g] had stopped at Laurin, about two miles from where they overtook me, where Ives fired five shots at the bottles on the shelves because the bartender refused them whisky, which accounted for the fact that only one charge was left in his revolver.

But I am getting away from the lumbering subject, so I am going back to the camp, where Mr. Evenson, the next day, disfigured my face badly in extracting the powder. So with my face bandaged up, in the cold and snow, we managed to build a brush road on grade around a steep mountain to our mill location on the creek. We made a hand sled with cross beams extending outside the runners far enough, so when necessary with a hand spike on each side we were able to nip it along.

With this hand sled we removed our outfit to the creek and we did all the logging this way during the entire winter. We first built a cabin and a blacksmith shop, but this soon became more of a machine shop, for when we came to erect the sawmill we met with what seemed insurmountable difficulties. As I knew nothing about a sawmill, I had left the purchase of the outfit to Mr. Evenson, who claimed to be a millwright by profession, but it developed that he had either been very careless in inspecting this machinery or he had not understood it, for so much of it was missing that it seemed impossible to get a working mill out of the material on hand. As there was no foundry or machine shop in this part of the country we were at a loss to know what to do, but were determined to erect a sawmill of some kind; so out of our rubber coats and whipsawed lumber we made a blacksmith bellows, then we burned a pit of charcoal, while a broad axe driven into a stump served as an anvil. Mr. Evenson knew a little about blacksmithing, so I began to feel somewhat at ease, but soon discovered what seemed to be the worst obstacle yet. This was that we had no gearing for the log carriage, not even the track irons or pinion—and to devise some mechanism that would give the carriage the forward and reverse movement, became the paramount problem. After a great deal of thought and experimenting we finally succeeded in inventing a device which years later was patented and widely used under the name of "rope feed." Incidentally I might say that we found this to be such an excellent appliance that we later used it on most of our portable mills, and I have been informed that several manufacturers used and recommended this, charging an additional $300 for it on small mills.

However, returning to the point, in order to construct this, we had to first build a turning lathe, and when we came to turn iron shafting, it took much experimenting before we learned to temper the chisels so they would stand the cutting of iron. To turn the shafting (which we made out of iron wagon axles) Evenson would hold the chisel and I with a rawhide strap wrapped around the shafting, taking hold with a hand on each end of the strap, would give a steady, hard pull with the right hand until the left touched the shaft, then reverse, repeating the process until the work was finished.

These were strenuous days and we worked early and late in the face of the most discouraging circumstances. We manufactured enough material for the sixteen-foot overshot waterwheel, the flume, etc. As we were short of belting, we made it out of untanned ox hides, and it worked well enough in the start. We finally got the mill started and sawed about 5,000 feet of lumber before we ever had a beast of burden in the camp.

Before we could get any of this lumber out we had to employ some help, and the first thing necessary to do was to grade a wagon road on the side of the mountain to get to the top of the divide. It required a great deal of labor to get a road in shape to put teams on. There had been much comment as to our lack of judgment in building a mill at the location we had selected, as it was estimated that it would take at least $10,000 to construct a road which would enable us to get the lumber to the top of the divide, and there was no one in this section with this amount of money (or half of it) who would consider putting it into any such enterprise as our small mill.

Now as the mill had been tried and proven satisfactory, a crew employed and the mill started, I felt at ease, as I imagined all obstacles had now been overcome so I left the mill and went to Nevada City, a flourishing camp three miles below Virginia City, and opened a lumber yard.

When I got the yard opened at Nevada City, the lumber commenced arriving from the mill and was disposed of as fast as landed. When we began selling lumber we made only two grades, namely, sluice or flume lumber, which we sold at $140 per M. and building lumber (including waney edge), for which we got $125 per M. in gold dust. The demand for lumber was greater than the supply, and quite often some of the larger mining companies would send a spy out on the road, in order that they might be informed when a load of lumber was approaching. Then they would have a crew of men arrive at the yard simultaneously with the load of lumber, and when the team stopped, without consulting me at all, they would unload the lumber and carry off every board to their mines.* Soon a man would come along to me with the pay for the lumber, and they always settled according to the bill of lading of the road at the established price so that no loss was incurred by this summary method of marketing our product. Some time after this we also started a yard at Virginia City.

But this prosperous business soon came to a standstill, for rainy weather set in and the untanned belting began to stretch from the damp atmosphere, until it could no longer be kept on the pulleys, so the mill had to be closed down. We heard of a man at Bannack, eighty miles from Nevada City, who had eighty feet of six-inch two-ply belting, and we decided to try to get this. Partly by walking and partly by riding a very poor excuse for a horse I found the owner of this belting and tried to purchase it from him. No price seemed to attract him, and I finally offered him my entire wealth, consisting of $600 in gold dust—equal to $1,200 in currency—but he would not consider the offer. Six-inch two-ply belting would be worth 30 cents per foot in Helena at the present time, or a total of $24 for this piece. Failing to get this belting, I returned to Virginia City, where I learned of a man who owned some canvas, which I succeeded in purchasing. I got a saddler to stitch it by hand, and this made a very good and efficient belt for our purpose.

Everything was now moving along smoothly, with the exception that the head sawyer got killed by coming in contact with the circular saw, and another man was also killed by getting in front of a rolling log on the side of the mountain.

Among other things that occurred to vary the monotony of the days was a visit I one day received from an acquaintance from Pike's Peak, George Seymour by name. He was very much excited and threatened to thrash me because I had "taken his living away," according to his story. It seems that he had been whip-sawing lumber, receiving for it $750 per M. and he complained bitterly that we had cut the price to $140 per M.

Three miles across the divide was the flourishing mining town

* Somewhat similar practices were resorted to in the serious lumber shortage of 1946!

of Bevin's Gulch. The gulch was rich in gold, but short of water for mining, so at a miners' meeting of about five hundred men, resolutions were passed to take the water of Ramshorn Gulch, and it did not take long before they had the ditch constructed, taking the water out above the sawmill, leaving the creek dry. Without water we were forced out of business, but the miners needed more lumber, so they agreed to turn in the water to get the required amount of lumber sawed. When this was going on I was busy getting out an injunction and had to see to it that the sheriff got it served before they again got possession of the water, but the miners, depending upon the strength of their organization, disregarded the order of the court and again turned the water into their ditch, which left the creek dry, and the mill again shut down, and as they had placed an armed guard at the head of the ditch we had to again appeal to the court. This resulted in the sheriff and some deputies arresting the guard for contempt of court. About a dozen miners were convicted. We obtained a judgment for a few thousand dollars' damages, of which only a part was collected, and there was no more attempt to deprive us of the water.

During this year Cover & McAdow started a steam sawmill on Granite Gulch, and started a yard at Virginia City. This was then the best mill in the territory. Without any understanding in regard to prices of lumber they were maintained, and business went along satisfactorily, but we wanted more and better machinery, so we agreed that Evenson should go East to purchase a portable steam sawmill, with planing, shingle and lath machinery. He started by stage and stopped at Denver, and apparently having forgotten what he went for, he purchased some oxen and wagons, loaded principally with flour and nails and a primitive planing mill. On his return he got as far as Snake River, Idaho, when he was snowed in, leaving the outfit in charge of strangers. Being refused passage on the stage, he made himself a pair of skis and took a streak across the mountains for Virginia City, arriving at my office in a fearful snow storm, without having seen a human being since leaving Snake River until he arrived at Virginia City.

The stage on which he had been refused passage arrived three days later. Many of the cattle perished and considerable of the merchandise disappeared. What was left was shipped to Virginia City in the early spring of 1865 by pack train, at 30 cents per pound freight. It consisted of two kegs of ten penny nails and 26 sacks of flour. I disposed of the nails at $150 per keg and the flour at $100 per sack, all in gold dust.

During Mr. Evenson's absence I heard of a quartz mill at Bannack, which had a portable boiler and engine in it, and as the quartz mill was a failure I thought it might be for sale, so I struck out on horseback the second time. I found the owner and was very much pleased to find a man entirely different from the man who had the eighty feet of belting, for he wanted to sell.

I accompanied him to his mill, where I inspected his engine. It was a portable Lawrence Machine Co. boiler and engine, cylinders 10 inches in diameter, 12-inch stroke. His price was $1,200, which I paid him in gold dust. (Two years later I was offered $6,000 for the same engine, and refused to sell.)

During the winter of 1864–65, when we had decided to remove the portable sawmill to Helena (then called Last Chance), as the engine and boiler needed repairs, we looked about us for means of doing what was needed. Machine work was required, but as there were no machinists to be had in those days we had to content ourselves with the help of two blacksmiths that we found and who seemed to be willing to do what they could. I had made arrangements to meet them in Nevada City, and I started from Virginia City (three miles distant) with a load of supplies, including a 125-pound anvil—of which more later—and a team of mules. When I reached Nevada City the men had not appeared and it seemed expedient to return to Virginia City and hunt them up. Realizing that the team had a hard day's work ahead, I thought best to walk back, which I did, and found them sitting comfortably over a fireplace. They demurred at going with me, saying it was too cold and too stormy, but they finally accompanied me to Nevada City, from where we started on our way. For the first six miles we had good sleighing, but when we got through the canyon, the snow gave out so we could ride no further. When we reached Bevin's Gulch the snow was so deep that we still had to walk, as it was all the team could do to pull the sleigh and load of supplies. Indeed in many places the load would have to be removed, and when the sled was gotten through the drift, the load carried over and re-loaded. This was not so bad except the aforesaid anvil, which seemed to get very heavy by the time I had carried it over all the big drifts in the gulch. My men would not assist me any in this work, so I was getting pretty well exhausted. To add to my fatigue

and discomfort, the lines were too short to permit me to walk behind the sled and drive, so I had to struggle through the snow beside the sled.

Finally after dark we reached the mining camp of Bevin's and I
found a cabin where I could put the mules for the night and give
them the feed that I had carried for them. I was very anxious to
reach the mill that night, but the men refused to go any further
with me, and the team could not go on. I had been keeping at this
place a pair of skis for use in getting to the mill, but some one had
"borrowed" them, so I had to set out on foot without them for this
last piece of the way. I had eaten nothing since early morning and
was rather exhausted. I got on well enough for part of the way, but
soon the snow was so deep that in order to get on I would have to
lie down on it, press it down as much as possible, then walk a few
steps and repeat the process over and over again. It got so that I
could only go a rod or two without resting. I began to imagine that
I heard voices around me and among them I recognized those of
some of my childhood's playmates, and that of my mother, who was
still living at that time.

Then a new danger confronted me. In resting an almost irresistible impulse to sleep would possess me, but having experience
in this direction before, I realized that if I gave way to it, the sleep
would be my last, so with almost superhuman effort I would get on
my feet again and go on, resuming the struggle. Finally I reached
the divide where there was almost half a mile of practically level
ground with little snow. Slowly my senses seemed to return and
the sound of voices ceased. I had now come about two miles, and
had only about a mile more to go, so I commenced to regain hope
that I would reach the mill. Hard blasts of wind would strike me
now and then and I felt as though they were passing through my
body. I encountered a few drifts, but managed as before to get
through them. Then getting to the down grade towards the mill, I
found the snow too deep for me on the wagon grade, so I attempted
to go straight for the mill, but the slope of the mountain was very
steep, and not having sufficient strength left to keep up the mountain side, I was beginning to have a desperate struggle to get there. I
encountered a good many fallen trees, and was now so weak that
where it was possible I crawled under the trees instead of over them
to save strength.

I finally got to the creek about a third of a mile below the mill, where there was a deserted cabin. The snow was very deep, and fortunately here I found a board about ten inches wide and fourteen feet long. So I took this and laid it on the snow and crawled its length, then pulled it along, and repeated the process until I finally reached the mill cabin. The snow was shoveled away a distance from the door, and I took quite a little rest on the snowbank, from where I could look in through the window and see a brisk fire burning in the fireplace. I laid there and planned how I could get strength to walk in and reach a stool that I could see in front of the fire. I did not want to make any disturbance and wake up the men sleeping in the cabin, and it seemed almost impossible to again get on my feet, but I felt sleep overcoming me again, so I made another start and got to the woodpile in front of the door, where I fell, and again almost went to sleep. This warned me, so I made an effort to reach the door, grasped the latch with my left hand, opened the door and stepped in. I tried to get hold of the inside of the door with my right hand and close it, and reach the stool, but I dropped on the floor, when Evenson, who was sleeping in the room, awoke and rushed to assist me. The men sleeping in the other part of the cabin now awoke and naturally supposing me to be frozen, they all rushed to my assistance. They soon had mittens, boots and socks off, but found that while my clothes were frozen stiff on the outside, they were damp with perspiration on the inside. I knew that I was not frozen, so asked to be let alone, as all I needed was rest and some food. Soon they gave me a dish of cold boiled beef—all the food to be had at that time, as there were no vegetables or flour in that part of the country. I remember that I thought that never had anyone enjoyed such luxurious rest as I lying on the floor in front of the fire, and weakly trying to eat the cold beef. After a time they put me on the bed, stripped me and gave me a brisk rubbing with rough towels, then put on some warm dry clothing, covered me up, and left me to sleep and recover from my exhaustion. Being very strong and having great recuperative powers, strange as it may seem, the next morning, although I felt quite rocky, I was able to get about, and I got on some skis, and, accompanied by some of the mill hands, went back to Bevin's, hitched up my mules and drove back to Virginia City, reaching there the same evening without further trouble.

During the winter of 1865 the discovery of gold in Last Chance Gulch became public, and a town started up named Helena, now the capital of Montana, so instead of changing the water mill into a steam mill we managed to construct another mill pretty much the same as the first one. This outfit we located at the mouth of Colorado Creek, eight miles southwest of Helena, and got started sawing lumber in April. By this time provisions of all kinds had become scarce. Virginia City had already had its notable flour riot. We had to suspend work at Ramshorn and the last sack of flour we obtained for the Helena mill cost us $150, so we all had to get along on beef straight.

A man that I will call Van for short, had already had a lumber yard started in Helena. His sawmill was a water power mill, about the same style as our Ramshorn mill. He was selling building lumber at $100 per thousand feet, and I do not remember his price for sluice and flooring lumber. I had heard of him before as the wealthiest man in Montana. I happened to meet Mr. Van on my first day in Helena. He was quite abusive, and told me that the lumber business belonged to him, as he was there first and wanted me to remove my mill somewhere else, and said if I did not he would reduce the price of lumber down to $40 per thousand feet, if necessary.

The Holter and Evenson business in Helena was now in charge of W. S. Benton, a competent business man, well qualified for the lumber business, so I returned to Virginia City and Ramshorn, where affairs were less satisfactory. Evenson had a large crew of men employed, trying to start the mill with a new water wheel, an invention of his own. We had no lumber at the mill or yard, so the business was at a standstill, but still under heavy expense. I wanted Evenson to start the overshot wheel, but did not succeed.

I made Virginia City my headquarters during the summer, and as there were three stage lines operating between Virginia City and Helena, schedule time fifteen hours, I made frequent trips to Helena.

The freight outfit that had been left at Snake River finally arrived with the empty wagons and the long-looked-for planing mill. It was a primitive looking machine. The frame was made of pine lumber, and the feed gearing looked very delicate, but we put it up and by having one man to pull and another to push to help the feed gearing when passing the boards through the machine, we got along fairly well, as we were getting $40 per thousand feet extra for surfacing and matching, and I believe we charged $20 per thousand feet for surfacing only. I sometimes became disgusted, but when strolling about the premises there was some satisfaction in realizing that I was part owner of the first engine and boiler that ever turned a wheel in Montana. It was a small portable engine and boiler, twenty-five or thirty horse-power, manufactured by the Lawrence Machine Company in 1859, I believe, and shipped from St. Louis to Fort Benton in the spring of 1862, by the American Fur Company. I was also part owner of the first saw mill, a part of which was made at Pike's Peak and completed at Ramshorn, Montana, and last but not least, the planer and matcher, also made in Colorado during her Pike's Peak days.

Mr. Van had already started to drive us out of business. He kept the price up, but privately allowed large discounts for cash. I had no time to give Mr. Van my attention, for I had to get back to Virginia City to get the Ramshorn mill started. On my arrival at Virginia City I learned that I was reported to have left the territory for parts unknown.

This news had already reached the mill and some of the employes had already arrived in town and seemed highly pleased to see me. They did not appear to need their money as much as they had imagined, and all of them wanted to go back to work but one man, and he had $400 due him and wanted to return to the states. I succeeded in borrowing this amount from one Mr. Brown, then doing a sort of banking business, but when I saw the kind of gold dust he was going to let me have, it was so poor that I had to object to the quality. I went after my man and told him that the dust was poor, but the man was satisfied with it after he examined it. I gave my note for thirty days with interest at the rate of 10 per cent per month, in bankable gold dust, that is, gold dust free from black sand and adulteration, worth at least 20 per cent more than the kind of gold dust loaned.

I soon returned to Helena and the sawmill, and learned from Mr. Benton that Mr. Van had dropped prices $10 at a time until lumber was now selling at $60 per thousand feet, with a discount of $10 per thousand feet, so Mr. Van was doing a good business and getting the money, while we were getting the credit, and collections were not sufficient to pay running expenses. There was a good demand for building lumber in Helena at this time, so I concluded to pass by Mr. Van. I instructed my yard man to reduce the price of building lumber from $60 to $40 per thousand feet, and to allow no credit, as we could not afford to employ a collector, and the lumber was to be paid for before it left the yard.

I then went to the sawmill, where I had a consultation with the mill employes, and also with the loggers who were supplying the mill with logs on a contract. I informed them of my instructions to the yard man, and told them that I wanted them to keep the sawmill running and told the loggers to get in all the logs they possibly could before winter, as there would be no feed for the stock. I wanted the mill operated to its full capacity also, but would not remove any more lumber from the mill than could be sold for cash, the surplus to be stacked at the mill.

In purchasing my partner's interest in the business I had allowed him to take the cash on hand, so the only promise I could make in the way of salaries was to supply them with the necessities of life until the lumber could be disposed of; so I had a roll call and told them to answer "yes" if they cared to remain and "no" if they did not care to work on this basis. Every man answered "yes."

The next day I returned to Virginia City, where the mill had gotten started and business was in pretty good shape. I then returned to Helena after an absence of about two weeks. The man in charge of the yard told me what lumber there was in the yard was sold and paid for, and that he could not get it from the mill fast enough to supply the demand; also that Mr. Van had quit shipping lumber to Helena. I took the money on hand in the office and went to the mill. I met the men at supper time, and after ascertaining the amount wanted, I told them that it amounted to less than half of what I had expected they would need and they could double up just as well as not, as it was as convenient for me to pay now as it would be any other time; but they had all they wanted. However, it had the effect of establishing confidence among the men.

I spent the greater part of the summer at Virginia City and the Ramshorn mill. About this time I took my brother, M. M. Holter, in as a partner and adopted the firm name of A. M. Holter & Bro. In the fall I left my brother in charge at Virginia City and moved to Helena.

I knew of three water mills and two small portable sawmills that had either started or were under construction when the fall in the price of lumber came; so after a thorough investigation I found that none of them had any supply of logs on hand and were not prepared to do any logging after the winter weather started. I was logging with all the force I could possibly press into service, and waiting anxiously for the first snow to fall. Finally on a Sunday morning, while at the Helena office, a snow storm started in good shape. The lumber sold when I dropped the price to $40 was still stacked in the yard, so I told the office man to go to the owners and notify them to remove the lumber the next day or to offer to pay them the same price they had paid me. He returned and reported having purchased every board. I then told him to fill all orders on hand at $40 per thousand feet, but from this time on to sell no lumber at less than $60 per thousand, and that he could extend credit, especially to prospectors, wherever he thought there was reason to believe they would be successful. I also instructed him to employ more teams to haul lumber and to get the yard stocked with a good assortment. My man protested very hard against a raise of $20 per thousand feet, and my reply was that it was still too cheap in comparison with other commodities. I avoided an argument for I did not want to expose my future plans. We soon had some snow, so I raised the lumber to $70 per thousand feet, and received no complaint. The demand kept increasing, so I had to operate the mill night and day.

Business went on without any interruption until January 12, 1866, when a snow storm set in that lasted until the morning of the 14th. The snow was then very deep, and this snow storm was followed by a spell of the coldest weather that I ever experienced. I do not remember how cold it was, but I do remember that the quicksilver in the thermometer froze solid. This storm is referred to yet by the old pioneers as the Sun River stampede, on account of so many people freezing; some were frozen to death and a large number became cripples for life.

I owned a hay ranch three miles from Helena, where I had plenty of hay, so I had all the live stock removed to the ranch. Several of the men got badly frosted in getting there. I found I had a surplus amount of hay, so sold it for $100 per ton. This price was considered cheap, for the winter of 1861 and 1862 at Central City, Colorado, I had paid $200 per ton for hay to feed my stock.

Everything moved along all right until about the middle of July, 1866, when I had the saw ruined. This apparently ended the supply of lumber, but I found a man that had two fifty-two-inch circular saws in transit for Helena, and I agreed to take one of them at $500.

297

When they arrived, however, he did not want to separate the pair, and offered to sell them both to me for $1,000. I accepted the proposition, but before I could get the gold dust weighed out, he changed his mind again and wanted six yoke of my logging cattle in lieu of the gold dust. I finally got the saws and let him take the cattle. The market value of the team was $1,200, but as I did not have them to spare they were worth considerable more.

We got the mill started once more, but I had to get more oxen. I learned of a herd of unbroken Texas cattle, and from it I selected as many as I wanted. They were not broken for work, and we had a grand circus in getting them broke and trained to work.

I had no trouble in finding laborers enough, but I could not find anyone that had had any experience in the lumber business, or keeping accounts. The man in charge of the Helena office had left for the States. The man I installed in his place proved to be a man of good education, and competent, but I could not find anyone to assist me at the mill. It had become my custom to rise at 4 o'clock in the morning, call the cook, then start a fire under the boiler, then start loading and measuring and making bills of lading. There were often as many as eight teams to get ready and I had to get up early enough to enable them to get to Helena and return before dark. Everything was supposed to be in readiness to start the mill running at 6 o'clock. I would usually get the teams loaded by 9 o'clock, get my breakfast and then attend to the orders for lumber that was to be sawed and shipped. I would then saddle my horse and take a trip to the place where the choppers and loggers were working, to give them orders as to size, length, etc. the lumber was to be, as considerable lumber was sold at the mill. In this way, I had the accounts as well as the chores to attend to, and it kept me quite busy.

I had commenced to think that the Helena office needed looking after, so after getting the book entries finished and having had my supper, I would get into the saddle and ride to Helena, a distance of about eight miles. I concluded to do a little detective work in order to ascertain what were the habits of the man in charge after business hours, and who his associates were. I gathered up a few of my acquaintances and invited them to see the town under the lamplight, which meant to visit such places as gambling halls, hurdy-gurdy (dance) houses, etc. By being a "good fellow" around these places, it would not take long to ascertain if the Helena manager had any bad habits and if he was spending more money than he should. No admission fee was charged to these places, but it was expected that one would at least treat the crowd at the bar. I had not yet seen my office man, and did not want to, but I pretended that I wished very much to see him on important business, and made many inquiries as to where he could be found. I learned a good deal from my friends and from such of their friends as we met, and during an evening's stroll I gathered about all the facts that I needed to know, so I began investigations at the office, and as soon as the manager saw what I was trying to do, he disappeared, and I later learned that he had left a shortage of $11,000.

During August, 1868, we had all the machinery of the Ten Mile mill over-hauled and made a better plant of it than it had ever been before. We started operation on January 2nd, 1869, and everything moved along in a very satisfactory manner until February 15th. Early in the morning of this date the man in charge of the plant arrived in Helena to inform me that the mill had burned down that night, and also considerable lumber. I hastened to the ruins and started the men to clearing the ground and rebuild. My mind was somewhat relieved to find the boiler and engine had not been damaged beyond the possibility of repair. As I had no one competent to put in charge of the rebuilding of the plant, I undertook the task myself, so I started in getting up at 4 o'clock in the morning, driving to the mill, and returning in the evening, getting the needed supplies (stores were then kept open in the evening until 10 o'clock) and giving orders for parts of machinery, etc., that mostly had to come from the other mills. I kept this up for about three weeks, when we got the mill started sawing lumber, but it took some additional time to replace the shingle and lath machinery.

The planer and matcher that I had purchased in Chicago two years before was still in transit, wintering at Cow Island, a place on the Missouri River, about 200 miles below Fort Benton. It had to be brought this 200 miles, and then about 140 miles overland, which meant much valuable time. Now was the time if ever that Montana, and especially Helena, needed this kind of machinery, for Helena's great fire occurred on April 28, 1869, when nearly seven blocks were burned over, including most of the best business portion of the town. There was now a very great demand for all kinds of building material. It is worthy of note, however, that in spite of the demand, prices were not advanced.

Late in the fall I started East to purchase more and better machinery. In April, 1867, I shipped, by way of St. Louis and Fort Benton, a complete sawmill, shingle and lath machine, also door and sash machinery, but it took over two years for a part of this machinery to reach Helena. Freight by steamer from St. Louis to Fort Benton was then $250.00 per ton in currency and $200.00 per ton from Fort Benton to Helena, in gold dust.

I left St. Louis on April 13th, on the steamer "Gallatin," and went as far as Jefferson City, Missouri. Then by railroad, then steamer and railroad again to Salina, Kansas, where I got permission to ride inside the railing on the hurricane deck of the Overland stage. There were seventeen persons on this coach. Each was supplied with a rifle and ammunition and revolvers. We were much annoyed and delayed by Indian war parties. The distance to Denver from Salina was about four hundred and fifty miles, and ought to have been driven in two days, but it took us seven to reach Denver. I arrived in Helena the 17th day of May.

Shortly after I had left Helena in 1866 the cutting of prices began, and from this time on the custom of selling for what you could get prevailed. The prices obtained by A. M. Holter & Brother for the year 1867 up to August, 1868, averaged about $50.00 for common lumber and $60.00 per thousand feet for sluice, flume and the better grades, but during the month of August we reduced these prices $10.00 per thousand without consultation with the other dealers. We had reduced the price of planing mill work to $25.00 and $20.00 per thousand, according to quantity, and $10.00 for surfacing. Shingles sold for $6.00 and lath for $12.00. We maintained the prices on the last three items, as we had no competition on these.

In 1868, we built a sash and door factory and set in motion the machinery that he had imported the year before. This was the first of its kind in Montana. Many of my friends had warned me against this expenditure. They reasoned that within a short time the gold placer mines would be worked out and we would have to move elsewhere. However, we operated this plant continuously for eleven years, up to October, 1879, when it was destroyed by fire. As we had no fire insurance, we suffered quite a loss, but we rebuilt as speedily as we could and on the fifteenth day after the fire, we had the engine and planer running. Six years later, in 1885, we disposed of the machinery to Getchell & Dunwall, who removed it to their shop in Helena.

By this time we had sold the Ramshorn and also the Jefferson mill, but still continued to start new mills about the territory. Within the next few years we had started mills on the Blackfoot River, near Lincoln, Wolf Creek, Skelly Gulch, Buffalo Creek, Whiteman Creek, Strawberry Creek, Dutchman Creek, and Stickney Creek.

Most of these mills produced lumber for the Helena market, but the Stickney Creek mill, which was started in May, 1880, had Fort Benton and surrounding country as its prospective market, and we established a lumber yard on the west bank of the Missouri River below the mouth of Sun River, where we located a section of desert land and made the first payment, but never found time to get the water on it, so we let it go by default. This land extended from Sun River down the Missouri River for two miles and takes in what there is of Great Falls on the northwest side of the river, the concentrating plant and the smelter.

The lumber was hauled about six miles from the mill to the raft landing and then rafted down the river to the Sun River yard, a distance of about seventy miles. In the Spring of 1884, the river was very high and swift, and they were unable to stop the raft at Sun River, so they shoved the horses over-board, and I believe they also saved the wagon. The men swam to shore, but the raft went over the falls and broke up and was lost. The nearest neighbor to this lumber yard was Mr. Robert Vaughn, twelve miles off. People had commenced settling up the country, so a few of us during the Winter of 1885-6, put in a ferry across the Missouri River to where Great Falls is now, and in February, 1886, we moved the lumber across the river to Great Falls.

In 1889, as there was no saw timber left on Stickney Creek, we moved the mill to Great Falls, so instead of rafting the lumber from the mill, we now floated logs to the mills. We had secured considerable of the best timber tributary to the Missouri River by cutting it into logs, for possession was considered good title in those days.

In 1869, when gold was still at a premium, the merchants commenced to receive United States currency, which was called "greenbacks," at par.

The lumber business at and about Helena had been in a deplorable or "go as you please" condition from 1866 to 1888. During these twenty-two years merchants and all classes of trade, except lumber dealers, were prosperous. The lumbermen were playing a freeze-out game, apparently, to ascertain who could last the longest. The large majority of those who had started in the lumber business in the early sixties had dropped by the wayside. Even my competitor, Mr. Van, had disappeared, and it was rumored that he was owing his employes alone over $10,000.00 when he quit.

During this trying period I heard of but one call for a lumberman's meeting. I did not attend, but was informed of the schedule adopted, and the next day we were to bid on what we considered then a large bill, and the contract was awarded to the parties who were instrumental in calling the meeting, at $3.00 per M. less than schedule price adopted the day before.

For some years past the lumber business had been conducted at a loss, and I can think of only four parties who, from the time the first slab dropped until 1888, had made any apparent profit, and none of them any more than a reasonable amount. It would seem that with the establishment of the Montana Lumber & Manufacturing Co., in 1888, the freeze-out game disappeared.

By the disposal of the Montana Lumber & Manufacturing Co., [in 1898 to Marcus Daly], I felt that I was a new and free man, for with the exception of the Holter Lumber Co. at Great Falls, my thirty-five years of annoyance and anxiety in Montana, concerning sawmills, logging, lumber hauling, lumber yards, sash and door factories, etc. had come to an end.

Most of the music of the Montana cattle range, at least most of that which has been recorded, came up the trail from Texas. E. C. "Teddy Blue" Abbott reports in *We Pointed Them North,* the excellent book of recollections in which he collaborated with Helena Huntington Smith (Farrar & Rinehart, 1939), that the three of which portions are printed here were popular in the 80's. He intimates that he introduced "The Little Black Bull" to Montana; it was the oldest range song, he says, and probably originated in the Ozarks. It is not in the noted Lomax collection, *Cowboy Songs and Other Frontier Ballads* but various versions of the other two are in that book. They also were widely sung in Montana, Abbott declared; in fact, he says "Bury Me Not" was sung to death: "it got so they'd throw you in the creek if you sang it."

The Little Black Bull

THE little black bull come down the mountain;
  Hoorah, Johnny, and a hoorah, Johnny—
  The little black bull come down the mountain,
 Long time ago.
A long time ago, a long time ago,
And he run his horn in a white oak sapling,
 Long time ago.

The Cowboy's Lament

As I walked out in the streets of Laredo,
As I walked out in Laredo one day,
I spied a poor cowboy wrapped up in white linen,
Wrapped up in white linen as cold as the clay.

"Oh, beat the drum slowly and play the fife lowly,
Play the dead march as you carry me along;
Take me to the green valley, there lay the sod o'er me,
For I'm a young cowboy and I know I've done wrong.

"I see by your outfit that you are a cowboy"—
These words he did say as I boldly stepped by.
"Come sit down beside me and hear my sad story;
I am shot in the breast and I know I must die.

"It was once in the saddle I used to look handsome,
It was once in the saddle I used to go gay,
First took to drinking and then to card-playing;
Got shot in the breast and I'm dying today."

The Dying Cowboy

"Oh, bury me not on the lone prair-ee"—
    These words came low and mournfully
From the pallid lips of a youth who lay
    On his dying bed at the close of day.

    "Oh, bury me not on the lone prair-ee,
    Where the wild coyotes will howl over me,
    Where the rattlesnakes hiss and the crow flies free;
    Oh, bury me not on the lone prair-ee."

"Oh, bury me not—" And his voice failed there;
But we took no heed of his dying prayer.
In a narrow grave just six by three
We buried him there on the lone prair-ee.

I LEARNED TO RIDE

WILL JAMES

Few have been so superbly qualified by experience to portray the West as was the late Will James. This lonely and unhappy man produced, in little more than a dozen years, some of the West's finest literature and illustration. His birth in a wagon in Montana's Judith Basin interrupted his parents' overland trip to Alberta. They settled down in this state, but when he was a year old his mother died and his father followed her three years later. Will was informally adopted by a family friend, a French-Canadian trapper whom he called "Bopy," but when he was fourteen years old Bopy drowned. Bopy had taught him to write; Will never went to school. He drew incessantly throughout his childhood, and at twenty-eight sold his first sketch. No one has ever surpassed his drawings of the Western horse and horseman. The drawings needed stories, so he began to write and turned out nineteen books, several of which won wide acclaim. *Smoky* received the Newbery medal; *Lone Cowboy,* his autobiography (Scribner, 1930), was a Book-of-the-Month Club selection. Here is a chapter from *Lone Cowboy;* when the events described in it occurred, Will was fourteen or fifteen years old. During most of his productive period, he lived at his ranch in Pryor, Mont., or in Billings. The later years of this ill-starred genius brought tragic decline of his powers and he died, after a long illness, in a Hollywood hospital on Sept. 3, 1942. He was fifty years old.

I'VE often wondered what power keeps drawing a human or animal back to the place where daylight was first blinked at. Many a time a man will go back to the country of his childhood when there's not near as much for him at that home spot as where he just left. I've seen horses leave good grassy range and cross half a state to get to a home range where feed and water was scarce and the country rocky.

That same power must of drawed me, but I was hitting for better country instead of worse when I, so natural like and without thought, drifted to where I first stood up and talked. . . . After I left the ranch and crossed the river, it wasn't but a few days that I begin to notice something mighty familiar about the country. The further South I went the more familiar it got and I begin to feel mighty contented, like as if I was at home and amongst my own folks. There was no people and no landmarks that I recognized to let me know I was in my home grounds, nothing but the general lay of the country itself. I'd ride acrost coulees, crossed creeks, and rode over bridges, passes and hogbacks which made me feel as if Bopy was near and just ahead of me a ways.

I kept a watching out for the camp where I passed my first winter with Bopy, and I also scouted some for the big cow outfit where I got my little sorrel horse. But I had no luck finding any of the camps nor the outfit and I didn't meet a soul that'd ever heard of Trapper Jean. All I really could go by to know that I was in my home country was the name of a little range of mountains which I skirted.

I expect I crossed many a place that I'd crossed while I was with Bopy, and, when I finally left the mountains, I know I must of rode down many a draw and over many a bench where my dad's horses had left a footprint. I tried to find out just where in that country I was born, but nobody seemed to know and nobody could tell me of my dad. A few had heard of him, but the ten years that'd passed since his death didn't leave much to remember.

It was pretty late spring when one day, down country a ways, I sees a herd a skirting along swale after swale. Scattered out a bit and grazing the way they was, it looked like the whole country was moving. There was only about half a dozen men with that big herd when I first spotted it, but as I rode up on a knoll to get a better look I could see more riders on both sides of me drifting down from all directions and passing the main herd, each rider was bringing along more cattle and was careful not to let 'em mix with the main herd because in the new bunches that was being brought in was many calves that had to be branded. When that was done the new bunches would be throwed in the big herd too, making it still bigger.

I'd seen quite a few big herds of cattle before, but this was the biggest I'd ever seen up till that time. There must of been at least eight thousand head of cattle in the main herd alone. I wondered why they was moving so many cattle at that time of the year. Then I got to thinking that it was on account of wanting to save that part of the range so as the beef herd could be throwed onto it to mature later on. As I found out later, I'd guessed right, and the cattle I seen that day was only a good sized herd as compared to what that one outfit owned.

Further on, down country and past the big herd, I could see the

Remuda * and on a little flat in the creek bottom was the round-up wagon and camp of the outfit.

Leading my pack horse, I fell in with a couple of the riders that was coming in off circle and I helped 'em shove their bunch in to the cutting grounds not far from camp. While riding along with them there was hints dropped that the outfit was short handed. I didn't pay much attention to that because I knowed, even then, that all riders like to see many more come in and hit the foreman for a job, and get it. The more riders there is, the shorter the nightguard shift is cut, and the further apart comes the dayherd shift. Them is two things the coyboy hates to do most, specially dayherding, too slow and monotonous.

Dayherding means grazing and holding a herd in daytime, a herd that's to be shipped or moved to some other part of the range. On a well-run and full-handed cow outfit the dayherd shift comes every two or three days for half a day at the time. Range cattle are not herded only, as I've just said, when a bunch is held to be shipped or moved. There's three shifts in dayherding, morning, afternoon and evening shift. The evening shift is called "cocktail." Two to four men go on them shifts at a time, all depends on the size of the herd that's being held. After the evening shift the nightguard begins, from eight o'clock till daybreak, when each rider takes a shift of from one to two hours (sometimes half the night and more). The last guard is "relieved" by the first dayherd shift.

Many riders like to take a "rep" job (representing a neighboring outfit) because with that job there's no day herding. The reason for that is that the "rep" has to be on the cutting grounds so as to look thru every fresh herd that comes in off every day's "circle" (round-up), cut out and brand the cattle that belongs to his outfit, and throw them in the main herd.

I helped the two riders bring their bunch to the cutting grounds, and being I had a pack horse to contend with, I rode on into camp. I unpacked and unsaddled, but I didn't turn my horses loose because I figgered the wrangler would be bringing in the remuda for a change of horses pretty quick. It's a bad point to turn a horse loose at that time because, being the wrangler has to get *all* the loose horses in, that would only give him the extra work of getting mine, besides the unnecessary corralling of 'em.

I was just unsaddling when a rider which I figgered was the

* Remuda: a trail outfit's horse herd.

foreman rode into camp. He didn't turn his horse loose either, not till the wrangler run the remuda in the rope corral. Then he unsaddled and turned him in with the others. Then all the cowboys rode in, all but a few that was left to hold the cattle that'd been gathered that morning, also the few others that was with the main herd. There must of been at least twenty cowboys with that round-up camp.

The boys got to the chuck box and made the rounds from there to the skillets and ovens for all that was needed to make a meal. After they all was set I started in and done the same. . . . I was still eating when most of the boys was thru, had caught their fresh horses and gone. The "relief" men was the first to go. They rode to take the place of the riders that was with the main herd and the others that was holding the morning's drive. There's fast riding during them reliefs because the men that's relieved still have to eat and change horses and be on the job for the afternoon's work. A "drag" is sure not thought much of in a round-up camp.

There was some mighty good men with that outfit and they was riding some mighty tough horses, tough as a Northern range horse can get, and I got to wondering a bit if I'd better try and get a job there after seeing how some of them ponies acted. One of the riders had told me that each rider had three bronks (unbroke horses) in his string, also a couple of spoiled horses. The rest of the string was made up of the gentler ones.

I was by the corral as the last man was catching their horses. The foreman was coiling up his rope when I walked up to him and asked.

"Are you taking on any more riders?" . . . Just like that.

He looked at me and grinned. "Why yes, Son," he says, "when I can find any. . . ."

I didn't say anything to that, then after a while he asks.

"Looking for a job?"

"Yessir," I says.

The foreman shook out two coils of his rope and made a loop.

"I don't know how I'm going to fit you up with a string of horses," he says, as he looked the remuda over, "but maybe I can rake up enough gentle ones out of the two strings that's left. . . . The next rider that comes along and wants a job will have to be some powerful rider."

On many outfits I've rode for, a string was never split. Each string was made up of ten or twelve head of horses for each rider. There was unbroke horses for the short circles (rides), spoiled horses for long circles, good all around horses for any work, cow horses for dayherd and cutting out, and then there was the night horses. About two of each of them horses went to make up a string and ten to twenty of them strings went to make a remuda. As I said before, them strings was never split. If a rider quit or was fired the horses in his string was not used till he come back, or till another rider took his place.

On a few outfits, instead of scattering unbroke or spoiled horses amongst the cowboys, they have a couple of riders who take on and ride nothing but them worst ones. Their string is called the "rough string."

The foreman, being short of riders and having a big herd on his hands, split two strings that day and turned eight head of the gentlest over to me. What was left of the two strings could easy been called "rough" by the best of riders.

I knowed that by the fact that two of my "gentle" ones bucked me off regular and most every time I rode 'em. Two others was bronks, full grown but little fellers. They was mean to handle while on the ground but I got along all right once I got in the middle of 'em. They couldn't buck very hard. My other four horses was pretty good, if the mornings wasn't too cold or wet. One of 'em was hard to get on to.

At that outfit was where I first got initiated with rough ponies. The others I'd tried to ride before had been just for fun and that makes a big difference. I was handed gentle old horses while "wrangling" for the big outfit to the North, but now I wasn't wrangling no more, I was on circle, dayherd, nightguard and being a regular hand.

I felt mighty proud of that, but I found out right there that there was grief and sweat on the way to any ambition. My string furnished me with plenty of that. Thinking of what horse I had to ride was the cause of me eating mighty light breakfasts and other meals. The thought of what they might do to me sort of made me lose my appetite. I wasn't exactly what you'd call scared, I was just nervous, very nervous.

Then again, the boys kidding me about what this and that horse of mine did to this man and that man, sure didn't help things any, even tho I knowed they was kidding, the laughs I'd hand back at 'em wasn't what you might call right hearty.

It might be wondered at why I took on a job that was too much for me when there was so many other jobs that I could of started in at easy. But I didn't wonder. I never wondered and I never thought of any other work than what I'd started with at the outfit. There was nothing else in the world mattered to me but what went with a horse, saddle and rope, and when I took on that job I done it unthinking, like as if there was nothing else. There was nothing else, for me.

Of course I could of rode on to some other outfit where I wouldn't have to ride horses that was so rough on me from the start. But, there again, the start would of been slower, and I might of had to take on the wrangling job too. As it was now, I was started as a regular hand, and, outside of the wrangler and the nighthawk, I had the gentlest horses in the outfit to start in with. Of course that outfit had a great reputation of having tough horses, but mine wasn't really tough, only too tough for me that's all. I was too new yet, and too young, and they just played with me. Any grown cowboy could of handled and rode 'em blindfolded and with both arms tied behind his back.

I stayed on with the outfit. I kept a piling on my ponies and they kept a piling me off. Finally and gradual my piling off got to happen less and less often. I was getting to know my horses. After ten years of riding I was learning how to ride, and come a time, as the boys kept a slapping my hands with a quirt so I'd leave go of the saddle horn, that I begin to straighten up in my saddle and to stay.

It wasn't long after that that most of my *nervousness* begin to leave me. I was getting so used to handling and riding my ponies in whatever they done or which ever way they jumped, that I got to fit in natural with the work, like a six-month old pair of boots. I got so I never thought ahead of time what horse I was to ride next no more and, being so used to things that way and hardened in, my appetite wasn't hindered by any thoughts of any bad horse. The boys begin to quit kidding me about them horses too, because now I was coming back at 'em with laughs that was sure enough hearty.

It took me about a month or so to get the hang of how to set my ponies when I couldn't see their heads. There was two good reasons why it took me so short a time. One was that I'd been amongst the cowboys and riding pretty steady from the time I could walk and riding had got to be a lot more natural to me than walking. The second reason was that them ponies wasn't very hard buckers. Then again, all around me was the best of teachers, the cowboys themselves. They didn't coach me as to how to set, but they done better, they'd laugh at me when I'd buck off and they'd pass remarks.

"You can ride him, Kid," I'd hear one holler just about the time I'd be hitting the ground. . . . What used to make me sore was to have one of the boys come along and pick me up and brush the dirt off my back with a sagebrush and say something like, "You'll ride him next time sure, but you got to stick closer to your riggin'."

Sometimes, when I'd get pretty high up in my saddle, the boys would ride beside me, reach up in the air and set me back in it. "Now set there and *ride*," they'd holler.

I finally did get to *ride*, specially when the foreman had a talk with me a week or so after I'd started with the outfit. It was during the "cocktail" shift and he was riding along as me and a few of the boys was grazing the herd towards the "bed grounds." He rode by the side of me and begins saying,

"I think you better catch your private ponies in the morning, Son, and hit back home where you belong. Your dad ought to have plenty enough riding for you, and horses you can ride, too. This string I handed you is a little too rough for a kid like you."

That talk from the foreman layed me out pretty flat for a spell. Finally I came to enough to say, "I haven't got no dad, and no home to go to."

The foreman had figgered that I'd just got wild and run away from the home range. . . . Here was another time I had to tell the story of my life. I told it short and quick and there was a funny look in the foreman's eyes when I got thru. As a wind up I added on,

"And if you'll give me a little more time I'll be able to ride 'em, I think."

"But you're all skinned up now," he says.

"Sure," I comes back at him, "anybody is liable to get skinned up."

I know I won out when I seen him grin, and I sure begin to snap out of it from then on. If I ever meant to ride I started in from there and if I got throwed off I sure left marks on my saddle as to how come.

But the foreman had got to watch me pretty close after that talk I'd had with him. Learning that I had no home sort of worried him, and I think he felt like he ought to be sort of a guardian over me. I caught him trying to swap my best bucker off to the wrangler for a gentler one one day, and I made such a holler that the trade didn't go.

"I rode him easy the last time he bucked," I says, "and, besides he's in *my* string."

Well, I kept on riding and also kept my string as it was first handed me, and came a time when it was hard for any of them ponies to loosen me. It wasn't so long after that when they couldn't loosen me at all, and then is when I got to thinking I was *some* rider.

But riding wasn't all I was learning while with that outfit, and, even tho I'd growed up with handling stock pretty well, I learned a lot more there. I wasn't playing now, and I had to be something else besides somebody setting on a horse. I had to know how to find and "shove" cattle while on circle, I had to know where to be at the cutting grounds, what to head off and how. Then I took on calf wrassling while branding was on. Of course I took only little fellers there.

A writer said one time that on account of doing nothing else but riding a cowboy's muscles are not developed, only from the waist down. I never seen a cowboy yet who looked that way, and I'm thinking that if anybody swings a rope for hours at the time, like is done during branding, or wrassles big husky calves for as long, there'll be some exercise found that takes in the whole body, and exercise of the kind where hide-bound muscles would never do, because there's something else besides strength needed in that work.

It's ticklish work at times, such as saddling or handling a mean horse while on the ground, and our horses are not as small as most people think. Few are smaller than the average polo horse, and many size up with the *hunter* of the East. *Wild* horses of that size can jerk a man around pretty well if he don't know how to handle himself. Then while that horse is quivering and about ready to blow up, if anybody is doubtful of the cowboy's shoulder muscles, try and slip forty pounds of our saddle on such a horse's back with one hand. The cowboy does it because he has to hold the horse's head with the other.

With the big herds that was handled on that outfit I had to keep my eyes and ears well opened if I was to do my work right. There was brands to read and tally up on. That, along with making out the earmarks, wartles and vents, was my grammar while I was riding. There was many other things, too, that had to be noticed and which, while only shifting a herd, would take quite a size book to explain.

There was my shift on nightguard where I was bawled out on for getting off my horse too close to the herd. I was bawled out for many things I done now and again but never more than once for any one thing. I always remembered.

I also remember once when I started to sing while on nightguard. I'd started sudden and on a pretty high note and come doggone near causing a good stampede. There's writers who say that cowboys sort of sing cattle to sleep and sing on nightherd only for that reason. That strikes me funny, specially when I think of how I near caused a stampede by doing just that. If a cowboy sings on nightherd it's only because he wants to, and not to sing any cattle to sleep. Sometimes, on real dark and spooky nights, a rider will hum or sing or whistle while going around the herd, but that's only so they'll know of his coming and won't scare as they might if they didn't see him till he got near.

The cattle we was handling on that outfit was pretty wild. Over half of 'em was Old Mexico longhorn and the other half was of the same breed only crossed some with Durham and White Face. Them last two breeds hadn't made much of a showing in the herds as yet. Myself, I liked the old longhorn best and always will even tho they don't bring as much *money*. And, regardless of what's all been said about the longhorn being of the past, . . . popular talk, I'm saying now that I've rode for many outfits that owned many a thousand longhorn; and I don't have to go any further back to tell of the time than 1914, only sixteen years ago.

I know where I can produce many herd of longhorn cattle, thousands of miles of wide open country, thousands of wild horses right in this time of fast airplanes and 1930. . . . And, for the past forty years, it's been handed out by *desk-hounds* that the

313

West and the cowboy is gone. That's good small-town boosting, but, like all boosting, very far from the truth.

Well. . . . Getting back to the outfit, the herds was shifted, the cattle was graded and throwed on the range they belonged, I done my little best to be of some help and, outside of wanting to "push" the cattle too hard and dragging a rope, which I got bawled out for some more, I think I made a pretty fair hand of myself. Anyway, I'd got so I could ride my horses. But "that's nothing," said the cowboys, "you've only been riding *pets.*"

PULLING OUT

RUTH HAMILTON

"Pulling Out" is from Vol. I, No. 2 of *The Frontier*—the first appearance of the magazine under that name, since the first issue of the Montana State University literary journal appeared as *The Montanan* in May, 1920. No. 2 appeared in November. Miss Hamilton had been a member of the creative writing class of H. G. Merriam, sponsor of the quarterly; she was graduated in 1920, went East and married. At this time *The Frontier* was published by the writing class, but after 1927 the publisher's role was taken over by Dr. Merriam, who is head of the English department of Montana State University. By hard work and considerable personal sacrifice, he kept it going as a medium of regional expression until 1939. Several years before this, *Midland*, published in Chicago and edited by John T. Frederick, had merged with the Montana quarterly. William Saroyan and Vardis Fisher are among the writers whose early work appeared in *The Frontier*.

A WESTERN, sunbaked town whose population ebbs;
Where daily, drooping houses board their doors to die,
Spiders with evil faces starve on fruitless webs,
And the long prairie road runs coastward with the sky;
Dry-farmers who have known five cropless years,
A stream of Homestead folk blocked now against the sun,
An old Ford, heaped with household goods, a girl in tears,
A child, clutching of his poor toys the salvaged one;
A thresher, drawn by one unwilling pioneer,
A white horse, staring-eyed, ending the straggling file,
An ancient cattleman uplifts his glove to peer
At the departure with a lean malignant smile.

KISSINEYOOWAY'O

JOSEPH KINSEY HOWARD

This is a portion of a chapter from *Montana: High, Wide, and Handsome*, published in 1943 by Yale University Press. It describes the spectacular end of the open-range cattle industry.

. . .

EVEN today some old-timers will insist, speaking of the range era: "It would have been all right, if it hadn't been for the weather."

Always and eternally, the weather: always in Montana the bitter conviction that its vagaries are exceptional and malevolent, though they were so unexceptional and periodic that they ruined, impartially, cattlemen, sheepmen, and wheat raisers.

But most of the veterans will say that the weather could have been contended with successfully—never conquered—had it not been for the settlers cluttering up the range.

That is not the whole truth, either. No industry which functioned as haphazardly as did that of the range could have long endured; nevertheless, the weather came along at the right moment to finish a job begun by other elements, and then so terrible was its onslaught that it was easy to credit grumblings of supernatural malice.

In less than thirty years of cattle drives to Montana from the southwest, more than thirty-five thousand Texans rode into the state. A large share of this number turned right around and rode back, shivering. The inability of the Rio Grande cowboy to withstand Montana's winters was the subject of countless cook wagon jokes, songs, and barroom brawls.

But in the end the Texas cowboy had a free choice: stick it out in Montana until he was acclimated—and at considerably higher wages than he got in Texas—or pack his war bag and go home. The Texas longhorn was not so fortunately situated. Hundreds of thousands of these poor beasts stumbled off the gale-swept plains to die by frozen streams, or staggered on trembling legs into concealed drifts at the heads of coulees, there to be held fast while they slowly starved; or they pushed each other under the ice of the rivers in their frantic stampede to drink at the treacherous air holes.

The wasteful sacrifice of animal life on the open range is hard to credit today. A 10 per cent winter loss was "normal" in Montana; thus a cattleman running 10,000 head could consider his operation reasonably successful if he did not lose more than 1,000 head each winter, though each of these animals had a potential market value of about $50!

The winter toll was heaviest, of course, among the calves, and especially those trailed in that same season from the hot plains of Texas. These losses were increased by the fact that during their first winter on the range the Texas dogies would stand around the ranch house and bawl for their food instead of going out and rustling it for themselves. "This practice is not encouraged" (by feeding), a Miles City newspaper commented callously. "It is hoped they will absorb enough cow sense to go out on the range and eat." Most of them did, when they got hungry enough.

The cattlemen could do little to reduce the 10 per cent loss ratio. Half of it might be attributable to wolves and rustlers, and a constant war was waged against them; but the other half could only be offered on a sacrificial altar to the gods of storm, who would not be placated thereby, either.

Nor was it only winter weather which gnawed at the cattleman's profits. Summer drouth, because it meant a shortage of feed, invariably meant heavier winter kill. There were heavy summer losses, too, through consumption by the stock of poisonous plants which they would not touch when there was sufficient grass. And drouth brought fire.

Nothing in Nature is as terrible as a prairie fire; not even a blizzard. Where such a fire had been, nothing could live; and out of such disasters grew the legends of country so desolate that magpies flying over it had to carry their own provisions. Gophers would come up from their cool chambers and starve to death in the ashes. Game which escaped the holocaust would start a long and hungry trek to find water, grass, and brush, and die before finding them.

Grass fires moved with the speed of the wind. Only the most terrible forest fires, those which are "crowning"—flame leaping from treetop to treetop—can do that; and forest fires, usually in rough country, pause due to shifts or breaks in the wind. The prairie fire did not pause: it swept on at forty or fifty miles an hour, faster than a horse could run, widening its front all the while, a low wall of flame above which rolling masses of black smoke heaved in the wind and then spread to curtain the sky for weeks.

Such a fire would force a range operator to move thousands of head from their customary grazing grounds to a new district strange to him and his stock and perhaps already precariously near overstocking. On his old range no cattle could subsist until the new grass came in the spring; and then, though greener than before, it would lack the nourishment it had had, and because the moisture-retaining mulch would be gone it would not be as hardy.

This move must be made quickly; and so these were the worst drives of all. The cattle would scuffle through mile upon mile of ashes, their hooves bringing up great clouds of sooty, weightless dust until the air was like hot smoke and the world was blotted out. Their hides and the skin of the cursing riders would turn black; flesh would crack and burn with the dryness, despite the scarf flung up to protect the face. Eyes ached from the grayness and the baking heat, and tears which dried before they could be shed gummed eyelids with mud.

Soon the cattle would bawl for water, and there would be none. The rider would curse a little louder, lest the heat and his wretchedness put him to sleep; for now he must be watchful. Many miles away, perhaps in the direction whence they had come, there might be a little stream—too small to water this herd. But a sudden wind might carry the scent of that water to the cattle; if it did, the herd would swing instantly and be gone on a run. It might be impossible, under these conditions, to head them, and they would die—every last cow—of exhaustion, starvation and thirst.

So the rider tried to straighten his aching back and open his aching eyes and watch the herd for the first sign of madness. He had to watch his horse, too, sometimes; and he caught himself musing over strange fancies which left him even unsure of himself. But above all he must see that the herd, if it were going to stampede, stampeded in the right direction; then the boys were in position to handle it. . . . If they were still there; if he were not riding alone in a dead and desolate world, alone with thousands of filthy, half-mad cows. He pulled the bandanna down from his nose and sang out to his partner, riding "point" on the other side of the herd. His voice was cracked; so was the reply, when it came back. But, anyway, it came.

Such were the drives from burned-out range. It is little wonder that cattlemen would spend prodigally, that they and their cowboys would even risk their lives, to forestall such disasters. Owners would not hesitate to have their men slaughter $50 steers and drag their expensive carcasses—drawn by ropes from saddlehorns—over the burning prairie. Sam Remington, who ran a few head of cattle, was told by his neighbor, a big operator: "If a fire starts, strip the hide off one or two of my cows; I can spare a few head." But whether they could "spare" them, like this operator, Sam Spencer, or couldn't—it was better to take this loss than take a chance on losing the whole herd. When there was no time to skin the animal, the carcass was dragged between two horses, one on the burned-over side of the flames, the other in the unburned grass, both riders going hell-for-leather, in an attempt to smother the fire with their "drag." It was a sickening ride, but sometimes it worked. In later years a chain "drag" with an asbestos blanket was devised but few had come into use before the open-range period ended.

It took an empire of grass to feed such fires, and they will never be seen again. One of the last, as well as one of the worst, occurred in the '90's. It crossed an international border, leaped a large river and numerous creeks, and was stopped only after it had started a forest fire, too.

This blaze, started by lightning, broke out in the Cypress Hills of southern Saskatchewan, approximately forty miles north of the boundary. Pushed by a screaming northwest gale, it swept straight south to the Milk River in Montana, which is forty miles south of the boundary, fired a cottonwood tree, and rode across the river on a wind-borne blazing branch. Swiftly it caught in the grass south of the river and flew on as desperate riders of two of Montana's most famous outfits—Stuart's D H S and the Coburns' Circle C—tried to beat it out. Thirty miles farther south the flames entered the pine forests of the Little Rocky Mountains, where the weary cowboys, one outfit working from the east and the other from the west, finally "pinched" the fire out. It had

319

destroyed all the grass in an area more than one hundred miles long and from five to thirty miles wide.

Lightning started most of these fires, but there were other, less innocent agents. Indians resentful of being driven off their buffalo range were responsible for many of the earlier ones; a cattleman coming onto range which had never been used before for domestic stock had to watch constantly for this. Indian hunters occasionally started a fire to stampede a herd of cattle deliberately in order that they might cut out some and get away with them; these hunting parties also set fires to drive game. White rustlers set a few. Some were the result of carelessness—a cigarette (though the cowboy's hand-rolled smoke, which goes out when dropped, is not such a hazard as the tight "tailor-made") or a spark from the chuck-wagon stove. Such a spark started the disastrous fire on the X I T ranch in Texas in the fall of 1885, and the cook who started it lit out in a hurry, fearful he would be lynched.

These fires, in addition to destroying the grass, wiped out cattle herds, ranch houses, and sometimes humans. Several men died in a blaze which swept eastward from the Sweet Grass Hills following the drouth of 1884, blackening the tinder-dry grass for seventy miles in a strip thirty miles wide. Indians set it.

But it was the winters—when icy gales shrilled across the crusted prairies and sliced through the sturdy logs of the ranch houses, when the deadly "white cold" crept slowly down from the Height of Land in Canada's Northwest Territories, when snow fell interminably, burying range, stock, and ranch house—it was the winters which finished the cattlemen.

Even as the first big herds moved onto the plains of central and eastern Montana, the first in a series of bad winters which was to dog the industry was wiping out the herds in the west and on the Sun River–Rockies slope. This was the winter of 1880–81, when blizzards began in December and continued with hardly a break until May: temperatures were seldom less than 20 below and for weeks at a time stayed at 40.

Most of the cattle on the Sun River range had been brought in a few months before the blizzards struck; still unfamiliar with the country, they drifted desperately with the incessant wind and died finally of exhaustion as much as of hunger. Losses on that range were 90 to 98 per cent; thousands of cattle lay dead in the water courses and their ruined owners said, "you can walk from Sheep Creek in the Belts to the Dearborn in the Rockies and never take your foot off a dead cow." Some of the stockmen made frantic efforts to get feed to their animals, but hay was scarce. Ten strawstacks sold for $1,000 at Cascade, though straw was "stuffing," not nutritious feed.

Central and eastern Montana did not suffer so badly that winter because there were as yet few herds on that range, grass was plentiful and the wind kept it freer of snow, and there was still tall brush in the coulees to afford shelter. Nevertheless there were catastrophic instances: an English company which had driven in 5,000 head the previous fall (the cattle thus were thin and weak) had 135 head left in the spring and went bankrupt. Granville Stuart's loss, however, was but 13 per cent and wolves and rustlers accounted for all but 3 per cent of that. He had carefully selected his range, not so much for grass as for shelter, and an early "freak" chinook which apparently blew nowhere else also contributed to his good fortune.

The wolves' toll increased sharply in such winters, as the herds were driven to unfamiliar country. One outfit which had been running 10,000 head of cattle including 3,000 cows found, at the spring roundup, not one calf. Another counted 700 calves lost to wolves and found its cows bitten in the hams, their tails chewed off, and otherwise bearing the marks of battle with the wolves: the range cow, especially the wild longhorn, would fight fiercely to save her calf from the shrewd gray killers which surrounded her in packs of 15 or 20.

Sometimes it was a race between the wolves and the "grubbers." These latter were skinners who took to the range in the winter and early spring to strip the hides from the dead stock. The first on the field got as much as $5 or $6 a hide, but the market was soon glutted after disastrous blizzards, and it became known as a "grubstake" job—just sufficiently lucrative to keep the skinner alive.

Most adept at this industry were the wolfers and trappers, who posted themselves in coulees and waited grimly for the cattle to totter in to die, stripping the hides while the body was still warm. Frequently they did not wait until the cows were dead and while this was perhaps merciful during the winter (the wolves were

321

waiting) it caused considerable complaint when the practice continued after spring had come and there was some chance of recovery for the feeble survivors.

The bad winter of 1880–81 started the overcrowding of the central Montana range and thus led directly to the climactic disaster of 1886; but there were signs and portents in the five intervening years for those who could read. There was, for instance, the Starvation Winter of the Pikuni.

A day or two after Christmas, 1883, a luminous and glittering mist formed over the northern and eastern Rockies slope—where Glacier Park is today. Frantically the Pikuni-Blackfeet prayed to Aisoyimstan, the Cold Maker, not to persecute their people; pleadingly they sought of their Indian agent a few extra rations. But rations were low: the agent had reported (seeking to make a record for himself) that the Blackfeet were now nearly self-supporting.

The mercury dropped to 40, 50 below zero, and stayed there for sun upon sun. All travel ceased and the hungry Blackfeet huddled in their lodges. Every day was as the day that had gone before; the sun was a faint light in a colorless void, and it set far to the south. There would come slightly warmer days, and it would snow, silently, thinly, hour after hour; tiny, icy crystalline particles which glittered in the gray light.

Now the hunters would go forth to seek game afoot, for their horses had long since died or been killed for food; and when there was no more game, they brought back the inner bark of the fir and pine trees, or tissue scraped from buffalo skulls, or the hooves of cattle, left by the wolves—or even rats hunted out of their homes in the rocks.

They were deserted by their agent, who was being replaced; his successor arrived in the midst of the worst suffering and did his best. Word of their plight reached Montana towns, and rescue expeditions were organized. George Bird Grinnell, famous naturalist and friend of the Blackfeet, stirred the government to action. Cursing freighters fought their way over drifted trails to the reservation with wagonloads of food. They found some of the survivors mad with hunger and grief among the bodies of their kin; they found coyotes and wolves fighting in the lodges of the unburied dead; they found six hundred Indians—one-quarter of the tribe—starved to death.

The next winter was nearly as severe, and the *Mineral Argus* remarked casually in January, 1885: "Many of the Piegan (Pikuni) Indians are reported frozen to death." The *Chicago Times* printed a special dispatch from Montana's cowboy capital, Miles City:

Since December 1st there has been no break in the cold . . . until it culminated last night in the dreadful temperature of 52 degrees below zero. The whole valley on all sides of Miles City is filled with cattle, seeking what protection the scant shrubbery affords. Even in the streets of the town great droves of cattle wander back and forth, but there is no food for them.

Losses were mounting annually, but still new herds were being crowded onto the Montana range, as the established cattlemen appealed for opening of the reservation. Market conditions also were worrying them. The average beef price per hundredweight on the Chicago market in 1882 had been $4.75; in 1883 it was $4.70, and in 1884, $4.40. The next year it dropped to $3.90, partially because of the distressed selling of some of the herds Cleveland had forced out of Indian Territory.

The bonanza days were gone, and some of the old-timers recognized the fact. "There was no way of preventing the overstocking of the ranges," Stuart admitted, "as they were free to all. . . . The range business was no longer a reasonably safe business; it was from this time on a gamble, with the trump cards in the hands of the elements."

It soon became apparent that the elements were not going to help the situation any. The summer of 1885 was dry; that of 1886 was parching. Great fires swept the range; those cattlemen who could find new grass began the move through a haze of smoke which hung over Montana for months. "There has hardly been an evening in the last week," said the *Rocky Mountain Husbandman* in August, "that the red glare of the fire demon has not lit up our mountain ridges, while our exchanges bring news of disastrous fires in all parts of the Territory."

The grass began to die in July and all but the largest streams and water holes dried up. Water in the creeks became so alkaline that cattle refused to drink it. Cinders, ashes, and hot alkali dust covered the range and even the furniture in the ranch houses.

That fall wild game moved early from its favored shelters in the Missouri badlands and hurried south and west. Birds which customarily remained all winter fled, too. The horses' winter coats appeared earlier than usual; "even the range cattle," said Stuart, "seemed to take on a heavier, shaggier coat of hair."

Nature had set her stage for the last act.

Kissin-ey-oo-way'-o, the Crees said; "it blows cold." The Crees were the northern people, from the Height of Land; they had many words for cold, degrees of coldness, the effects of cold—but none more literally translating into speech the condition it described: in *kissineyooway'o* the north wind sang, softly at first, then rising to a wail and a howl. . . . It blows cold.

It began November 16, though Montana seldom has severe cold or heavy snow until after Christmas. The gale was icy, and it had substance: it was filled with glassy particles of snow, like flakes of mica; it roared and rumbled. After the first day the tonal pitch rose: from a roar it became a moan, then a scream. The snow rode the wind, it thrust forward fiercely and slashed like a knife; no garment or hide could withstand it. The gale piled it into glacial drifts; when cow or horse stumbled into them the flesh on its legs was sheared to the bone.

Now suddenly there appeared white owls of the Arctic. The cattlemen had never seen them before; but the Indians and the métis knew them—and like the beasts and birds, they fled south.

Slowly the temperature moderated. The stockmen prayed for what the Indians called "the black wind" from the arch of black cloud on the western horizon from which it emerged; but it was too early in the season for the chinook. The drifts dwindled but did not disappear; they spread, crusting the range.

In December there were two more blizzards.

January is the Moon of Cold-Exploding-Trees. On the ninth day of that month it snowed without an instant's interruption for sixteen hours—an inch an hour; and the temperature fell to 22 below zero. Intermittent snow continued for another ten days, with temperatures ranging from 22 to 46 below in central Montana; in some other sections it was 40 below day in and day out for more than two weeks.

There was a respite of a little more than a week; then, on January 28, the great blizzard struck. For three days and three nights it was impossible to see fifty feet in any direction and ranch thermometers read 63 below zero. A sudden break in the cold and a wind shift gave promise of a chinook, but the storm set in again and lasted through February 3. A rider who dismounted dropped into snow to his waist on level ground.

Cattle which had been pushed over the Missouri in the fall to the better grass on the northern range drifted back, for there was little shelter on the steppes north of the river. Half dead from cold and hunger, their bodies covered with sores and frozen blood, bewildered and blind in a world of impenetrable white, they blundered into the barbed-wire fences, crumpled against them, and perished. They were trapped in drifts above their bellies and stood erect until their bodies froze. They slid into air holes in the rivers.

Cowboys donned two suits of heavy underwear, two pairs of wool socks, wool pants, two woolen shirts, overalls, leather chaps, wool gloves under leather mittens, blanket-lined overcoats, and fur caps. Before putting on the socks they walked in the snow in their bare feet, then rubbed them dry vigorously. After pulling on their riding boots they stood in water, then stood outdoors until an airtight sheath of ice had formed on the boots. Sometimes instead of the riding boots they wore moccasins and overshoes or sheepskin-lined "packs."

Thus prepared, they mounted and fought their way through the snow to extricate cattle stuck in drifts, tried to herd the dying beasts into sheltered ravines and head them off from treacherous rivers. They blacked their faces and eye sockets with lampblack or burnt matches to forestall snow blindness, or they cut holes in their black neckerchiefs and masked their faces, bandit-fashion. They strained and gasped as the icy air stabbed into their lungs and stomachs; they froze hands and feet, and many of them died. Their bodies, frozen stiff, were lashed on the backs of their horses and borne back to the ranch house, to be thrust into a snowbank until a chinook came because the ground could not be broken for graves.

For all this they got no medals, nor expected any. A cowboy's job was to look after the herd; he was being paid for it—$40 a month. But hundreds of ranchers and riders underwent such hardships in that dreadful winter that they forsook the range forever, crippled in body and spirit.

As the storms and cold continued through February, the tragedy of the range was brought into the towns. Starving cattle staggered through village streets, collapsed and died in dooryards. Five thousand head invaded the outskirts of the newborn city of Great Falls, bawling for food. They snatched up the saplings the proud city had just planted, gorged themselves upon garbage.

Kaufman and Stadler, Helena cattlemen, wrote to their foreman in the Judith Basin to inquire about their herd. When the delayed stage delivered the letter, the foreman tossed it with a derisive grin to one of his riders, a young Missourian who had attained some bunkhouse fame for his pencil and water color sketches.

"Got a postcard?" asked the young artist, whose name was Charley Russell. On it he swiftly sketched in water color a gaunt steer, legs bowed and head down, standing in a drift with a coyote waiting near by. Below he printed a terse legend: "Last of Five Thousand." The card was mailed back to the Helena men without other comment. It was the first Russell work to attain wide circulation; under the title he had originally given it or the later one, "Waiting for a Chinook," it made the artist famous throughout the cow country. It is now owned by the Montana Stockgrowers' Association and hangs in its Helena office. Russell died in Great Falls in 1926; his last painting sold for $30,000.

The chinook did not come until March—a month later than it could have been expected. Before the spring roundups were held to determine the extent of the disaster, the Montana Stockgrowers' Association met in Miles City, scared but hopeful.

"We are not here to bury our industry, but to revive it," said Joseph Scott, association president, whistling bravely in the dark. Then he went on to admit: "Had the winter continued twenty days longer, there would not have been much necessity for this association."

Sadly the stockmen went home for the May roundup. They were in no great hurry to learn the truth; most of them, in short rides near their homes, had seen thousands of rotting carcasses on the plains. There were coulees and sheltered valleys which they could not enter because of the stench of decomposing beef.

The popular estimate of the cattlemen after the roundups had been completed was 60 per cent loss for the state, or about 362,000 head of cattle.

More conservative were official figures, showing a 40 to 50 per cent loss. The drop in cattle on assessment rolls was 200,000, but this did not account for all the loss by any means, since thousands of cattle, including all the fall calf crop, had not been assessed.

Officially, it was reported cattle worth $5,000,000 had perished; actually the cattlemen estimated the loss amounted to $20,000,000. They had to figure in the deterioration in their potential assets, including unborn calves, the cost of restocking, and other more indirect results of the disaster.

Nelson Story of Bozeman, who twenty years before had brought the first trail herd from Texas, lost more than 66 per cent of his stock. On the Yellowstone range losses reached 95 per cent. The Home Land & Cattle Co. had put 6,000 head across the Canadian border; 2,000 survived. James Fergus sold 1,500 hides from his dead stock for $2,000.

The great Swan Cattle Co. of Wyoming, Scotch financed, which had large Montana holdings, went bankrupt. The Niobrara Cattle Co., founded in Texas, collapsed; it had 9,000 head left out of 39,000 and it was $350,000 in debt. Gibb Brothers, typical of the smaller operators, counted 320 head left out of their 2,500. They sold the 320 and quit. Theodore Roosevelt decided the cattle business was not for him and sold his ranch just east of the Montana line in North Dakota. The French Marquis de Mores closed up shop in his ill-fated packing plant at Medora, N. D., and went off to India to hunt tigers.

Nevertheless, the *Yellowstone Journal* in Miles City commented sarcastically on the disaster: "It is comforting to reflect on the number of reputations that were saved by the 'hard winter.' It never killed half the cattle that were charged up to it. . . . The story was told of one manager who reported 125 per cent loss."

The newspaper's reference was to the strange bookkeeping practices of the range industry, which also accounted for the wide variation in estimates of the loss. There were two ways of totaling one's herds: the "book count" and the "tally." The latter— actual count of every cow, calf, and beef steer on the range—was

327

the only way to determine one's true assets. The "book count" was easier and much more popular, especially among managers for absentee owners. It was based upon the number of cattle originally placed on the range, to which was added, annually, the normal expectancy of increase, and from which was subtracted, ostensibly, "normal" losses to rustlers, wolves, disease, and "winter kill." This paper computation bore little relation to the actual number of cattle on the range. It speeded the collapse of some of the large speculative companies.

But regardless of whether the losses were all valid or partially "paper," a panic had gripped the industry. Ranchers who intended to stick it out but who needed cash found that the forced liquidation of livestock assets had smashed the already tottering Chicago market. Prices slid until the going figure was $3.15 a hundred pounds—less than $38 for a 1,200 pound steer, of which there were few left. Then, on October 8, 1887, came word that a shipment of Montana cattle had been sold in Chicago for $2.50 a hundred—not much more than $25 a head, and with a freight charge of $6 a head to be deducted.

Eastern and foreign investors had lost interest and thrust their companies into bankruptcy; the big herds had nearly vanished. Hundreds of Montanans now became disgusted. "A business that had been fascinating," said Stuart, "suddenly became distasteful. I never wanted to own again an animal that I could not feed and shelter."

. . .

But the snow which had brought ruin in the winter brought rich new grass in the spring and helped the transition to a new type of operation—fewer cattle, more limited but better range, supplemental feeding. Ranchers could restock in 1887 for less than $20 a head; more than 100,000 came in by trail from the south that year. By 1893 Montana had 100,000 more cattle than it had had before the great storm—but individual herds were smaller so that they could be maintained on owned range, fed and sheltered.

Montana old-timers recall that one of the biggest roundups of all time occurred in the middle '90's, along the Canadian border from the Sweet Grass Hills to North Dakota—three hundred miles. It is significant that nearly one thousand riders representing nearly a score of ranches participated; a decade earlier there would have been a few hundred, representing half a dozen companies.

Most of the ranches in this big roundup now owned or leased at least a part of their range. One of these outfits was the famous Circle Diamond of Colorado, which had begun as Thatcher Brothers of Pueblo and became the Bloom Cattle Co. At this writing their foreman, John Survant, is still a prominent citizen of Montana. The Circle Diamond was destined to be the last big outfit on the northern range.

This company's shipments in the '90's had reached an annual total of 9,000 to 12,000 head. In 1902 the firm acquired, by lease, a dozen linked townships along watercourses in Saskatchewan. In the fall of 1906 on this range and in Montana the Circle Diamond had 12,000 head; that winter 9,000 of them perished. The company survived, but within two years it closed out its Montana and Canada cattle operations, and the big herds had disappeared forever from the open range.

In that winter of 1906–07 railroad tracks snapped in the cold and for two months freight shipments were tied up as wreck crews struggled to keep the trains moving. Again starving cattle invaded the towns; one old steer, little more than a scurfy skeleton, stood in the yard of a Chinook newspaper plant until he died. There was nothing to feed him.

Losses would have been as severe as twenty years before were it not for the fact that livestock practice had changed. The story of human heroism in a futile effort to save the stock was repeated: sheepmen and cattlemen rigged up flatboard scrapers to clean the snow off the range in long strips so their animals could get at the grass; again the herders underwent great hardships in efforts to save their charges from accident or starvation.

In April, 1907, the state sadly tabulated the winter's cost: 727,136 head of sheep, 110,628 head of cattle, 6,423 head of horses. It was the worst loss in all America, though it had been a bad winter nearly everywhere. The national average winter kill was 3.49 per cent for cattle, 6 per cent for sheep; Montana's was 12 and 13 per cent. The last open-range roundup had been held in the fall of 1906; little interest had been shown in it and it had been hard to organize because there were so few outfits left using unfenced grass. In the spring of 1907 it was apparent that there never would be need for another.

. . .

GOOD SHEPHERDS

HUGHIE CALL

Hughie (Florence) Call, a Texan, married a Montana sheepman and
came north to manage his household on a ranch near Ennis in the
Madison country. Out of her experiences grew the book *Golden Fleece*,
published by Houghton Mifflin, in 1942; "Good Shepherds" is a
chapter from that book. *Golden Fleece* was popular in Montana, as
it well deserved to be; it is amusing, but always friendly, and it is
accurate but always interesting. In this chapter the much-maligned
sheepherder at long last finds a sympathetic witness. Another chapter
from the book will be found elsewhere in this collection.

THE men were looking for a wool sack. I heard six
drawers open and shut. The cellar door slammed twice.
Finally they dragged a ladder under the trap door of the
attic. I know it was a wool sack they found, because I heard the
camp-tender tell the chore boy, as they lumbered down the steps
together, that the attic was a *helluva* place to keep wool sacks if
you asked him. (I had thought it was a good place when I cached
it there last spring.)

I also gathered that the camp-tender wanted the wool sack
for a herder's mattress. The wool sack is as versatile as it is popular. It can be used for a mattress, when stuffed with straw, a saddle blanket, a meat sack or an irrigation dam. It might also have
been used as the foundation for a hooked rug if I had taken the
precaution to lock it in a trunk.

I want that wool sack badly, but there's no use to dash down
and claim it now. I could put up a fight and cow any member
of this outfit into returning my lawful property, but I can't
handle the camp-tender. He knows my weakness for herders and
takes advantage of it. If that herder needs a mattress, he needs
it, and that's that.

Tom shares my weakness to a certain point. He is pleased to see
me hand over the last can of corn or the last jug of syrup because
the camp-tender forgot we were 'out'; but he isn't so pleased when
he misses his favorite pair of overshoes, mittens or the current
issue of a magazine in which he is reading a serial.

He has no recourse. It is understood on this ranch that while the 'Missus' merely accepts, of necessity, the fact that the sheep come first, she's a stern defender of their herder's rights. Not that it ever gets her anywhere. The herders still prefer a calling down from the Boss to a word of praise from the 'Missus.'

The herder is a strange person. (Tom calls this statement a piece of colossal conceit. Why, asks he, is a herder strange? Because he doesn't like women?) I have known two types of herders, and both believe this is a man's world. The first because he knows too little about women, and the second because he knows too much.

The first, a bachelor by choice, reluctantly admits that woman is a necessary cog in the usual scheme of things, but not in his scheme. He boasts that he can best any woman in her own field. He can cook, sew, scrub and clean, and he can do all this in a tenth the time, with a fourth the fuss and effort.

The second has been unpleasantly involved in marriage at some time or other, and has kicked over the traces and taken to the hills. In spite of his disillusionment, he misses the comforts of home. He usually does his housekeeping grudgingly, in hit-or-miss fashion. He values his isolation for obvious reasons, but he is pathetically grateful for a loaf of home-baked bread or a bucket of doughnuts or cookies.

It is well to sort the herders into their separate types as soon as they come on the job. Once I lost a cook during threshing because I neglected to do so. The camp-tender was leaving for a new herder's camp. The cook had just fried a large batch of doughnuts and I hastily packed a few and sent them along.

The very next time the camp-tender went to that camp he returned with a present for me. It was a ten-pound bucket, filled to the brim with golden sugar-crusted doughnuts. I was touched, and showed them to the cook.

'These,' I remarked tactlessly, 'are the best-looking doughnuts I ever saw. Imagine a man making them!'

The cook did not share my enthusiasm. Her face went blank and her silence should have warned me.

'Let's have some for supper,' I said, getting out a plate.

'I baked cookies for supper,' she replied stiffly.

'Save them for tomorrow.' I was lifting the doughnuts out of the bucket now.

331

Her back went as rigid as a flagpole, and her lips poked out. I got the idea that she wasn't pleased but I didn't know just how to handle the situation without a loss of face. I left the kitchen hastily.

At supper we had both cookies and doughnuts. The men did not touch the cookies but they cleaned the plate of doughnuts. When the dishes were washed up, the cook folded her apron deliberately and asked for her time.

'I thought you liked it here,' I said reproachfully.

'No herder can insult me and get away with it,' she returned sullenly. 'If you folks like his cooking better than mine, give him my job.'

She had lived in the country longer than I and knew the herder's challenge for what it was. Nothing I could say would dissuade her. She left in a huff. A week passed before we found another cook, and long before that week was up I had lost my taste for doughnuts. But I still liked herders.

I had not lived here long enough to understand their peculiarities (and doubt that I ever will), but I had learned something that caused me to overlook even the loss of a cook. I had learned the meaning of the word *loyalty* in its truest sense. The word *shepherd* has always been a synonym for loyalty. I believe that this accounts for the fact that in no other business is a man of the herder's caliber entrusted with assets representing so great an amount of capital.

The herder is solely responsible for the welfare of approximately eighteen hundred head of sheep. An hour's neglect or carelessness on his part could turn the balance from profit to loss on the entire year's operation, and nobody knows it so well as he. There are few sacrifices the herder would not make to keep his flock intact.

In this country the herder is liable to a term in the penitentiary if he abandons his sheep in the mountains for any reason whatever; nor can he quit his job without first serving five days' notice to the woolgrower. The quality of a good herder's loyalty can be gauged by the fact that only once have I known one to abandon his sheep, and that man was crazy. Fear of the law does not influence them, because the penalty has been exercised so seldom that it has taken on the status of a myth. I doubt if half the herders in Montana even know of its existence. We have had herders who went to heartbreaking lengths to stay with their sheep, and one who laid down his life for them.

Years ago we had a herder whose name was Ed. He was one of the finest men I have ever known as well as the best herder we ever had. I can see him yet—on the crest of some wind-swept hill, with his dogs and sheep about him. A tall, gaunt man, with straight-seeing blue eyes and a ready smile.

His sheep were always fat and he prided himself on the fact that he could usually keep them that way on grass. They seldom required the cottonseed cake or corn that is often so necessary for the welfare of sheep in bitter winter weather. He used his head and planned each day's grazing as carefully as a pilot maps out his flight.

He knew every foot of the range and if there was grass to be had, Ed drove his sheep to it. No mountain was too high, no snow too deep. He never spared himself, and his pride in his flock was a splendid thing to see. He would trust them to no other herder and we could never persuade him to take so much as a few days' vacation. We were surprised and pleased, then, when one day the camp-tender brought word that Ed wanted a leave of absence.

We later discovered that he had spent all of two days' vacation in a Butte clinic and had been told by the doctors there that he had an incurable cancer of the stomach. He did not tell us, he never complained, and for a full year after the doctors had diagnosed his case, he stuck to his job.

At last the time came when the pain grew so intense that it was difficult for him to leave his wagon. He knew the end was near, and he worried for fear he might die on the range and leave his sheep unprotected. He selected a day when he was sure the camp-tender would bring supplies; bathed, shaved and dressed himself in his best suit of clothes. Then he lay down on his bunk, put his revolver to his head and shot himself. He had planned it all very carefully, at least two weeks in advance. The camp-tender told us later that he had noticed a penciled ring drawn about the date on Ed's calendar a fortnight before and had wondered about it.

Ed left a note for my husband. He explained the whole tragic situation and apologized for leaving his sheep alone even so short a time. He said he'd counted them an hour before and that they were all there. But should any be missing when the camp-tender came, he wanted pay for them deducted from his time.

333

To this day I can remember every word of that note. The last stark sentence still has the power to bring a lump to my throat:

Thank you for all your kindness to a fellow who did not know enough to appreciate it.

His poor tortured mind . . . Counting all those years of loyalty as nothing against the fact that he felt he was betraying us in the end. . . .

His death saddened every man on the ranch, but you would never have known it. Death is a mystery that ranch men take in their stride. When I first came to Montana it seemed to me that they were casual and cold-blooded about it. I did not realize that there is no more sensitive or tender-hearted creature alive than the average ranch man or herder; that their casualness is merely a shell built up to conceal their real feelings.

I remember the weatherbeaten, hard-boiled chore boy (a man of fifty or thereabouts) who was given the unpleasant task of cleaning the wagon in which the suicide had taken place. The wagon had been pulled into the home ranch and I was forced to pass it on my way to the garden. The chore boy was scrubbing away. He had not heard me come and I was about to speak when I caught sight of his face. It was twisted with emotion and the tears were streaming down his leathery cheeks. I was humbled . . . and ashamed for my intrusion. I would have slipped away quietly but he looked up and saw me. Instantly his expression changed to one of surliness.

'Looks like Ed'd ought to of remembered that some of us fellers 'ud have to clean up this mess,' he complained. 'Looks like he could've gone outside if he was hell-bent to splatter his brains around.'

We had another herder who shot himself accidentally while cleaning a gun. This herder could have reached the ranch in an hour had he deserted his herd to do so. Instead, he drove his flock in, over a period of four hours, and arrived at the ranch on the verge of collapse from loss of blood and exposure. We rushed him to the nearest hospital, and when he had had a blood transfusion Tom asked him how he had managed to travel that far in his weakened condition. The herder told him quite cheerfully that he had crawled the last half-mile. And he told the truth, for when

334

the sheep were driven back over that same trail the next day, we found his loyalty patterned in a crimson ribbon on the snow.

As a rule the herder's sense of responsibility is confined to his own flock, but this is not always the case. Several winters ago two of our herders were camped within five miles of each other, with a mountain between. Once a week the camp-tender brought them supplies, and this was their only contact with the outside world. On a morning following the camp-tender's visit, a fierce blizzard swept the mountains. It raged for twenty-four hours, and shortly after it had died down one of the herders, a man whom we called Jean, picked up a hundred or more ewes whose brands he recognized as belonging to the flock of his neighbor.

He gave the matter little thought, but when toward nightfall another bunch wandered into his herd, he was puzzled and concerned. The next morning twenty more ewes sought sanctuary in his flock, and now Jean was convinced that all was not right in his neighbor's camp, else by this time the other herder would have corralled his band at the shearing pens (which was only three miles the other side of his camp) and he and his dogs would be scouring the country for lost sheep.

Jean did some tall thinking. He could not leave his own sheep to investigate, and yet if he failed to do so that other herd would be scattered beyond recall and perhaps half of them destroyed by coyotes before the camp-tender's next visit. Aside from that, he felt sure the other herder was ill or had met with some accident. He decided to go to his aid and he turned his flock toward his neighbor's camp.

The journey was fraught with hazards. The snow was deep and soft. His sheep floundered about in it and many times he was forced to dig some of them out of great drifts. It was dusk before he reached the other camp and he was tired to the point of collapse.

He was alarmed by what he saw. No ewes were on the bed-ground, and there was not a dog in sight. Nor had the sheep bedded there the night before; there were no tracks in the new snow about the wagon. But the thing that concerned him the most was the fact that no welcome curl of smoke rose skyward from the stovepipe. He tried the door and found that it had been locked from the inside. His fingers were stiff from cold, and none too steady. Ten minutes elapsed before he managed to break the lock.

Once Jean got inside, he could see the dim outline of the other herder's figure on the bunk. He was angry and disgusted. 'I figured I'd gone to all my trouble for a skunk who would hole in and sleep while his sheep ran loose,' he told us. 'I grabbed him by the shoulder and shook him . . .'

He jumped back then and stared down in shocked dismay. The man on the bunk was dead; his body was stiff and cold. When he got hold of himself Jean covered him with a tarp. Then he kindled a fire in the stove and sat down to think.

At this point I wish I could say that he knew he had only to make himself comfortable and presently the dogs would return, driving the missing herd before them. I've read about such dogs, but ours are not of that breed. (Just once before I die I hope I can see or hear of a Montana sheep dog which has gathered up a flock of lost sheep and brought them in alone.)

It didn't take Jean long to piece the story out. A high wind had been blowing for three days. Sheep have a habit of traveling in the direction of the wind. In the absence of the herder they had set out and the dogs, lacking their usual instructions, had followed. They would continue to follow, striving to keep the flock together. Their efforts would be futile, but they would stick with the herd until their feet gave out and then they would return to camp alone.

For Jean to corral his own sheep at the shearing pen and set out for help would mean the loss of a day, in which time the lost sheep would be scattered all over the country. He did not relish the idea of spending several nights alone with a dead man, but he stayed just the same. The next morning he corralled his sheep and set out in the direction of the wind. Eventually he picked up most of the sheep and the dogs, and drove both herds into the ranch.

Surprisingly, he was little the worse for his experience, which he related in minute detail. I could scarcely wait for him to be through because, woman-like, I was curious to know where he had slept all those nights. I finally asked him. For the first time he displayed a touch of resentment. His face became crimson with embarrassment. 'Where could I sleep?' he demanded heatedly. 'There ain't but one bunk. I had to sleep if I hunted those sheep, so I just shoved Bill over and slept long side of him.'

I stared at the man for a moment and then left the room abruptly. When I later voiced my horror, Tom reminded me of something

I had forgotten. Jean had risked his life, and the welfare of his own flock, to go to the aid of his fellow herder. And it was Jean who later 'shot his stake' to place a fitting marker on his grave.

If men are rewarded in the Hereafter for what they endure on earth, the herder has something to look forward to. I think I can say, with no fear of contradiction, that sheepherding is the hardest, most harrowing job on earth. Ditch-digging is child's play beside it. In all other professions there is a limit to the number of hours a man may work. The shepherd's job is a twenty-four-hour job. He can never be sure when he collapses in his bunk at night that he will be able to stay there until morning. It is second nature for him to sleep with one ear on his sheep and the other on his dogs.

If the dog gives warning that a coyote is stalking the flock, the herder jerks out of a sodden sleep, grabs his gun and fires a shot which he hopes will frighten the marauder away. It seldom does. Sometimes he is forced to repeat the procedure four or five times before morning.

One of the most aggravating habits sheep have is that of wandering off the bed-ground at night. In winter a high wind is almost sure to precipitate an epidemic of wanderlust. In summer, the mosquitoes will have the same effect. Sometimes a lead sheep will decide that she has not had her fill of green grass and set out to remedy the lack; whereupon every sheep in the herd will do likewise. Sometimes they just leave—for no good reason at all. It may be simply an idea that can be promptly squelched, or it may become an obsession. If the latter, there will be little sleep for the herder.

But his nocturnal problems sink into insignificance before the problems of his days—especially in winter. Our winters are always cold, but several years ago we had an unusually bitter winter. The wind blew for days on end with no letup and the thermometer dropped down to thirty below and stayed there. Thirty below is not bad in this country if it's calm, but a high wind can drive it into the marrow of your bones. It can also drive it through any sheep wagon that has ever been built.

We had a good thirty days of this before we got any reaction from the herders, and then one morning the camp-tender brought word that a herder wanted to quit. He was brought by the ranch to get his time and Tom asked him what his grievance was. He refused to say at first, but when Tom insisted he sullenly replied that he didn't see why he had to have the coldest camp on the range.

'Nonsense,' Tom told him. 'Your camp isn't any colder than Joe's (a herder with a camp some four miles away), and he isn't quitting.'

'It is colder too,' the disgruntled one replied. 'Joe's only slept with his spuds four nights this winter and I've had to sleep with mine every night for a month.'

And sleeping with potatoes to keep them from freezing represents a very small share of a herder's trials. If a sheep gets her fill in the winter she must forage from sunup until dusk. If she fails to get a 'fill' every day, she grows gaunt and has to be trucked to the home ranch and thrown into the hospital band. The hospital band is composed of weak sheep, which could not weather the winter without corn or cottonseed cake. At best there are always a few sheep which normally swell this band—very old sheep or lame sheep. A herder's efficiency is judged in relative proportion to the number of sheep he turns into the hospital band in a winter.

If he values his reputation or even his job, the herder must drive his sheep off the bed-ground at sunup, blizzard or no. Before he leaves camp his potatoes and canned goods must be wrapped securely in his roll of bedding, to prevent freezing.

His lunch consists of one sandwich, which he tucks in the pocket of his sheepskin. At night he returns to his wagon, having trudged many miles in the wake of his sheep, to find his fire in ashes and his water bucket frozen hard. He builds his fire, thaws out his water bucket and cooks a sketchy meal for his dogs and himself. His menu seldom varies. Day after day his food is fried food, since he has neither time nor energy to prepare any other.

Good weather or bad, herders have their troubles. I spent most of my first winter in Montana feeling sorry for them. Every time a blizzard whistled through the sturdy windows of our house, I remembered the herder's flimsy shelters, and when the blizzard broke and the sun came out, I was always relieved. I didn't know then that the blinding reflection of the sun on the snow could cause the herder pain, or at best discomfort.

The sun's rays can penetrate the best of smoked glasses and cause the eyes to throb and sting. Loss or accident to his glasses renders the herder helpless and often results in the tragedy of snow-blindness. The native herder would never dream of starting to work without his colored glasses, but it is hard to convince a herder who comes up from the Southern States that these are a necessity. They usually buy a pair or two when they first arrive, as a sort of keeping-up-with-the-Joneses gesture, but they are constantly breaking them or forgetting to take them along.

Tom seldom employs out-of-state herders, but there are times when herders are scarce and he is forced to hire anyone he can get. This was true immediately after the First World War. During that time, he employed a herder from Arizona. One morning in February the man was digging into the pocket of his sheepskin coat for a sack of tobacco. His colored glasses were caught in the drawstring, and they fell against a rock and were broken into bits.

It was cloudy that morning and he suffered no discomfort for a time. Later the sun came out and reflected on the snow, but the herder was a long way from his camp and second pair of glasses, and he was not as energetic as he might have been. Some people's eyes are more sensitive to snow glare than others, and the herder proved to be one of these people.

He did not recognize the danger signals as a native herder would have done. His eyes began to smart, but he was in acute pain before he realized the seriousness of the situation. He sent the dogs around the sheep, turned them and started back for his camp. He had covered only about half the distance when he lost his vision. Panic took him. He did not stop to think or reason; he had but one plan and that was to reach his wagon as soon as possible, and he stumbled along in that general direction as fast as he dared.

There was an abandoned prospect hole directly in his path and he walked right into it, striking his head a nasty lick on supporting timbers as he fell. He also fractured an ankle and his collarbone. He would surely have died from exposure if a Ranger had not been searching for a strayed horse that day.

The Ranger spotted the sheep from a hill and rode down to them, hoping their herder had seen his horse. By then the sheep were a good half-mile from the prospect hole. The Ranger was puzzled when he failed to find the herder and thoughtful enough to ride by the ranch and report the matter to Tom.

Herders who are new to this section have such a capacity for getting into trouble that Tom was alarmed and sent three riders out to search. The snow was fresh and it did not take them long to track him. The man was unconscious and could be no help to them. One of the riders was lowered into the hole with a rope which he tied about the injured herder, and the rescue was accomplished. Months passed before the Arizonan could get about again, but the moment he was able to discard his crutches, he took a south-bound train.

Out-of-state herders do not have a corner on this capacity for trouble. Strange things can happen to veteran native herders, through no act of carelessness on their part. One of our friends had a herder who went through a harrowing experience a few springs past. The day was warm and sunny and the herder was tired. He was also sleepy. Coyotes had scattered his flock the night before, and he had spent a good many hours rounding them up and driving them back to the bed-ground. The sheep were now grazing contentedly in an area where the grass was thick, so the herder sat down with his back against a big rock and promptly dozed off. One of his arms rested along the top of the boulder.

He was awakened by a stab of pain in his finger and he leaped to his feet in time to see a huge rattler slithering along the ground a short distance away. The herder was petrified with fear. He had a fever sore on his lip and he knew that should he attempt to suck the poison from the wound, this would be suicide.

There was no time to think. His hand was beginning to swell and two angry pin points of red were plainly discernible on the tip of one of his fingers. Before he could possibly reach help, he would die, and the thought of dying a tortured death, alone in the mountains, was more than he could contemplate.

There was but one thing to do and this he did quickly. He always carried a big knife which he used to pelt his dead sheep. He got the knife out of his pocket and performed a neat job of surgery on the injured finger, cutting it off to the first joint. Then he sped back to his wagon and stopped the bleeding with soot from the inside of the stovelid.

The Lord has his arms around that herder. By every law of science and medicine, an infection should certainly have resulted. Six hours elapsed before he received a doctor's care, and yet the finger healed perfectly.

SOCIAL LIFE

"Face to face with each other, they were confronted with the newness of the land, with ignorance of its geography, topography, resources, climate—and above and beyond all with the fact that they were strangers each to the others."

STAR IN THE EAST

FRED WARD

This simple little story of Christmas in an isolated foreign-language community in Montana is an editorial from a country newspaper, the *Meagher County News*, White Sulphur Springs. Fred Ward, the editor, wrote it three times before it was simple enough to suit him. Ward, born in Wisconsin in 1891, was brought up in Miami, Ariz., a mining town; he attended a normal school in Wisconsin, was graduated from Montana State University, and obtained his master's degree at the University of California; but, he reports, "I have always said that if anyone could recognize those degrees in any of my writing I would be a complete flop." He was in schoolwork for twenty-three years, but in 1934 bought the Montana weekly. He has written editorials or features for several metropolitan newspapers and done some magazine work. Another story by him appears elsewhere in this book. "Star in the East" appeared in the *Meagher County News* on Dec. 26, 1945.

T HE Christmas story that I remember best is not one that I read. It is one that I saw and it happened down in the "breaks" of eastern Montana over thirty years ago.

They were putting on a program in the Lame Jones school beyond the "breaks" of Upper Sandstone. I had visited this unit frequently, for it was in the district where I was superintendent; and one afternoon I listened to the children practice. I promised them that I would come again the night they gave it.

It was snowing when I left home but when I got to Lame Jones I found that the whole community had turned out. They had a tree that someone had brought in from the pine hills of Pennel Creek and they had lighted it with candles.

There were fourteen children in the school and every one had some part in the program. There was one dialog with five of the smaller children in it. I remember this much of it: it started out with a boy named Ralph Sandaas coming out dressed like Santa Claus. He said: "I brekt the chimney off because 'twas much too small for Santa Claus."

But the big event of the evening was the final number. In this a little girl named Heisley Stockfisch was the mother of a brood of children; someone knocked at her door and she came out and she said: "My day, who can this be, knocking at my door so early on Christmas morning?"

They had an intermission while they hung sheets in front for a curtain and the crowd had got to talking among themselves. Thinking to help the teacher, I pounded on the desk for silence.

That was a mistake, for when I pounded, Heisley came out and exclaimed: "My day, who can this be, knocking at my door so early on Christmas morning?"

The teacher, who had been behind the curtain helping the other children make up for their parts, rushed out and led Heisley back.

The crowd was still talking so I pounded on the desk again. And again Heisley rushed out and she said: "My day, who can this be, knocking at my door so early on Christmas morning?"

Again the teacher rushed out and retrieved this little girl. I knew better than to hammer on the desk again, so I bellered, "Quiet!" A woman standing within a foot of me almost jumped out of her skin.

Order was finally restored. The mailman knocked at the door, but this time Heisley was not to be fooled. The teacher had to lead her out on the stage, and she said, with a sigh of deep resignation: "My day, who can this be, knocking at my door so early on Christmas morning?"

Two of the Diesterhaft girls that evening sang a song in the tongue of their ancestors:

"O Tannenbaum, O Tannenbaum,

"Wie treu sint deine Blatter."

It had been snowing and I had to go as soon as the presents were given away. I had left my car at the Stockfisch homestead, for there was no road down through the "breaks." I had found deep drifts walking to the schoolhouse, but they explained that there was a shorter path by the coal mine. Heisley volunteered to show me the way.

When we walked out into the night, the sky was clear. A slim moon hung over the rim of the prairie. Heisley clutched at her Christmas gifts as we waded through the heavy snow. She pointed to a big yellow star that was rising in the east.

"Lookit," she said. "Just like the story in the book. The star in the east."

I might have told her that the light of the star and of the Prince

344

of Peace was not something which existed only in the ages of long ago, but like the brightness I had seen that night in the eyes of little children who were glad, it was something eternal and unchanging. But that thought did not strike me for thirty years. It had to await the coming of war and the uneasy peace after the war; then war again and another peace ushered into the world.

The homesteaders on Lame Jones Creek were mainly Ukrainian Russians. They spoke German and English with equal fluency. When I finally got the cold car started, I leaned from the driver's seat: "Guten Abend, Heisley."

And the little girl called back: "Gute Nacht, Herr Professor. Lustige Weinacht."

WHEN BRYAN CAME TO BUTTE

CHARLES H. EGGLESTON

This is undoubtedly Montana's most famous and best-remembered newspaper poem. It appeared in *The Anaconda Standard,* Aug. 13, 1897, the day after the beloved Commoner, whose free-silver platform was popular in silver-producing Montana, visited near-by Butte. The *Standard,* established by Marcus Daly, copper king, was published in Anaconda to get an Associated Press franchise, but distributed in Butte. Eggleston, a Syracuse, N. Y., newspaper man, came to it in 1889 as associate editor. He was a state senator for two terms. He died in Anaconda, April 28, 1933.

I HAVE read of Roman triumphs in the days when Rome played
    ball,
    When she met all other nations, taking out of each a fall;
When victorious Roman generals marched their legions home
    in state,
With the plunder of the conquered—and the conquered paid the
    freight.
Gorgeous were those vast processions rolling through the streets
    of Rome;
Mad with joy went all the Romans welcoming the veterans home.
Gold there was for fifty Klondikes, silver trinkets big as logs,
Marble statues by the cartload, gems enough to stone the dogs.
Following chariot cars were captives, dainty damsels by the score,
Ballet dancers from far harems, savage men and beasts galore.
Millions cheered and yelled and thundered; shook the earth as by
    a storm;
All Rome howled—and yet Rome's howling after all was not so
    warm,
For these monster Roman triumphs, at which not a stone was
    mute,
Couldn't hold a Roman candle—
           When Bryan came to Butte.

I have read of the convulsions of the fiery men of France
When Napoleon came from Elba, eager for another chance.

346

Marble hearts and frozen shoulders turned the generals to their
    chief,
But the people hailed their master with a rapture past belief.
What though France lay stunned and bleeding, she arose and got
    too gay;
What though he had cost her fortunes, still the devil was to pay.
Though he'd slain a million soldiers and returned to slay some
    more,
The survivors stood there ready to pour forth their inmost gore;
And they wept and sang and shouted, whooped and roared in
    sheer delight,
On their knees they begged, implored him to pull off another
    fight—
Sure the champion was in training, and in training couldn't lose;
Thus they laughed and cried and acted as if jagged with wildest
    booze.
But the passion that they cherished for this brilliant French galoot
Was as zero to that witnessed
          When Bryan came to Butte.

I have read of Queen Victoria and her diamond jubilee.
London rose and did the handsome—it was something up in G.
Long and glittering the procession—beat old Barnum's best to
    death;
When the queen is on exhibit, even cyclones hold their breath.
Troops of white and black and yellow—regiments from East and
    West—
All the glory of Great Britain—pomp until you couldn't rest.
Russia also cut a figure when she crowned the reigning czar.
In the line of fancy blowouts Russian stock is up to par.
There were balls and fetes and fireworks, bands played on and
    cannon roared;
Monarchy was at the bat, and all their royal nibses scored.
Add the Moscow show to London's, take the paralyzing pair,
Put the queen and czar together, yoke the lion and the bear—
Swell these pageantries of Europe till you get a dream to suit—
And it's pretty small potatoes—
          When Bryan came to Butte.

Bryan has had many triumphs, some ovations off and on
Just a little bit the biggest that the sun e'er shone upon.

You remember the convention in Chicago, do you not,
When the party went to Bryan and the goldbugs went to pot?
You remember the excitement when he rose and caught the crowd,
When for fully twenty minutes everybody screamed aloud.
Oh, the mighty roar of thousands as he smote the cross of gold,
As he gripped the British lion in a giant's strangle hold!
Oh, the fury of the frenzy as he crushed the crown of thorns,
As he grabbed the situation, as he held it by the horns!
Some there were who leaped the benches, some who maniac dances
    led,
Some who tried to kick the ceiling, more who tried to wake the
    dead.
'Twas a record-breaking rouser, down to fame it shoots the chute,
But it wasn't quite a fly-speck—
                When Bryan came to Butte.

Ah, when Bryan came to Butte! greatest mining camp on earth;
Where the people dig and delve, and demand their money's worth.
Though the Wall street kings and princes spurn and kick them as
    a clod,
Bryan is their friend and savior and they love him as a god.
Did they meet him when he came there? Did they make a little
    noise?
Were they really glad to see him? Do you think it pleased the
    boys?
'Twas the screaming of the eagle as he never screamed before,
'Twas the crashing of the thunder, mingling with Niagara's roar,
All the whistles were a-screeching, with the bands they set the
    pace—
But the yelling of the people never let them get a place.
Dancing up and down and sideways, splitting lungs and throats
    and ears,
All were yelling, and at yelling seemed wound up a thousand
    years.

                • • •

Of the earth's great celebrations 'twas the champion heavyweight,
'Tis the champion forever and a day, I calculate,
For it knocked out all its rivals, and, undaunted, resolute,
Punched creation's solar plexus—
                When Bryan came to Butte.

WHEN BRYAN CAME TO BUTTE—
YESTERDAY

BERTON BRALEY

This looks like sardonic comment on the hazards of political glory—
but as a matter of fact Bryan was just passing through Butte when
Berton Braley saw him at the station. Braley, long one of this country's best known writers of popular verse, was born in Madison, Wis.,
in 1882 and came to Butte in 1905 soon after finishing college. He
worked a year on *The Intermountain,* where his facility with rhyme
was not appreciated, then three years on the *Evening News* under the
renowned Montana editor Dick Kilroy. In 1909 he quit Butte and
went to New York to launch his career as a free-lance writer and
foreign correspondent. *Who's Who* credits him with more than ten
thousand published poems in addition to many articles and stories.
His home is now in Connecticut. His entertaining autobiography,
Pegasus Pulls a Hack (Minton, Balch, 1934), contains a section on
his life in Butte.

D ARKNESS hung about the city when the Peerless Leader
came;
P. C. Gillis smoked and jollied at a little solo game,
Robert Haydn read his Shakespeare 'mid the comforts of his home,
John O'Rourke was dozing, dozing, in the glimmer of the gloam.
Yet while Democrats by the hundreds flitted all around the town
Not a one was there to greet him when the train was slowing
down—
Not a bell clanged out a welcome, there was not a whistle's toot,
But a News reporter saw him, when Bill Bryan came to Butte.

Charlie Nevin never knew it, Wally Walsworth hadn't heard,
Tommy Walker, John MacGinness didn't know it had occurred.
So the silver tongued and matchless, whom the city used to cheer,
Looked in vain for greeting from them—no one knew that he was
here—
No one, save a News reporter, who was loafing at the train,
And who recognized the features of the Leader once again.
Democrats were dead or sleeping, whistles, bells were silent, mute,
When, upon this sad occasion, Mr. Bryan came to Butte.

COWBOY'S COURTSHIP

CON PRICE

Born in Iowa in 1869, Con Price accompanied his parents to the
Black Hills ten years later, and landed in Montana as a cowboy in
1886. He was a close friend and at one time ranch partner of Charles
M. Russell, and for many years operated a cattle spread in the Sweet
Grass Hills. The girl he married, not without difficulty—as told here
—was Claudia Toole, sister of the late E. B. Toole of Shelby. In 1910
Price sold his Sweet Grass Hills ranch and moved to western Montana, and thence to Pasadena, Calif., where he has lived for many
years. "Cowboy's Courtship" is an excerpt from *Memories of Old
Montana* by Con Price, published by the author in Pasadena (725
Michigan Boulevard) in 1945. It contains a score of authentic and
often amusing incidents of the closing days of the open-range era and
simply written sketches of people and places.

. . .

I THINK everybody has more or less trouble in their courting
days, but it seemed to my wife and I that we had more than our
share. As I said before, my wife's parents didn't know we were
keeping company at all—in fact, didn't hardly know me. There
was a very noted dance coming off about 20 miles from her home
that we had planned to attend, when, lo and behold, a few days
before the dance a very wealthy and refined gentleman (and an
old friend of her father's) with a fine team and top buggy (which
was very rare in those days) came to her father's ranch to ask her
parents to take her to the dance. They at once gladly said yes and she
in order not to tip her hand had to consent, and mind you, we were
engaged to be married at this time. Of course, with me not knowing anything about this transaction it placed her in a very precarious
position, and she had a terrible time getting in touch with me to
explain to me what had happened. It didn't set too well with me,
but in order to keep everything under control we agreed that she
would go to the dance with this man and I would go alone. I guess
the fellow must have had some suspicion of the way things stood,
as he told her the next day when he was taking her home that he

350

noticed she and I seemed to feel very much better when we had our first dance together. He tried to question her about me and told her I didn't even own a cabin. She acted very innocent and unconcerned about the matter, but he must have figured he was out of the race, because he never came to call on her again.

When we got married we had to steal away like we did when we were courting. I borrowed a team and spring wagon and we had to drive forty miles and the snow was about belly deep on the horses. Then we had to wait over in Shelby until the next day to go to Great Falls. The job of getting her away from the ranch was the hard part of it. My wife's room was upstairs in her home and we agreed that she would throw her stuff out the window about eight o'clock at night and I would pick it up and carry it to the wagon I had parked about 100 yards from the house. I didn't have any idea how much stuff she had until she began throwing it out—clothes, suitcases, shoes and everything else that a woman ever wore, and besides, she used to play the piano and she had great bales of sheet music and every time one of those bales of music hit that frozen ground it sounded like someone had shot a high powered rifle and the stuff fell right in front of a window down stairs and the window curtains were up. Her father sat reading about ten feet from where I was picking it up. I would take all I could carry on my back to the wagon and come back for another load, and as she was still throwing stuff out while I was gone there would be a bigger pile than ever when I got back. I believe she would have thrown the piano out too if the window had been big enough, and the worst part of it was her father had two bloodhounds and they bellowed and howled every time she threw out a fresh cargo. It was a very cold night and I wore a big fur overcoat and every time I bent over to pick up a package they would howl louder than ever. They thought I was some kind of animal. I tried whispering to them to get out and keep still and that would bring a bigger howl than ever. I was watching her father pretty close through the window and every once in a while he would cock his head sideways to listen and acted like he was going to get up and come out, then would settle down and go to reading again. During those intervals, my heart was sure pounding and I was all sweaty with fear. I have often heard of people being very nervous when they placed the bride's ring on her finger, but I know that is nothing compared to the ordeal I went through. I forgot, and left a lot of things around where I loaded the wagon and it snowed a lot after that. Every time my wife missed something of hers, we would go to that spot and shovel snow.

Neither one of us had any idea of what it took to set up house-keeping and it is amazing what we bought. One thing we both agreed on was a carpet, as we intended to move into an old cabin that had big cracks in the floor. When we got home and checked our outfit, it seemed to be mostly carpet. Then I think every friend we ever had gave us a lamp for a wedding present, so we had a whole wagonload of carpets and lamps. We had hanging lamps, floor lamps and lamps to throw away, but hardly anything else in the way of housekeeping. When we arrived back in Shelby there were about 25 cowboys in town that had come to celebrate Christmas (it being Christmas week we were married) and they were all at the train to meet us. Most of them had a good sized Xmas jag on and the different congratulations I got from that bunch would sure sound funny today if I could remember them all. They were all old time cowboys that I had worked with for years. We all went to a saloon to celebrate the event. Each one would take me aside to pour out his feelings and congratulations, and give me hell for stealing away to get married without telling them. Some of the names they called me wouldn't look good in print but that was their way of showing their true friendship. One old bowlegged fellow that I had known from the time I was a kid had a little more joy juice aboard than the others. He didn't have much to say, but stood at the end of the bar and drank regularly while the celebration was going on. He had one cock eye and kept watching me all the time until he got an opportunity to attract my attention. He nodded to me to come over to where he was. I went over to him and he looked at me silently for a moment and said, "Well, you're married, are you?" I said yes, and he asked, "Did you marry a white woman?" I answered yes, and he said "You done damn well, but I feel sorry for the girl." In the meantime, while we were away getting married, my wife's father wrote her a letter to Shelby where we had our team and wagon and told her all was forgiven and to come home, which we did.

I went to work for him and as he owned plenty of cattle and horses I seemed to be just the kind of a son-in-law he needed, but we sure had a supply of carpet and lamps that we didn't know what to do with.

RED RIVER VALLEY

Undoubtedly the best known "country party" song of the Montana plains and mountains is the familiar "Red River Valley," which was probably brought in by the earliest settlers from Dakota. It is also the most popular song in English among the French-speaking métis or halfbreeds, who were popular fiddlers and singers at early-day parties and whose "home," in so far as the unfortunate wanderers had any, was the Red River Valley of Canada. Carl Sandburg notes in *The American Songbag* (Harcourt, Brace, 1927) that an optional last line for the refrain is "the halfbreed that's waiting for you." Only a couple of verses and the chorus are given here; there are many stanzas and many different versions, some of which may be found in the *Songbag* or in the Lomax collection, *Cowboy Songs and Other Frontier Ballads*. Sandburg says the song was originally "In the Bright Mohawk Valley" and underwent many transmutations as the frontier moved westward.

FROM this valley they say you are going,
We will miss your bright eyes and sweet smile,
For they say you are taking the sunshine
That brightens our pathway awhile.

CHORUS:

Come and sit by my side if you love me,
Do not hasten to bid me adieu,
But remember the Red River Valley
And the girl that has loved you so true.

For a long time I have been waiting
For those dear words you never would say,
But at last all my fond hopes have vanished,
For they say you are going away.

THE RURAL TELEPHONE

HUGHIE CALL

All states have rural telephones, but the isolation of many Montana ranch homes gives the precarious link with civilization which the "party line" represents an added importance. Many are the tales— mostly funny but a few tragic—about these phone lines, some of which are strung on barbed-wire fences. This is another chapter from Hughie Call's *Golden Fleece*.

ALL the problems of that first summer were problems of adjustment to fixed customs and a way of living foreign to anything I'd known before. I was new and the customs and standards of living were as old as the state itself. I was convinced that I'd have to fit in with the accepted way of living as quickly as possible, but some of the customs were a little more than I could take.

Foremost among these was the habit our neighbors had of 'listening in' on the country telephone line. This practice was general, and its matter-of-fact acceptance was revolting to me. I could scarcely conceal my distaste when anyone related a bit of news in my presence and casually admitted that he'd heard it while listening to a telephone conversation which I felt sure was not meant for his ears.

I can 'listen in' as brazenly as the rest now. It's one of my favorite diversions, but in those days, before my children were born, I could no more have stooped to 'eavesdropping' than I could have tampered with Uncle Sam's mail.

This lack of tolerance and understanding was unfortunate. Had I spent even a small part of my time 'listening in' that first summer I should not have been lonely and I should have been encouraged to learn that other ranch wives had problems which, if not the same, were as hard to iron out as my own. But a lot of water ran under the bridge before I became convinced that there was nothing secret or shameful about 'listening in' and regretted my smugness.

The country telephone is something more than mere wires strung on tall poles, than receivers and mouthpieces. It is a living, vibrant

354

thing which welds the interests and problems of isolated communities in a way that is past understanding.

The telephones are even equipped with a convenience for the eavesdropper—a little gadget on the left side of the instrument which can be released if you want to talk or left in place if you'd rather listen. Thus is quiet ensured. A mother can balance a fretting baby on her hip and get the news without having to worry lest the noise disturb her neighbors.

Many ranch wives do their own work and have only snatches of time between dishwashing and potato-peeling and the cooking and serving of three huge meals a day. They may have a spare moment to listen, but no time to become involved in talk. The country telephone has all the advantages of the radio or the talking machine. It can be turned on or off at will. No danger of your pies burning while you learn the latest local news, for you can leave your post without seeming rude, take a peek at the pies and come back again. You may have missed a little, but you can always catch up if the conversation interests you enough.

I shall never forget my first contact with 'listening in.' I walked into the dining-room one morning to find Jennie leaning indolently against the wall, the receiver glued to her ear. This surprised me. Until that day I had never seen Jennie idle. Ordinarily she whizzed around with a purpose and energy that put me to shame. I was pleased to see her take time off for—I supposed—a chat with a friend.

I had come downstairs to ask some question and I went on into the kitchen to wait until she was through. She didn't get through. Moments elapsed before it dawned on me that Jennie was eavesdropping.

Grim with disapproval, I came back to the dining-room, pulled a chair out from the table and sat down. Jennie might have me bested and on the defensive where ranch work was concerned, but I felt I could teach her a thing or two about ethics and I meant to do it.

I waited and Jennie listened.

The moments ticked on and finally I said, 'Jennie, I'd like to speak to you.' I was not handling this matter well and the knowledge put an edge of sharpness to my voice.

I expected her to drop the receiver sheepishly, but not Jennie. She gestured for silence and listened ten minutes longer. When at last she put the receiver back on its hook and turned about, I was too angry to care what I said and I voiced my distaste in no uncertain terms. Her calm eyes widened with surprise.

'Why, Missus,' she told me, as though conveying a fact I'd be delighted to hear, 'that's all right. Everybody listens. You're supposed to. It's a good thing I did. Ellison's ditch broke and flooded the road for a quarter of a mile. Old man Thayer's stuck down there with a truck full of hogs and Jim Anderson's taking a team to pull him out. He . . .'

I cut her short and explained with all the patience I could muster that I was not interested in other people's business. I should have said more, but she interrupted excitedly: 'But Missus, it *is* our business. The Boss's trucks was coming that way with cottonseed cake. If they get stuck, it'll take a block and tackle to get them out. I'm going to ring down the line and ask the Thextons to send them up through the field.'

That took a little of the wind out of my sails, but I was still unconvinced and indignant. When she had delivered her message, I warned her that I never wanted to see her 'listening in' again.

She took me literally. I never *saw* her do it, but oh, how she listened! That woman knew everything that happened within a radius of fifty miles and she naïvely regaled the ranch hands at meal time with the gossip. She knew that the Ellisons had sowed their oats before the 'shiftless Burtons' had more than broken their ground. She knew when the Lawtons sold their hogs and what they got for them. She was righteously indignant when the doctor in a near-by town refused to bring the Burton baby into the world, because he hadn't yet been paid for the last five Burton heirs. This story shattered my heroic reserve and I urged Jennie to go right down and see what she could do; I even offered to take her down.

'Grandma Bassett'll go. She's the closest.'

'But she may not know about it. It would be criminal to leave that poor woman alone at a time like this!'

She looked me squarely in the eye before she turned back to her work. 'Don't worry,' she said. 'She *knows*.'

She did know. I later learned that Grandma Bassett had taken immediate charge of the Burton affairs, had browbeaten the doctor into making another entry on the debit side of his ledger, and furthermore had stayed with the mother until she was up and about again.

Several months later a lamb buyer telephoned Tom and offered him nine dollars per hundredweight for his lambs. Tom would not commit himself, but promised to think it over. No sooner had he put down the phone than our ring came through. I answered, and a woman's excited voice called over the wire: 'Tell Tom not to take nine dollars for his lambs. I heard that lamb buyer make Jim Anderson the same offer last night and Jim upped him to nine dollars and a quarter.'

I did a sum in mental arithmetic before I replaced the receiver. That message would make Tom some money. Jennie eyed me expectantly as I turned away from the phone, but I took a mean advantage. I refused to relay the message until Tom and I were alone.

These two incidents gave me food for thought, but it took something that struck even closer to bring me into line. Leigh was not quite a year old at the time. Jennie had married a 'dry farmer' and we had a man cook. I wouldn't admit that it was dull without Jennie, for if it was, I knew why. I missed her chatter—and her 'listening in.'

One afternoon during the first lamb drive of the season, the ranch was deserted save for Cy, the cook, my young son and I. Cy adored the baby and spent all his spare time amusing him. I had letters to write, so I left them together on the back porch and went upstairs to my desk. Cy had been peeling green apples, and upon my return I found the baby alone, gurgling gleefully, with his small mouth full of apple peelings. I was frightened, of course, and worried throughout the balance of the afternoon because I couldn't be sure just how many peelings he had swallowed.

By ten o'clock that night I knew he had swallowed too many. He grew restless, cried out repeatedly in his sleep and began to run a temperature. I did everything I knew to do, but my efforts were futile. Around midnight his body began to twitch and draw. I considered calling Cy, but to do so I should have to go to the bunkhouse, some eight hundred yards away, and I dared not leave my son.

Terrified, I sped down the stairs and tried to call the doctor. His wife answered the telephone. She told me he was out in the country, on a maternity case; she doubted if she could get word to him.

'You've got to get word to him!' I gasped. 'I'm all alone, and I'm afraid my baby is having convulsions!'

She assured me she would try, but she didn't sound encouraging. I was frantic with fear, and for a moment I clung shakily to the receiver, wondering if there was anything else I could do. Even now Leigh could die before the doctor got back to town and then drove all those miles to our ranch. . . . Just as I was on the point of returning the receiver to the hook, a woman's voice called out:

'See here, child, have you any hot water?'

'Yes . . . *Yes.*'

'Put your baby into a warm bath right away, and get some cold compresses on his head. Jeff's backing out the car this minute and I'll be with you as soon as I can make it.'

If you've ever been alone, ignorant and helpless, with someone you love slipping away before your eyes, you'll know what that message meant to me. I carried out her instructions, eased the small, rigid body of my son into a warm bath and placed cold compresses on his head. After what seemed hours to me, my neighbor arrived.

She took charge with the efficiency that comes of long practice, while I carried out her orders. We fought shoulder to shoulder—I, white and shaken and no doubt clumsy and ineffectual; she, grimly, but very, very surely. Ah, that woman, that blessed woman. I can hear her now . . . 'There, he's comin' out of it . . . Look, his eyes is back natural . . . Now his breathing's easier . . . You ain't sick, you onery rascal. You're just tryin' to scare your poor ma to death.'

When the doctor's car drove up to our door, Leigh was sleeping quietly and naturally. The doctor assured me that everything had been done as he himself would have done it.

There are some things you can't thank people for, things that are too big for words, but I clung to my neighbor's work-worn hand and did my feeble best. She patted my shoulder in her friendly fashion and laughed.

'Lord, child, you needn't thank me, just give thanks for the party line. I knew nobody would be ringing town that time of night unless they were in trouble. I just naturally had to get up and listen.'

She didn't think she'd done anything unusual. She'd have done the same thing for anybody. But I had learned a lesson. From that time on I 'listened in' brazenly and I was never dull any more.

One afternoon I overheard a rancher's wife call him in town and tell him to bring home some bread. They expected the threshers the next day, and she couldn't bake because something had gone wrong with her yeast. Her husband was so absent-minded that he was a community joke, and I worried about that bread until I heard his car rattling down the hill. It was a mere skeleton—that car. A box, nailed to a few boards, formed the seat. Nothing was hidden; even the engine had no hood. If the bread was there I couldn't help but see it, and I rushed out to the yard to have a look. Sure enough, he'd forgotten the bread. Before I had time to think, I found myself running down the road in his wake.

'You've forgotten Bertha's bread!' I shrieked. 'We baked today. You'd better take some of ours.'

The car stopped with a sudden grinding of brakes. He got out and thanked me sheepishly. As I packed the still warm loaves in a box it never occurred to him to ask, 'How did you know that Bertha needed bread?' and it never occurred to me to enlighten him.

Another time, in the busiest part of haying season I overheard a hardware merchant in town telling a rancher that it would take three days to get new teeth for a broken rake. 'Hay-diggers' work against time in this country. The season is so short that every hour counts. I knew that the laying up of a rake for three days was nothing short of a tragedy. We had the same kind of rakes and some extra teeth. I got into my car and took them down to him. He was grateful, but not a whit surprised.

I don't think I ever knew the real meaning of neighborliness until I came to Montana. Ours was a large, closeknit family. We were sufficient unto ourselves, and had few contacts with our neighbors. In my home city I sometimes sent flowers when I happened to learn that a neighbor was ill. In this country, with the doctor miles away, illness can assume alarming proportions. You always know about it, via the rural telephone line. You don't send flowers, you *take* an extra hot-water bottle, a bag of ice or a change of bed linen. Sometimes the only help you can give is releasing a worried mother from the kitchen, for ranch work must go on, illness or no. But whatever there is to do, you do it gladly, knowing full well that when trouble strikes, the same will be done for you.

I never complain now when I'm trying desperately to hear over long distance, although every receiver that goes down weakens the telephone circuit more and more. I just yell a little louder.

I'll have to confess that there are times when I wish I had the courage of a Forest Ranger in our district. There was a rumor abroad that the Government intended lowering grazing fees on the Forest, and this was a matter of vital importance to every sheep-man on the line. All the receivers were down and it became increasingly harder for the Ranger to hear. Presently he could no longer hear. Patience exhausted, he slammed the receiver down on the hook and gave the general ring.

'Listen, folks,' he begged, 'I can't make head nor tail of what the supervisor says unless you hang up. Do it as a favor to me and when I'm through talking, I'll ring back and tell you what he says!'

He didn't keep his word, though, and I've always had a grudge against him. I had to learn the Government's decision from a neighbor who was 'on to him' and wasn't taking a chance on missing a single thing.

PREFACE TO A BLUE BOOK

"JOHN BOYLE O'REILLY"

Butte, the incomparable, has had everything any other city has had and some things other cities never dreamed of. New York had a Blue Book, so Butte had one, too—just one, published in 1901 and apparently greeted with something less than acclaim, since it was never reprinted, even though the lines of social distinction were "not too closely drawn." (Somehow or other, "Personnel of the Press" got in, along toward the back.) Present residents of Butte say they think the book was compiled by a barnstorming outfit from "outside." The introduction, some of them insist, was written by a Butte wag and was intended all the time to be a joke (which is the most charitable way to look at it). At any rate, whoever wrote it chose to remain anonymous, taking as a pseudonym the name of the great Irish patriot of that time, a hero to a large share of the population of the greatest mining camp on earth. Joke or no joke, Butte's society took itself seriously in those days, and had the money (and frequently the cultural background) to support its pretensions.

ALL of Butte's society ladies have dreaded the task of preparing a list of guests for a reception or other important social function. The cards of calling acquaintances, and the invitations of other hostesses, even if preserved, do not furnish complete data. Then, too, man, like the feathered tribe, has strong migratory instincts which he gratifies to the extent of occasionally changing his address, to the perplexity of his would-be hostess and calling acquaintances.

It is the design of the compiler of the Butte Blue Book to lighten the task of arranging lists, and to furnish a family directory that will be of practical use.

Every possible effort has been made to secure a complete list of the prominent people of the community, with special reference to those who figure conspicuously in the social world, where it will be found that the lines have not been too closely drawn. In its arrangement, the plans adopted by the publishers of similar books in the larger cities have been followed, with the result that several features of special interest and value and new to Butte have been introduced.

The chief claim of merit made for the Butte Blue Book, however, is that it is up to date and will fill all needs for such a work for a considerable time to come.

THE MOOR IN ALDER GULCH

EDWARD B. NEALLEY

This early venture in social survey and dramatic criticism is taken from "A Year in Montana," published in the *Atlantic Monthly* in August, 1866. It was probably the first magazine article about Montana. Its author, Edward B. Nealley, was United States attorney for Montana Territory at the time he wrote it. Not only was it the first magazine article and the first nationally read comment on the Montana theater; at the end of the excerpt here reprinted the reader will find the first study of distinctive Montana speech terms, all of which are still familiar today. Nealley was a keen, though critical, observer.

THIS was the beginning of Virginia [Alder] Gulch, from which twenty-five millions of dollars in gold have been taken, and which has today a population of ten thousand souls. The placer proved to be singularly regular, almost every claim for fifteen miles being found profitable. From the mouth of the canon to its very end, among snows almost perpetual, are the one-storied log cabins, gathered now and then into clusters, which are called cities, and named by the miner from his old homes in Colorado and Nevada. In travelling up the crazy road, with frowning mountains at our left, and yawning pit-holes at our right, we pass seven of these cities—Junction, Nevada, Central, Virginia, Highland, Pine Grove, and Summit.

Virginia, the chief of the hamlets, has since developed into an organized city, and the capital of the Territory. Its site was not chosen for its natural beauty. Along the main gulch are the mines—huge piles of earth turned up in unsightly heaps. At one side of the mines, and up a ravine which crosses the gulch at right angles, lies the city. In shape it was originally like a letter T, but its later growth has forced new streets and houses far up the hillsides. Not so much regard was paid, in laying the foundations of the new city, to its future greatness, as Penn gave when he planned Philadelphia. The miner only wanted a temporary shelter, and every new-comer placed a log cabin of his own style of architecture next the one last built. Where convenience required a street, lo! a street appeared. There were no gardens, for beyond the narrow center of the ravine only sage-brush and cactus would grow. But the mines thrived, and also grew and thrived the little city and its vices.

Gradually a better class of buildings appeared. What were called hotels began to flourish but it was long before the monotony of bacon, bread and dried apples was varied by a potato. And for sleeping accommodations, a limited space was allotted upon the floor, the guest furnishing his own blankets.

A theater soon sprang up. And either because of the refined taste of some of the auditors, or the advanced talent of the performers, the playing was not the broad farce which might have been entertaining, but was confined to Shakespeare and heavy tragedy, which was simply disgusting. This style of acting culminated in the *début* of a local celebrity, possessed of a sonorous voice and seized with a sudden longing for Thespian laurels. He chose the part of Othello, and all Virginia assembled to applaud. The part was not well committed, and sentences were commenced with Shakespearean loftiness and ended with the actor's own emendations, which were certainly questionable improvements. Anything but a tragic effect was produced by seeing the swarthy Moor turn to the prompter at frequent intervals, and inquire, "What?" in a hoarse whisper. A running colloquy took place between Othello and his audience, in which he made good his assertion that he was rude in speech. Since then, Shakespeare has not been attempted on the Virginia boards. "Othello's occupation's gone"; and all tragic efforts are confined to the legitimate Rocky mountain drama. "Nick of the Woods" has frequently been produced with great applause, though the illusion is somewhat marred by the audible creaking of the wheels of the boat in which the Jibbenainosay sails triumphantly over the cataract.

Gold dust is the only circulating medium in the Territory, and is the standard of trade. Treasury notes and coin are articles of merchandise. Everybody who has gold has also his little buckskin pouch to hold it. Every store has its scales, and in these is weighed out the fixed amount for all purchases according to Troy weight. An ounce is valued at eighteen dollars, a pennyweight at ninety cents, and so on. It is amusing to notice how the friction of the scales is made by some men to work them no loss. In *weighing-in,* the scale-beam bows most deferentially to the gold side; but in *weighing-out,* it makes profound obeisance to the weights. The same cupidity has given rise to two new terms in the miners' glossary—*trade dust* and *bankable dust*. Bankable dust means simply gold, pure and undefiled. Trade dust is gold with a plentiful sprinkling of black sand, and is of three grades, described very clearly by the terms *good, fair,* and *dirty*. The trader, in receiving our money, complains if it does not approximate what is bankable, but in paying us his money, pours out a combination in which black sand is a predominating ingredient. Many merchants even keep a saucer of black sand in readiness to dilute their bankable gold to the utmost thinness it will bear.

In all new and thinly settled countries, many ideas are expressed by figures drawn from the pursuits of the people. Among the Indians, more than half of every sentence is expressed by signs. And miners illustrate their conversation by the various terms used in mining. I have always noticed how clearly these terms conveyed the idea sought. Awkwardness in comprehending this dialect easily reveals that the hearer bears the disgrace of being a "pilgrim," or a "tenderfoot," as they style the new immigrant. To master it is an object of prime necessity to him who would win the miner's respect. Thus the term "adobe," the sundried brick, as applied to a man, signifies vealiness and verdancy.* A "corral" is an enclosure into which herds are gathered; hence a person who has everything arranged to his satisfaction announces that he has everything "corralled." A man fortunate in any business has "struck the pay-dirt"; unfortunate, has "reached the bed-rock." Everything viewed in the aggregate, as a train, a family, or a town, is an "outfit." I was much at a loss, on my first arrival, to comprehend the exact purport of a miner's criticism upon a windy lawyer of Virginia,—"When you come to pan him out, you don't find color." But this vocabulary is not extensive, and the pilgrim soon learns to perceive and use its beauties.

* Because the basic component of "adobe" is soft mud.

THE HORRORS OF ANACONDA

C. H. EGGLESTON

One of Montana's bitterest—and, this long after the event, funniest —political struggles developed in the fight between Helena and Anaconda for the state capital, decided by popular vote in 1894. Helena won. The battle is reputed to have cost a million dollars, most of it spent by two of the "copper kings"—W. A. Clark, who backed Helena, and Marcus Daly, who backed Anaconda. The contest also gave rise to one of Montana's best political hoaxes, the pamphlet titled *Helena's Social Supremacy.* It bore a Helena imprint and was ostensibly published by that city's capital committee as one of a series, following two others which actually had been published there; but in fact it was written by C. H. Eggleston, assistant editor of Daly's *Anaconda Standard.* That newspaper incautiously let the cat out of the bag by commenting on the little book's popularity and reporting a new edition under way. Clark's *Butte Miner* raved: "Coarse . . . insulting . . . vulgar . . . libel . . . slander . . . forgery." Culprit Eggleston, secure in his anonymity, chuckled and went on writing *Standard* editorials needling Helena. Another Eggleston product, the poem "When Bryan Came to Butte," appears elsewhere in this book. And here's a sample chapter of *Helena's Social Supremacy,* one which follows several describing the manifold beauties of Helena, including its Montana Club—the state's only men's residence club and still functioning.

IN contrast to Helena with her elegance and ease, her manifold graces and refinements, the supreme niceties and brilliancies of her drawing rooms, what do we find in Anaconda? A rude, rough smelter town, rooted in vileness and vulgarity; a town nine-tenths of whose population toil the year around at manual labor; big, strong, coarse workingmen, who could not tell a german from a wheelbarrow; with so erroneous a conception of the proprieties that, so far from exhibiting a sense of mortification and chagrin, they seem to take a sort of conscious pride in going to and from their work in soiled overalls and with huge dinner buckets; laborers, mechanics, artisans, bricklayers, copper dippers, whose average wages reach only $105 a month; living in small cottages with ridiculous wives and children; spending their spare time cultivating their little, sawed-off gardens, going to low picnics, and organizing and perfecting labor unions, which, as Helena is informed and believes, are the greatest curse of the modern world.

The Helena capital committee has no desire to speak disrespectfully of Montana's working classes. The constitutional convention in 1889 saw fit to give them the right to vote. Helena will not dispute the wisdom of the constitutional convention. Its work is done and further argument is useless. But we submit to the candor, the honesty, the intelligence, the patriotism of the workingmen themselves whether they will vote to locate the capital of this great state, destined, as it undeniably is, to be one of the richest in the union—whether they will vote to locate the capital of Montana in a town where their own class so overwhelmingly predominates. They surely must perceive the peril of such a procedure. According to all history and all tradition and all experience, legislative bodies must be removed from contact with the common people. To fulfill their purpose, to realize their ideals, the lawmakers of a state, or of a nation, must, while they are in session at least, be surrounded constantly by people who can feed them on culture and champagne. In Montana this desideratum is found, and found only, in the city of Helena—Helena the refined, the fascinating, the fastidious, the magnificent!

Mark the vivid and powerful contrast presented by Anaconda, the very antipodes to Helena in this as in all essential regards; a town literally swarming with thousands of plain, common people of humble origin and modest means; more than that, a town within 45 minutes' ride of Butte, the greatest mining camp on earth, with its hordes upon hordes of miners, with their big hands, and big feet, and big labor organizations, and big notions of what they want in the way of legislation, aggregations of men who would certainly keep cases on the legislature, and bother and annoy and worry its life. God forbid that the legislation of Montana shall ever be subject to such dangerous influences.

The workingmen of Montana, the miners and ranchers, the smelter men, the railroad men, the timber cutters and loggers, the cowboys and sheep herders and bull punchers, these men are not fools: they recognize the self-evident truths we have asserted: they see at a glance the incomparable advantages of Helena with her fine ladies and gentlemen, her personages of birth and distinction, her hosts of aristocrats with their courtly grace and polished

366

demeanor and Broadwater baths, generously devoting all their
time and energy to the upbuilding of a society of Parisian magnificence—the working-men of Montana, we repeat, admit the immeasurable superiority of Helena over Anaconda, with nothing
but her mobs of clodhoppers; good enough people, some of them,
perhaps, in their way, but without a title to their names, or a
four-in-hand to their barns, or a *femme de chambre* to their wives,
or a nursery maid to their children, or a cask of wine to their
cellars, or a skeleton to their closets—or, saddest and most pitiable
of all, a dress suit to their backs!

ROADHOUSE GIRL

JASON BOLLES

Montana has sun and space and clean air and countless fishermen along a thousand streams. It also has a tradition of reckless living, free spending, and late hours; to satisfy these urges it has a profusion of bars and roadhouses. Some of these are not far removed from the hurdy-gurdy house of the gold-rush frontier, which was a dance hall and saloon, sometimes with what we now call a "floor show" but what was then a music hall "turn." (The hurdy-gurdy was not, contrary to the belief of some who read about it today, a house of ill repute.) Here, in a poem by the late Jason Bolles of Bozeman which appeared in Vol. XI of *The Frontier*, May, 1931, and later in his book *Magpies' Nest,* is a vivid picture of "a new joint." This was in the dry era, but the "joint," minus the slot in the door, is probably still running. One wonders what has happened to Baby. Other selections from the work of Jason Bolles and notes on his life appear on pages 403 and 404.

O UT by the Ten Mile Hill where the white road lifts,
     Curved like a striking snake to the gaunt hills sunning,
     Where aspens green and hawthorn petal drifts,
And the river ripples, there is a new joint running.
The headlights swerve where the red gate opens wide,
    There's a slotted door where you stand while keen eyes peek,
There's a big log room with tables around the side
    And a wheel and a bar and a glare and a blare and a reek.

There's a slim kid sitting, and banging on the box,
    Over in the corner by the slot machines,
Black eyes flashing through black tossing locks,
    With a jiggling glass beside her, and she's only in her 'teens.
White fingers flashing, deep voice rolling,
    Strong sweet shoulders, jouncing to the jazz;
Whispering, pleading, moaning, and cajoling,
    Brother, what it takes, she has!
"Take me down to that town in old Virginny"—
    "He's my man, an' he done me wrong!"—
"Some likes a gal with a shape that's skinny,"—
    "How long, Baby, how long?"

Outside the wall are the crags and the moonlit ranches,
  And a man who is hired to rummage the unlocked cars.
The long white headlights sweep through the balsam branches,
  And a lone coyote howls to the marching stars.

  The kid's got a sweetie in the Copper Rivet mine,
    Cranking on a liner in a long, dim vault,
  Sweating in a crosscut by the carbide shine—
    Jesus watch above him if they run into a fault!
  "How long, Baby, how long?" that's your chorus.
    The loose slabs fall while they're mucking out the round,
  If one lights on him he will come home porous—
    Sing! while your white hands pound.
  There'll be no more loving when the Copper Rivet hugs him,
    Though your arms be white and tender and your shoulders
      sweet and strong.
  No more kisses when the gray granite mugs him,
    How long, Baby, how long?

  Bright shoes fumble on the new oak floor,
    Girls can drink a lot before their feet forget to dance,
  Six more suckers hammer on the door,
    Eager to gamble where they haven't got a chance.
  Step, slide, shuffle, shuffle (God, that stuff is heady)
    Moonshine highballs rattle on the bar,
  Flushed girls slump against partners none too steady.
    Whoop! "He's mah man—" Stamp! How the windows jar!

  Tramp the shiny pedals with slim legs silken gay—
    Never clap your hands, boys, that's no way to do!
  Say, "Waiter, bring the little lady something and I'll pay."
    (Tony, make it wine, please, my throat is split in two!)
  Throat ache—head ache—ache in lovely shoulders,
    "Only one o'clock, kid, let's have another song!"
  Drag at your inside like your shape was full of boulders,
    How long, Baby, how long?

There's a path from the porch to a spring, and a grove uprearing,
  And a shadowy great rock, half as large as the house.
Wild lilies under the moon at the side of the clearing,
  And the chirp of a bird, and a yell from the big carouse.

How long can you keep up that husky, honeyed singing?
  How long can you keep hitting the liquor every night?
How long can you stand to have the lily buds upspringing,
    And you shut from your sweetheart and the hawthorn
      boughs so white?
How long's that slick-haired gambler had his eyebrow cocking?
  How long d'you think he's carried that Chinese strangling
    thong?
How long before you wake up with a bill inside your stocking?
  How long, Baby, how long?

By the Ten Mile Hill, where the road swoops down to the river,
  Where the trim square ranch fields crowd to the greening
    wood,
There's a new joint open, with stuff that will crisp your liver,
  And a mamma who shouts the blues, and the kid is good!

HANS

MARY HARTWICK

Appearance of this story in the section of this volume titled "Social Life" may seem odd, yet the chief value of the tragic little piece, in the editor's opinion, lies in its strong picture of a Montana neighborhood in a time of crisis, when the quick friendliness and the will to action born of frontier living are seen at their best. There are countless such instances—neighbors rallying to rebuild the burned farm or help the suddenly crippled farmer with his crops, and many others. This story appeared in *The Frontier*, Vol. VIII, No. 3, May, 1928. Mrs. Mary Hesse Hartwick's home is near Holland Lake, north of Missoula; she was a frequent contributor to *The Frontier* and an account of her own homesteading experience in the mountains won her an award in a *Scribner's* "Life in America" contest.

THIS is the story of Hans, my neighbor, whose homestead lies beyond mine a mile farther from the Ranch. It begins on a November night five years ago.

The moon came up from behind the long white scarp of Holland Peak. Across the narrow valley, it lit up the snowcaps of the Mission Range, so that they stood out clear against the steel-blue of a winter sky. The light crept down over the glacier fields and fell on the green shoulders of the forest. It searched out the canyons and little swales of the foothills. And the clearing and the little cabin of Hans.

The slanting moonbeams struck fire to the snow crystals. Clean and smooth and glistening lay the clearing of Hans. Gone the blackened stumps, the half-burned logs, the piles of stones and brush. Gone the wee lake and meadow, little intervals of grace here in the deep woods. Sunlit pool and field of waving blue monkshood lay deep in their winter sleep. There was nothing to break the surface of the snow, except the little cabin, crouching bravely and incongruously in the center of the clearing, defying with its bright-shining windows the utter solitude and the palpable spirit of the wilderness that pressed in from the shadowy walls of forest.

Inside the cabin, Hans sat on a bench tediously turning his furs rightside out. Anna was putting records on a tinkling phono-

371

graph. And up and down the floor spun the two children, Nord-land elves, silver-haired, with fringed gentian eyes, dancing with inherent grace. And as they danced, they let out squeals of ecstatic joy, like the bubbling over of some pure fountain of delight.

The young mother, in whose great dark eyes lay always some mystery of sadness and a far-away calm, was listening apprehensively now, for her quick ear had caught a crunching on the snow down by the gap. She sat still and waited, looking at Hans, but he was rustling the dry furs and did not hear. Anna sprang up with alarm at the sound of a knock on the door.

Hans, too, was startled. Dropping his work he hurried to the door. Then he began to chuckle, "Ha, ha, Oskar, where you going a night like this without your clothes on? Come on in, you must be froze." Then Hans stopped laughing, for Oskar, coming into the light, was deathly sick—and falling.

They got him into a chair and pulled off his steaming underwear and took the gum shoes off his half-frozen feet. "No, no, Hans, leave 'em on, I gotta go."

"Where did you come from, Oskar?" asked Hans.

"From the Ranch, of course. They had me in bed and my clothes hid. I left anyhow. I gotta get home and feed my dog and cat." And looking down at himself, "I can wear this blanket. You len' me some socks, will you, Hans? I gotta go."

Oskar wasn't going anywhere. After he had swallowed the hot milk that Anna brought, he caved in. Hans, after a tussle, hefted the overgrown boy onto the bed in the corner and imprisoned him in the blankets. And after a while, drowsily, "You feed my cat and dog, will you, Hans? You feed 'em."

Later, when the boy in the corner seemed to sleep and Hans slept in his chair, Anna crept softly over to the other bed and lay down with the children. She covered them up and put her arm around them. But Anna did not sleep.

In the morning Hans fed and cared for the boy and persuaded him to stay in bed. "You stay here, Oskar, while I go and feed your dog and cat, will you?" Oskar would. Hans would find some meat under a box on the porch and some canned milk under the floor by the stove. "Feed 'em good, Hans."

Incredibly swift went Hans, down his long lane in the forest.

Hans was used to skis and he was strong. And fear nipped at his heels and love lent wings. Hans flew.

Incredibly soon he fetched up at the door of the Ranch house. Still on his skis he was listening to the doctor from town.

"We can't let you come in. We are full of flu here—patients from the homesteads. Where did you come from?"

"Me?" Hans stared. "Me," he said dumbly. Then he started to chuckle. "Why, I came from another house full of flu—full by now, I guess."

Then he stopped his ghastly chuckling and told the doctor. And they followed him with a sled. For Hans had gone, as he had come.

Again he stood in his own door. When he could see, there was Anna in the corner, bending over the boy, rubbing something into his chest. She came forward. "He had a bad spell—coughing and choking. His lungs are rattly."

Hans went in and told Anna—very quietly, making light of it. She kept her whitening face turned away from the questioning eyes of the children. "He's too sick now to move. They can't take him out in this cold. We will have to move—into the shed."

Quickly, Hans picked up the still warm stove and carried it into the shed, leaving Anna's range, for Oskar would not want much heat. Then Hans went up a ladder nailed to the wall and threw down a lot of rugs, goatskins, homewoven blankets of purest wool, a featherbed, and big square downy pillows, treasures from the homeland. And Anna and the children snatched them up and ran to the shed.

"Tan we take the dolls and moosic and everysing, Daddy Hans?"

"Yah, take everything, run, quick." This was fun. So was the bathing and scrubbing and gargling, for they must be going somewhere, they were getting into their wraps and hurrying so. And the wee girl ran to find her muff of white rabbit skin, that Mother Anna had made. It had a red ribbon to go over her neck and a rosebud with green stem, nestling in the fluff. She loved her little muff and red mittens. They were bundled up and set out on a table in the sun, to air. And presently, Anna, herself scrubbed and renovated, took them into the shed.

It was evening when the sled came. The horses had had a hard

373

time in the lane, breaking road. The doctor went in for a while with Oskar. Then he came out and talked with Anna and looked into the shed and after giving Hans some medicine and instructions for Oskar, he went back to his other patients.

And Hans had to go in and tell Oskar. First Anna handed out some milk toast from the shed and Hans coaxed Oskar to eat it. Then he told him.

Oskar got mad and cursed. "The old son of a gun, comin' 'way up here to tell you that, 'stead o' doin' somethin' for me. Why, the missus has me almost well now—he's crazy, the dam old fool." And cursing and choking and arguing with himself, he fell back exhausted and lay still, staring.

Then in the gathering dusk—"Oh, Hans, come here. Hans, you do something for me. You tell me—it can't be, can it, Hans? Oh, I don't need to die, I want to live—I can get well, can't I, Hans?"

Hans was filled with a great compassion. He gathered his friend in his arms and steadily, soothingly, like a mother, comforted him. Then—"Take it like a gentleman, Oskar, go out like a gentleman. We all have to go, maybe soon. You shouldn't act like a baby, Oskar, you're a grown man. Attaboy, like a gentleman, now."

At long last, the boy turned his wet face from the wall. "Like a gentleman it is, Hans." And he tried to smile.

And as the long hours of the night wore out, peace came into the cabin of Hans. The two men were boys again, back in their homeland. Inarticulate Hans grew eloquent. He spoke with authority and persuasion. He got down books and read, and to make Oskar laugh sang some of the songs of their early days. And talked of their early teachings. When breath was scarce, the boy signalled, "Go on."

Hans, seeing how things were going, remembered his boyhood prayers:

> "Gud Fader, Son och den Helige And'
> Med all sine englars skara . . ."

When the moon withdrew its shining shaft from the west window, the soul of the boy went with it. Like a gentleman he went.

The next evening the sled came again. And went. Hans, turning from staring after it, began to dig a hole in the deep snow. He brought out Oskar's bed and things and burned them. Then he took off his own clothing and flung it into the flames. Taking a header into the soft snow, he came up chuckling and ran into the cabin. Soon there was such a smoke coming out through the shakes, that Anna called to know if he was burning the cabin down. Hans was fumigating, himself included.

After a few days they moved back. Hans let go some of the fear around his heart and took up his work. In the evenings Anna played the phonograph for the children while they danced. When they were asleep, she sat under the pedestal lamp that Hans had made out of the enlarged bole of a lodgepole pine and she was working the tiniest, most exquisite rosebuds on a tiny dress. Anna had the fingers of an artist. She had beautified the rude cabin with her handwork so that it was something like the homes she and Hans had grown up in. Mother Anna, whose children were always so becomingly dressed and their belongings so beautified. Anna who loved the little lake and the blue monkshood and waited for the coming of summer.

Sometimes Hans was writing letters. Hans loved to write, and wrote in several languages, a very fine hand. One letter he was writing was making the sweat stand out on his forehead and he spent a long time at the task. This was a letter to a girl overseas, waiting to hear from Oskar.

Then swiftly, Anna was stricken. The doctor came back on the day that he had set, to look in on them. He found Anna in bed and Hans waiting for him. He stayed two days. Looking at the children, he made a superhuman effort for the life of Anna. She was better when he returned to the Ranch. "I will come again day after tomorrow." And he told Hans what to do. And that her heart was getting weak.

Anna slept until towards evening. Then she began coughing or lying in a stupor. When she grew worse Hans propped her up and tried to help her. Later she begged not to take the medicine or treatments on her lungs. "I am tired, let me rest." She seemed better and breathed easily and her lungs did not fill up like Oskar's.

Later in the night, when Hans had been sleeping with his head dropped on the edge of her bed, she called to him. "I will not be here with you in the morning, Hans, I'm going too." She told him

375

calmly, with resting from the exhaustion of speech, and made him be still and listen. "No, you will only make me worse, it's my heart; don't disturb me."

Hans was broken; he felt paralyzed. Still, he could scarcely believe, for Anna was so quiet and at ease. And once he read from her English Bible, at some of the places that opened easily from long wear—all running along the same theme—"Where wast thou when I laid the foundations of the earth—when the morning stars sang together? For He sayeth to the snow, be thou on the earth; likewise to the small rain, and to the great rain of His strength." And when Hans was reading about the green pastures, which Anna had marked in her book, he looked up to see if she were sleeping. Anna was more than sleeping. Anna had gone away. Gone quietly, without rebellion, without fear, facing forward.

And Hans sat in the light of the moon through the west windows, and waited for the morning. And with the first light of another day, he set to do the things Anna had told him to do.

Hans got the children up, first pulling the curtains about the other bed. He had already prepared their oatmeal and toast and cut the toast in tiny strips as Anna had done. The boy could mostly dress himself, except for the garters. And the little girl laughed at his awkwardness, and the boy told him how the girl's things went on.

Very dignified and straight they sat, like lady and gentleman, and did not cram. Very patiently, eyeing each other, they folded their little floursack napkins with the lovely initial topside. Then they both said at once—"Tak for Maden, Daddy Hans."

He lifted them down from their homemade high chairs and they stood quietly at attention, these well-mannered children of Hans, waiting to see what this brand new day would bring to them.

"We will go for a ride, while Mother Anna sleeps." He had already collected their wraps, making sure to get the muff and everything. Wrapping the little girl in a woollen blanket he stood her in his packsack and tied her mittens on at the wrists, and fastened her little red cap on with a big silk scarf. He took a lot of pains with her, then he set her outside, where the boy was waiting on the skis.

Then Hans went back inside. Soon they began to call him.

"We's waiting, Daddy Hans, hurry, tum on, es do." He came out and secured the door. When he turned to the children he was ironing out his countenance with the palm of his hand and Hans' smile, which he generally managed for his children, was all awry.

Picking up the packsack he put it on his shoulders and the head-band across his forehead. Stepping into the skis, he took the boy in his arms and started again down his long white lane in the forest. Not so swiftly, but with a great effort at haste.

So—he came into my clearing that day. Seeing the torture of his progress, I went to meet him and took the sleeping boy from his cramped arms. He slid the band off his wet forehead and swung the girl into his arms.

"Fru—Ma'am, I bring my children to you. They both sleep. Anna, my wife, is dead."

And even while I was unwrapping the bewildered children, now awake and yearning toward Daddy Hans, he was going. Refusing to wait for the food I offered to bring, he was going. "I go to get the sled for Anna."

Out through my clearing, back to the road, gaining momentum as he went—to get the sled for Anna.

WHISKEY

CHARLES M. RUSSELL

Charley Russell, Montana's beloved "cowboy artist," provides here not only a gay essay on the evils of drink—of which, it appears, he was not altogether convinced—but also a shrewd comment on liquor laws which discriminate against his friends the Indians. Peter Koch, in one of his pieces in the *Contributions*, gives this recipe for Indian whiskey: one quart of alcohol, a pound of rank, black chewing tobacco, a handful of red peppers, a bottle of Jamaica ginger, a quart of black molasses, and water from the Missouri River. This Russell story is from *Trails Plowed Under* (Doubleday, Doran, 1937).

WHISKEY has been blamed for lots it didn't do. It's a brave-maker. All men know it. If you want to know a man, get him drunk and he'll tip his hand. If I like a man when I'm sober, I kin hardly keep from kissing him when I'm drunk. This goes both ways. If I don't like a man when I'm sober, I don't want him in the same town when I'm drunk.

Remember, I ain't saying that booze is good for men, but it boils what's in him to the top. A man that beats his wife when he's drunk ain't a good man when he's sober. I've knowed drunks that would come home to mama loaded down with flowers, candy, and everything that they thought their wife would like. Other men that wouldn't take a drink never brought home nothing but laundry soap. The man that comes home drunk and licks his wife wouldn't fight a chickadee when he's sober. The drunk that brings home presents knows he's wrong. and is sorry. He wants to square himself. The man that licks his wife ain't sorry for nobody but himself, and the only way to make him real sorry is to beat him near to death.

There's a difference in whiskey—some's worse than others. Me and a friend drops into a booze parlor on the Canadian line. The man that runs this place is a friend of ours. I ain't mentioning no names but his front name's Dick. He's an old-time cowpuncher. He's bought a lot of booze in his day but right now he's selling it.

When me and my friend name our drink we notice there's

378

about ten men in this joint. Their actions tells us they've been using some of Dick's goods, but there ain't no loud talk. They are all paired off, talking low like they're at a funeral. I get curious and ask Dick if these gents are pallbearers that's spreading sorrow on his joint.

"No," says Dick, looking wise. "This ain't no cow-town no more. It's one of the coming farmer-cities of this country, and the sellers of all this rich land don't want nothing that'll scare away farmers, and I'm here to please the folks. Most of these tillers of the soil come from prohibition states where men do their drinkin' alone in the cellar. When you drink that way, it don't cost so much. The old-timer that you knew was generally on the square. When he got drunk he wanted everybody to know it and they did, if they were in the same town. Folks to-day ain't been able to sweep all this old stuff out but, like some old bachelors I know, they've swept the dirt under the bed, and what you don't see don't look bad.

"The gent that sold me this brand of booze told me there ain't a cross word in a barrel of it, and he told the truth. All these gents you see in here are pleasant without the noise. This bunch, if they stay to the finish, will whisper themselves to sleep. This booze would be safe for a burglar. I call it," says Dick, "whisperin' booze."

But as I said before, there's different kinds. I knowed a old Injun trader on the Missouri River that sold another kind. Back in the '80s the cowmen of Judith country was throwing their cattle north of the river. This old trader had a place on the river right where we crossed the cattle. All summer we were swimming herds.

I never knowed what made an Injun so crazy when he drunk till I tried this booze. I always was water shy and this old stream has got many a man, but with a few drinks of this trade whiskey the Missouri looked like a creek and we spur off in it with no fear. It was sure a brave-maker, and if a man had enough of this booze you couldn't drown him. You could even shoot a man through the brain or heart and he wouldn't die till he sobered up.

When Injuns got their hides full of this they were bad and dangerous. I used to think this was because an Injun was a wild man, but at this place where we crossed the herds there's about ten lodges of Assiniboines, and we all get drunk together. The squaws, when we started, got mighty busy caching guns and knives. In an hour we're all, Injuns and whites, so disagreeable that a shepherd dog couldn't have got along with us. Some wise cowpuncher had persuaded all the cowpunchers to leave their guns in camp. This wise man could see ahead an' knowed things was going to be messy. Without guns either cowpunchers or Injuns are harmless—they can't do nothing but pull hair. Of course the Injun, wearing his locks long, gets the worst of it. We were so disagreeable that the Injuns had to move camp.

It used to be agin the law to sell an Injun whiskey, but the law has made Injuns out of all of us now. Most new booze is worse than trade whiskey. Whiskey made all men brave. If nobody got drunk the East Coast would be awful crowded by this time. Maybe the leaders of the exploring party didn't drink, but the men that went with them did. It's a safe bet there wasn't a man in Columbus' crew that knowed what a maple-nut sundae was.

In the old times, when the world had lots of wild countries and some brave explorer wanted men to go up agin danger and maybe starvation, he don't go to the fireside of home lovers; he finds the toughest street in a town where there's music, booze, and lots of fighters—he ain't lookin' for pets. When he steps in this joint, he walks to the bar and asks them all up. He don't bar nobody, not even the bartender. He starts with making a good feller of himself. This sport don't ask nobody who he is, but while he's buyin' drinks he's telling about others that has gone to these countries and come back with gold in every pocket, an' it ain't long till all have signed up and joined. If there's any danger of them weakening, he keeps them drunk. There's been many a man that got drunk in St. Louis, and when he comes to out of this debauch he's hundreds of miles up the Missouri, on a line dragging a boat loaded with trade goods for the Injun country. If he turns back he's liable to bump into war parties, so he stays. This game is played on sailor, woods and river men. Cowpunchers were of the same kind of goods—all careless, homeless, hard-drinking men.

Fur traders were the first and real adventurers. They went to countries unknown—every track they made was dangerous. On every side were unseen savages. Such people as Colter, Bridger, and men of their stamp, these fellers were not out for gold or great wealth—they asked for little but life and adventure. They had no dreams of palaces. Few of them ever returned. The gold-hunter who came later loved the mountains for the gold he found in them, and some when they got it returned to the city, where they spent it and died in comfort. But most trappers kissed good-bye to civilization and their birthplace—took an Injun woman, and finished, nobody knowed how or where.

The cowboy was the last of this kind, and he's mighty near extinct. He came from everywhere—farms, big cities, and some of them from colleges. Most of them drank when they could get it.

As I said before, they're all Injuns now since the Volstead law. Just the other day I'm talking to a friend. Says he, "It's funny how crazy an Injun is for whiskey. A few days ago I'm riding along—I got a quart of booze in my saddle pocket. I meet an Injun. He sees what I got, and offers me the hoss he's riding for the quart. To a man that wants a saddle hoss, this one is worth a hundred dollars. I paid six for this moonshine."

"Did you make the trade?" says I.

"Hell, no!" says he. "It's all the booze I got!"

THE PEPPER SONG

This song (unfortunately its melody has been forgotten) is one of the few known to have been of native Montana origin. An old-timer, Lon Swan of Gardiner, recalled it in an interview with "Elno" which was printed in the Montana Newspaper Association's inserts for weeklies, on Nov. 28, 1938. Swan said it was sung in Emigrant Gulch (near Gardiner) and arose from an incident during a party there in 1878. A miner, disgruntled for some reason, sprinkled pepper on the dance floor and sneezes temporarily broke up the ball. Angry celebrators drew guns and a general slaughter threatened, but wiser counsels prevailed, the floor was swept, and the dance went on. The guilty man was never found. The song also had a chorus, which Swan had forgotten; it was mostly yodeling anyway, he said. The "gum slippers" mentioned in the first verse were the miners' rubber boots.

NEAR the Yellowstone River at a small mining town
    There lives a tribe of great fame and renown.
    They've naught but gum slippers to wear on their feet;
Their pants are all broken and out at the seat.

Their bald heads are full of mischief and fun;
    They shine like a mirror in the bright morning sun.
Their shirts never see either water or soap,
    And they have a strong odor like a poor antelope.

In getting up parties, they take great delight,
    If things don't suit 'em, they soon raise a fight;
They go get their pistols, they froth and they roar,
    And sprinkle red pepper all over the floor.

SUNDAY AT THE MINES

A. K. McCLURE

This account of life in the mining camps in the '60's is from *Three Thousand Miles through the Rocky Mountains,* by A. K. McClure, published by Lippincott in 1869. Its author was one of the keenest observers among the early travelers to Montana.

I HAVE seen the Far-Western people in almost every phase of life, and I have never, in a single instance, found respectful conduct on the part of a stranger met in any other way than with a just, if not a generous, measure of respect. I have already written of their horse-races, their theatres, their churches, their reading-rooms, and their proverbial hospitality. That they are merciless on "bilks" and pretenders generally, is true; but no matter how humble the straightforward visitor may be, he is received with the warmest cordiality, and will meet with generous hearts and welcome boards wherever he may find the camp of the miner. Every settlement in Montana, and every city as well, is a mining-camp. Virginia City is but the centre of the great Alder camp; and Helena is the same for the various gulches which surround it. They are sustained solely by the mining-interests about them, and the cities advance or recede with feverish haste just as the mines improve or degenerate. There are agricultural settlements in Deer Lodge, Jefferson, Madison, and Gallatin; but there is not a farmer—or ranchman, as they are called—who has not his claims, or fractions of claims, on various gulches and leads, and he is merely farming to live until his slumbering wealth is developed by others more able than himself.

As a rule, the successful gulch-miners are most improvident; and of the scores of men who came here without a dollar and made from ten to fifty thousand dollars of gold out of Alder Gulch, there are very few indeed who could to-day command one thousand dollars, while most of them are utterly "broke." Their necessary expenses were very heavy, but their needless expenses were usually much heavier. A newspaper would bring from one to two dollars in gold in the days of gulch-mining, but three years ago. A letter

383

usually cost five dollars. Flour cost from fifty cents to one dollar a pound; and everything else in proportion. A cat would sell very readily in the days of gulch-mining for one hundred dollars in gold, and the display of pets of any kind was one of the easiest means of reaching the miner's well-filled buckskin bag. Then came the gambler's claim, and the fever of speculation, and what the indulgence of the appetites left was mostly sure to be swept into the faro-bank or frittered away in some fancy purchase.

This restless, profligate, and heterogeneous mass has long since departed from Alder Gulch. Many of their rude and now tenant-less cabins remain; and the continuous ridges through the gulch for more than ten miles tell of the thousands of sturdy men who here delved for the precious metal, gathered it in fabulous sums, and scattered it as lavishly as they found it. Now most of them are spending their time in prospecting, and earn a precarious subsist-ence by resuming legitimate labor when stern necessity leaves them no other channel through which to find bread. I have al-ready spoken of this class of men. How much they do for the world, and how little for themselves, but few can appreciate. It is to them that the nation at large, and all who profit by mining-operations, are indebted for unlocking the vast wealth of the moun-tains; but the fruits of their labors are in most cases gathered by strangers. They sow through merciless storms and spiteful snows, while others reap in the sunshine of golden harvest.

Although there seems to be general safety to person and property in Montana, and a leaven of healthy moral tone apparently per-vades all circles, the outward signs of morality, as recognized in the East, are among the novelties of the Territory. Sunday is the main business-day of Virginia City. On that day the gambler's saloon, licensed by law, is gayest and receives its largest profits. Most of the stores are open and drive their briskest trade on that day. The streets swarm with miners, who gather in their week's wages or "clean up" in their pockets, and commerce readily ac-commodates itself to their wishes and wants. Every corner in the main street has an auctioneer, whose stentorian voice is raised to its utmost volume to compete with that of his rival who is bawl-ing out his bargains on the opposite corner; and through the crowd the horse-jockey and his mounted salesman ride, John-Gilpin-like, expecting everyone to look out for his own neck and limbs. "Cheap John," whose sign I have seen in every Western town, deals out heavy pepper-and-salt suits for thirty-five dollars each, and sends a score or two of the mountaineers home every Sunday in his favorite costume. He had trouble in fitting me when I called for a suit, and invited me to come on the following Sunday, when he would open his new goods. In answer to my inquiry whether Monday would not answer as well, he gave me a look of pity, as if he considered me totally unfitted for life in this region, and expressed the belief that I would soon "get over that Eastern notion." Of the six mills in this section, that of the Montana Gold and Silver Mining Company is the only one that suspends operations on Sunday.

Such a thing as a sermon I have neither heard nor heard of since I have been in Union City. Occasionally a stray shepherd comes along to look after his lost sheep wandering through the mountains; but as a rule the shepherd gets lost among the sheep, and seems to prefer glittering nuggets of gold from the gulches and mines to the promised glittering stars in his future crown for the salvation of souls. I have had bishops and divines at my frugal board; but they were merely viewing the confines of their commands, and did not tarry to expound the gospel.

There is now some show of Sunday in Union City, but by most Eastern observers it would be regarded as a microscopic view. The miners and other laborers reluctantly leave their work, and the mill stands in apparently uneasy solitude. Here may be seen an innocent game of quoits; there a pair of bronzed arms kneading the bread for the coming week; yonder the sounds of the axe tell that there will be a bountiful supply of firewood to serve through the days allotted to regular labor; and thus throughout the city the odd chores are done up to save what is regarded as the more precious time when wages can be earned. Some gather in their ponies—for many miners keep their ponies, letting them graze and roam at pleasure until wanted, when they seldom search in vain for them—and take a pleasure-ride; others, armed with pick and shovel, devote the day to prospecting for new mines. There is no Sunday-school, no church, no public observance of religious ceremonies in the city.

THE DANCE

D'ARCY McNICKLE

D'Arcy McNickle, of Irish and French-Indian parentage, spent much of his childhood on Montana's Flathead Indian Reservation, and wrote vividly of reservation life in *The Surrounded*, novel published in 1936 by Dodd, Mead, and copyrighted by the author. Born in 1904, he was educated in a government Indian school and public schools before majoring in English at Montana State University, from which he was graduated in 1925. He studied subsequently abroad and at Columbia University, and is now a field representative of the Office of Indian Affairs.

*D*E-DUM, *de-dum, de-dum, de-dum, de-dum . . .*
The drum had been beating since early morning, faintly, regularly, as if the earth had begun to pulse. It was a sound to quicken the blood. People still at home, going about their daily chores, listened, and then hurried to complete what was still to do that they might be free. The throb of the drum lifted their spirits, urged them forward. It was an intoxicant.

Dust rose from every road leading to St. Xavier and disappeared against the cloudless sky. The sun was at white heat. People were on the move, traveling in spring wagons, in carriages, on horseback, afoot. Every roadside barn and nearly every telephone pole was placarded with the announcement: "FOURTH OF JULY CELEBRATION: BUCKING CONTESTS: HORSE RACES: BASEBALL GAME: BIG INDIAN DANCE: DANCING AT NIGHT WITH RAGTIME MUSIC: COME ONE! COME ALL! RIDE 'EM COWBOY!"

In St. Xavier groups of men stood before the pool-halls, talking and laughing. Women passed, surrounded by their children; the little girls in starched dresses and ribbons flying, the boys rigged out like baseball players.

In the dusty streets horses reared and plunged at the sound of exploding firecrackers. The riders cursed, to the amusement of the onlookers. When one rider was hurled through a store window the crowd was delighted. On the Fourth of July everybody was a little bit crazy. They shouted "Let 'er buck!"

386

The older boys and girls eyed each other's new clothes and made remarks. They went about in groups, the girls with arms entwined, giggling, screaming. When a group of boys went down the street, girls followed—not too near, but not far behind.

Dogs fought in the street, firecrackers exploded, babies cried, mothers were worried. Nobody above the age of twenty had a really good time, but they wouldn't have been found enjoying themselves at home for anything.

Beneath all other sounds, and giving to movement as well as to sound a conscious rhythm, was the throb of the drum. . . .

Dum, de-dum, de-dum, de-dum, de-dum . . .

The dancing ground was a mile below St. Xavier, in a grove of willows and cottonwoods near Buffalo Creek. The circle of white tepees, with their smoke-stained tops, contained more than a hundred camps. People streamed out of St. Xavier, where many had left their rigs, going toward the encampment and the sound of the drum. Dust rose chokingly from the ground. The air seemed to be turning to fire.

In the early morning Archilde went to Modeste's lodge, one of the few old-time hide-covered tepees, and one of the handsomest. Within it, he found the old man sitting with his hands in his lap, in an attitude of contemplation, calling to mind the sweet peace of the past; his lips moved, his eyelids fluttered; in different dress he might have been taken for a priest preparing himself for some ceremony.

Modeste's old woman, a dried-up creature, but possessed of her sight and of surprising energy, was preparing Mike for the dance, and enjoying herself with the detached, suave humor of the aged. She was painting his face, applying red in a band across his cheeks, and then placing six white dots under each eye. In the old days this would have signified that each eye was to have the strength of six; today it signified no more than an old woman's fancy. She chuckled. Bells were attached to his ankles, and she shook each leg in turn to try the effect. Her smile exposed her toothless mouth.

Mike was quiet, but not dull, as he had been too much of late. Archilde watched him closely. His eyes were active, examining the old woman's paint pots and following her agile fingers. At odd times, he looked guardedly at Modeste, revealing a shyness which expressed his awe of the old man and his excitement at the drama he was to have a part in. If Modeste was a priest, Mike was his altar boy, and each was absorbed in the part.

Archilde did not wait for them to quit the lodge. Occasions of that sort, he knew, required a decent privacy. Intruders were not wanted, strange voices were unkind. The old man with the boy leading him would move across the prairie in their own dignity, and anyone would show them small respect who sought to share the honor with them.

He quit the lodge and went to his mother across the encampment. She too was occupied, making Narcisse ready. Watching her, Archilde felt suddenly happy. She was pleased with her duties in the way that only an old art or an old way of life, long disused, can please the hand and the heart returning to it. She took up the folded garments of beaded buckskin and placed them on her grandchild in a kind of devotional act that derived satisfaction from minute observances; in a matter so simple, the least part has its significance or it is all meaningless. Narcisse submitted to her mood and to her ministering, even to her hands removing his underclothing and leaving him momentarily naked.

Archilde could see that for his mother this was a real thing, and he had felt the same way a moment before in Modeste's lodge. For these old people it was real, almost real enough to make it seem like a spirit come from the grave. Watching his mother's experienced hands, he could guess how she had lived, what she had thought about in her childhood. A great deal had happened since those hands were young, but in making them work in this way, in the way she had been taught, it was a little bit as if the intervening happenings had never been. He watched the hands move and thought these things. For a moment, almost, he was not an outsider, so close did he feel to those ministering hands.

Upon leaving her lodge he went toward the dancing ground— and at once his feeling changed. There was nothing real in the scene he came upon. The rows of carriages and wagons were bad enough, but that wasn't the worst. The idea was of a spectacle, a kind of low-class circus where people came to buy peanuts and look at freaks.

The dancing ground was a round pavilion, about thirty feet in diameter, with upright posts supporting a roof of fir boughs laid across poles. A tall post was planted in the center of this circular ground, and its upper end, protruding above the roof of boughs, flew the American flag. Benches were placed inside for the dancers.

This pavilion was surrounded by selling booths decorated with bunting, and the crowd was coaxed to buy "ice col' pop" and "strawb'ry ice cream" and to win a "cute Frenchy doll" on the roulette wheel. The crowd was dense and perspiring.

The drum was placed flat on the ground within the pavilion and the drummers sat around it, beating it with short sticks, the ends of which had been covered with red flannel. As they beat time they also sang, without words, a sort of "HI-yih, hi-yih, hi-yih, HI-yih, hi-yih . . ."

The ground within the pavilion had already been beaten bare by the stamping feet. Only a few tufts of the tough prairie grass remained. A fine dust rose, parching the throats of the dancers and causing the women spectators to wave their handkerchiefs before their faces. "Phew! My! My! What dust!" they exclaimed sweetly.

All that was part of the circus atmosphere. The dancers, meanwhile, enacted their parts and showed no concern because of the staring eyes and the distractions beyond the pavilion.

"Ho! Let it be as it was in old times!" The aged Modeste had begun the dance with those words and there were cries of approbation. The dancers went forward like actors in a play and lost themselves in their game. In the pauses between dances bottles of soda water were passed around and old men told stories. These were cheered as if the actions they described had taken place only yesterday.

Archilde had wedged himself into the front line of spectators, but when he got there he was sorry. It was a sad spectacle to watch. It was like looking on while crude jokes were played on an old grandmother, who was too blind to see that the chair had been pulled away just before she went to sit down. He felt the hurt which the old men suffered unknowingly.

They echoed the war cry from time to time and made threatening gestures with a feathered carpenter's hatchet, which was fierce enough to cause a white woman to grow pale and draw back, it was true—but what a small matter that was! The white husband made a joke of it, as well he might.

"Let it be today as it was in old times!"

389

The throbbing drum, the voices chanting in unison, the bells on the dancers' legs, the stamping feet, each in its way added to the simple rhythm and swelled the volume of sound until it traveled to the surrounding mountains and rolled back upon the prairie. On no other occasion did the Indians make so much noise.

But he had come to see Mike and he would stay until he had satisfied his eyes. He wanted to watch the expression on the boy's face and try to guess how he was taking this medicine for his "sickness."

At first he did not locate him, but after a moment Mike seemed to appear out of a cloud, partly dust and partly moving figures. And then he came forward with a slow, weaving, muscular movement that was inexplicably graceful—a detached element of rhythm, moving unhindered through space. Behind the boy, the dry bones of Modeste advanced with a minimum of variation from normal locomotion. As the pair passed, Archilde stood but two feet away and the vision he had of Mike's face was stirring.

For a moment he felt everything Mike felt—the rhythmic movement, the body's delight in a sinuous thrusting of legs and arms, the wild music of drum and dancing bells, and best of all, the majesty of the dancers. It really seemed, for a moment, as if they were unconquerable and as if they might move the world were they to set their strength to it. They made one think of a wild stallion running free—no one could approach him, no one would ever break his spirit.

That was what he shared with Mike, but it was for a moment only. Then he heard the spectators laughing. They were making fun of an old man, too weak to move in the circle, who stood in one place and bobbed himself up and down. His face showed his inner contentment and he was oblivious of the laughter at his expense. Someone shouted "Hi, gran'pa! Does your mama know you're out?" Archilde went away, making a passage for himself through the dense crowd.

. . .

The drum was silenced at sundown and the white people went away. Then the women brought forth the horses and decked them with fancy gear—with saddles of the whitest and softest of buckskin, stirrup leathers reaching to the ground, and painted and fringed caparisons covering the horses from withers to tail. There were horsehair bridles with colored rosettes, martingales spangled with silver, and bells hanging from cinches and saddle backs. When the men had eaten they mounted their horses and began a procession, going round and round the circle of tepees. The chiefs rode in front, each in turn delivering a speech to the encampment, and those who rode behind responded. The bells on the horses rang out, *ca-ring, ca-ring, ca-ring,* measuring the stately pace. Fires glowed within the tepees and children stood at the entranceways. The dogs sat on their haunches but made no outcry.

As Archilde sat in his mother's tepee he wondered at the expression of peace which had settled over her. From the depths of his own turmoil he looked upon her with searching eyes. At first he had an impulse to tell her what had happened, but when he studied her calm, half-smiling face, he realized that it would not do. Her hands had taken her far back into the past that day and he would not drag her forth again.

She stirred the fire and he watched the sparks fly upward, alive, then dead. They lived just long enough to know. A man's life was too long by comparison. It dragged out his misery, or if he had happiness that too was dragged out until it turned into misery. And he didn't die until he had tasted all of it. One had just to go on, taking everything that came, somehow. . . .

Ca-ring, ca-ring, ca-ring . . .

"My people! Listen to my words! When I was young . . ."

The old lady sighed. She stirred slightly, then returned to her dreaming.

A full yellow moon had risen above the grove of cottonwoods. The fires within the tepees glowed at the base of the gloom.

Archilde sat quietly and felt those people move in his blood. There in his mother's tepee he had found unaccountable security. It was all quite near, quite a part of him; it was his necessity, for the first time.

THE REDEMPTION OF COLONEL CRULL

E. J. CRULL

This harangue is a more or less freely transcribed version of an actual plea delivered in an actual court by "Colonel" E. J. Crull of Roundup, Dec. 17, 1909, and inserted in the court records. The case originated in the court of Justice of the Peace Martin of Roundup. Before him came the owner of a horse which had lost a race; it had been a traditional "hoss for hoss" event, and he had lost his horse. He complained that the race was "framed" and demanded return of his horse. "Colonel" Crull, an attorney, was his counsel in the action, but during the hearing a charge was made that the "Colonel" himself had been a party to the conspiracy which cost his client his horse. And the race had been run on Sunday, which was illegal. As a result of the uproar which followed these allegations or disclosures, both the horse owner, B. F. Bruckert, and Crull were charged in Tenth district court, Lewistown, with participation in an illegal horse race. (The technical offense was participating in a race which was not run on an inclosed track, a legal device aimed at "outlaw" races in hidden coulees, such as this one.) Both pleaded guilty, and a fine of $100 was assessed against each culprit. This was Crull's speech in his own defense to Judge E. K. Cheadle. It was recorded, under some difficulty because of the mirth it caused in the courtroom, by H. B. Gibson, the court reporter. Gibson subsequently reported that in transcribing it he did some revising (apparently the speech was completely extemporaneous) and that it was further "embellished" by Tom Stout, editor of *The Lewistown Democrat-News,* and the late John B. Ritch of Lewistown, who became librarian of the Historical Society of Montana, from whose files this copy was taken.

MAY it please the Court, I have a few brief words to say. Not in my defense, Sir, not in palliation of any offense I may have committed to bring me to the humiliating position which I now occupy, standing before this honorable Court as a conspirator and violator of our sacred laws—but I do sincerely desire to offer the Court a short explanation of why I am in your honorable presence, suppliant to Your Honor's clemency.

It was on a balmy Sunday afternoon in the month of October, may it please the Court, that I wended my way to attend a meeting of the Epworth League in the beautiful, hustling, thriving metropolis of the Imperial Valley of the Musselshell; and while on this truly commendable mission I was so unfortunate as to overtake a party of friends who were going in the same direction—to a horse race.

Your Honor, I remember now how the sun laved our little city in a brilliant, opal sheen; how the bracing winds from the west stirred my fast-aging pulses at the thought that I, too, might be a witness to and participant in, as it were, that noblest and most thrilling of all sports yet devised by mankind to separate the sucker from his money. And forgetting for the moment my obligations as a Christian gentleman, pillar of the Wesleyan denomination and one of the most faithful participants in the services of the Epworth League, I permitted myself so far to forget my religious privileges and responsibilities as to depart from the prosaic paths of rectitude and follow in the serpentine and deeply beaten trail that leads eventually to degradation and humiliation.

I have noticed, Your Honor, that in every city now rising to power and affluence in our great Westland, as is now the modern little city of Roundup, the spirit of chance penetrates the very being of every enthusiastic, progressive resident. It seems as if the "builder" is always and ever a devotee of Dame Fortune, ready to stake his last dollar on his judgment that he will win—and, as I would have you understand, Your Honor, Roundup is a glaring exemplification of this time-proven fact.

We arrived at the race track, and there before us and around us were gathered in gallant array the beauty and chivalry of the "Miracle of the Musselshell." There were strong men, poor men, beggar men, men strong in the anticipation of things to come, wise in their day and generation, men who looked like horse thieves, and, Your Honor, a few honest men—all the concomitants of a horse race in these decadent days.

And there *was* a horse race.

Prancing up and down the track before me, I saw the Pride of Forsyth, fleeter than the wind, more beautiful than the gazelle and more promising to some than the mines of Golconda. There also, champing at her bit, was the invincible, unbeaten and unbeatable Dixie. And there, Your Honor, was where I fell. Aye, harder than ever Lucifer fell. And, Your Honor, they were ready for the start. . . . Even honest men and beggar men in that assemblage were ready to wager their all on the outcome of this, one of the greatest speed contests yet recorded on the musty pages of history. And, Sir, witnessing such a scene, I exclaimed:

> "Lives there a man with soul so dead
> Who never to himself has said
> 'Here is where I get even on my whole life'?"

So, Sir, I frisked myself and found that I was the humble but honest possessor of twenty-six—yes, count 'em—twenty-six simoleons, and I played the chuck on the Pride of Forsyth.

Some narrators of this event have said that Chance was eliminated and Honesty was annihilated in the frameup previous to this speed contest. It may have been so, Sir. Yes, I really think it was.

It is alleged by some of the participants, Your Honor, that this race *was* held within an inclosure, in order that there might not be a violation of the law; and according to the broad-minded view held by us who have lived in the days of the unfenced range, it *was* an inclosure. As fragile memory serves me, there was a barbed wire fence partially bounding the inclosure on the east; to the north, by the elasticity of my imagination, I could discern the aurora borealis; on the south was the procession of the equinoxes, and on the west, Sir, was Eternity, the end of time. As I recall now, Your Honor, those sturdy horses could still be running and not have covered one-fifth of that half-mile, straightaway course.

And, Sir, as I said before, there was a race, and with the permission of this Court, asking its pardon for this digression, I desire to ask you, Sir, have you ever been placed in a position where twenty-six simoleons, shekels, pesos, yen, and those things known in this country as dollars, represented an overwhelming majority of your capital stock? And, Sir, has it ever been your misfortune to have taken fair Chance by the forelock and cast the die, to win or lose your all, on the result of a scrub horse race? If so, Sir, you are placed in a position to appreciate the poignant pain which permeated my more or less ponderous avoirdupois when I saw the Pride of Forsyth falter in the stretch and lope leisurely under the imaginary wire like a winded range cow—long after the unbeaten and invincible Dixie, carrying the colors of the sourdough coat and coonskin cap, had been twice curried down in a nearby stall.

Sir, that was my day of grievous disappointment, dire humiliation, and financial engulfment.

But, Your Honor, I was not the only sucker in that concourse of spectators. There was a wail that could be heard from Lavina to Melstone, the reverberations of which waved the nearby cactus as though they were breathed upon by a South Sea simoon, and caused the tipple of Mine No. 3 to wobble in its socket. Trouble was on. Conspiracy was rife, and, Your Honor, had been rife from the moment I was met on my way to the Epworth League; and the warmer waxed the controversy, the rifer it became, Sir.

I am trying to make an honest living practicing law the best I know how with what little stock I have in trade. The owner of the Forsyth horse, having lost his money and his "Pride" in the race, asked me, in my capacity as an attorney, to undertake for him the recovery of his horse. Then I was also unjustly branded as a conspirator, and by that familiar process I am now before this honorable bar of justice pleading to an information. I wish it understood in this presence, with these honorable men congregated around, that I am ashamed of myself, deeply humiliated, and feel the consequence of this false position more than I am gifted to tell at this time, may it please this honorable Court.

I might say more. It would possibly have become me better to have said less; but I desire, here and now, in this presence, to state that hereafter, on these golden Sunday afternoons, when the sun laves with its warm breath that bibulous Babylon the City of Roundup—that, if there is a horse race in one direction or a dog fight in the other direction, I shall attempt as nearly as possible to steer in a straight line diametrically opposite.

Your Honor, I am only an ordinary, sinful, wicked man, but I will say that I plead guilty, with humiliation and with shame, to the crime charged in this information. I know the flesh is weak; that we are filled with the lust of sin, environed by the lechery of temptation; but with me the spirit will be willing, and I shall hereafter walk piously in the pleasant furrow of rectitude and righteousness.

And never more will I be accused of horse racing where the race is jobbed, whether it be in a legal inclosure or not!

NOSTALGIA

BERTON BRALEY

"Nostalgia" is from Berton Braley's autobiography, *Pegasus Pulls a Hack*. The other poems by Braley in this book are from the Butte newspapers *Intermountain* and *Evening News*, neither of which is now published. The former became the *Butte Daily Post*, still operating; the latter, which was owned by F. Augustus Heinze, great foe of Anaconda Copper during the famed mining wars, folded. "Nostalgia" was written shortly after Braley had left Butte, which, he wrote, always would seem "home."

I'M goin' home where the mountains are,
Where a man's own eyes kin see as far
And farther, too, in that atmosphere
Than a man with a telescope kin here.

I'm goin' home to the minin' town
Where the boys is sinkin' the deep shafts down
Where the hills is steep and the scenery's bare
And there ain't no foliage anywhere.
    I'm goin' home.

I'm goin' home to the raw old camp
Where the whistles hoot and the engines stamp
Where nobody asks you, "Who are you?"
But only, "Hey, there, what kin you do?"
Where the slag-dumps glow an' the ore-cars bang
An' the six-horse teamster shouts "g'lang!"
Where the chimneys flare with a hundred hues;
Where you play the game with a stack of blues,
Whoop if you're winner and grin if you lose;
Where the pace is fast an' the blood runs hot
An' you blow in all of the cash you've got.
    I'm goin' home!

I'm goin' home to my own again,
To the breezy girls and the six-foot men,

NOSTALGIA

To the rocky hills and the sage brush plains
Where it always pours an' it never rains;

Six thousand feet above the sea
Where the heart beats swift an' the soul is free.
Where you live like a live one, an' when you die
They bury you under the alkali
An' drink to your soul in a whiskey straight
An'—match for the drinks at the graveyard gate.

You can have my job an' my office space;
I want to get out to the good old place
Where the peaks are white as the ocean foam,
I'm goin' home!

Ave, Atque Vale—Butte.

BACK AGAIN

BERTON BRALEY

"We are grateful to be home once more," said former Alderman John L. Doidge of Walkerville, who has just returned from Australia, in company with Mrs. Doidge. "America is the only country on earth for me, and Butte is the only city in it."—News item.

MR. DOIDGE is back again;
    Tickled, too, as he can be,
    Happiest of mortal men,
  "Butte is good enough," says he.
"I've been to Australia
  But the country didn't suit,
U.S.A. will do for me;
  Thank the Lord I'm back in Butte."

Mr. Doidge is back again,
  Back from the antipodes
Where he went to live, and then
  Found the prospect didn't please.
He's come back from overseas
  By the fastest kind of route;
Now he's saying things like these,
  "Thank the Lord I'm back in Butte."

Mr. Doidge is back again
  From the southern hemisphere;
Gee! his grin expanded, when
  Butte's familiar slope drew near.

"I shall never go from here,"
  Sayeth Doidge, with wink astute,
"I'm too happy—have a beer—
  Thank the Lord I'm back in Butte!"

398

BACK AGAIN

Mr. Doidge says "Here I stay
Till the judgment horn shall toot;
And I'll murmur every day
Thank the Lord I'm back in Butte."

ANIMALS

"It was one of the most prolific
and one of the largest game
preserves on the globe."

COYOTES

JASON BOLLES

Jason Bolles, beloved minstrel of Bozeman and one of the finest poets
Montana has produced, died suddenly of a heart attack while on a
camping trip in 1942. He was born in 1900, came to central Montana
in 1911 with his widowed mother when she took up a homestead,
was educated at Montana State College and became an English in-
structor there. This and the rest of his poems in this book are from
his collected verse in *Magpies' Nest,* published in 1943 in Bozeman
by his widow, Martha Maxey Bolles.

A FLAKE of moon in a speckle of fire,
Lighting a barren lea;
And out of the shadows a goblin choir
Singing a ghostly glee:
   rrrrooooo

Now a single voice in a mellow yell;
Hark to the flirt and fleer!
Now hark to the raving chorus swell
The wild cadenza of fear:
   rr rk rr
rooeeeyihyihyihyrrr

'Rroyo and rimrock, bench and butte,
Pale in a whey of light,
While the voice of a mad, insouciant brute
Sings in the sage-sweet night:
   eee

COWS

JASON BOLLES

From *Magpies' Nest*.

MY cows come up from pasture, walking slow,
The biggest leading by a little space.
Their feet are lifted, moved, set down just so,
With stinginess of effort that is grace.
My cows come up from pasture before night,
Reluctantly, their bellies taut and round,
Their long heads swinging at their shoulders' height.
Stiffly they inch across the trampled ground,
And snuff the barnyard gate that blocks their way.
They feign torpidity, and seem to drowse;
But soon they bellow, malcontent that they
Have come, that they must halt, that they are cows.
In the faint shining of the early stars,
I bring the buckets and let down the bars.

THE STORY OF SCAMMON

MEMBERS OF THE LEWIS AND CLARK EXPEDITION

The first dog to traverse the western United States was a Newfoundland named Scammon. He trotted much of the way, too, though sometimes he rode in a boat with his master, Captain Meriwether Lewis, who was appointed in 1803 by President Jefferson to head an expedition into the Northwest. Before the expedition started, the Louisiana Purchase was consummated (April 30, 1803), so to the original objective of finding a route to the Pacific was added that of determining what we got for the $11,250,000 with which the United States purchased all French possessions west of the Mississippi. The Lewis and Clark expedition entered Montana in 1805, returned to St. Louis Sept. 23, 1806, still accompanied by Scammon. Historians have devoted years of study to Lewis and Clark and their famous girl guide, Sacajawea; none has bothered with Scammon. Here's the record of some of his exploits, as pieced together from the fragmentary notes in the *Journals* of Lewis and Sgt. John Ordway, edited by Milo M. Quaife (Wisconsin State Historical Society, Vol. 22, 1916) and *The Original Journals of the Lewis and Clark Expedition*, edited by R. G. Thwaites (Dodd, Mead, 1904). Note the entry for May 29, 1805, when Scammon probably saved the noted explorers' lives . . . but in the final entry the canine hero, just like any other dog, is howling over the torture of mosquito bites.

Lewis Journal

SEPT. 11, 1803 [on the Ohio River enroute to Illinois where the expedition party went into training during the winter of 1803-4]—I made my dog take as many [squirrels] each day as I had occasion for. . . . My dog was of the newfoundland breed very active and docile, he would take the squirrel in the water, kill them and swiming bring them in his mouth to the boat.

Sept. 14, 1803—Saw many squirrels this day swiming the river from N.W. to S.E. caught several by means of my dog.

Sept. 15, 1803—Saw and caught by means of my dog several squirrels, attempting to swim the river.

Nov. 16, 1803—One of the Shawnees a respectable looking Indian offered me three beverskins for my dog with which he appeared much pleased, the dog was of the newfoundland breed one that I prized much for his docility and qualifications generally for my journey and of course there was no bargain. I had given 20$ for this dogg myself.

Clark Journal

Aug. 25, 1804—Our Dog was so heeted and fatigued we was obliged [to] Send him back to the Creek.

Ordway Journal

April 18, 1805—One man killed another goose. Scannon b[rought] out.

Lewis Journal

April 22, 1805—Walking on shore this evening I met with a buffaloe calf which attatched itself to me and continued to follow close at my heels untill I embarked and left it. it appeared allarmed at my dog which was probably the cause of it's so readily attatching itself to me.

April 25, 1805—My dog had been absent during the last night, and I was fearfull we had lost him altogether, however much to my satisfaction he joined us at 8 oclock this morning.

Clark Journal

April 25, 1805—The Dog which was lost yesterday, joined us this morning.

Ordway Journal

April 26, 1805—Saw a flock of geese swimming the river this morning near to our camp. Capt. Lewes dog Scamon took after them and caught one in the river. Drowned & killed it and swam to shore with it.

Lewis Journal

April 29, 1805—Antelopes are yet meagre and the females are big with young; the wolves take them most generally in attempting to swim the river; in this manner my dog caught one drowned it and brought it on shore; they are but clumsy swimmers.

May 5, 1805—And my dog caught a goat, which he overtook by

superior fleetness, the goat it must be understood was with young and extreemly poor.

Clark Journal

MAY 5, 1805—And our Dog caught an antilope, a fair race, this animal appeared verry pore & with young.

May 19, 1805—Capt Lewis's dog was badly bitten by a wounded beaver and was near bleading to death.

Lewis Journal

MAY 19, 1805—One of the party wounded a beaver, and my dog as usual swam in to catch it; the beaver bit him through the hind leg and cut the artery; it was with great difficulty that I could stop the blood; I fear it will yet prove fatal to him.

Ordway Journal

MAY 19, 1805—Semon Capt. Lewiss dog bit by a beaver.

Lewis Journal

MAY 29, 1805—Last night we were all allarmed by a large buffaloe bull, which swam over from the opposite shore. . . . He then allarmed ran up the bank . . . still more alarmed, he now took his direction immediately towards our lodge . . . when he came near the tent, my dog saved us by causing him to change his course a second time.

Clark Journal

MAY 29, 1805—Alarmed by a Buffalow . . . landed opposit the Perogue in which Capt. Lewis and my self were in   he crossed the perogue . . . our Dog flew out & he changed his course & passed without doeing more damage than be[n]d a rifle.

Ordway Journal

MAY 29, 1805—The dog flew at him which turned him from running against the lodge [in] which the officers layd   He passed without doing more damage than bend[ing] a rifle a[nd] breaking the stalk and injuring one of the blunderbusses in the perogue as he pass through.

Lewis Journal

JUNE 19, 1805—After dark my dog barked very much and seemed extreemly uneasy which was unusual with him . . . [One of the party] reported that he believed the dog had been baying a buffaloe bull.

June 26, 1805—My dog seems to be in a constant state of alarm with these bear and keeps barking all night.

June 28, 1805—They [bears] come close arround our camp every night but have never yet ventured to attack us and our dog gives us timely notice of their visits, he keeps constantly padroling all night.

July 15, 1805—Drewyer wo[u]nded a deer which ran into the river   my dog pursued caught drowned it and brought it to shore at our camp.

July 26, 1805—My poor dog suffers with them [prickly pear and cactus] excessively, he is constantly binting [biting] and scratching himself as if in a rack of pain.

Aug. 17, 1805—The b[l]ack man york and the sagacity of my dog were equally objects of admiration [to the Indians].

Clark Journal

AUG. 17, 1805—Every thing appeared to astonish these people [Indians] the appearance of the men, their arms, the Canoes, the Clothing, my black Servent & the Segassity of Capt Lewis's Dog.

Lewis Journal

APRIL 11, 1806 [on Columbia River below the Dalles]—Three of this same tribe of villains the Wah-clel—lars [Chinook] stole my dog this evening, and took him towards their village; I was shortly afterwards informed of this transaction by an indian who spoke the Clatsop language . . . and sent three men in pursuit of the theives with orders if they made the least resistance or difficulty in surrendering the dog to fire on them; they overtook these fellows or reather came within sight of them at the distance of about 2 miles; the indians discovering the party in pursuit of them left the dog and fled.

Ordway Journal

MAY 7, 1806—One of the hunters wounded a deer only broke its leg Capt Lewises dog Scamon chased it caught it and killed it.

Lewis Journal

MAY 23, 1806—Sergt. Pryor wounded a deer early this morning in a lick near camp; my dog pursued it into the river.

Clark Journal

MAY 23, 1806—Sergt. Pryor wounded a deer at a lick near our camp and our dog prosued it into the river. Two Indians which happened to be at our camp Mounted their horses and swam across the river chased the deer into the water again and pursued it across to the side on which we were, and as the deer came out of the water Sgt. Pryor killed it. we derected half of this deer to be given to these two Indians.

Lewis Journal

JULY 15, 1806 [near Great Falls]—The musquetoes continue to infest us in such manner that we can scarcely exist; for my own part I am confined by them to my bier (protective covering) at least 3/4 of my time. my dog even howls with the torture he experiences from them.

THE PASSING OF THE BUFFALO

B. F. LAMB

This is an "eyewitness story" of one of the most dramatic episodes in Montana's economic history. Many have written about it, but there are few alive who saw it. Lamb, who was born in 1857 in Jasper County, Iowa, came to Montana when in his twenties. He described the slaughter of the great buffalo herd in a talk to the Rotary Club of Laurel on June 22, 1943—seven days before his eighty-sixth birthday. He had been a resident of that town for many years. In editing this account, which appeared the next day in *The Laurel Outlook*, interpolations of the news writer have been eliminated.

I HAVE nothing to tell but what I saw and can remember, and it is a long time since I gave much thought to it.

It is about the passing of the buffalo. It is as I saw it. It takes me back to the early 80s and the scene is on the north side of the Yellowstone River, near Miles City. The area comprised quite a strip of country, commencing on the west at a creek called Froze-to-Death and extending north to the Bull Mountains and Mussel-shell Valley, and east (down the Yellowstone) to where Glendive now is.

At that time the country was not settled, and in 1880 vast herds of buffalo drifted in to take the place of other kinds of game, such as antelope, deer, elk, and some straggling bands of buffalo already there. I never saw stock cattle to anywhere the equal of the buffalo that were on the range then. Anywhere from five to ten miles from the Yellowstone River you could look in any direction and see buffalo on every hill and ridge, in every valley, as far as the eye could reach. You could see millions at one time.

If one had not seen it, it would be almost unbelievable. But they were there—and were gone in the course of one year. The last cleanup of the herd was on the prairie south of Dickinson in North Dakota.

In the late summer there were no hunters in that country, but by the first of November it was more thickly settled than I think it will ever be again. The hunters came and the slaughter of buffalo commenced. Every day that was not too stormy you could hear the constant roar of the big guns.

410

You can draw some idea of how many buffalo were killed by the number of hides that were shipped out by steamboat from as far west as Froze-to-Death to the Sunday Creek bottom 12 miles east of Miles City. There were over 5,000,000 hides shipped by steamboat by actual count.

Buffalo hunters' camps were made in every conceivable place— some at the heads of coulees, some on the banks of bluffs, a great many cribbed up with poles or built of rock and alkali mud and a ridge pole covered with buffalo hides. (There was a surplus of old bulls whose hides were not good for anything else.) The most common were tents put up Indian fashion, or just a pup tent made of green buffalo hides stretched over a pole and used to sleep in or store goods in.

A camp outfit generally consisted of a team and wagon, and a saddle horse or two. Some of the larger outfits had more horses— some four head of work horses and three or four head of saddle horses.

The camp cooking outfit consisted of a good-sized frying pan, a Dutch oven, good-sized kettle, dishpan and smaller pans to put food in to serve. Also included were knives, forks, tin plates and cups. It is quite an art to cook on an open fire and not blacken your vessels or burn them.

A hunter's supplies consisted of a fifty-pound sack of flour, fifty pounds of sugar, fifty pounds of coffee, a side of bacon, beans, baking powder and fifty pounds of different kinds of dried fruit. The most essential item was the ammunition, consisting of 100 to 500 pounds of lead, fifty to 100 pounds of powder, primer caps, 500 shells, reloading outfit and one or two Sharps rifles. Some used 45-120 and a great many used 40-90 calibre rifles.

The animals divided into large family groups when grazing on the range. The hunters found it convenient to utilize that habit and prevent stampedes. The leaders had to be killed first. It was not well to shoot into a herd, for an injured animal would run and stampede the herd. The usual technique was to shoot the outermost ones, the leaders or guards, through the lungs. They appeared to become numb from the resulting internal hemorrhage and would 'hump up' and lie down.

There were two kinds of hunters. One kind went out and began shooting when he got close enough. Maybe he would get one or two, or sometimes three. Probably that would be all he could skin.

The other kind was the man who wanted to get a stand on a bunch and kill anywhere from eight to ten or thirty or forty, and sometimes more. These were called the big hunters. They would go out and stalk a band of buffalo. This was where a good hunter came in, for he generally had to shoot from 500 to 1,000 yards for the first ten or twelve shots. If he made good on them he could work his way sometimes to a position within 100 to 200 yards. The greatest difficulty was to gauge the distance. A man to be a good hunter had to be a good judge of distance.

Only the hides and tongues of the buffalo were saved; the rest was allowed to rot. Hides brought from $1.50 to $3.50 and the tongues were worth 25 cents a pound, dried.

The hides had to be taken to the camp or somewhere near it and spread flat on the ground and stretched clear of wrinkles, then staked down so they would not shrink up, using twelve wooden pegs to the hide. When dry the hides could be taken up and put in piles. They were doubled down the center (fur on the inside) and placed alternately to make a solid pile.

The tongues were cleaned and put in curing vats. The brine was of salt and saltpeter (potassium nitrate). The vats were made by digging a square hole in the ground and lining it with old buffalo hides, green and staked down around the top, and covered with dry hides weighed down with anything convenient. When cured the tongues were taken out and hung on poles or placed on rocks to dry. Then they were tied up in bundles.

Next came the job of getting the stuff to market. There were trading posts along the river where there were always buyers or trading post operators who would buy from one to any number of hides, tongues or cured meat the hunters had to sell.

Stormy weather and snow covering the grass did not bother the buffalo so long as the snow was not crusted. They would use their heads as brooms and sweep or brush the snow from the grass so that they could get down to it. You could get on a vantage point and watch them for hours, swinging their heads from side to side and moving as much snow as a man with a snow shovel. Buffalo always faced and went against a storm, never with it.

I had spent two years, previous to the time of this story, in the country along and north of the Missouri River and north of Miles City. At the time of the beginning of this story I was located on the head of Horse Creek, some twenty-five or thirty miles north of

Rosebud. I was in a camp consisting of Sam McGuire, head hunter; Ernie McGuire, general man; John Fargo, teamster, and Benjamin F. Lamb, skinner. During the four months we saved and marketed 3,800 buffalo, 1,800 antelope, and some 4,000 buffalo tongues. I have skinned as many as sixty buffalo in a day.

Probably half of the buffalo killed were never touched, never skinned. They went to waste. That was the last of the buffalo. What was left of the once vast number went away when spring came and never returned. Elsewhere there was a final roundup in 1881 and 1882, when 300,000 were slaughtered.

Extermination of the buffalo tamed the Indians of the West. After the Custer battle the Sioux had gone north into northern Montana and in 1881 they got to the head of Fallon Creek after crossing the Missouri. Soldiers from Fort Keough went out and brought in 3,000 Sioux who were destitute and hungry and in a miserable state through loss of the buffalo. They had resorted to killing their dogs and horses for food. The Indians were later shipped to Standing Rock reservation in the Dakotas.

THE STARTING OF SMOKY

WILL JAMES

This is a portion of the first chapter of *Smoky*, by Will James, which many, especially in the West, consider the greatest horse book ever written. Published in 1926 by Charles Scribner's Sons, it has been reprinted many times. This fragment should go a long way toward explaining the appeal of the book; it should explain, too, why most Montanans love horses. (But for the other side of the picture, from someone who simply doesn't *like* horses, read the chapter "Horse Rides Man" in Donald Hough's merry book about life in the Western mountains, *Snow Above Town*.) Another excerpt from James's works, with notes on the author, appears on page 305.

IT seemed like Mother Nature was sure agreeable that day when the little black colt came to the range world, and tried to get a footing with his long wobblety legs on the brown prairie sod. Short stems of new green grass was trying to make their way up thru the last year's faded growth, and reaching for the sun's warm rays. Taking in all that could be seen, felt, and inhaled, there was no day, time, nor place that could beat that spring morning on the sunny side of the low prairie butte where Smoky the colt was foaled.

"Smoky" wouldn't have fitted the colt as a name just then on account he was jet black, but that name wasn't attached onto him till he was a four-year-old, which was when he first started being useful as a saddle horse. He didn't see the first light of day through no box stall window, and there was no human around to make a fuss over him and try to steady him on his feet for them first few steps. Smoky was just a little range colt, and all the company he had that first morning of his life was his watchful mammy.

Smoky wasn't quite an hour old when he begin to take interest in things. The warm spring sun was doing its work and kept a pouring warmth all over that slick little black hide, and right on thru his little body, till pretty soon his head come up kinda shaky and he begin nosing around them long front legs that was stretched out in front of him. His mammy was close by him, and at the first move the colt made she run her nose along his short neck and nickered. Smoky's head went up another two inches at the sound, and his first little answering nicker was heard. Of course a person would have had to listen mighty close to hear it, but then if you'd a watched his nostrils quivering you could tell that's just what he was trying to do.

That was the starting of Smoky. Pretty soon his ears begin to work back and forth towards the sound his mammy would make as she moved. He was trying to locate just where she was. Then something moved right in front of his nose about a foot; it'd been there quite a good spell but he'd never realized it before; besides his vision was a little dim yet and he wasn't interested much till that something moved again and planted itself still closer.

Being it was right close he took a sniff at it. That sniff recorded itself into his brain and as much as told him that all was well. It was one of his mammy's legs. His ears perked up and he tried nickering again with a heap better result than the first time.

One good thing called for another and natural like he made a sudden scramble to get up, but his legs wouldn't work right, and just about when he'd got his belly clear of the ground, and as he was resting there for another try at the rest of the way up, one of his front legs quivered and buckled at the elbow, and the whole works went down.

He layed there flat on his side and breathing hard. His mammy nickered encouragement, and it wasn't long when his head was up again and his legs spraddled out all around him the same as before. He was going to try again, but next time he was going to be more sure of his *ground*. He was studying, it seemed like, and sniffing of his legs and then the earth, like he was trying to figger out how he was going to get one to stand up on the other. His mammy kept a circling around and a talking to him in horse language; she'd give him a shove with her nose then walk away and watch him.

The spring air, which I think is most for the benefit of all that's young, had a lot to do to keep Smoky from laying still for very long. His vision was getting clearer fast, and his strength was coming in just as fast. Not far away, but still too far for Smoky to see, was little calves, little white-faced fellers a playing and bucking around and letting out wall-eyed bellers at their mammies, running out a ways and then running back, tails up, at a speed that'd make a greyhound blush for shame.

415

There was other little colts too all a cavorting around and tearing up good sod, but with all them calves and colts that was with the bunches of cattle or horses scattered out on the range, the same experience of helplessness that Smoky was going thru had been theirs for a spell, and a few hadn't been as lucky as Smoky in their first squint at daylight. Them few had come to the range world when the ground was still covered with snow, or else cold spring rains was a pouring down to wet 'em to the bone.

Smoky's mother had sneaked out of the bunch a few days before Smoky came, and hid in a lonely spot where she'd be sure that no cattle nor horses or even riders would be around. In a few days, and when Smoky would be strong enough to lope out, she'd go back again; but in the meantime she wanted to be alone with her colt and put all her attention on him, without having to contend with chasing off big inquisitive geldings or jealous fillies.

She was of range blood, which means mostly mustang with strains of Steeldust or Coach throwed in. If hard winters come and the range was covered with heavy snows, she knowed of high ridges where the strong winds kept a few spots bare and where feed could be got. If droughts came to dry up the grass and water holes, she sniffed the air for moisture and drifted out acrost the plain which was her home range, to the high mountains where things was more normal. There was cougars and wolves in that high country, but her mustang instinct made her the "fittest." She circled around and never went under where the lion was perched a waiting for her, and the wolf never found her where she could be cornered.

Smoky had inherited that same instinct of his mammy's, but on that quiet spring morning he wasn't at all worried about enemies. His mammy was there, and besides he had a hard job ahead that was taking all of his mind to figger out: that was to stand on them long thin things which was fastened to his body and which kept a spraddling out in all directions.

The first thing to do was to gather 'em under him and try again. He did that easy enough, and then he waited and gathered up all the strength that was in him. He sniffed at the ground to make sure it was there and then his head went up, his front feet stretched out in front of him, and with his hind legs all under him, he used all that strength he'd been storing up and pushed himself up on his front feet, his hind legs straightened up to steady him; and as luck would have it there was just enough distance between each leg to keep him up there. All he had to do was to keep them legs stiff and from buckling up under him, which wasn't at all easy, cause getting up to where he was had used up a lot of his strength, and them long legs of his was doing a heap of shaking.

All would of been well maybe, only his mammy nickered "that's a good boy," and that's what queered Smoky. His head went up proud as a peacock and he forgot all about keeping his props stiff and under him. Down he went the whole length of his legs, and there he layed the same as before.

But he didn't lay long this time. He either liked the sport of going up and coming down or else he was getting peeved; he was up again, mighty shaky, but he was up sure enough. His mammy came to him. She sniffed at him and he sniffed back. Then nature played another hand and he nursed, the first nourishment was took in, his tummy warmed up and strength came fast. Smoky was an hour and a half old and up to stay.

The rest of that day was full of events for Smoky. He explored the whole country, went up big mountains two feet high, wide valleys six or eight feet acrost, and at one time was as far as twelve feet away from his mammy all by himself. He shied at a rock once; it was a dangerous *looking* rock, and he kicked at it as he went past. All that action being put on at once come pretty near being too much for him and he came close to measuring his whole length on Mother Earth once again. But luck was with him, and taking it all he had a mighty good time. When the sun went to sinking over the blue ridges in the West, Smoky, he missed all the beauty of the first sunset in his life;—he was stretched out full length, of his own accord this time, and sound asleep.

LEPLEY'S BEAR

CHARLES M. RUSSELL

One of the funniest of the many hilarious tales by Charley Russell, this is from *Trails Plowed Under* (Doubleday, Doran, 1937).

OLD Man Lepley tells me one time about a bear he was near enough to shake hands with but they don't get acquainted. He's been living on hog side till he's near starved. So, one day he saddled up and starts prowling for something fresh. There's lots of black-tail in the country but they have been hunted till they are shy, so after riding a while without seeing nothing he thinks he'll have better luck afoot. So, the first park he hits, he stakes his hoss. It's an old beaver meadow with bluejoint to his cayuse's knees, and about the center (like it's put there for him) is a dead cottonwood snag handy to stake his hoss to.

"After leaving the park he ain't gone a quarter of a mile till he notices the taller branches of a chokecherry bush movin'. There's no wind, and Lepley knows that bush don't move without something pushing it, so naturally he's curious. 'Tain't long till he heap savvys. It's a big silvertip and he's sure busy berrying. There's lots of meat here, and bear grease is better than any boughten lard. So, Lepley pulls down on him, aimin' for his heart. Mr. Bear bites where the ball hits. It makes Old Silver damn disagreeable—he starts bawlin' and comin'.

"As I said before, there ain't no wind. It's the smoke from his gun hovering over Lepley that tips it off where he's hiding. He's packing a Sharp's carbine an' he ain't got time to reload, so he turns this bear hunt into a foot race. It's a good one, but it looks like the man'll take second money. When he reaches the park his hoss has grazed to the near end. Lepley don't stop to bridle, but leaps for the saddle.

"About this time the hoss sees what's hurrying the rider. One look's enough. In two jumps, he's giving the best he's got. Suddenly something happens. Lepley can't tell whether it's an earthquake or a cyclone, but everything went from under him, and he's sailin' off; but he's flying low, and uses his face for a rough lock, and

418

stops agin some bushes. When he wakes up he don't hear harps nor smell smoke. It ain't till then he remembers he don't untie his rope. The snag snapped off, and his hoss is tryin' to drag it out of the country, and Mr. Bear, by the sound of breaking brush, is hunting a new range and it won't be anywhere near where they met. When his hoss stops on the end of the rope, that old snag snaps and all her branches scatter over the park. I guess Mr. Bear thinks the hoss has turned on him. Maybe some of them big limbs bounced on him and he thinks the hoss has friends and they're throwing clubs at him. Anyhow, Mr. Bear gives the fight to Lepley and the hoss.

"Lepley says that for months he has to walk that old hoss a hundred yards before he can spur him into a lope, and that you could stake him on a hairpin and he'd stay."

JOB, *39:18*

(What time she lifteth up herself on
high, she scorneth the horse and his rider.)

ELLIOTT C. LINCOLN

Two or three years ago a horse whose owner died suddenly wandered
in from the range daily to the hitching rack behind a Choteau bar—
until townspeople, moved by his loyalty, found him a pasture for
life. The owner of the horse in this poem was unhappily alive, but
Nig's habits were similar; and a horse is a creature of habit. This is
another selection from *The Ranch* (Houghton Mifflin, 1924).

LEMUEL Keno Birch, that's him
 Ploddin' along out there in the dust
  With his head hung down. A she girl's whim
It set him afoot, an' his heart went bust.

Lem, the ridin'est son-of-a-gun
 That ever straddled a range-bred colt
Or a squealin' outlaw—well, he's done,
 He's a walkin' man till the angels moult.

≫≪

Us fellers that worked at the Flyin' A
 Was willin' to take our oath,
An' own right up to it, proud an' free,
Lem Birch was the best that ever we see,
 Fer women an' horses both.

≫≪

His own pet black, that he rode to town
 On his monthly pay-day toot,
Was standard bred, an' his best girl, Nell,
Was the lookin'-queen of the Musselshell,
 An' the boss's daughter to boot.

An' the only trouble with Nig, the hawse,
 Was, nobody knowed what he'd do;

420

An' the only trouble with Nell, the fair,—
Well, speakin' plain, she had red hair,
　　An' a temper to match it, too.

But Lem, he's a-gettin' along right fine
　　Until one day in the spring
When the meaderlarks was chirpin' love—
Or so he thought—an' the sky above
　　Was blue as a bluebird's wing.

Then Nell, she says, with her nicest smile,
　　"Say, Lem, I'm a-goin' to town,
'Cause the Baptis' ladies is givin' a feed, .
An' I sorter said—fact is, I agreed
　　Fer to help 'em to pass things roun'.

"But Dad, he's busy, an' Goldie's lame,
　　So I jest gotter borrow a hawse.
Could you lend me Nig?" Lem, he gets hot
An' picks at his collar, an' sweats a lot,
　　An', stutterin', says, "O' course

"He's never been rid by a lady none,
　　An' he might be sorter mean;
But he knows the road, an' he orter do
His level best fer a girl like you—
　　The prettiest ever I seen!"

So Nell, she does like a lady should
　　Till both of 'em lose their breath.
An' then she saddles, an' rides away,
While Lem, he picks fer the weddin' day
　　Sunday, June twentieth.

Come noon, there ain't much farther to go,
　　An' Nell lopes happy along
Till she turns into Main Street, head in air,
Right tickled at making the town folks stare,
　　When sudden—things busted wrong!

Fer the hitchin'-rack at the Mint Saloon
  Was home, sweet home, to Nig;
An' seein' she aims fer to pass it by,
He stops right short, gives a grunt, an' a sigh,
  Then spins like a whirligig.

He makes three jumps to his usual place
  Right next to the door, an' stops.
Jest shuts his eyes, an' humps his back,
With his nose glued tight to the hitchin'-rack,
  Till blazin' hell sure pops!

She fans him up, an' she fans him down,
  She scratches him plenty an' free,
But every time, when the dust cloud clears,
He's a-standin', hunched, with pinned-back ears;
  So the crowd comes runnin' to see.

Nell, she gets redder, an' redder yet,
  Till her face most matches her hair,
But findin' he wouldn't budge that day
She jest climbs down an' stomps away,
  An' leaves him standin' there.

Now, jest what happened I never quite knowed,
  But subsequent I hear tell
That Lem, when he loses his chance fer a wife,
Swears off from hawses the rest of his life
  An' from female girls as well.

>>> <<<

Young man, when you plan them sprees, jest think
  Of the fate that lit on Lem K. Birch:
Don't make no odds where you take your drink,
  But hitch your hawse by the Baptis' church.

THE ELKHORN MONUMENTS

LT. JAMES H. BRADLEY

This odd fragment is another of the scores of such stories for which Montanans are indebted to Lt. James H. Bradley's manuscripts, which after his death were given to the Historical Society of Montana. Other excerpts from his records appear elsewhere in this book. This one is from Vol. IX of the *Contributions*.

THE Elkhorn monuments are among the mysteries of the West destined never to be unraveled. They were three in number, situated on Elkhorn Prairie, on the south side of the Missouri River, just below the mouth of Poplar Creek. The largest was about twenty feet high and twelve feet in diameter at the base, tapering gradually to a rounded top; the other two were somewhat smaller, and all stood within a few hundred yards of each other, about two miles from the Missouri.

They contained many thousand horns, all evidently shed by living animals. They were first discovered in 1831, and appeared to have been built a good many years, as the horns were somewhat decayed and the superincumbent weight had pressed the base of each mound several inches into the hard prairie soil. Major Culbertson made diligent inquiries concerning them among all the surrounding tribes, Assiniboines, Blackfeet and Crows, but none were in possession even of a tradition concerning their origin. Such a number of horns could only have been gathered by great labor from a vast area, and it seems improbable from the known character of the neighboring Indians that they could have been the architects of the mounds. There is nothing to indicate the purpose of the monuments, which remains wrapped in as deep mystery as their origin. They seem not to have been discovered by Lewis and Clark in 1805 or 1806, but must then have been in existence. A belt of timber partially interposed and they might readily have been overlooked by men toiling at the line of a keel boat or seated upon its low deck.

There is but one known monument of a similar form within a radius of hundreds of miles, which is of stone and located near

Belly River [Alberta]. Like the Elkhorn mounds, no account of it could be obtained from the surrounding Indians and the builders of all must evidently be sought among other people. The Elkhorn monuments were taken down by the American Fur Company in 1850 and the best horns selected and carried to St. Louis in the hope that they would find a ready sale among workers in horn, but the speculation was not very remunerative. Had they not been torn down these monuments would have stood for ages, and it is to be regretted that the greed for money has deprived us of these interesting memorials of a possibly extinct people.

TWO ANECDOTES

FRANK B. LINDERMAN

Frank B. Linderman's special field was Indians, but there was no facet of life in Montana which did not attract the interest of this loyal citizen, one of the Northwest's outstanding writers. He contributed these unusual animal sketches to Vol. VIII, No. 2 of *The Frontier*, March, 1928. Other work by Linderman will be found elsewhere in this book.

I

IN a magazine that came to my home the other day I read an article dealing with strange comradeships among animals and birds. It recalled to my mind two very exceptional examples of association between natural enemies, and I will tell them to the readers of *The Frontier*.

Back in 1869 Joe Henkel, now of Kalispell, was employed as night watchman over the store and warehouses of Durfee & Peck at old Fort Belknap, Montana. In the spring of the year that Henkel began his nightly vigils for the company a Blackfoot Indian brought two cub bears to the post and traded them to Abel Farwell, the manager of the store. The cubs thrived, and always playing together around the post became favorites of the engagees and the steamboatmen who came up the Missouri river from St. Louis.

One day in the summer when a band of Indians were trading at the company's store Club-foot Tony borrowed a bow from one of them and shot an arrow straight up into the air. When the arrow came down it struck one of the cubs and killed it. The other, lonely now, took up with an old sow and several growing pigs, and began at once to live with them in the bastion of the old fort. They became inseparable, the bear, knowing herself to be wisest, assuming leadership over the strange company that ate and slept together.

The steamboats brought many strangers from the States to Fort Belknap, and one night the company's store was entered by way of its front window. The glass had been broken out of the sash, and the ground beneath littered with its pieces. Henkel had heard nothing in the night, and when confronted the next morning with proof of the burglary could only say the thing must have happened while he was eating his midnight lunch. "I'll charge you up with everything they have taken," declared the irate manager. "All right," agreed Henkel, duly meek under the circumstances, "I'll pay."

But nothing was missed from the stock in the store. The mystery grew until one moonlight night in the late fall—past midnight, when Henkel, seated on a crockery-crate in the deep shadow of the store building, saw the bear coming up from the bastion. The post was deserted. There were no sounds in the stockade except the rippling of the river, and an occasional ribald shout from the camp of some rivermen down stream. The bear was the only living thing in sight. She stopped in front of the store and sat up on her haunches to look craftily about, as though she intended studied mischief and feared interruption. "Woof—woof!" she snorted, evidently smelling Henkel, but uncertain of his position. Down she dropped to all fours, walked a step or two, and stopped again. She was a little worried.

Henkel sat very still. Every movement of the now nearly half-grown bear was easily discernible in the bright moonlight that shimmered on the store's windows. Once more the bear sat up, head turning, nose lifted so that the faint night breeze might tell her if her plan was feasible. It brought her no weighty warning, and dropping again to all fours she shuffled hastily to the window, smashed the glass with one blow of her heavy paw, and disappeared into the store. Henkel, in great glee, ran to the sleeping quarters of the manager. "Wake up— Wake up!" he panted. "That feller's in the store again right now!"

The manager called another man, and the three ran to the store. One stopped by the broken window, one at the back door, and the other, Henkel himself, who knew he had only to face a pet bear, unlocked the front door, and entered. The two outside waited, with their rifles ready. Henkel, inside, struck a match! His companions saw the small flame flicker through the windows. "The fool!" they thought. "He'll be shot—killed!"

But instantly there was a terrible racket. Things began to tumble, glass to jingle—and out through the broken window bolted the bear with a small wooden keg fast to her head. The keg had held cookies; in her greed to secure the very last one she had wedged her head so tightly into the keg that she could not get it out again.

426

Blinded by it and terrified, she ran to the safety of the bastion and her friends.

Of course she would have to be killed now that her bad habit was formed. The men waited for her to come out of the bastion. But she didn't come. And strange to relate, not even a pig showed himself, for two whole days and nights, in spite of feeding calls. She would not permit them to leave their quarters. It was as though she knew the men had sentenced her to death, and believed that like punishment would descend upon her companions because of their association with her. The bastion was besieged until the morning of the third day, when the bear herself, yielding to hunger, came out alone, and was shot. Somehow, during the siege, she had rid herself of the keg.

II

The anatomies of the common house cat, and the cougar or mountain lion, are almost identical. Size is about the only difference. The cats, all of them, are natural enemies of the deer. Everybody knows that the mountain lion is the greatest destroyer of deer; and I believe a full-grown lion will each year account for from twenty to fifty. But not everybody knows that the smaller varieties of wild cats sometimes kill deer. I have myself seen a lynx spring from a spruce tree upon a deer. (And I killed the lynx.) Often when I was a young man I found deer I believed had been killed by bob-cats; and many times I have trapped a bob-cat at such a kill, so that, naturally, all members of the cat family must look somewhat alike to a timid deer.

In 1888, when the forest reserves were new, Link Lee of Big Fork, Montana, was appointed ranger with quarters on Tobacco Plains. The government had not yet set up its forestry stations, and the one in Tobacco Plains was established temporarily in a cabin built and owned by a squatter named Mike Petery. The Petery cabin stood on the edge of a meadow near Edna creek, and was jointly occupied by Petery, N. M. Dudley, and the newly appointed forest ranger, Lincoln Lee, who had trapped with me in the earlier eighties.

When Lee took up his quarters in the cabin the only pet about the place was Petery's cat until Lee, one day, caught a fawn in the meadow, and brought it in. A young deer tames very easily, and within a day or two the fawn was given its liberty. It soon learned that the men would feed it, and it always showed up at mealtime, greedily lapping condensed milk from the same pan with Petery's cat. The cat and deer were friends from the start, and never quarreled over their food, even when the men tried to make trouble between them. When the pan was emptied the fawn would lick the cat while the latter relicked the pan and purred contentedly. After the meal the deer would slip away into some willows that grew at the lower end of the meadow and sleep until another mealtime arrived. He seemed to know the exact time to return to the cabin to share the men's bounty with the cat.

When fall came the deer had grown husky and more playful. His spots were nearly gone, and his coat was "short blue." Now he and his friend, the Petery cat, made a game which they played together for nearly a year. It gave both opportunity to display their natural instincts; and the most astonishing feature about it was its demonstration that both players perfectly understood their unnatural relationship. The trail out of Tobacco Plains passed the Petery cabin over level ground. On the far side of the trail from the cabin door was a grindstone set in a frame, which permitted a person to sit upon it and by peddling with his feet grind an axe or other tool. The deer and the cat made good use of it, and their daily performances were watched by many a man besides those who regularly occupied the cabin.

The cat, after purring a proposal to the deer, would spring upon the grindstone's frame, and crouch. Her claws would prick nervously from their cushions, her body grow tense, her tail-tip twist threateningly, like that of her big cousin, the mountain lion, when he is crouched to spring upon his prey in the forest. The deer, thus challenged, would trot up the trail a little way, then turn to face the cat. Planting his sharp hoofs carefully, he would move them often to better positions, the fine muscles of his shapely shoulders alive and dancing with excitement. There was much preparation by both. It was part of the game itself. There seemed to be agreed signals between them. It was as though the deer asked, "Are you ready?" and the cat replied, "You bet!" Then the deer would race past the grindstone, and the cat would spring, reaching out with clawed front paw to strike, just as a lion strikes a deer. But she always missed. The deer was too cunning for her. She could never land on his shoulders, probably because he could see her, and knew what was going to happen. Her countless failures did not

428

lessen her love for their game, however, and she was always ready to try once more. Determined to win, she would spring again and again to the grindstone's frame, go through the same old preparation of pricking out her claws and twisting her tail-tip, while the deer, as though laughing at his friend's lack of luck, would turn to race back. This went on every afternoon until the following fall. Then—when the October moon was full—the young buck slipped away into the dark forest where he was killed—or found better company, and forgot to come back.

MIKE

MERLE T. HAINES

This unusually vivid story of an outlaw horse—and what made him an outlaw—is from *The Frontier*, Vol. VIII, No. 3, May, 1928. Its author, a junior at Montana State University when this story was published, had lived with horses all his life and had been a packer.

MIKE threw up his head to watch the riders who were trotting leisurely toward him and his band of wild horses. Standing on a small knoll, he saw the strangers when they left the timber. He snorted, stamped and held his head high, rolling his big eyes from the horsemen to his band. His nostrils flared as he caught their scent, and he whistled savagely.

Mike was an outlaw. He had been captured when a three-year-old and had been nearly killed by a man who had tried to break him with a club; he had caught the man off his guard, struck him, breaking his shoulder, and had escaped; he had run wild since then, hating and fearing men. These men knew him only as a big, strong horse, well built and fast.

When Mike judged the men were too close he whirled and single-footed across the flat, followed by his excited band.

With wide nostrils thrust out to catch the wind they followed their leader heading for the rough, timbered ridges behind Lava mountain. The riders leaned low over their straining ponies, chasing the cloud of dust that ran before them, scarfs and saddle strings snapping in the wind.

Mike made the timber and ran along a broad trail holding his head low to avoid branches. He was running too hard to see or smell clearly, so he plunged into the blind corral. He sensed that something was wrong before he saw the barrier across the trail. His four legs stiffening, his hind quarters sank back till they nearly touched the ground as he ploughed to a halt, his nose against the logs and brush. The herd piled in upon him, a kicking, squealing mass.

The horses untangled and ran wildly around the enclosure, seeking a hole. Men were rolling up heavy logs at the entrance.

Mike screamed as he leapt at the fence, striking at it with his fore-feet and tearing it with his teeth. He fell back; got up; tried again. The sweat poured out of him, soaking his coppery hide and drip-ping to the ground.

Two men rode inside. Mike rushed them, his teeth bared, his ears flat on his neck. They parted and as he swerved towards one a lariat clutched him around the neck, biting into the hide, cutting off his wind and almost jerking him off his feet. He caught his balance and started for the man holding the rope. The second rider flipped a noose over his head. He fought till he fell. Then the rope slackened and he caught some air. It was heavy with dust but it eased his lungs.

Mike was snaked down to a ranch between two rope horses. If he fought he was choked down and the saddle horses were too wise and well trained to let him get near them. But Mike fought. It was his nature. Occasionally he was forced to take short breathing spells, then he went at it again till his legs trembled under him and his lungs grew raw and sore.

At the ranch they tied him to a snubbing post in the round corral. He stood there in the sun for two days, without water and with a small bunch of hay. He had never eaten hay. It was dry and dusty and smelled strongly of man. His flanks became gaunt, his eyes sank.

The third day Mike was put in a shute and harnessed. As the straps slapped his back and sides he crouched, quivering and snort-ing—four years ago this same thing had caused him pain. They opened the shute and he sprang out, bawling, bucking and kick-ing. He lunged against the fence and a rider from the outside beat him back. One foot caught over a hold-back strap and ripped it loose. The breeching slipped to one side and in a minute the harness was broken straps. Another harness was put on and one forefoot was tied up. This time it stayed. Mike hobbled around the corral all day, fighting the bit and kicking at the straps when they touched him. After dark he got down to the water and drank in big sucking gulps. He waded into the creek and splashed water on his belly with his forefoot. Snorting, head up, eyes burn-ing, he scrambled up the bank. Far off in the night a horse whinnied. Mike answered with a piercing cry and strained against the fence, his muscles quivering, his heart pounding.

For several days he wore the harness and hated it as much on the last as on the first. He was nervous, frightened and starved. He'd jump at the least sound or movement. They threw him some freshly cut hay. It was wet and sweet; he ate it and looked for more.

One morning they led out a sleepy grey and hitched him to Mike, tying their tails together. For two days the team was driven in the corral. Mike dragged Oak, the big grey, and Marks, the two hundred-pound man, all over the corral. He foamed and sweat, circled and backed. Marks, cursing, jerked and sawed on the lines.

The alfalfa was ready to cut. Marks was short on work horses so he and Little Bill decided to hitch Mike to the mower. They milled for an hour to get Mike backed up to the machine. Marks held the lines while Little Bill tried to hitch them up. He got the neckyoke in place but in reaching over to snap it to Mike's collar he got in front.

Mike's right front foot flashed up, out and down. Little Bill tried to jump back. The ragged, unshod hoof slashed down his chest, skimming clothes and skin from it. Little Bill landed on his shoulders, a scream of pain and fright in his throat. With agility born of terror, he rolled under the fence and lay gasping for breath.

Mike snorted and plunged forward, eager to bite and trample. Marks dug his heels in the dirt and leaned back, seesawing on the reins. The bit clamped on Mike's lower jaw, bringing the blood, cutting his swollen tongue. It forced him to rear, shaking his head and pawing at the air. He came down with one foot over the neck-yoke and another straddling the tongue of the mower. In a mad effort to free himself he fell and was unable to get up.

Marks wrapped the lines around a post and ran to Little Bill. When he got there the boy was sitting up, cautiously exploring his bruised and bloody chest.

"I'm all right," he told Marks, trying hard to smile.

"Better go to the house and get fixed up," said Marks and turned back to the team.

He soft-footed up to Mike's back. He hesitated a moment to take a deep breath, then quickly planted one knee on the horse's neck, just behind the ear. Grasping Mike's nose in his right hand, he twisted it back until it pointed straight up. Mike groaned and writhed. Marks unsnapped the breast strap with his left hand, loosening the neckyoke and freeing Mike's front foot. Then he leapt back and got the lines firmly in his left hand. In his right he held a ten-foot blacksnake.

432

The heavy whip hummed through the air and snapped as it bit into Mike's hide. It brought him to his feet with one movement. He tried to run away but could only follow the corral fence. Marks pivoted in the center, jerking on the lines and swinging the whip.

"Swish-snap! Swish-snap!" The blacksnake writhed back and forth through the air.

When Marks' arm grew tired and his anger cooled he stopped the horses. He forced Mike into the barn and tied him with a heavy rope hackamore. When the harness came off Mike shook himself, a long breath of relief whistling from his lungs. But Marks came back. Mike grew tense. His muscles bunched, ready to snap into action. Marks climbed up on the outside of the stall and leaned over, sliding a broad, heavy strap over Mike's cut and bloody back. Mike flinched and crouched in anticipation.

It came in a minute, before he knew what to expect. Marks reached under his belly with a long wire hook, drew the strap-end to him, slipped it through the end-buckle and reared up on it. Mike's breathing was restricted; the strap hurt his back. With a bawl of rage and pain he threw himself backwards. The hackamore tightened over his ears and around his nose. His eyes bulged. He crashed forward into the manger. He kicked and struck, threw himself and floundered up again. But the band still cut into him. He stopped from exhaustion, his breath rasping through his nostrils, sweat dripping from his belly and flanks. As he stood with legs braced, Marks buckled a hobble strap on each front foot. Then he put the foot rope on, running it from the right hobble, through the ring on the belly band, down to the left hobble, back through the ring and on out behind him. He threw the harness back on and holding the foot rope, led Mike out.

The hobbles and rope frightened Mike. He walked awkwardly, throwing his feet far to the side to get away from them. He made a startled leap, jerking away from Marks, when the harness scraped the side of the door. Marks pulled on the foot-rope. At the third jump Mike's front legs snapped up to his belly. He went down on his nose. A grunt was wrenched from him as his neck twisted back. Then his feet were released and he got up. He started to run, and again his feet were pulled up.

All afternoon he was driven around the corral; every time he tried to fight he was jerked to his nose. He was put in the barn for the night and given a very little hay and water. In the morning

433

he was more gaunt and wild-eyed than ever, and still vicious. When Marks tried to go behind him he slashed out his right hind foot, barely missing him. He tasted the whip for that and bruised and battered himself in trying to break away.

That morning they got him hitched to the mower. Oak, the big grey, pushed and dragged him where he didn't want to go, and bit him when he fought too much.

So they went around and around the field of alfalfa at a tiresome plod with a noise dragging behind them.

Green, damp hay lay under his feet and waved in the breeze beside him, tickling his shoulder, but he couldn't get a mouthful. His tongue was swollen, his jaws and mouth tender and raw from the clamping bit always pressing tightly on his lower jaw, crushing it. His shoulders, under the collar, were sweaty and sore; the hobbles dragged at his feet, chafing them.

When a grouse, springing from the alfalfa with a hum of wings, jarred Oak from his sleepy calm, Mike shied against him and plunged forward. Marks yelled, dropping the foot ropes and lines as he fell backwards off the seat. Oak was frightened and tried to keep up with the running sorrel. The mower bounced and jolted behind them.

The sickle guard caught a rock and snapped off; a wheel broke on another rock. They jumped a ditch. A trace parted, the tongue dropped, plowing into the ground. There was a ripping of leather, a crashing of iron and wood as the mower rolled free. The team gradually slackened, their terror lessening. They stopped in the corner of the field, crowded against the fence.

Marks caught them there. He punished Mike, with a fence pole. Mike kicked back and got more for his resistance. He was taken to the barn half dead.

"I'll put you on the merry-go-round tomorrow. I'll damn well show you," Marks promised.

The merry-go-round, a contraption for taking the fight out of bad horses, had never yet failed. It was made up of two sixty-foot logs bolted to a center post and extending outward in the form of an A. On the end of each was a wagon wheel. About the middle was another wheel fastened between the two to keep them from sagging. On one log was a seat. Between the logs, at the outer ends, the horses were hitched. They were tied to the log in front of them.

As long as the harness held the horses could do nothing but go forward in a circle. After dragging the heavy logs around the center post a few hours almost any horse would "stand without hitching."

But in the morning Marks had to help his men rush in the hay, so Mike had a reprieve. There were no men around, no horses. They were all out in the hay field. An old rooster strutted across the corral talking foolishness to the hens following him. Mike was too tired to chase them out. He stood with his nose on a fence rail to protect it from stinging nose flies. There was no shade then, but in the afternoon the barn would lay its shadow across the corral. Already it was beginning to creep out.

The sneezing of the work horses and the rattling of the harnesses as they came in at noon aroused Mike. He watched them go to the creek and drink deeply, then trot back to the barn, whinnying for oats.

The men paused to look at him.

"He's sure a hell-bender," said one.

In the afternoon Mike stuck his head in the shade of the barn and slept, as peaceful as though he were under his favorite pine tree out on the range. He paid no attention to Little Bill as he sat on the porch whittling. He flipped one ear forward when the cook stepped out slamming the door behind her, then he flipped it back again.

Evening, and the men came in from the field. They watered Mike and fed him a little. Night, and the cool air drifted down from the mountains. Morning—

Marks blindfolded Mike to hitch him to the merry-go-round. With the lines and the whip in his hands he braced himself in the seat. Little Bill was around again so he rode a saddle horse alongside of Mike and jerked the blindfold.

Mike ran till he was winded, dragging Oak and the merry-go-round with him. Then he tried to stop and fight, but Oak went ahead, forcing him along. Marks pulled on the lines to get him used to them.

Around and around they went. The sun was hot. The merry-go-round dragged heavily. The day wore on—slowly! One hour, two hours. The wheels groaned and sent up the choking, pulverized dirt. Blood dripped from Mike's mouth making little spots in it. He got a short breathing spell while Oak was taken out and a fresh horse put in. They started again, around and around on the endless trail.

When Mike lagged he got the whip. Then he would run awhile, fighting the bit, kicking at the man. Finally the whip failed to arouse him. He had no feelings. His feet mechanically carried him around in a circle like a locoed horse trying to catch the shade around a bush too small to throw any shade. Unless stopped, he would go like this till he fell.

At last he was pulled up and driven down to another mower. A fresh horse was put with him. Mike gave no sign. Marks could see he was about done for. He leaned carelessly over to hook the breast strap. Mike's eyes blazed, his muscles quivered as his upper lip curled back. A cry came from Marks as Mike's teeth crushed his arm. The ragged hoof was a blurred streak as it went out. Marks was thrown several feet and lay crumpled in an unnatural position. Mike was an outlaw!

Men came running and they carried Marks away. Then Little Bill got a rifle. He leaned it against the fence, mounted his saddle horse and riding alongside of Mike cut the harness straps with his jack-knife. Guiding his horse with his knees, the rifle in one hand and the hackamore rope in the other, he led Mike up the lane. Out on the flat he slipped the hackamore over his ears.

Mike backed away and stood free with the open range stretched before him. He shied and started to single-foot across the prairie. Little Bill jerked down the lever and watched the shell slide into the barrel. He looked up. Mike was running now, running smoothly, with his head up. Bill lined the sight on the coppery streak and squeezed the trigger.

TRAVEL AND TRANSPORT

"We were isolated . . ." Communication was often "tedious and expensive."

TWO SONGS OF THE TRAIL

Every overland party had its songs, which were sung around the campfire after supper on the trail. Here are two with special historical significance for Montanans, for they were the favorites of the Edgerton party during their trip in 1863 to the Territory, of which Edgerton became the first governor. Journals of Lucia D. Park, Edgerton's niece, and of Mrs. Martha Edgerton Plassman, his daughter, in the Montana State Historical Society library describe the singing of these songs by a man who joined their party, Mr. Everhard, who apparently made a profound impression upon the young ladies of the company. He played his own accompaniment on the violin; but his enunciation was indistinct and he sang "with a pronounced lisp." Such vocal shortcomings, however, did not detract from his popularity and may, in fact, have foreshadowed the style of some of today's radio favorites. Both songs have several more verses; only portions are reprinted here.

Fairy Belle

THE pride of the village and the fairest in the dell
Is queen of my heart, and her name is Fairy Belle.
The song of her light step may be heard upon the hill
Like the fall of the snowdrop or the dripping of the rill.

CHORUS:

Fairy Belle, gentle Fairy Belle,
Star of the night and the lily of the day;
Fairy Belle, queen of all the dell,
Long may she revel in her bright sunny way.

Down the O-hi-o

Oh, the river is up, the channel is deep,
And the wind blows steady and strong,
Let the splash of your oars the measure keep
As we row the old boat along.
Oh! the water is deep and flashing like gold
In the rays of the summer sun—
And old Dinah's away up out of the cold
Agetting the hoe cake done.

439

CHORUS:
Oh, the river is up and the channel is deep
And the wind blows steady and strong;
Let the splash of your oars the measure keep
As we row the old boat along.
Down the river, down the river—
Down the O-hi-o;
Down the river, down the river—
Down the O-hi-o!

Oh, the master is proud of the old broad horn
For it brings him plenty of tin—
The crew they are darkies, the cargo is corn,
And the money comes tumbling in.
There's plenty on board for the darkies to eat,
There's plenty to drink and to smoke;
There's the banjo and bones and tamborine,
There's the song and the comical j-o-o-o-o-o-ke.

Oh, the river is up, etc.

THE NEW NORTHWEST PASSAGE

CAPT. JOHN MULLAN

This is the introduction and first two chapters of Mullan's *Miners'
and Travelers' Guide,* published for the author by William M. Frank-
lin, New York, in 1865. Captain Mullan is listed on the title page
as "late superintendent of the northern overland wagon road and
commissioner of Northern Pacific Railroad." He was appointed by
Gov. I. I. Stevens of Washington Territory in 1859 to construct a
wagon road connecting Walla Walla with Fort Benton and completed
it in 1863. This road, which today is suitably marked in Montana,
was of tremendous importance in opening up the Northwest. It
crossed the Rockies a few miles north of the present McDonald Pass
highway between Helena and Missoula; the Northern Pacific Railroad and a county road now use Mullan Pass. A mural painting by
Irvin (Shorty) Shope featuring a six-horse stage on the Mullan road
hangs in the highway department building at Helena. Most of the
advice given by Mullan herein would be indorsed by the skilled mountain packer today; note especially his suggestion that the animals be
governed "as you would a woman, with kindness, affection, and
caresses," in order to win their "docility and easy management."

. . .

DURING the past fourteen years the entire emigration that
has sought the Pacific Coast, with the view of there making permanent homes, has taken either the route across
the continent, via the South Pass, involving 2,000 miles of land
travel, or via the Isthmus of Panama, involving 6,000 miles of sea
travel; both fraught with heavy expense, danger and discomfort.

The great desire of all has been to secure a route where the sea
travel would be avoided in toto; and at the same time have the land
transit the shortest minimum. The geography of the section of the
Continent west of the Mississippi shows that this can only be attained by ascending the Missouri river to its highest point practicable for steamers, and thence cross to the navigable waters of the
Columbia, where we find the land carriage only 624 miles.

Having been occupied for a number of years in the exploration
and construction of the wagon road via this route, I feel warranted
in placing in a brief form such advice, facts, and statements as our
labors in the field have developed.

Those who desire to make this trip should apply for further information to Charles P. Chouteau, of St. Louis, or to John G. Copelan, of St. Louis, both of whom are interested in forwarding passengers and freight from St. Louis to the Rocky Mountain region, at the headwaters of the Missouri and Columbia rivers. Their steamers are generally ready to leave St. Louis somewhere between the 4th of March and 1st of May—starting thus early in order to take advantage of the June rise which they meet at or near Sioux City, and which enables them to run over all the bars and shoals found in the difficult stream of the Missouri.

These boats make the trip but once a year, and hence all travelers should make their preparations in time to take the boats by 1st April, either from St. Louis or from Walla-Walla. John G. Copelan will keep constantly a steamer between Fort Benton and the Yellowstone for the accommodation of travelers who wish to return east in early spring, or late in the autumn. Wagons and outfits of all kinds can at present be secured at Fort Benton.

Travelers will probably find fresh vegetables at Sun River, on the Big Prickly Pear, in the Deer Lodge Valley, Hellsgate Valley, at the Coeur d'Alene Mission, on the Spokane River, on the Touchet River, Dry Creek and Walla-Walla, and fresh beef at each and all of these points.

Fresh animals can be purchased at nearly all these points, and blacksmith shops will be found at the Deer Lodge, Hellsgate, and Coeur d'Alene Mission.

No fear need be apprehended from Indians along the entire route. The trip from St. Louis to Fort Benton will involve from 35 to 40 days, and from Fort Benton to Walla-Walla about the same length of time.

The following more detailed statistics published in an official report will be found to contain much of interest to those who have never made the trip:

Recommendations for Travele s

For persons who desire to leave St. Louis in the spring on steamer for Fort Benton, where the passage is from $100 to $200, and freight from ten cents to twelve cents per pound, and who desire to make the land transit by wagon, I would advise that they provide themselves with a light spring covered wagon in St. Louis, also two or four sets of strong harness, and transport them to Fort Benton, where they can procure their animals, mules or horses. The former can be had from $100 to $150, the latter from $50 to $75; oxen, from $100 to $125 per yoke. Let them provide themselves with a small kit of good strong tin or plated iron mess furniture; kettles to fit one in the other, tin plates and cups, and strong knives and forks; purchase their own supplies in St. Louis; brown sugar, coffee, or tea, bacon, flour, salt, beans, sardines, and a few jars of pickles and preserved fruits will constitute a perfect outfit in this department. I have found that for ten men for fifty days, the following is none too much on a trip of this kind: 625 pounds of flour, 50 pounds of coffee, 75 pounds of sugar, 2 bushels of beans, 1 bushel of salt, 625 pounds of bacon sides, 2 gallons of vinegar, 20 pounds of dried apples, 3 dozen of yeast powders, and by all means take two strong covered ovens, (Dutch ovens.) These amounts can be increased or diminished in proportion to the number of men and number of days. If your wagon tires become loose on the road, caulk them with old gunny sacks, or in lieu thereof, with any other sacking; also, soak the wheels well in water whenever an opportunity occurs. In loading the wagons, an allowance of four hundred pounds to the animal will be found sufficient for a long journey. For riding saddles, select a California or Mexican tree with machiers and taphederos, hair girth, double grey saddle blanket, and strong snaffle bit.

If the intention is to travel with a pack train, take the cross-tree packsaddle, with crupper and breeching, and broad thick pads. Use lash-rope, with canvas or leather belly bands. Have a double blanket under each saddle. Balance the load equally on the two sides of the animal—the whole not to exceed two hundred pounds. Have a canvas cover for each pack. A mule-blind may be found useful in packing. Each pack animal should have a hackama, and every animal (packing and riding) a picket-rope, from thirty-five to forty feet long and one inch in diameter. For my own purposes, I have always preferred mules to horses. Packages of any shape can be loaded upon the aparejo more conveniently than upon the packsaddle. A bell animal should be always kept with a pack train, and a grey mare is generally preferred. Every article to be used in crossing the plains should be of the best manufacture and strongest material. This will, in the end, prove true economy. Animals should be shod on the fore-feet, at least. Starting at dawn and camping not later than 2 P.M., I have always found the best plan in marching. Animals should not go out of a walk or a slow trot, and after being unloaded in camp they should always be allowed to stand with their saddles on and girths loose, for at least fifteen minutes, as the sudden exposure of their warm backs to the air tends to scald them. They should be regularly watered, morning, noon, and night. Never maltreat them, but govern them as you would a woman, with kindness, affection, and caresses, and you will be repaid by their docility and easy management.

If you travel with a wagon, provide yourself with a jackscrew, extra tongue, and coupling pole; also, axle-grease, a hatchet and nails, auger, rope, twine, and one or two chains for wheel locking, and one or two extra whippletrees, as well as such other articles as in your own judgment may be deemed necessary. A light canvas tent, with poles that fold in the middle by a hinge, I have always found most convenient. Tables and chairs can be dispensed with, but if deemed absolutely necessary, the old army camp stool, and a table with lid that removes and legs that fold under, I have found to best subserve all camp requisites.

Never take anything not absolutely necessary. This is a rule of all experienced voyageurs.

Advice to Emigrants by This Route

Those who start from the Upper Mississippi frontier can replenish their supplies at Fort Union, at the mouth of the Yellowstone; at Fort Benton, and, in addition, at the other points hitherto alluded to.

Those who travel by the central or Platte route, and desire to take the western section of the road to Walla-Walla, can deflect either at Fort Laramie, the Red Buttes, or Fort Hall, and connect with it at the Deer Lodge Valley.

The road from Fort Laramie to the Deer Lodge Valley has never been worked, but was passed over with wagons by Captain Reynolds, of the army, in 1859 and 1860, and by miners in 1863–64. It passes through a beautiful, easy, and interesting region.

The road from Fort Hall to Deer Lodge has been used by wagons for many years, and though not worked is quite practicable.*

* There follows a detailed itinerary of the eastbound trip by wagon from Walla Walla to Fort Benton, logging daily moves and stops, and showing 47 days' travel time for 624 miles; probable time, however, allowing for delays and accidents, is put at 55 days. For a pack train, Mullan estimates 35 days for the trip. The construction of the road, Mullan reports, "involved 120 miles of difficult timber-cutting, twenty-five feet broad, and thirty measured miles of excavation, fifteen to twenty feet wide. The remainder was either through an open, timbered country, or over open, rolling prairie."

HOW BIG SANDY GOT ITS NAME

The Fort Benton River Press carried this story June 4, 1890. It gives Big Sandy a more interesting origin than have the scores of towns in Montana which were dully named after obscure and forgotten officials of transcontinental railroads!

THE town and creek of Big Sandy take their name from "Big Sandy" Lane, who was formerly a mule skinner on the old freight road out of Fort Benton, and who is now whiling away a peaceful existence in Helena dealing faro. The legend is that Big Sandy came to the creek one evening with a train of time freight * due at Fort Assinniboine next day, consisting principally of bacon and hard tack upon which the life of the soldiers depended. It had been raining hard all day and the wheels were often clogged with gumbo, but Sandy had such a persuasive way of addressing the mules that good headway was made until the creek was reached. Here he found the banks so treacherous and the water so swollen that after much shouting and rattling of chains he found it impossible to cross. Sandy then began cursing his luck, the weather, and the mules so vehemently that in a short time the creek dried up, and he crossed on dry land, reaching his destination in time to save the garrison from starvation. Many old freighters are yet living who will vouch for the truth of this legend. Even to this day at certain seasons the creek sinks where Sandy crossed—reappearing, however, a short distance below.

* Time freight: "rush"; perishable goods.

THE PONY EXPRESS

LT. JAMES H. BRADLEY

This is one of the invaluable Bradley manuscripts in the possession of the Historical Society of Montana, described elsewhere in this book. The excerpt is from "Account of the Attempts to Build a Town at the Mouth of the Musselshell River," in Vol. II of the *Contributions*, 1896.

. . .

D URING the year 1867 the government let a contract for the establishment of a pony mail route from St. Paul, Minnesota, to Helena, Montana; Fort Hawley being one of the stations, and the point of departure from the Missouri River for Diamond City. The service, however, was very ill-performed, and a measure that might have been of great benefit to the country became a positive detriment from the repeated losses of the mail matter forwarded by the route. The pony-riders had long and difficult journeys to make between the different stations, they found fuel scarce and newspapers heavy, and with happy ingenuity got over both difficulties by burning the papers, and developing still farther their inventive talent made excellent cigar lighters out of the letters in the mail sack. To receive a letter over the route at all soon became a matter of surprise, and at last the government refused payment for the ill-performed services and the route was abandoned.

In the spring of 1868, Al. Bradbury, superintendent of the western section of the route—which, we will remark, was exceptionally well conducted—arrived at Musselshell, having been engaged in collecting the material of the company and closing up its affairs. About the middle of April he set out for Helena accompanied by Henry McDonald, a daring and successful rider on the route, and four other men, the party having in its possession some five or six horses. The route chosen led them over the Judith Mountains, and, as they neared their base, they discovered at a distance a party of about thirty Sioux Indians whose movements were threatening and the party sought a commanding knoll and prepared for defense

447

by digging small rifle pits with their butcher knives. The Indians came up and attacked them vigorously, making repeated charges against their position, which were all repulsed. Here under a hot fire they maintained a stubborn defense for two hours, when night fell.

They had lost all their horses, killed in the course of the attack, and two of the men were wounded though not disabled. As soon as the darkness screened their movements they abandoned their position and were enabled to elude the vigilance of the savages, and Bradbury with four of his companions subsequently reached the settlements without further adventure. But not so the other, named Dennis. During the night he became separated from his companions and with all his efforts was unable to rejoin them. He floundered about in the darkness in a state of no little anxiety, and when morning broke discovered to his dismay that the Indians were upon his trail. He fled at his best speed, but found that he was being rapidly overtaken. Escape now seemed impossible, but with the desperation of despair he pressed on.

He was now entangled in the "bad-lands" prevalent in that region, which is seamed and scarred by the combined action of wind and water until it presents an illimitable dismal prospect of barren mounds, naked ridges and deep, steep-walled ravines, difficult to traverse and almost completely shunned by every form of animal and vegetable life. As he struggled on he came upon one of those sinks, so common in such regions, where the water has worn a subterranean channel from the high ground to the bottom of some ravine. The Indians were now close at hand and into this he plunged, crawling forward till he found an indentation in the side, into which he sank and lay motionless. The Indians were not long in reaching the spot and discovered his hiding place. The winding course of the hole hid the white man from their view and they hesitated to follow him into his cavern. But one could advance at a time, and should the white man be armed—as seemed probable— the leader at least must be killed. It was a desperate enterprise and all shrank from it.

But at last they discovered the exit of the sink in the ravine below. An entrance here was less perilous, as it was supposed the white man's attention would be directed to the other opening and he might be surprised by a cautious advance. Three young warriors stripped and entered. As they crept slowly and noiselessly up the narrow way, by an instinctive feeling Dennis became aware of their approach. He was armed with a revolver, and shrinking close in his little cavern he nerved himself for a desperate defense. He was unaware of the number of his foes; but resolved if the leader passed him without discovery to permit him to do so, and thus get two in range before firing. On they came, and as Dennis had hoped, the foremost savage, peering straight forward, glided by on his hands and knees as noiselessly as a mouse. Close behind him followed a second and aiming as well as he could through the intense gloom, Dennis pulled the trigger. Before the savage who had passed him could recover from his astonishment Dennis fired another shot with the muzzle almost touching the body of his foe. Then all was still except the hurried scrambling of the rearmost Indian as he retreated by the way he had come, leaving Dennis alone with the motionless forms of his two victims.

The shots came to the ears of the Indians above, and they anxiously awaited the result. But no shout of triumph came from their comrades in the sink and presently the sole survivor of the three rejoined them with the story of his companions' probable fate. Then a yell of rage and lamentation went up outside, and Dennis listened in trembling apprehension lest the desire of revenge should urge them to a still more desperate effort against his life. But it was not made. Their "medicine" proved too weak and they sought their recompense of scalps in the pursuit of some less hazardous enterprise.

All day Dennis remained in his cavern, tortured with suspense, listening for the movements of his foes without, but for hours all was still. When night came he crept past the bodies of his victims and ventured forth, choosing the outlet into the ravine. To his great joy the enemy was gone, and he lost no time in putting all possible distance between himself and the scene of so much mental suffering. But his troubles were not over, for during two days he wandered without food or water, and then had the good fortune to reach a camp of Crow Indians, where he obtained refreshment and repose and the next day made his way to Musselshell.

SONG OF THE OVERLAND STAGE-DRIVER

NAT STEIN

Montana, as noted elsewhere in this book, has created few folk songs. Here, however, is one born in Virginia City, where its author, Nat Stein, was the agent for the Overland Express, succeeded soon after the song was written by Wells-Fargo. The song, which used the tune of "The High Salary Driver on the Denver City Line" (and don't ask us what that tune was!) first appeared in *The Montana Post* in Virginia City, Montana Territory, April 8, 1865. It caught on with the drivers (Stein, though an "office" man, was popular with them) and was sung by them until they vanished from the Montana scene with the coming of the railroad.

I SING to everybody, in the country and the town,
A song, upon a subject that's worthy of renown;
I haven't got a story of Fairyland to broach,
But plead the cause of sticking to the box-seat of a coach.

CHORUS:
Statesmen and warriors, traders and the rest,
May boast of their profession, and think it is the best;
Their state I'll never envy, I'll have you understand,
Long as I can be a driver on the jolly Overland.

There's beauty never-ending, for me, upon the plains,
That's worth a man's beholding, at any cost of pains;
And in the Indian country it offers me a fund
Of glee, to see the antelope and prairie dogs abscond.

Statesmen and warriors, etc.

The mountains and the canyons, in turn afford delight,
As often as I pass them, by day or in the night;
That man must be a ninny, who'd bury up alive,
When all it costs to revel through creation—is to drive.

Statesmen and warriors, etc.

Alike are all the seasons and weathers, to my mind,
Nor heat nor cold can daunt me, or make me lag behind.
In daylight and in darkness, through rain and shine and snow,
It's my confirmed ambition, to be up and on the go.

    Statesmen and warriors, etc.

You ask me for our leader, I'll soon inform you then,
It's Holladay, they call him, and often only Ben;
If you can read the papers, it's easy work to scan
He beats the world on staging now, "or any other man."

    Statesmen and warriors, etc.

And so, you must allow me, the Agent at his books
And selling passage-tickets, how woe-begone he looks!
'Twould cause his eyes to twinkle, his drooping heart revive,
Could he but hold the ribbons, and obtain a chance to drive.

    Statesmen and warriors, etc.

The Sup'rintendent, even, though big a chief he be,
Would find it quite a poser to swap off berths with me;
And if Division Agents, though clever coves and fine,
Should make me such an offer, you can gamble I'd decline.

    Statesmen and warriors, etc.

The Station Keepers nimble, and Messengers so gay,
Have duties of importance, and please me every way;
But never let them fancy, for anything alive,
I'd take their situations, and give up to them my drive.

    Statesmen and warriors, etc.

And then the trusty fellows, who tend upon the stock
And do the horses justice, as reg'lar as a clock,
I love them late and early, and wish them well to thrive,
But theirs is not my mission, for I'm bound, you see, to drive.

    Statesmen and warriors, etc.

451

A truce to these distinctions, since all the hands incline,
To stick up for their business, as I stick up for mine;
And, like a band of brothers, our efforts we unite,
To please the traveling public, and the mails to expedite.

 Statesmen and warriors, etc.

It's thus, you're safely carried throughout the mighty West,
Where chances to make fortunes are ever found the best;
And thus, the precious pouches of mail are brought to hand,
Through the ready hearts that centre on the jolly Overland.

 Statesmen and warriors, traders and the rest,
 May boast of their profession, and think it is the best;
 Their state I'll never envy, I'll have you understand,
 Long as I can be a driver on the jolly Overland.

THE STAGE RIDE

FRANCES M. A. ROE

This is from *Army Letters from an Officer's Wife,* by Frances M. A. Roe, published in 1909 by D. Appleton. Mrs. Roe spent ten years in Montana, in which time she lived at most of the Territory's army posts. Historical researchers frequently complain that contemporary reporters fail to record adequately the little things—clothing, food, shelter, transport—the familiar things which were a part of the mechanics of living in a certain period. No such criticism could be brought against Mrs. Roe, to whom everything about life in Montana was fresh and interesting. Hers is one of the best books of memoirs of that time.

Camp on Marias River, Montana Territory
September 8, 1878

. . .

I was glad enough to get away from that old stage. It was one of the jerky, bob-back-and-forth kind that pitches you off the seat every five minutes. The first two or three times you bump heads with the passenger sitting opposite, you can smile and apologize with some grace, but after a while your hat will not stay in place and your head becomes sensitive, and finally you discover that the passenger is the most disagreeable person you ever saw, and that the man sitting beside you is inconsiderate and selfish, and really occupying two thirds of the seat.

We came a distance of one hundred and forty miles, getting fresh horses every twenty miles or so. The morning we left Helena was glorious, and I was half ashamed because I felt so happy at coming from the town, where so many of my friends were in sorrow [Helena had just suffered serious losses in a sudden flood] but tried to console myself with the fact that I had been ordered away by Doctor Gordon. There were many cases of typhoid fever, and the rheumatic fever that has made Mrs. Sargent so ill has developed into typhoid, and there is very little hope for her recovery.

The driver would not consent to my sitting on top with him, so I had to ride inside with three men. They were not rough-looking at all, and their clothes looked clean and rather new, but gave one the impression that they had been made for other people. Their pale faces told that they were "tenderfeet," and one could see there was a sad lacking of brains all around.

The road comes across a valley the first ten or twelve miles, and then runs into a magnificent canyon that is sixteen miles long, called Prickly-Pear Canyon. As I wrote some time ago, everything is brought up to this country by enormous ox trains, some coming from the railroad at Corinne, and some that come from Fort Benton during the Summer, having been brought up by boat on the Missouri River. In the canyons these trains are things to be dreaded. The roads are very narrow and the grades often long and steep, with immense boulders above and below.

We met one of those trains soon after we entered the canyon, and at the top of a grade where the road was scarcely wider than the stage itself and seemed to be cut into a wall of solid rock. Just how we were to pass those huge wagons I did not see. But the driver stopped his horses and two of the men got out, the third stopping on the step and holding on to the stage so it was impossible for me to get out, unless I went out the other door and stood on the edge of an awful precipice. The driver looked back, and not seeing me, bawled out, "Where is the lady?" "Get the lady out!" The man on the step jumped down then, but the driver did not put his reins down, or move from his seat until he had seen me safely on the ground and had directed me where to stand.

In the meantime some of the train men had come up, and, as soon as the stage driver was ready, they proceeded to lift the stage—trunks and all—over and on some rocks and tree tops, and then the four horses were led around in between other rocks, where it seemed impossible for them to stand one second. There were three teams to come up, each consisting of about eight yoke of oxen and three or four wagons. It made me almost ill to see the poor patient oxen straining and pulling up the grade those huge wagons so heavily loaded. The crunching and groaning of the wagons, rattling of the enormous cable chains, and the creaking of the heavy yokes of the oxen were awful sounds, and above all came the yells of the drivers, and the sharp, pistol-like reports of the long whips that they mercilessly cracked over the backs of the poor beasts. It was most distressing.

After the wagons had all passed, men came back and set the

454

stage on the road in the same indifferent way and with very few words. Each man seemed to know just what to do, as though he had been training for years for the moving of that particular stage. The horses had not stirred and had paid no attention to the yelling and cracking of whips. While coming through the canyons we must have met six or seven of those trains, every one of which necessitated the setting in mid-air of the stage coach. It was the same performance always, each man knowing just what to do, and doing it, too, without loss of time. Not once did the driver put down the reins until he saw that "the lady" was safely out and it was ever with the same sing-song, "balance to the right," voice that he asked about me—except once, when he seemed to think more emphasis was needed, when he made the canyon ring by yelling, "Why in hell don't you get the lady out!" But the lady always got herself out. Rough as he was, I felt intuitively that I had a protector. We stopped at Rock Creek for dinner, and there he saw that I had the best of everything, and it was the same at Spitzler's, where we had supper.

We got fresh horses at The Leavings, and when I saw a strange driver on the seat my heart sank, fearing that from there on I might not have the same protection. We were at a large ranch—sort of an inn—and just beyond was Frozen Hill. The hill was given that name because a number of years ago a terrible blizzard struck some companies of infantry while on it, and before they could get to the valley below, or to a place of shelter, one half of the men were more or less frozen—some losing legs, some arms. They had been marching in thin clothing that was more or less damp from perspiration, as the day had been excessively hot. These blizzards are so fierce and wholly blinding, it is unsafe to move a step if caught out in one on the plains, and the troops probably lost their bearings as soon as the storm struck them.

It was almost dark when we got in the stage to go on, and I thought it rather queer that the driver should have asked us to go to the corral, instead of his driving around to the ranch for us. Very soon we were seated, but we did not start, and there seemed to be something wrong, judging by the way the stage was being jerked, and one could feel, too, that the brake was on. One by one those men got out, and just as the last one stepped down on one side the heads of two cream-colored horses appeared at the open door on the other side, their big troubled eyes looking straight at me.

During my life on the frontier I have seen enough of native horses to know that when a pair of excited mustang leaders try to get inside a stage, it is time for one to get out, so I got out! One of those men passengers instantly called to me, "You stay in there!" I asked, "Why?" "Because it is perfectly safe," said a second man. I was very indignant at being spoken to in this way and turned my back to them. The driver got the leaders in position, and then looking around, said to me that when the balky wheelers once started they would run up the hill "like the devil," and I would surely be left unless I was inside the stage.

I knew that he was telling the truth, and if he had been the first man to tell me to get in the coach I would have done so at once, but it so happened that he was the fourth, and by that time I was beginning to feel abused. It was bad enough to have to obey just one man, when at home, and then to have four strange men—three of them idiots, too—suddenly take upon themselves to order me around was not to be endured. I had started on the trip with the expectation of taking care of myself, and still felt competent to do so. Perhaps I was very tired, and perhaps I was very cross. At all events I told the driver I would not get in—that if I was left I would go back to the ranch. So I stayed outside, taking great care, however, to stand close to the stage door.

The instant I heard the loosening of the brake I jumped up on the step, and catching a firm hold each side of the door, was about to step in when one of those men passengers grabbed my arm and tried to jerk me back, so he could get in ahead of me! It was a dreadful thing for anyone to do, for if my hands and arms had not been unusually strong from riding hard-mouthed horses, I would undoubtedly have been thrown underneath the big wheels and horribly crushed, for the four horses were going at a terrific gait, and the jerky was swaying like a live thing. As it was, anger and indignation gave me extra strength and I scrambled inside with nothing more serious happening than a bruised head. But that man! He pushed in back of me, and, not knowing the nice little ways of jerkies, was pitched forward to the floor with an awful thud. But after a second or so he pulled himself up on his seat, which was opposite mine, and there we two sat in silence and in darkness. I noticed the next morning that there was a big bruise on one side of his face, at the sight of which I rejoiced very much.

It was some distance this side of the hill when the driver stopped his horses and waited for the two men who had been left. They seemed much exhausted when they came up, but found sufficient breath to abuse the driver for having left them; but he at once roared out, "Get in, I tell you, or I'll leave you sure enough!" That settled matters, and we started on again. Very soon those men fell asleep and rolled off their seats to the floor, where they snored and had bad dreams. I was jammed in a corner without mercy, and of course did not sleep one second during the long wretched night. Twice we stopped for fresh horses, and at both places I walked about a little to rest my cramped feet and limbs. At breakfast the next morning I asked the driver to let me ride on top with him, which he consented to, and from there on to Benton I had peace and fresh air—the glorious air of Montana.

Yesterday—the day after I got here—I was positively ill from the awful shaking up, mental as well as physical, I received on that stage ride. We reached Benton at eleven.

A TOWN IS BORN

This sardonic comment on the enthusiasm of Montana's "boosters" in the railroad era is from Leeson's *History of Montana* (1885). The Utah & Northern (now Union Pacific) entered Montana in 1880, the Northern Pacific in 1881, Great Northern in 1887, Chicago, Milwaukee & St. Paul in 1906.

APROPOS of the building of this [the Northern Pacific] road and its effect upon the settlement of the central belt of Montana and its growth from east to west, the following story is told as related by a locomotive engineer:

"One day I was driving my engine over the prairie at the rate of forty miles an hour, without a house in sight, and supposing the nearest town to be thirty miles distant. But as I glanced ahead I was astonished to see that I was approaching a large city. I rubbed my eyes thinking it was a mirage.

" 'Jim,' says I to the fireman, 'what's this place?'

" 'Blamed if I know!' says Jim, staring out of the cab. 'I declare, if there ain't a new town growed up here since we went over the line yesterday!'

" 'I believe you're right, Jim. Ring the bell or we shall run over somebody.'

"So I slowed up, and we pulled into a depot, where more than five hundred people were waiting to see the first train come into the place. The conductor learned the name of the town, put it down on the schedule, and we went on.

" 'Jim,' says I, as we pulled out, 'keep your eyes open for new towns. First thing you know we'll be running by some strange place.'

" 'That's so!' says Jim. 'An' hadn't we better git one of the brakemen to watch out on the rear platform for towns that spring up after the engine gets by?' "

458

THE LAST SPIKE

GEORGE A. BRUFFEY

The Northern Pacific, first northern transcontinental railway, was started in 1870 and completed Sept. 8, 1883, with the driving of the "golden spike" at Gold Creek, Mont.—site of the James and Granville Stuart gold prospect of 1858. Eyewitnesses to the ceremony, including the one quoted here, said the spike wasn't gold. This is how the ceremony looked to the average Montana visitor, who took his lunch, was bored by the financiers' speeches about their troubles in world money markets, but liked Ulysses S. Grant because he gave the credit to those to whom it belonged. This account is from *Eighty-one Years in the West* by George A. Bruffey, published by the Butte Miner Co. in 1925. Bruffey was a pioneer miner, merchant, and farmer. His story passes over one prominent figure in the "last spike" ceremony, the black horse Nig, which was one of the two that drew the cars bearing the last rails into position. Nig wore a sign, and stepped proudly along the rows of spectators so that all might read: "My name is Nig; I have drawn the iron car 750 miles."

THE Northern Pacific was completed, except for the laying of a few rails to connect the eastern portion with the western. The road-building had advanced from St. Paul and the Pacific coast to their junction on the Hell Gate River in Deer Lodge County, and the last spike was to be driven at Gold Creek, near where the Stuart boys had discovered gold in 1858.

With my young friend, George Scott, and an old and truly-tried friend of years, Frank E. Curtis, one of the Fiske party who came in by the northern route with Jim Fiske in 1862, we made a party of three to go and see the driving of the "last spike."

With two good Montana horses, one of John W. Lowell's two-seated spring buggies, with Scott as driver, we made Butte City, twenty-eight miles distant, in one afternoon. After a pleasant night's rest we took on our old friend, Joseph Ramsdell, a boon companion of years; he was one of the dauntless few of the party of 1863. We were now a gleeful party of four, bound for pleasure, and to witness one of the most significant events of our time.

We drove forty miles down through the beautiful Deer Lodge Valley, then covered with fine productive ranches all free from debt

459

and taxes. Horses and cattle were to be seen everywhere, and every home seemed surrounded by comfort and plenty. After a night's rest at Mr. Ramsdell's ranch, four miles below Deer Lodge, we again started out, this time being equipped with a big box of grub put up for us by one Louis Coleman at Doctor Higgins' store. Our hostess at the ranch, Mrs. Tedrow, added a few loaves of bread and two or three pounds of her golden Montana butter to our box of lunch. We had the pleasure of dividing this among a hungry crowd some twelve miles down the Hell Gate River.

The trains, driving on schedule time from the East, were bringing many guests of the company. Many of these were from foreign lands—Holland, Germany, and other countries. They were the representatives of the money-lenders in foreign lands who had loaned money to complete the railroad and were now specially invited guests of the president of the Northern Pacific, Mr. Villard. General Grant was among the guests from the East, as well as the governors from Wisconsin, Minnesota, and Dakota, and many officers of the company.

Two well-equipped trains from the West came in bringing the governors of Washington and Oregon. With them was the old builder of Oregon, who was one time the head of the Columbia Navigation Company. He was now old and on crutches, and known all over the West as "Colonel" Baker. There was also the builder of the well-known Mullan road, which was built from Fort Benton on the Missouri, the head of navigation, to Fort Walla Walla in Washington Territory, started in 1858 and completed in 1862. It was one of the greatest arteries of the West. He, Mullan, was a jubilant guest at this eventful meeting. Many old St. Louis people were there, now residents of Butte and Philipsburg. R. D. Leggat, C. S. McClure, John Noyes, James Mills, and many other good citizens of Montana were present.

The exercises commenced by the booming of a six-gun battery, planted on a slope, manned by a contingent of about one hundred men, officers and soldiers. The soldiers presumed to police the meeting. A large grandstand had been provided for the distinguished guests and visitors and some smooth planks for a crowd of laymen. An officer with about twelve soldiers marched down to guard the gangway between the grandstand and the seats to prevent intrusion on the specially reserved grounds. The unsophisticated miner, nothing loath, strode down the aisle, pushed through the guards, pressed between each gun and went up to the front. Villard came down and asked the officer if he could not keep those men back. "Yes, by bayonetting them!" he said, "but we don't want to do that." They then stretched a rope, but these gentlemen of the West dodged under it or stepped over it, whichever was convenient, and went on up to the front. I will never forget the genial smile of General Grant as he viewed these intrepid miners of the time.

After this feeble attempt to govern the crowd, now numbering over two thousand, Villard came down and released the guard. They went back to their brass battery, to the great satisfaction of the crowd.

The speaking was now on. Villard opened with a long history of the coming of the railroad—its attendant trials and failures. He told us that the company had spent the enormous sum of seventy million dollars and how he, with little assistance, had secured loans from European financiers. Representatives of those financiers were there at the meeting. He believed they would see that the money invested would bring big returns. The road traveled a vast country where many people would flock and build homes and where peace and plenty would abound.

He was followed by a professor from one of the famous schools of learning in Germany. He spoke well of the project and its land grant so generously given to the road by this great government (every other section for forty miles each side of the right of way.) Next, Frederick Billings, an ex-president of the company, spoke of the hard times and other untoward circumstances on account of which he had failed to accomplish much. Next, General Grant spoke. He commended the work, and said: "You fellows talk of who built the Northern Pacific Railroad. I say it was these hardy miners represented here today that built the railroad. For twenty years they have developed the mines, sending millions to the East, proving to the world its hidden wealth. It is already a land of plenty, with many comforts and every necessity."

It was now time to close the gap between the East and West. Two loaded cars, one from the East and one from the West, bore the material for the track. Each car was manned by a crew of well-trained workmen. Two well-trained horses, one at each car, drew the rails into place, bringing the West and East closer and closer until in less time than it takes to tell it the gap was closed. Villard

461

appeared, holding aloft an old rusty spike that had been drawn from the road at the terminal near the Great Lakes. "This," he said, "is the Golden Spike! We will proceed to drive it here to commemorate the extension of the Northern Pacific from the Great Lakes to the Pacific Coast—the union of the East with the West." There was a mad scramble to "hit the spike a lick." Miss Villard, General Grant, and others tried. Rod Leggat, one of the Butte delegation, had a hammer in his hand all the time and was hitting the spikes as they were driven by the workmen. "Let General Grant drive it!" he cried, but no one will ever know who drove the Golden Spike. The engines hissed, and all was over.

After the exercises we stayed at Mr. Ramsdell's overnight and then went on to our homes.

JOURNEY

FRED J. WARD

Fred J. Ward, whose country-weekly editorial, "Star in the East," is to be found in another section of this book, wrote "Journey" for *The Frontier*, Vol. XIII, No. 3, March, 1933. In this straightforward story may be read "life in Montana" at its most dramatic: this could be any Montanan's journey any time in the unpredictable winter, anywhere except on the main highways which are cleared for essential bus travel—and sometimes even there. Imminent death is implicit on every page of this story, yet thousands of Montanans who have survived similar experiences might wonder why Mr. Ward chose such a familiar incident as a theme for his tale, and fail altogether to recognize its dramatic value. Why, this could happen to anybody in Montana! And it does.

JOVIS HOLT turned on the light in the rear of the garage and made his way to the single-seated coupé that was parked in the corner. He pushed it by hand through the big door that opened into the repair shop, swung the jack under the differential and raised the hind wheels off the floor. Methodically he tested the air in all four tires, struck the spare with his fist to see if it was hard. He slung a chain round each of the rear wheels and fastened them with cross springs. Letting the rear down, he dragged the jack to the front of the car and set a pair of chains to the front wheels.

The side door of the garage opened and Henry Rourke came stumbling through, accompanied by a gust of wind and a spatter of rain.

"Say, Jovis," he demanded, "you are not trying to go to Montana City tonight?"

Jovis Holt, now sitting in the seat, had just touched his foot to the starter. He nodded his head in the affirmative. The old car gave a roar. Jovis turned off the switch, climbed out of the driver's seat and raised the hood.

Henry Rourke touched him on the arm. "Don't tell me, man, that you are going out in such a storm."

Jovis did not answer.

Henry Rourke caught him still more urgently by the arm.

"There isn't a thing you can do. What's happened is likely past all mending. Wait until morning."

Jovis Holt turned lusterless eyes on his friend. "By morning there will be two feet of snow on the divide."

Henry directed a flashlight under the hood for Jovis, who was now examining the timer. "Why don't you take my car? It's a new car, enclosed—"

"This old car has three inches more clearance. I'm expecting to run into snow."

Henry turned away. He opened the side door of the garage half-way. Stray flakes of snow eddied across the floor. He closed the door and turned back to the man working over the motor.

"If you're bound to go, Jovis, I'll go along."

"The car stands a better chance to get across the ridge road without a load. I'll go alone."

"Have you got plenty of clothes? I'll get you another overcoat." Henry stumbled out through the door.

Jovis emptied the contents of a glycerine bottle into the radiator and added water until the solution rose to the overflow pipe. He examined the gasoline in the rear tank, poured a quart of oil into the crank case. He unlatched the big door and pushed it against the driving wind until it was wide open; climbed into the driver's seat and buttoned the side curtains fast. Before Henry Rourke returned Jovis had driven out into the night.

Jovis turned the car westward through the main part of the village, swung south at the bank corner toward Ash creek. A half-dozen windows at the edge of town glowed dimly in the storm. The car splashed heavily through pools of water that collected in the parallel ruts marking the road up Ash creek. Water was running in rivulets in every coulee crossing. Where the highway traverses the bottoms by the Crown-W ranch it had gathered in a shallow pond, but the ground beneath the wheels was firm. Jovis pressed on the accelerator until the speedometer registered twenty miles an hour, then twenty-five, finally thirty. At this point he held it steady. Rain beat against the side curtains, drove through the crack at the bottom of the windshield in tiny bubbles. It showed in the twin lights of the headlamps like oblique scratches against the black prairie ahead.

A flood had gathered on Tussler creek at the point where it crosses the road. Jovis brought the car to a stop. He got out, clutched

464

at his heavy cap, and braced his body against the gale. He stood at the edge of the stream, measuring the width of the water with his eye. There are no bridges across Tussler draw, but during the summer an enterprising farmer had hauled three loads of gravel to the roadbed at this point. Whether the gravel had been washed away the man could not tell. Some driftwood had lodged under the fence below the road. Russian thistles, which had rolled into the coulee during the dry summer months, had washed against the driftwood, and now formed a dam, over which the muddy waters were pouring.

Jovis unstrapped the shovel from the rear of the car and using it as a balancing staff, climbed perilously out on the lower wire a third of the way across. Bracing himself against the wind, which tore at every loose fold of his clothes and drove the streaming rain against his face, he jabbed at the thistles until he had cut a narrow path for the water to pour through. He set the blade of the shovel under the foremost piece of drift and pushed, but failed to move it. He pried at a second piece, which also held fast. The third piece, however, gave way with a suddenness that almost tumbled him into the water.

Jovis Holt climbed back to the edge of the stream and again measured the width of the flow with his eye. He strapped his shovel onto the back of the car, got in and started the motor, then threw the clutch into low. The car splashed, hesitated, gave a lurch as the hind wheels caught the mud and gravel on the bottom, shook itself out on the opposite bank.

The road leads into higher ground south of Tussler draw. Jovis thought the air was getting colder. Although the wind still ran high, the rain had diminished. The trail was firmer, for there is sandy soil among the buttes. Again he accelerated the car to thirty miles an hour.

At the Emmet Mills corner he was brought to a sudden stop. A four-wire fence had been strung directly across the way. Jovis now recalled that there had been trouble between Emmet Mills and the commissioners of the county about a right of way, and that to vent his resentment the owner had fenced in this corner of his land. To get past, the driver had to detour down into the bottoms and cross Tussler draw in two places.

Jovis again unstrapped the shovel from the rear of the car. With the point he pried staples loose from several posts on both sides of the road. He laid a stone on the loosened wires to hold them to the ground so that he could drive over them. The air was now bitter cold. The rain had ceased. A strip of moon gleamed between two flying clouds.

From this point the road winds among the buttes to the higher ground known locally as the Sheep Mountain Pines. At the end of a mile the driver had to get out and take down the fence where it shut off the road at the southern boundary of the Mills property. The sky was completely overcast again. It had grown warmer. The odor of storm was still in the air. Jovis took up his thirty-mile gait along the deserted road, as he approached the last climb to the Yellowstone divide, within twenty miles of Montana City. He looked at his watch under the light of the dash lamp. Nine o'clock. The night was completely black.

A gust of rain spattered against the windshield. This was followed a moment later by a shower of snow pellets which pounded off the hood like soft balls of hail. The ground halfway up the Sheep Mountain hill was covered with snow. The flakes swirled in the light of the car. The wheel tracks of the prairie road were half filled. Jovis felt the car slowing down. He shifted into second; then into low. As he neared the divide the wind increased in velocity. The storm had turned into a whirlwind of snow, which clung like sticky plaster to the cowl. Every hundred yards he had to get out and wipe off an area of windshield big enough to see through.

The Yellowstone ridge, seen by day, is a naked stretch of gumbo hill marked here and there by a tiny cedar no taller than a man. From the top of the climb on the north, to the point where the road begins to wind its way down into the Cherry Flats, is scarcely more than a mile.

The car lurched along this narrow trail like a blind thing. Sticky snow formed on the windshield so fast that clear vision was impossible. Jovis felt a swift wrench at the wheel as the machine skidded on an unseen obstruction. He brought the car to a stop and got out to look. He had a feeling that he was turned, but whether he was now facing to the right or to the left of his true direction he could not tell. He examined the land in the light of the lamps. Two dim marks could be discerned on the left. He started down this trail but stopped again, for the wind, which should have been on his right, was directly behind him. Again he got out to examine the way. The trail took a turn to the right a few feet in front of the car.

Reassured, Jovis cleared the windshield and attempted to follow the marks of the road, but he had gone scarcely a dozen rods when he felt the nose of the machine dip suddenly downward. There was a violent jolt as the front wheels stopped dead against a bank.

Jovis again got out of the driver's seat. The first glance at the land in the flood of the headlights told him where he was. He had left the road within a few yards of the turn to the Cherry creek hill and had followed the old trail that led to the gravel pit on Sheep mountain, which road builders had opened up the summer before in repairing the highway below the divide. He tried to back out, but the wheels spun on the steep sides. The trap he had stumbled into was not more than twenty feet below the level surface of the ridge. The way leading down to it was not very steep, but it ended in a two-foot drop where the gravel had been dug away.

Tightening his sheepskin jacket around him, Jovis began smoothing down the abrupt sides of the depression with his shovel. He worked without pausing for half an hour. By quick manipulation of the low gear and the reverse he got the car into a rocking motion, back and forth, gaining momentum for the backward scramble out of the gravel hole. But when he opened the throttle for the final trial he felt the wheels lose their hold. The machine stopped halfway out. He turned the motor off.

On the side of the gravel pit there was a hump which had caught the running boards and raised the rear wheels off the ground. It would take three hours to work the frozen earth down smooth enough to allow the car to make its way up, and by that time the place would be filled with snow.

Jovis now remembered that a tunnel had been dug beneath this gravel pit, so that trucks could be backed in and then loaded through a trap door. With his flashlight he examined the ground at the edge of the hill. To the right of the tunnel the hillside fell away almost perpendicularly to the old trucking road. If he could get down to that point he might make his way along the trail which the road workers had followed to the main highway at the foot of Sheep mountain.

He dug the gravel and snow from under the running board and started his motor again. It was easy to get the car moving into the pit. He began working the machine back and forth again, gradually turning it so that it faced westward toward the edge of the hill.

467

Guided only by his sense of direction, for he could not see what lay beyond the rim of the gravel pit, he drew the car to the right of the tunnel. The wheels ground in the loose gravel and the front end of the car plunged over the bank.

There was a grinding sound when the running board and the frame caught on the edge. The car stopped, hung a moment as if in mid-air, and then gave a sudden plunge headlong down the hill. Jovis caught the brake, but yet the machine gained momentum as it fell. He could see nothing except the whirlwind of snow.

But as suddenly as the fall had started, the car stopped. It was not the sudden stop caused by an obstruction, but rather as if a brake had been applied quickly. Jovis was thrown against the windshield. The snow had drifted under the hill and now lay in a heavy fold, which caught the car and brought its wild career to a halt. From this point downward the slope was more gentle. He was able to ease the machine to the right along the base of the hill. A sudden bump told him that he had reached the road again. He knew the divide over Sheep mountain hill had been crossed.

It is ten miles from Sheep mountain to the railroad at Montana City. By a freakish whim of the treacherous prairie climate, the snow lay deeper south of the divide. Jovis could hear the grinding sound it made as the chained wheels bit into it. Depressions were filling rapidly under the swirling storm. The parallel ruts which had once been traced by wandering sheep wagons and now served these isolated settlers as an automobile road to the railroad, were drifted level with snow. The car crept ahead in low gear. But in the swale across Cherry creek the wheels spun without moving forward.

Jovis threw the gear into reverse. He backed the car until he was out of the deepest part of the drift, then swung the wheel to the right and pulled the car onto the vacant prairie. Out of the wheel tracks the snow was not so deep. He managed to cross the lowland in safety.

The driver now kept to the prairies, guiding himself as well as he could in the darkness and storm by the marks of the road to his left. The prairie is flat for five miles beyond Cherry creek; and the wind had kept it fairly well swept of snow. Progress here was more rapid. Jovis held his watch under the dash lamp—twenty minutes to two.

He had barely put away his watch when he saw a vague nothing-

ness appearing out of the storm. A second later he felt himself falling as though the earth had been pulled out from under him. The
front of the car dove downward, and then came to rest. In a flash
Jovis knew that he had plunged off the cutbank by the mouth of
Mink creek.

He got out and waded down into the ditch in front of the car.
The wheels were entirely buried in snow, which came up even
with the headlights. There was no use trying to shovel in a storm
like this, for the wind was piling snow faster in the draw than he
could shovel it out. Jovis began to scoop away with his mittened
hands the snow which obscured the light of the lamps. Of a sudden
it gave way. The car was swept downward into the bottom of the
draw and, standing deep in the snow, Jovis could not escape. When
the car came to rest he was wedged into the snow under it.

The car was lying on its side with a wheel resting across his leg.
The snow was soft and sticky, else the bone would have been
broken. Jovis wriggled his face to the surface and by working his
body was able to get the one free leg and his two arms applied to
the bottom of the car, but in such a position he could not raise the
machine. His efforts buried him deeper. Working his free foot until he could reach under the wheel which held him fast, he began
digging at the snow under the wheel with his shoe. How long he
kept at this task he did not know, but in time he was able to twist
his leg under the wheel, finally to pull it free. He wormed his way
from under the machine.

His leg was numb and his clothing was soaked with the water
squeezed out of the snow. Here under the lee side of the cutbank
there was scarcely any wind. Great fluttering snowflakes were being
swept into the coulee by the gale which howled above its brim.
Jovis pounded his arms and legs to restore the circulation.

He pulled a knife from his pocket and managed to open the
blade with chattering teeth. He cut loose the curtain behind the
driver's seat. From the tool kit he took a heavy wrench, and using
it as a lever tore loose the ball-and-socket connection between the
top and the frame of the windshield. With a pair of pliers he pulled
the cotter-pins which held the two top bolts to the side of the seat.
With a jerk on these bolts the top came free.

He dragged the top to the side of the car on the floor of the coulee
and with the shovel dug away the snow from under it. He placed
the cushion under this improvised shelter, which was now free

from snow and almost completely sheltered from the storm. He turned off the gasoline at the tank, and, wading to the front of the machine, raised the hood and feeling about with numb fingers located the connecting nut that held the pipe line to the vacuum tank. When the nut was unscrewed he returned to the gas tank and pulled the copper pipe until it was completely free. He curved this pipe so that it led to the ground just in front of the car top.

He climbed inside his shelter and with his knife made a long slit in the seat cushion, from which he pulled out three handsful of wadding. He laid them at the end of the feed pipe. He was working now as he had worked in the garage before starting on this journey, without hesitation but without undue haste. He climbed outside and gave a quarter turn to the spigot on the gasoline flow.

He returned to his shelter and held the end of the gas pipe over the pile of waste until by bending over it he could catch the odor of gasoline. He pulled off his water-soaked gloves and rubbed his hands on the sheepskin lining of his jacket until they were fairly dry. Reaching again into the slit in the cushion he extracted another handful of waste. With this he wiped the wrench carefully. From an inner pocket he brought out a match, and although his fingers were stiff and his hand refused to stop shaking, he managed to strike it on the dry handle of the wrench. He held it to the pile of waste, which immediately burst into flame. When his fire was going he pushed it farther out from under the car top so that the fumes were carried away.

Although the front of his shelter was open, he was now almost completely screened from wind, and the gasoline fire warmed the inside of the place. He held his stinging hands to the blaze, spread his wet mittens on the edge of the cushion. He pounded his leg, which was still numb. A feeling of warmth and comfort came stealing over him. Housed like this, a man could stay out a blizzard two days or more. His head nodded.

Jovis Holt came as abruptly awake as a man who has a sudden dream of falling into a great darkness. The fire had melted the snow about the entrance of his shelter and the water had collected in a shallow puddle at the base of the flame. He pulled on his steaming mittens, rebuckled the high tops of his overshoes and drew the collar of his sheepskin up about his ears. He cut a round piece of celluloid from one of the side curtains, rolled it up, and stuffed it into his pocket.

Outside, the wind had not abated a bit of its fury. The coulee was now drifted from bank to bank. He heaved himself through the deep snow to the opposite side. There he stood in the full sweep of the gale. By holding the strip of celluloid in front of his face to shield his eyes from the flying snow, he could look momentarily into the gloom ahead. With the stoicism of one who has discounted the meager chances of his gamble Jovis started afoot across the empty prairie. If the wind did not change direction, four miles with the snow stinging at his right cheek would take him to Montana City.

There was no trace of a road underfoot, no trace of house or light anywhere about him, no sign of moon or star in the sky—nothing but a vague whiteness of whirling snow. Once he detected a rising crescendo in the howl of the storm. Turning slightly to the right he came suddenly upon a tree. It was a pine tree scarce taller than a man. This was the only tree for miles on Cherry creek flat. It was called Lone Pine and it stood out as a landmark for the honyock- ers * of that region. The trunk was bent almost double now. The top branches were fluttering like the ribs of an umbrella turned inside out by the wind.

For a moment Jovis leaned against the swaying trunk and then trudged on. To his numbed consciousness there came the realiza- tion that he had been traveling too much to the left. He righted his course. How long he fought against the storm he never knew. For to him all sense of distance had been plumbed into a measureless void and time had locked hands with eternity.

The Munyon residence in Montana City is on the east side of the railroad tracks in the direction of the Cherry creek flat. Mrs. Mun- yon had risen at six-thirty, more through habit than necessity, for the storm which had been raging all night was still blowing, and little could be done today. She was adding coal to the kitchen fire when there came a heavy knocking at the front door. It was not the staccato tap of the polite visitor. It was a dull insistent pounding.

A man fell into the room as she turned the knob. He was covered from head to foot with snow.

"Frank," she screamed. "Come quick. There is a man here. He's all white. I think he is going to die."

Her husband, startled out of a morning nap, helped her drag the limp form into the room.

* Honyockers: homesteaders.

471

"God have mercy," he exclaimed, as he brushed the snow off the still face. "It's Jovis Holt from the north country. I heard yesterday they had telephoned for him."

But Jovis Holt did not die. He woke in a strange room of utter whiteness. The sun outside now flooded the windows with the reflected glory of a sea of snow. There was a white bandage on each hand. Two women in nurse's habit were standing close to his bedside.

There was another bed close to his. On it lay a woman as pale and colorless as the white walls of the room. Jovis caught a quick, grateful flicker of recognition from this woman, but now in the vague unreality of the situation the recognition did not seem to matter.

He closed his eyes and heard one of the white-clad figures speak to the woman on the bed opposite: "Your husband is here, and now you're going to get well."

Jovis Holt knew in his heart that she would get well. In common with all humble folk, he had learned the strength of woman when lying in childbirth, just as he had known how to gauge his own skill against the raging futility of the prairie storm.

The nurse spoke, but Jovis did not answer. He turned his head to the wall, and tears of complete exhaustion rolled down his cheek.

"See there," the woman whispered to her companion. "He's crying, because—"

The woman was wrong. Ordinary living does not wrench a tear from such a man as Jovis Holt. He was still enveloped in a feeling of utter isolation.

472

THE FIRST TRAIN'S COMING

THOMAS SAVAGE

Thomas Savage, better known to Montana friends in the Beaverhead country where he grew up as Tom Brenner, is a former State University journalism student. His novel, *The Pass*, published in 1944 by Doubleday, Doran, is a moving story of a young couple's life as they establish a ranch on Horse Prairie in the southwestern corner of Montana, the country in which Savage lived on the Brenner-H ranch as a boy. A central incident in *The Pass* is the coming of the Gilmore & Pittsburgh railroad in 1916, described in this excerpt from the novel.

AND here it was, the last day of Jess's haying, and no one mentioned beer. The stackers didn't come down from the stack between loads to mop their brows with damp red bandannas and to drink deep of the metal-tasting water in the milk can under the wagon. They pitched as fast as they could and called for more hay.

"More hay! Got sleeping sickness, you?"

And it showed in the fields, too, where the teams dragged rakes. Take Joe, the raker. They said around camp that Joe loved the old mare called Rosie. He said to her when she was slow, and Rosie was slow, "Come on, Rosie," like she was a girl, and was asking for a kiss. But today he said, "Hike, damn you, hike!"

At ten o'clock the derrick broke down. The crew worked feverishly to fix it, sweating, cursing their luck. Blue faded shirts and streaked on the back with sweat, long dark marks. Jess running his horse over the field toward the ranch for tools, hammers, crowbars.

"By God, we've got to get this stack done."

"It'll take two hours anyways to get to the city!"

You don't know what's happened.

It's the tracks. The tracks of the Salmon City and Pittsburgh. They're in the city. The first train—it's coming!

"At one o'clock in the afternoon," according to the Salmon City *Recorder,* "the crowd assembled at the track, where the speaker's stand had been erected, just above, or below, where the depot is go-

473

ing to be, in Hayes Williams' cow pasture. The Salmon City band came with a soulful blow of voluptuous music, and the thousand people present felt like the Fourth of July."

The speaker's stand was a rough yellow pine-board affair set high on stilts, a decorated gibbet. Yellow pine two-by-fours showed through where the alternate red-and-white-and-blue strips, wound spirally, had separated.

The steps leading to the platform quivered as a Mr. Clinton (they said) of Pittsburgh, Pennsylvania (they said), ascended. He covered the first few steps with dignity becoming the president of a railroad. Then, near the top, he scurried. But the prairie did not laugh, as the prairie would not laugh if the steps were golden and the climber were God. For Clinton was a kind of god. America, people said, needed his sort. His florid face, his jovial manner covered a shrewd and canny streak, but it pleased him when a venture could be successful and at the same time humanly decent.

He walked erect now to the rear of the platform to straighten one of the flags which served as a backdrop, a neat, patriotic gesture. Then, his voice friendly and intimate, he spoke.

"Friends, we are here"—everybody looked approvingly at one another—"we are here, not to dedicate the railroad, to watch the golden spike driven, not to watch the locomotive—and modern cars—pull in . . ."

A nervous murmur arose from the crowd.

"We are here," Clinton boomed, "to open up"—he paused for breath—"to open up the prairie!"

"That's the same thing," Amy whispered crossly. "I wish Cy would get back from the stable. He was all for keeping the buggy here. Said he wanted the blacks to see the railroad come, like human beings. I said—"

Clinton went on: "Those mountains that loom back of you will today witness the flowering of this country." Clinton gazed heavily at the mountains. The platform creaked, and he took a quick, dignified step forward. "At two o'clock the train will come rolling in, bringing new prosperity—to all."

Loud cheering.

Cy and Billy joined the group near the foot of the platform. Cy was scrubbed, his face shining like a child's. His hair had turned, in the past two years, almost as white as Billy's. He was deep in thought. The whole celebration seemed to rest on his shoulders.

474

Amy said, "Cy, you missed the first part of the speech. He said the mountains are going to flower. Isn't that nice?"

"Yes," he said absently.

"There you go thinking again! Look—there's Mrs. Cooper. Yoohoo! Doesn't she look lovely?"

Mrs. Cooper bore down upon them, Newt trailing, his face cynical. Mrs. Cooper wore a severe black suit which gave her the look of a rather handsome black mare. She clutched at her hat with the waving black plumes that looked bluish in the sun.

"*Mon Dieu!*" she called. "French for goodness. Newt made me late. Must wear his diamond stickpin. Hasn't worn it since—don't know when." She breathed heavily. "Man is vain."

"You look lovely," Amy said.

Mrs. Cooper was pleased. "Nonsense."

"I wish," Amy said wistfully, "I knew exactly what to do about clothes. I love them so. If I could just make up my mind what to wear when—"

"That would be a good starting point," Mrs. Cooper admitted.

"The trouble with me is," Amy said, "that I go into the clothes closet to pick out something to wear, and I lose confidence."

"I have a book," Mrs. Cooper confided, "about clothes. Beth had it at her school. 'The safest way is black or gray,' the book says. Black is my type."

"But black and gray are dull!" Amy cried.

"Life is apt to be dull," Mrs. Cooper reminded her.

Clinton's voice was far away. "Jess," Beth said, "can you make sense out of Amy or Clinton, either one?"

"No. Mrs. Cooper doesn't make any more sense than Amy. She didn't used to be like that."

"We're all changing, Jess."

"Not us. Not you and me."

"Shh!" Amy said. "Listen to Mr. Clinton."

". . . this long-awaited time." Clinton took a glass of water from the table, drained it. "This is an occasion on which I have long wanted to speak. But I wish that one among you, one of you who helped us to realize this dream, would step forward. Step forward and speak—dedicate this road." He took his gold watch from his pocket. "There will be just time." He glanced down in front, and eyes were turned away from the stand. People began to drop behind taller neighbors. The crowd was turning itself inside out.

Jess, suddenly uncomfortable, felt Clinton's eye on him. He pulled his hat down over his eyes and looked away. He would have been safe, except for Amy.

"Go on up." She laughed, wrinkling her nose. "You handsome! Make him go, Beth!"

Billy yelled, "Get up there, Jess!" His words spread like disease. The crowd had a victim. Get Jess up there. Then nobody would worry.

"Speech! Jess Bentley! Get up there!" Jess turned, almost panic-stricken, to Beth; his eyes pleaded with her to do something, to keep him from getting up there on that damned stand where God knew what could happen to a man. Shamed before his fellows. His knees were watery and his heart pounded. All those people. All those strangers. There was a low, weak feeling in the pit of his stomach.

"Beth!" he said, and felt his voice dry up like a spring on the dry flats. "I can't talk. I can't talk!"

She took his hand. "Go on, Jess. They've got to have a goat, I guess. And I'd like to see my husband speak for all of them. I want you to be—the biggest man on the prairie up there."

It's funny, what a woman can do.

"I'd just as soon go up there," Newt said loudly.

"You can talk big," Mrs. Cooper said. "You're safe as a lamb. He's going."

It was miles to the speaker's stand, a great gaudy platform covered with flags and banners the color of blood. Every step took him farther away from the only one in the world who cared for him, and just when he thought he'd reached the steps the whole damned business shook with heat waves and moved off. All those damned strangers . . .

The steps quivered and shook, like when you dream you're walking a log across a gorge.

You could stand it if there was a breeze, but the sun pressed in on the heavy, moist air and choked you; all you could smell was the sweat of a thousand people and the pitch oozing from the knots of the raw yellow pine.

And down there were people you used to know, just faces now, hundreds of grinning faces, waiting for you to make a damned fool of yourself.

But a little apart from them all Beth stood in her lady's-cloth suit, her hat back a little, her duster over her arm. But Jess saw only her eyes. Years ago she had looked at him like that, two, three years ago, in a hot, dusty corral. A horse quit bucking, and he saw her eyes, gray and quiet. Yes.

He spread his arms and gripped the sides of the table in each hand, steadying himself. Somebody laughed. Jess smiled out. It was going to be all right now.

"I guess you know," he began haltingly, "the only time I made a speech before was when I asked my wife to marry me."

He couldn't have begun better. Men who hadn't thought of their marriage for years remembered the embarrassment and chuckled; their wives made a pleased sound.

"When we got married," Jess went on, "we didn't ever think about a railroad in here. We thought everything would just go on like it was, quiet, and nothing big around like a railroad." The fear was gone; the crowd was with him.

"We planned to do just like everybody, work hard and swap horses and visit around, and maybe want to get outside sometime. But we knew we could never get outside. We were a long ways from the market and we couldn't get top prices for our cows because they lost weight on the trail.

"We knew there'd be shivarees when people got married and maybe camping trips, but we'd always know there was something we didn't have—a chance to be big—real big." He found now that he could relax his grip on the table.

There was quiet, not a sound, except for the flapping of one of the flags that moved listlessly in a hot little breeze that had sprung up.

Quiet, quiet; then, faintly, a sound unknown to the prairie. Far in the distance, but coming nearer. Huh-huh-huh-huh. Louder. Huh-huh-huh-huh. Jess turned, and his eyes moved up the glistening stretch of track, a ribbon of promise, on across the flat lonely fields around the town. A black dot at the end of the track grew bigger and bigger. Huh-huh-huh-huh.

He spoke quietly. "Folks, I can see it now."

He watched them. Watched them go out of their heads in that second. A thousand pairs of staring eyes, then a roar of cheering, and the Salmon City Band began to play.

The train came rolling on down, proud, two flags fluttering on

477

either side of the boiler, and bunting adorned its front from headlight to cowcatcher. It rolled slowly, majestically, forward, and the blast from the whistle sent the crowd cheering.

Mrs. Cooper was startled. She had long expected the railroad to come, but this whistling and clanking and hissing . . .

"Glory!" she gasped. "Don't go near it, Newt. No telling what it might do. Newt!"

But Newt and others were already running alongside the engine, shouting welcome to the fireman and engineer. The engineer grinned and answered by shooting steam out of the pistons, hiding the runners in a moist cloud.

Ladies called out and tried hard not to look at the wheels. No one heard. The band boomed away—"Stars and Stripes"—the cymbals crashed on the down beat. It was minutes before the train stopped and the officials from Pittsburgh, whom nobody noticed, slipped off the train.

There was no describing the engine. It was big and black, and it shone terribly in places. You would do well to stay at a distance unless you were crazy, like Newt and Cy, who had climbed into the cab.

"You ought to see the stuff they've got in there," Newt bragged. Cy smiled silently. Neither mentioned how they'd felt inside the cab, as if the train might suddenly bellow and carry them off.

They sniffed the thick black coal smoke and the hot, oily odor of the boiler.

They had forgotten Jess. He watched them, let down, tired. Now they had all left the speaker's stand, their shouts moving down the track, sweeping on down. . . .

But Beth stood there, just as she had, a little lost figure in a duster and a big hat. Jess smiled awkwardly. "I guess that wasn't much of a speech," he said.

Somewhere the Salmon City Band was doggedly playing "Stars and Stripes Forever." The sun glittered on the instruments, but Jess didn't hear them; he heard her say, "Jess . . ."

And that was the big moment of his life, that moment when her eyes said, "You are beyond doubt the most magnificent man who ever lived."

Afterward Beth remembered the time before it happened, the uneventful days. Her longing for them was like homesickness and tinged with self-reproach. Because in those tranquil days she had not felt tranquil, only bored.

She remembered the week's blizzard three months after the railroad came. A December blizzard that descended on the prairie like a savage, crushing animal. And she must stay inside the house.

On the second morning Jess came in after he had saddled his horse, hating to work facing the storm. He stood by the stove, his Mackinaw smelling hot and wool-like and of the barn. Mittens, Scotch cap, scarf around his throat. He stood spraddle-legged, rolling a cigarette.

"Please, Jess," she begged. "Take me with you to pitch hay. We can take an extra fork, and I can pitch to keep warm. I can put on trousers. It's not so cold out. I've seen worse. I've seen it really cold." She tugged at his arm. "I hate it here alone, Jess, in the blizzard." She was a little ashamed.

He was bluff. "With this going on you want to go out?" He turned to the window. Hard, dry snow slanted sharply. A hundred feet away the barn was a gray shadow. Jess's horse stood, head down, tied to the fence. "Not a chance. But I'm going to do something for you today."

She was a little appeased. "What, Jess?"

"I'm going to take some traps down, and after I get through feeding I'm going to try for some beavers. There's lots of them down the creek; three places I know of they're damming the stream and flooding things. And there's more over by Billy's on his land. Bet if I go over today and tell him you want some skins he'll get them for you. He likes to trap." He watched her, happy when she smiled. "You can have a long cape made with ten skins. Think of that, Beth!" He snatched up a Navajo blanket from the couch and threw it around her shoulders. "Look! Beaver cape!" He looked at her proudly. His wife walking down—somewhere—with a beaver cape on, and everybody looking. No thought of the drifts that rippled along the creek, the hours of freezing hands, the stumbling, the broken holes through the thick ice, and dark disappointment when a beaver gnawed its foot and got away.

"When Billy and I get ten good skins we'll take them to the city, and old Smith will make them up." He looked at her, musing. "Beth Bentley in a beaver cape. It looks nice on you."

She walked across the room, trailing the blanket, running her fingers across the rough wool. "It's soft, Jess. I'll take it." Laugh-

479

ing, she flung her arms around him. "But where will I wear it?"

"Where?" He gazed out the window at the storm. "London. Maybe New York." She laughed. "But I mean it, Beth." He wondered if she could see the places he could. Strange names, London, New York. Absurd to say them in a living room in Montana, with a blizzard at the windows wanting in. London. New York.

She endured the second day, the third. The fourth, and the storm raged. Calves lay frozen under the willows. The men carried axes with them to keep water holes open, the water only a thin trickle under thick ice. They counted the calves, and the lines deepened in their foreheads as if the wind had etched them there. Axes, frozen stock, storm. It was wrong to fret at her own inactivity. Wasn't it wrong to think of a beaver cape?

But she did think about it, and she did fret at the long hours. It wasn't that she wanted to go out in it. For a moment, perhaps, to get the feel of it, to try to understand it as Jess understood it. For a moment, watching the dry snow drift against the barn, she would wish passionately that she were a man, but not for long. The sixth day, when Jess froze an ear, she rubbed snow and grease on it, glad to be feminine and helpful. It was only that she missed him.

She would turn away from the window again and walk across the room and back again. "I have two beaver skins now. I have. Maybe Billy has two. New York. Oh, *damn!*"

On the fifth day she remembered the magazines. "All these nice magazines," Mrs. Cooper had said. "*National Geographics*. Wonderful. Takes you to faraway places."

"That's what I need," Beth said grimly to herself. "To be taken to faraway places." It was a month ago that Mrs. Cooper had brought them. Now Beth sat with the armchair pulled up to the stove and read and looked. Indian temples, a languid native leaning against an ugly stone torso. South American birds of brilliant plumage posing stiffly against tropical foliage. Tangled leaves and grasses.

". . . has a peculiar whistle and is found nesting in the higher altitudes of the pampas. Dr. Meade has counted no less than six different varieties, each one of them . . ."

Dr. Meade went on finding birds, and on the prairie the wind blew so hard the house shook and creaked, and in the fields the cattle hugged the willows, waiting for hay. New York . . . There had been a girl at school who had been to New York.

At school they had thought Beth strange, coming from a ranch. She didn't mind. The headmistress had called her the most lady-like of her class. She wondered if the headmistress had known what made her that way, studious, rule-abiding? When you were homesick it didn't help to break rules. When the girls climbed out windows for a dish of ice cream in town she would go to her room and write home, or paint a picture of a hill at home, just as she remembered it.

"That was a long time ago." Now she felt the same homesickness for the prairie in summer. Maybe if she painted the way the barn looked in summer . . .

She sat sketching, blowing against the window to melt the frost so she could see the barn. "I've got to *blow*," she thought, outraged, "even to see it!" Her browns were very brown and dry and hot and her greens bright and vivid. She sketched in a horse and rider, unable as usual to get the hind legs of the horse to resemble anything more horselike than a jackrabbit's. But the picture made her lonesome. She tore it up and dropped the pieces, one by one, into the stove.

"Tommy, those playing cards. Where are they?"

Solitaire at the golden-oak table. Cards slipped on the slick surface so you couldn't make a neat row across. A neat row was tremendously important just now. Calm, orderly neatness was what you needed on a day like this.

"Now, if I beat this game the storm will stop. The wind will die down, and nobody will ever know there was a storm." Shuffle, cards slipping. Ten on jack. Three on four. King up. Five on the— All right.

"Two out of three, then. If I win two out of three—"

The front door blew open, and the cards scattered like imps of hell before the iciness.

Beth stood up, furious, walked with deliberate calm to the door, and slammed it. She was about to kick it. "He's got to fix that door!" She almost sobbed. "He's got to fix it so it won't do that!"

If only Mr. Clinton had the telephone in now, instead of six months from now. Call up Amy or Mrs. Cooper and talk about the storm. Just to know that someone else hated it, caught in four walls. Why, it was dangerous not to have a telephone in weather like this. Suppose somebody got sick? Suppose somebody broke a leg?

"Tommy," she called, "do you think he'll be home early?"

The sixth night was the worst of the blizzard. When Jess came in he refused to talk about it and wouldn't look at the thermometer. He sat silent in the lamplight, drumming his fingers, and she, who had waited so long to talk, to be gay, sat silent too. Suppose she should start some conversation—about Dr. Meade and the birds in South America?

That night she lay beside him, aware of his warmth, and crept closer when the wind rattled the windows, drowning out the tick of the alarm clock. When the wind ebbed she heard it again, a comfortable sound. Tick-tick-tick. Tick—and she was asleep.

Suddenly she was sitting bolt upright, her heart pounding. "Jess!"

He turned in bed, grunted. "What, Beth?" He found her hand and took it.

"I don't know. Something. Something I don't like." Her throat was parched. "Listen."

In the darkness he listened intently to please her.

It wasn't that the wind was blowing harder than usual. That wasn't it. Nor the creaking of the house. Those sounds you learned to know, trust even.

It was the pitch of the wind. It moaned. It moaned like a human being. It penetrated the room and froze into something terrifying.

"It's just the wind," Jess said. He felt her hand tremble in his. Patting her shoulder, he got out of bed and put a Mackinaw on over his nightshirt. "I'll get you a cup of coffee." He lit the lamp. The flame flickered, leaped high, smoked, and cast wavering shadows over the room. His figure was enormous in shadow on the wall, and he appeared to lean over the bed. "You stay here and I'll go start a fire."

"I'm going too," she said quickly, and scrambled out of bed. "I'm not going to stay here alone." The floor was cold.

They brought their coffee to the bedroom and got in bed. "This is pretty funny." Jess laughed. "Breakfast in bed. What would the boys say?"

She sipped her coffee absently, looking over her cup. "I don't hear it now."

"I never heard it," he said lightly. "I think you had a nightmare."

"But, Jess"—she spoke slowly—"when you have nightmares you dream about something. I wasn't dreaming anything."

482

He kissed her briefly. "Don't be a crazy one." They put their cups under the bed, and Jess leaned over and blew out the lamp. "I won't let anything get you," he said seriously. "Snuggle up."

He breathed regularly and was asleep.

That morning the snow fell softly from a gauze sky, great lazy flakes drifting down. It was hard to see as they rode away from the barn. The mildness after the blizzard hung like a curtain about them, and Jess's voice was hushed and intimate.

"Watch when we come to those willows, Beth. Every morning I go by there's a coyote runs out." They watched. "See him, Beth?" Jess was triumphant. A grayish, indistinct shadow scurried ahead and disappeared into a clump of brush. "Yesterday I saw two weasels. Cute little devils." He was glad to have her with him again. There seemed a lot to say, as if she'd been gone.

"If the snow would clear up you could see it up on the Pass deeper than I ever saw it. So deep the timber low down is drifted over. Mornings I've watched it drift higher and higher."

"You love it, don't you?" She watched him fondly.

"The Pass?"

"Yes. And the prairie."

"I guess I do, Beth. Sometimes I get to thinking how good it is the railroad's in, how good for the prairie, open it up. That's good, isn't it?"

"It's fine, Jess."

They rode on while the clouds lifted.

"About all those new people that have come in, Jess, since the railroad. Those farmers."

Jess scowled. "Those. Beth, I went over the other day to that big piece of land one of them bought from Newt, and what do you think?" He turned indignantly in his saddle. "I saw a plow leaning against the fence. A plow! And I kicked up the snow and saw underneath where they'd been plowing." He shook his head. "I wasn't going to tell you." His voice was bitter. "Why couldn't they go to a farming country, instead of tearing up the land here? This is no place to—plow." He warmed to his subject.

"That's what the railroad did for the prairie, Jess. That's what it means when they say they're going to open up a country. The railroad's got to have people to ship things—wheat, carrots."

"Well, I knew that—but—"

"Jess, why are you always talking about how good the railroad is when you know you hate it?"

"But I don't. I think—"

"Is it because we'll have more?"

"Well, yes."

She watched him closely. "Because *I'll* have more?"

"Well, yes."

She began to hum to herself. She came first with Jess. She came even before the prairie.

MAJOR DONOHUE, COSEY AND HER FLYING MACHINE

This, a special dispatch to *The Great Falls Tribune* in which it appeared the next morning, illustrates some of the trials of barnstormers in Montana at the beginning of the age of flight. Several such outbursts occurred before Montanans could be persuaded that the early "aeroplanes," unlike horses, could not be sent forth regardless of wind and weather, and were somewhat less easily directed. A Great Falls crowd was infuriated when its first aerial performer failed to confine his flight to a small fairground area visible from the grandstand.

Glendive, Montana, July 4, 1911.

It required the services of a detail of the state militia today to prevent a long suffering but disappointed crowd from running an airship into the Yellowstone river because it would not, or could not, fly.

There were several thousand visitors in this city attending the biggest Fourth of July celebration ever held in eastern Montana. Many good attractions had been offered the crowds all day long in the shape of ball games, athletic events, vaudeville shows and concerts, but the star attraction advertised for the day was the airship flight.

The Curtiss Aviator company of New York City, after promising to send Aviator St. Henry here for a flight, had refused to keep the date and as a last resort an arrangement was made with George H. Webster of Fargo, N. D., who furnished all sorts of fair concessions, for a flight to be made by Felix Schmidt of Chicago, and $300 was paid down on the deal. The biplane arrived all right and with it came its alleged owner, Miss Cosey Smith, and a mechanician named Eugene Grubbin, together with Schmidt, the alleged birdman.

The crowd did not like the looks of the machine from the first and after waiting patiently until 5 in the afternoon, a wave of indignation surged over the crowd when word was passed around that the airship couldn't navigate the heavens today.

Someone suggested running the machine into the river and simultaneously a cowboy in the crowd lassoed the propeller with his

485

lariat and shouted for someone to bring him his good fast horse. A hundred willing hands seized hold of various parts of the contraption and in an instant it was headed for the Yellowstone river, a distance of only 200 yards.

The state militia under Major Don J. Donohue had been summoned early in the day to act as patrol to prevent accidents when the aeroplane should make its ascension. The soldier boys now came in handy in order to save the machine from utter destruction.

Aviator Schmidt and mechanician Grubb fled panic-stricken before the angry crowd. The airship was running swiftly on the ground and was about half way to the river when Major Donohue, who last Sunday at Billings ably impersonated the immortal General Custer in a vivid reproduction of the historic Custer massacre given on the original battlegrounds, threw a detail of militiamen in front of the crowd, surrounding the airship with a circle of bayonets, and saved it from destruction.

At midnight as soon as the holiday is ended the citizens' committee will serve an attachment on the machine and it is predicted that the city of Glendive will shortly own an airship, for no one believes the owners of the outfit will attempt to carry it away.

THE SPIRIT

Indian and white—"humility and
abounding fidelity . . . The ministers
of the Church did not consult
their ease."

THE HELPERS OF PLENTY-COUPS

FRANK B. LINDERMAN

In the opinion of many critics and readers, Frank Bird Linderman of Montana was the best writer on Indians this country has ever had; and of his dozen books *Red Mother* and *American* are usually held the crowning achievements. This is a chapter from *American: The Life Story of a Great Indian,* published in 1930 by John Day, and copyrighted by the author. This excerpt describes, with detail found in few accounts, the mystical experience we now call a vigil, sought by all young men of the Plains tribes. (Girls underwent a similar self-discipline but the procedure differed.) Note that, at least in this instance, the revelation was ethical and philosophical rather than purely religious: the dreamer, Plenty-coups, who became chief of the Crows, was instructed to develop himself to the fullest extent of his God-given powers, by will rather than by prayer. Linderman, born in Cleveland, Ohio, in 1869, persuaded his parents to let him come West when he was sixteen. He lived among the Indians as a trapper and guide, later became an assayer, merchant, newspaperman, state legislator, insurance man and hotel operator. His first book, *Indian Why Stories,* appeared in 1915. He established a home at Goose Bay on Montana's beautiful Flathead Lake and in his later years devoted all of his time to writing. In 1927 he received an honorary LL.D. degree from Montana State University. He died May 12, 1938, and Frederic F. Van de Water wrote: "His work is the flesh of a vanished epoch made words . . . He understood the Indian better than any man on this continent who has ever put pen to paper."

WHEN I was nine years old, a happening made me feel that I was a grown-up man, almost in a day," he said. "I had a brother. I shall not speak his name, but if there were four brave, handsome young men in our tribe my brother was one of them. I loved him dearly, and he was always an inspiration to me."

The names of the dead are seldom spoken by the Crows. "They have gone to their Father, Ah-badt-dadt-deah, and like Him are sacred." This custom makes the gathering of tribal history extremely difficult.

For a time Plenty-coups would not violate this tribal custom which was threatening my success in getting his story. But finally, as his interest in his tale grew, he realized it was necessary, and graciously, and I believe a little fearfully, he named many men and women who had passed away.

"One morning when our village was going to move, he went on the war-trail against our enemy, the Lacota [Sioux]. All that day he was in my thoughts. Even when we crossed Elk River [Yellowstone], where usually there was satisfying excitement, I kept thinking of my brother. Rafts had to be made for the old people and children, and these, drawn by four men on good horses, had ever given me plenty to think about. But this day nothing interested me. That night I could not sleep, even when all but the wolves [scouts] were sleeping. When the village was set up on the Big River [Missouri], news reached us that my brother was gone—killed by Sioux on Powder River.

"My heart fell to the ground and stayed there. I mourned with my father and mother, and alone. I cut my flesh and bled myself weak. I knew now that I must dream if I hoped to avenge my brother, and I at once began to fast in preparation, first taking a sweat-bath to cleanse my body.

"Nobody saw me leave the village. I slipped away and climbed The-buffalo's-heart, where I fasted two more days and nights, without success. I saw nothing at all and gave up to travel back to my father's lodge, where I rested.

"The fourth night, while I was asleep, a voice said to me, 'You did not go to the right mountain, Plenty-coups.' I knew then that I should sometime succeed in dreaming.

"The village was preparing to move to the Little Rockies, a good place for me, and before the women began to take down the lodges I started out alone. Besides extra moccasins, I had a good buffalo robe, and as soon as I reached the mountains I covered a sweat-lodge with the robe and again cleansed my body. I was near the Two Buttes and chose the south one, which I climbed, and there I made a bed of sweet-sage and ground-cedar. I was determined that no smell of man should be on me and burned some *e-say* [a root that grows in the mountains] and sweet-sage, standing in their smoke and rubbing my body with the sage.

"The day was hot; and naked I began walking about the top of the mountain crying for Helpers, but got no answer, no offer of assistance. I grew more tired as the sun began to go toward the west, and finally I went to my bed, lying down so my feet would face the rising sun when he came again. Weakened by my walking and the days of fasting, I slept, remembering only the last rays of the sun as he went to his lodge. When I wakened, looking into the sky, I saw that The-seven-stars [the Big Dipper] had turned round The-star-that-does-not-move [North Star]. The night was westward. Morning was not far away, and wolves were howling on the plains far below me. I wondered if the village would reach the Little Rockies before night came again.

" 'Plenty-coups.'

"My name was spoken! The voice came from behind me, back of my head. My heart leaped like a deer struck by an arrow. 'Yes,' I answered, without moving.

" 'They want you, Plenty-coups. I have been sent to fetch you,' said the voice yet behind me, back of my head.

" 'I am ready,' I answered, and stood up, my head clear and light as air.

"The night had grown darker, and I felt rather than saw some Person go by me on my right side. I could not tell what Person it was, but thought he beckoned me.

" 'I am coming,' I said, but the Person made no answer and slipped away in a queer light that told me where he was. I followed over the same places I had traveled in the afternoon, not once feeling my feet touch a stone. They touched nothing at all where the way was rough, and without moccasins I walked in the Person's tracks as though the mountain were as smooth as the plains. My body was naked, and the winds cool and very pleasant, but I looked to see which way I was traveling. The stars told me that I was going east, and I could see that I was following the Person downhill. I could not actually see him, but I knew I was on his trail by the queer light ahead. His feet stirred no stone, nothing on the way, made no sound of walking, nor did mine.

"A coyote yelped on my right, and then another answered on my left. A little farther on I heard many coyotes yelping in a circle around us, and as we traveled they moved their circle along with us, as though they were all going to the same place as we. When the coyotes ahead stopped on a flat and sat down to yelp together, the ones behind closed in to make their circle smaller, all yelping loudly, as though they wished to tell the Person something. I knew now that our destination was not far off.

"The Person stopped, and I saw a lodge by his side. It seemed to rise up out of the ground. I saw that he came to it at its back, that it faced east, and that the Person reached its door by going around it to the right. But I did not know him, even when he coughed to let someone inside the lodge know he was there. He spoke no word to me but lifted the lodge door and stepped inside. 'Come, Plenty-coups,' he said gently. And I too stepped into the lodge.

"There was no fire burning, and yet there was light in the lodge. I saw that it was filled with Persons I did not know. There were four rows of them in half-circles, two rows on each side of the center, and each Person was an old warrior. I could tell this by their faces and bearing. They had been counting coup. I knew this because before each, sticking in the ground, was a white coup-stick bearing the breath-feathers of a war eagle. Some, however, used no stick at all, but only heavy first-feathers whose quills were strong enough to stick in the ground. These first-feathers were very fine, the handsomest I had ever seen, and I could not count them, they were so many.

" 'Why have you brought this young man into our lodge? We do not want him. He is not our kind and therefore has no place among us.' The words came from the south side, and my heart began to fall down.

"I looked to see what Persons sat on the south side, and my eyes made me afraid. They were the Winds, the Bad Storms, the Thunders, the Moon, and many Stars, all powerful, and each of them braver and much stronger than men."

I believe the Persons on the south side of the lodge, the Winds, the Bad Storms, the Moon, and many Stars, were recognized by Plenty-coups as the great forces of nature, and that this is what he wished to convey to me.

" 'Come, Plenty-coups, and sit with *us.*' This voice was kind. It came from the north side.

" 'Sit,' said the Person who had brought me there, and then he was gone. I saw him no more.

"They, on the north side of the lodge, made a place for me. It was third from the head on the left, and I sat down there. The two parties of Persons were separated at the door, which faced the east, and again in the west, which was the head of the lodge, so that the Spirit-trail from east to west was open, if any wished to travel that way. On neither side were the Persons the same as I. All were different, but I knew now that they had rights in the world, as I had, that Ah-badt-dadt-deah had created them, as He had me and other men. Nobody there told me this, but I felt it in the lodge as I felt the presence of the Persons. I knew that to live on the world I must concede that those Persons across the lodge who had not wished me to sit with them had work to do, and that I could not prevent them from doing it. I felt a little afraid but was glad I was there.

" 'Take these, Plenty-coups.' The Person at the head of the lodge on the north side handed me several beautiful first-feathers of a war-eagle.

"I looked into his eyes. He was a Dwarf-person, chief of the Little-people who live in the Medicine-rock, which you can almost see from here, and who made the stone arrow points. I now saw that all on my side were the same as he, that all were Dwarfs not tall as my knee."

The Dwarfs or Little-people are legendary beings, supposed to possess great physical strength. In the story of "Lost Boy," a Crow saw one of the Dwarfs shoulder a full-grown bull elk and walk with it on his shoulder. They dwell in Medicine-rock, near Pryor, Montana. The Little-people made the stone arrow heads, the Crows believe.

All the Indian tribes of the Northwestern plains, with whom I am acquainted, possess legends that deal with the makers of the stone arrow points which are scattered so plentifully over North America. These legends, together with the knowledge that identical stone arrow points are found in Europe, led me, long ago, to the belief that our plains Indians neither made nor used them—that some other people made them. Careful inquiry among very old Indians, beginning in 1886, has not discovered a single tribesman who had ever heard of his own people making stone arrow points. These old men have told me that before the white man came their arrow points were of bone.

493

" 'Stick one of your feathers in the ground before you and count coup,' said the Dwarf-chief.

"I hesitated. I had never yet counted coup, and here in this lodge with old warriors was no place to lie.

" 'Count coup!' commanded the Dwarf-chief.

"I stuck a first-feather into the ground before me, fearing a dispute.

" 'That,' said the Dwarf-chief, 'is the rider of the *white* horse! I first struck him with my coup-stick, and then, while he was unharmed and fighting, I took his bow from him.'

"The Thunders, who sat at the head of the lodge on the south side, said, 'Nothing can be better than that.'

" 'Stick another feather before you, Plenty-coups,' said the Dwarf-chief.

"I stuck another first-feather in the ground, wondering what the Dwarf-chief would say for it. But this time I was not afraid.

" 'That,' he said, 'is the rider of the *black* horse. I first struck him with my bow. Then, while he was armed with a knife and fighting me, I took his bow from him, also his shield.'

" 'Enough!' said the Persons on the south side. 'No Person can do better than that.'

" 'Let us leave off counting coups. We are glad you have admitted this young man to our lodge,' said the Bad Storms, 'and we think you should give him something to take back with him, some strong medicine that will help him.' "

Plenty-coups had been speaking rapidly, his hands following his spoken words with signs, acting parts, while his facial expressions gave tremendous emphasis to his story. He was perspiring and stopped to brush his face with his hand.

"I had not spoken," he went on, "and could not understand why the Dwarf-chief had ordered me to stick the feathers, nor why he had counted coups in my name before such powerful Persons.

" 'He will be a Chief,' said the Dwarf-chief. 'I can give him nothing. He already possesses the power to become great if he will use it. Let him cultivate his senses, let him use the powers which Ah-badt-dadt-deah has given him, and he will go far. The difference between men grows out of the use, or non-use, of what was given them by Ah-badt-dadt-deah in the first place.'

494

...e to board for fifteen dollars a week, it is true. But I gave
...vant a dollar a week to come in to make up my bed and tidy
...om; afterwards, I gave a colored man $2.50 to come three
...a week and do the same. The other four days I did the best
...d for myself. I made a poor hand at it, however, as I did also
...acing buttons or sewing up rents. I was never made for a
...e, and have always needed the care of a woman. To fit up
...rnish the cabin cost me $244.75. I paid twenty-three dollars
...small sheet iron stove, thirty dollars for a pine bedstead;
...y dollars for a hay mattress, and forty dollars for a wool mat-
...The roof, moreover, was only pine poles covered with a foot
...of dirt. I soon found it leaking and was obliged to put boards
...he dirt at a cost of ninety dollars. A little calculation will
...that the winter's stay in the cabin was no saving over the
...The ladies, bless their hearts! soon managed to find out that
...not very comfortably fixed; so they went out and collected
...Then they came, and ordering me out took down my little
...and put in a better one, laid a carpet on the floor, and added
...ige and an easy chair.
...wever the cabin was better for me every way. It was my own
...ire to. It was a little bit homelike. I got a white cat, Dick, and
...resence added to the homelikeness.
...ouldn't always keep free from fits of dreary loneliness and Dick
...hen the greatest comfort to me. He would welcome me home
...my walks, with all the joy a cat can show, and in the cabin
...d crawl up on my shoulder when I was reading or writing.
...ight his place was on the buffalo robe at the side or the foot
...y bed. Often, however, if it got right cold before morning, he
...d crawl in between the sheets and lie at my side. Dear, faithful,
...dly old Dick! You were more of a help and a comfort to me
...winter than ever your cat's brains could know, and to this
...my heart warms to think of you!

"Then he said to me, 'Plenty-coups, we, the Dwarfs, the Little-people, have adopted you and will be your Helpers throughout your life on this world. We have no medicine-bundle to give you. They are cumbersome things at best and are often in a warrior's way. Instead, we will offer you advice. Listen!

" 'In you, as in all men, are natural powers. You have a will. Learn to use it. Make it work for you. Sharpen your senses as you sharpen your knife. Remember the wolf smells better than you do because he has learned to depend on his nose. It tells him every secret the winds carry because he uses it all the time, makes it work for him. We can give you nothing. You already possess everything necessary to become great. Use your powers. Make them work for you, and you will become a Chief.' "

A medicine-bundle contains the medicine or talisman of its possessor. Often the skin and stuffed head of an animal as large as a wolf is used. Sometimes, however, the bundles are small, containing the skin, claws, teeth, or heads of lesser creatures, depending wholly upon what animal or bird offered "help" to the dreamer. The medicine-bundle is of first importance, the possessor believing implicitly that the superlative power of the animal or bird that offered aid in his dream is always at hand and at his service when he is in need. The contents of these bundles are secret and sacred to the Indian.

"When I wakened, I was perspiring. Looking into the early morning sky that was growing light in the north, I went over it all in my mind. I saw and understood that whatever I accomplished must be by my own efforts, that I must myself do the things I wished to do. And I knew I could accomplish them if I used the powers that Ah-badt-dadt-deah had given me. I *had* a will and I would use it, make it work for me, as the Dwarf-chief had advised. I became very happy, lying there looking up into the sky. My heart began to sing like a bird, and I went back to the village, needing no man to tell me the meaning of my dream. I took a sweat-bath and rested in my father's lodge. I *knew* myself now."

ELLIOTT C. LINCOLN

From *Rhymes of a Homesteader* (Houghton Mifflin, 1920).

WHEN I'm out with the bunch, in town,
I'm jest as tough as I kin be;
It's pretty nearly ten to one
That God ain't apt to notice me.

But home here, where it's bare, brown plain
Fer miles an' miles on every side,
I sorter stick right up in sight;
God couldn't miss me if he tried.

'Tain't 'cause I like it, that I'm good,
The days I'm workin' on the ranch:
There ain't a soul fer God to watch
But me, I dassent take the chance.

THE RT. REV.

The Rt. Rev. D. S. Tuttle, D.D., LL.
tant Episcopal Bishop of Montana,
first bishop) in January, 1867. The
conducted by Thomas J. Dimsdale, s
Vigilante historian, in the office of J
Christmas Day, 1865. Dimsdale cont
three months. William J. Marshall sta
1867, and continued to do so until
Rev. E. N. Goddard on July 18. Th
in the town council hall July 21. Tu
until 1880, when he became Bishop o
farewell in a valedictory letter which
people of Montana," dated Dec. 8, 18
Rev. L. R. Brewer was to be consecra
is made over to him the name I have
loved, the Bishop of Montana . . .
themselves upon this hour, witness ho
to me. Let me say out my sadness. Th
nooks and crannies of your Territory.
loved! Good-bye! That means God be
bide with you, if you trustfully lean
are yours. With an almost bursting h
staff as Bishop of Montana. God help
of Montana, 1885.) The fragment of
counted below is extracted from his b
sionary Bishop, published in New York i

I LOOK back upon the winter of 1
as an important era of my life.
accomplish much. But my experie
and strengthen principles and habits
value to me in after life. . . .

But I was uneasy over personal exp
parson on $1,000 a year and I did not f
five dollars a week on my own living
to go into. . . .

In cool figuring I find my change to
much after all. My good friend, Mrs.

took
her se
the ro
times
I coul
at rep
celiba
and f
for a
twen
tress.
or tw
over
show
hotel
I wa
$200.
stove
a lo

H
to re
his
I c
was
fron
wou
At
of
wou
frie
tha
day

THEY WERE PERFECT LADIES

ALEX TOPONCE

Another extract from *Reminiscences of Alexander Toponce, Pioneer, 1839–1923*, privately published by Mrs. Katie Toponce in Ogden, Utah.

IN traveling about the West I frequently met Bishop Tuttle of the Episcopalian Church. He was a real pioneer and expected to rough it along with the rest.

I recall one trip I made on the stage from Helena to Salt Lake. There were about ten passengers and among them were two girls from a dance house in the mining camps, tough as hickory and hard as bull quartz.

I was interested from the start in the Bishop's attitude toward them. He talked to them as if they had been queens in disguise, not a word of preaching, no "holier-than-thou" talk, just plain everyday American.

They had to act the part of perfect ladies, because the Bishop expected them to. When we reached Salt Lake, one of them asked me, "Where is the church where he preaches? I am going to hear him next Sunday, if I have to crawl on my hands and knees to get there."

CLOSE-UPS OF BROTHER VAN

GEORGE MECKLENBURG

When "Brother Van," the Rev. W. W. Van Orsdel, D.D., Methodist, was called upon to give the prayer during dedication ceremonies for the Montana state capitol, his introducer referred to him as the "best-loved minister in Montana." He came to Montana in 1872, when in his early twenties, and died in 1919. He held meetings in saloons or dance halls; when he had no horse, he walked. (The walk in the first incident described here, Bozeman to Radersburg, was seventy-five miles.) He founded the Montana Deaconess School and rescued failing Deaconess hospitals. Incidents described here are extracted from *The Last of the Old West* by the Rev. George Mecklenburg, D.D., whose Montana ministry started at Valier about 1910 and who subsequently moved to Minneapolis, where he is now pastor of Wesley Methodist Church. The book was published by Capital Book Co., Washington, in 1927.

THE Wild West movies seem to many doubtless very much overdrawn. But I can vouch for an incident in Brother Van's life that would seem to justify the most extravagant of these movies. I learned first hand the narrow escape Brother Van had when he first came to Montana from being hanged for a horse thief.

. . .

Brother Van had but recently come to the Territory, and as yet had no horse, and so walked from one settlement to another. Having heard of Radersburg as a stirring mining camp, he set out afoot to visit it, walking from Bozeman with only one night's layover. Of course, when he reached Radersburg he was pretty dusty, and with his cowboy hat and clothes he looked like almost anything else than a preacher.

As he entered the little town he excited a good deal of attention. This he naturally expected. But it was not long until he saw signs of something more than curiosity: the men were gathering in groups and regarding him with anything but friendly eyes. As he passed the post office he was attracted to a poster beside the entrance: "$100 Reward," etc., for a horse thief who had been operating in an adjoining county. Brother Van did not stop long enough to see if the description tallied with himself. (Judging by the actions of the people, he decided that it did.) He hastened toward an open space and mounted a cast-off spring wagon and started singing the good old Methodist hymn, "O, Happy Day." This he followed with an earnest prayer, and then told the people who he was and why he had come among them.

The old lady who told this story to me was nearly ninety years of age. Brother Van sat by, clearing his throat as was his habit, apparently much embarrassed. I asked the sister if she believed he was the horse thief.

"Why, to be sure," she said half apologetically. "But as soon as he began to sing I knew we were mistaken."

>>> <<<

It was Fourth of July and the little town of Augusta, which nestled among the foothills of the Rockies, had planned a great celebration to which the people from a radius of over a hundred miles had been invited. There would be a rock-drilling contest for the miners. Single-handed and double-handed they would drive holes in a great block of granite while the judges stood with stopwatch in hand to see which team drilled the deepest hole in the allotted time. For the cowboys there were various contests and races. Roping and bulldogging, running races, and saddle and go races—all the events with which the East in the last few years has been made familiar through the professional rodeo.

To a ranch home a few miles from Augusta came the Methodist circuit rider, Brother Van. He was welcome in every home, welcome for his message, but doubly welcome because he brought the news and for his winning personality. Hospitality was the first virtue of the pioneer, but Brother Van would be welcome anywhere. His kindly nature, his genial smile endeared him to all who knew him, and he was as welcome and as much at ease in the home of the rich and influential as in that of the less important citizens of the state.

It was forenoon when he arrived. His horse was stabled and he was asked to stay for dinner. After the meal Brother Van retired to the living room for a good visit with the members of the family. It is safe to say that he was as great an attraction as the celebration in Augusta some miles away. He was noted for his voice, and of course it wasn't long until the strains of "Over and Over," "Die No More," and others of the old time songs could be heard. Time passed rapidly.

Meanwhile the cowboys were more interested in the rodeo in Augusta. Brother Van was like all Methodist preachers since the days of Asbury, a good judge of horseflesh, and he never rode any but a good one. The cowboys eyed his mare, saw possibilities in her, and took her with them to Augusta. Just before chore time, as the meeting in the living room was breaking up, they returned to the ranch in triumph, bringing back the preacher's horse and with her a five-gallon keg of beer which she had won for them in the races.

To them it was a good joke on the preacher, and the fact that he could laugh with them at his own expense is a partial explanation of his popularity.

→≫ ≪←

The Rev. George Logan tells a story of Brother Van as district superintendent which illustrates the spirit of comradeship that he shared with all men, even the saloon men and gamblers.

One Sunday morning Mr. Logan asked for a good collection to make up the district superintendent's salary, saying, "If I don't get it this morning, I'll come again tonight." The collection was not big enough, and true to his word the second collection was asked for. One man put a stack of six silver dollars on the plate, so the amount received was sufficient to make up the sum required for the unpaid salary.

Going downtown next day, Mr. Logan met the man of the silver dollars, who with a grin asked, "Did you raise Brother Van's money last night?"

"I did," was the pastor's reply.

"Did you notice that stack of silver dollars on the plate?"

"I did," said Mr. Logan again.

"Well, I'll tell you a story if you promise not to get angry about it."

"I promise," said the preacher.

"Two men at the service Sunday morning remembered afterward that Brother Van's salary was short, and they agreed to play for the money in the afternoon. If A won, the money was to be Brother Van's; if B did, Brother Van lost. Word went around and the saloon filled with sports to watch the game. If A won, the crowd yelled, 'The Lord gets that!' and if B was lucky, 'That goes to the devil!' "

A had won, and the unsuspecting district superintendent's salary was paid by the successful gambler. Mr. Logan looked the narrator in the eye and said, "I'm so glad I got the money; it has been in the hands of the devil long enough. Brother Van will put it to a better use."

»» «««

Another early time incident was narrated to Rev. Edward Smith by Thomas Hamilton, whose cattle and one cowboy were killed by the Indians. Mr. Hamilton was a settler on Upper Horse Prairie Valley who also acquired vast holdings and later built a fine modern residence on the early homestead site. Mr. Hamilton was the true type of the generous-hearted Westerner. He was a great friend of Brother Van to the day of his death.

In Brother Van's work, settlements were far apart. He often made the trip on horseback from Virginia City, Montana, to Salmon City, Idaho. Mr. Hamilton's cabin home was midway between these two points and made a fine stopping place for travelers. Mr. Hamilton explained this situation and then went on and told the following story:

"I had just come in with my team at noon. While giving hay to the horses a couple on horseback on the highway called over to know if they could feed their horses and get dinner. I said, 'Put in your horses and let them bust themselves on this fine hay, but you will have to see Mike about dinner.' (Mike was his nickname for his wife; the travelers, thinking it meant a man cook, took chances and put up their horses.)

"They came into the house and Mike soon had a fine dinner ready. But neither Mike nor I could make out who they were.

"When it came time for them to go one of the two asked: 'How much do we owe you?' 'Well,' said I, 'two kinds of fellows go through here wearing "biled" shirts; they are gamblers and preachers. I don't know which you are. If you are gamblers, I'm going to take it out in money; if you are preachers I'm going to take it out in prayer. There is the old Bible on the stand and it's up to you fellows.'

"Brother Van rose to the occasion. He said, 'My friend Riggin over there is a preacher. He will read a chapter from the Bible.' It was done. Then Brother Van sang and prayed."

"Now," continued Mr. Hamilton, "when I die I have already ordered that they send for Brother Van. He is at least one man who I believe will say something good about me."

503

A LETTER TO "BROTHER VAN"

CHARLEY RUSSELL

Providing a revealing comment upon the characters of two Montanans of good will, the writer and the recipient, this letter was sent to Brother Van by Charles M. Russell in March, 1918, when a special celebration of the beloved "sky pilot's" birthday was being held in Fort Benton. With the letter, Charley sent a water-color sketch for Brother Van—a landscape featuring a buffalo herd crossing the Missouri while a steamer waited for them to pass. The letter has been reprinted from time to time in Montana newspapers.

Dear Brother Van:

I think it was about this time of the year, 37 years ago, that we first met at Babcock's ranch, in Pigeye basin on the upper Judith.

I was living at that time with a hunter and trapper, Jake Hoover, whom you will remember. He and I had come down from the south fork with three pack horses, loaded with deer and elk meat, which he sold to the ranchers, and we had stopped for the night with old Bab, a man as rough as the mountains which he loved, but who was all heart from the belt up, and friends or strangers were welcome to shove their feet under his table. That all-welcome way of his made the camp a hangout for many homeless and prairie men, and his log walls and dirt roof seemed like a palace to those who lived mostly under the sky.

The evening you came, there was a mixture of bullwhackers, hunters and prospectors, who welcomed you with handshakes and rough but friendly greetings. I was the only stranger to you. So after Bab introduced Kid Russell, he took me to one side and whispered, "Boy," said he, "I don't savvy many psalm singers, but Brother Van deals square." And when we sat down to our elk meat, beans, coffee and dried apples, under the rays of a bacon grease light, these men who knew little law, and one of them I knew wore notches in his gun; men who had not prayed since they knelt at their mothers' knees, bowed their heads while you, Brother Van, gave thanks, and when you finished someone said "Amen." I think it was the man who I heard later was, or had been, a road agent.

I was 16 years old, Brother Van, but have never forgotten your stay at old Bab's, with men whose talk was generally emphasized with fancy profanity, but while you were with us, although they had to talk slow and careful, there was never a slip. The outlaw at Bab's was a sinner and none of us were saints, but our hearts were clean at least while you gave thanks, and the holdup said "Amen."

You brought to the minds of these hardened men and the homeless, the faces of their mothers. A man cannot be bad while she is near. I have met you many times since then, Brother Van, sometimes in lonely places, but you never were lonesome or alone, for a man with scarred hands and feet stood beside you and near Him there is no hate, so all you met loved you.

"Be good and you will be happy," is an old saying which many contradict and say goodness is a rough trail over dangerous passes, with windfalls and swift and deep rivers to cross. I have never ridden it very far myself, but judging from the looks of you, it's a cinch bet with a hoss called Faith under you. It's a smooth, flower-grown trail, with easy fords, where birds sing and cold, clear streams dance in the sunlight all the way to the pass that crosses the big divide.

Brother Van, you have ridden that trail a long time, and I hope you will still ride to many birthdays on this side of the big range. With best wishes from my best half and me,

Your friend,
C. M. Russell.

MRS. STATELER'S REBEL YELL

EDWIN J. STANLEY

This is a brief extract from a chapter in the *Life of Rev. L. B. Stateler, or Sixty-five Years on the Frontier*, by the Rev. E. J. Stanley, published in 1907 by the Methodist Episcopal Church, South, in Nashville, Tenn. Mrs. Stateler's rebel yell illustrated the strength of Confederate sentiment among the early arrivals in Montana Territory—and the discretion with which the poor woman guarded its utterance indicates the restraint under which ladies, especially missionaries' wives, labored in those days. Mr. Stateler and his wife came in 1864, penniless but with six cows and calves; they subsisted for a time on the sale of butter made by Mrs. Stateler. The cows produced three hundred pounds of this precious product in their first Montana summer, and the going price in the gold camps was $1.50 per pound. Stateler preached for the first time in Montana in July, 1864, in Norwegian Gulch, thirty-five miles northeast of Virginia City. The following February he began sharing the pulpit of Virginia City's new log community church with the Rev. Mr. Torbit, a Baptist.

SHE was a Southern woman by birth, a Southern Methodist from choice, and cherished the sympathies and attachments peculiar to a strong and sensitive nature living at that time. The fact of her husband being forced, without good reason, to abandon the field that he had helped to redeem from the wilderness, and of their home having been laid in ashes, compelling her to seek shelter on the bleak plains in midwinter, would naturally tend to arouse a spirit of resentment. But while possessed of a womanly nature and claiming a woman's prerogative, yet in all these trying experiences she observed the proprieties of prudent speech becoming to her position.

But after they had crossed the plains and were safely sheltered in the rugged mountains of the Northwest, the pent-up feelings of her somewhat impulsive nature could no longer be restrained. One day, while she was out watching the little herd of cows and the two faithful mares that had accompanied them (about all the property that had been saved out of the disaster) in one of the deep canyons tributary to Jefferson River, away where there was no human ear to be disturbed by the strange note, she raised her voice to its highest pitch and shouted *"Hurrah for Jeff Davis!"* with all the lusty life that thrilled her ardent nature, grateful to the Father above that she could give expression to her feelings where there was none to molest or make afraid.

To her surprise, a voice came back from a rocky crag in the distance uttering the same words with a force and distinctness that at first startled and then pleased her. Discovering that it was only an echo, she repeated the exercise again and again.

"I tell you, Brother Stanley," she remarked to the writer after relating the incident, "I thought I had never heard anything that sounded so well as the echo coming back from that rocky cliff."

Well, when Bishop Keener came from New Orleans to hold our Conference, as we were crossing the mountains not far from where the incident occurred, I told him the story, which greatly amused him. He laughed most heartily, and then remarked: "Well, I shall tell Jeff when I get back home (you know he is my neighbor) that he has at least one admirer out in Montana."

I suppose that he kept his promise, for in the course of time there came through the mail a neat little package addressed to Mrs. Stateler containing a photograph, cabinet size, of a fine-looking gentleman, on the back of which, in the neat, plain handwriting of the sender, was this inscription:

Beauvoir, Miss., December 7, 1887.

To Mrs. L. B. Stateler, with grateful affection and admiration both for herself and her husband, whose devoted service in the cause of Christianity is meet for a monument higher than man could build.

Faithfully,

JEFFERSON DAVIS.

"SAINT IGNATIUS, PATRON OF THE MOUNTAINS"

PIERRE JEAN DeSMET

Father Pierre Jean DeSmet, the great Jesuit missionary, was an extraordinary man on many counts. His travels covered more than 200,000 miles—an almost incredible figure for his time. He was a naturalist, geographer, and diplomat, frequently serving as intermediary between the whites and Indians. Born in Belgium in 1801, he ran away from a seminary because he wanted to be a missionary to the Indians and feared that his family would object, took ship to America and joined the Society of Jesus, being ordained a priest in 1827. Four years later the Flathead and Pend d'Oreille tribes of what is now Montana sent the first of four expeditions more than a thousand miles to St. Louis to ask for priests to come and instruct them in Christianity, of which they had heard from Big Ignace La Mousse, an Iroquois who had wandered west from Montreal in 1820 and joined the Flathead nation. Three of these Indian expeditions failed for one reason or another; on one of them Big Ignace himself was killed by Sioux. But the fourth, which included his son, Young Ignace, happened by chance to meet Father DeSmet at his mission among the Potawatomi near Council Bluffs. His pleas and those of the Bishop of St. Louis won him permission to go west, and in 1840, with Young Ignace as his guide, he crossed the plains and met the Flatheads at a rendezvous on Green River in Wyoming. Here is an account of his entry into Montana, July 24, 1840. Two days later, on the shores of Red Rock lake, the ultimate source of the mighty Missouri, he celebrated the first mass offered in this state. He returned to the east to recruit help and came back to Montana in 1841, establishing St. Mary's mission in the Bitterroot, Sept. 24. He introduced agriculture there in 1842. Reprinted here are extracts from his letters as they appear in Vol. II of *Life, Letters and Travels of Father DeSmet among the North American Indians*, by Hiram M. Chittenden and Alfred T. Richardson, published by Francis P. Harper, New York, 1905. After trips to Europe for money to support the Western missions, and many more journeys to the Oregon country, Montana, and Canada, Father DeSmet died May 23, 1873, in St. Louis. He is buried in Florissant, Mo., seat of the Missouri Province of the Society of Jesus.

508

I FOUND the camp of the Flatheads and Pend d'Oreilles in the valley called Pierre's Hole. This valley is situated at the foot of the Three Tetons, sharp-peaked mountains of a prodigious height, rising almost perpendicularly more than 10,000 feet, and covered with perpetual snow. There are five of them, but only three can be seen at any great distance. Thence we ascended one of the principal forks of Henry's [Fork of Snake] River, making every day little camps nine or ten miles apart. Often, in these little stages, we passed and repassed high hills, wide and swift torrents, narrow and dangerous defiles. Often also we came upon lovely valleys, level and open, rich in pasture grounds of a beautiful verdure, dotted with flowers, and where the mountain balsam (the travelers' tea) abounds. This tea, even after it has been crushed beneath the feet of thousands of horses, still perfumes the air with its delicious scent. In the valleys and defiles which we traversed, several more mountains drew our attention; some were in the form of cones, rising to a height of several thousand feet at an angle of forty-five to fifty degrees, very smooth and covered with a fair verdure; others represented domes; others were red as well-burned brick, and still bore the imprints of some great convulsion of nature; there were scoria and lava so porous that they floated on water; they were found scattered in all directions, and so abundantly in some places that they seemed to have filled whole valleys. In several places the openings of ancient craters were still to be distinguished. The argillaceous and volcanic strata of the mountains are generally horizontal; but in several places they hang perpendicularly, or else they are curved and wavy; often one might take them for artificial works.

On the 22d of July the camp came to Henry's lake, one of the principal sources of the Columbia; it is about ten miles in circumference. We climbed on horseback the mountain that parts the waters of two great rivers; the Missouri, which is properly speaking the main branch of the Mississippi and flows with it into the Gulf of Mexico, and the Columbia, which bears the tribute of its waters to the Pacific Ocean. From the elevated spot at which I was I could easily distinguish Mosquito [Red Rock] lake, source of one of the main branches of the north fork of the Missouri, called Jefferson river.

The two lakes are scarce eight miles apart. I started for the summit of a high mountain, for a better examination of the fountains that give birth to these two great rivers; I saw them falling in cascades from an immense height, hurling themselves with uproar from rock to rock; even at their source they formed already two mighty torrents, scarcely more than a hundred paces apart. I was bound to get to the top. After six wearisome hours, I found myself exhausted; I think I must have climbed more than 5,000 feet; I had passed snow drifts more than twenty feet deep, and still the mountain top was at a great height above me. I therefore saw myself compelled to give up my plan, and I found a place to sit down. The fathers of the Company [Jesuit Order] who are in the missionary service on the banks of the Mississippi and its tributaries, from Council Bluffs to the Gulf of Mexico, came to my mind. I wept with joy at the happy memories that were aroused in my heart. I thanked the Lord that he had deigned to favor the labors of his servants, scattered over this vast vineyard, imploring at the same time his divine grace for all the nations of Oregon, and in particular for the Flatheads and Pend d'Oreilles, who had so recently and so heartily ranged themselves under the banner of Jesus Christ. I engraved upon a soft stone this inscription in large letters: *Sanctus Ignatius Patronus Montium. Die Julii 23, 1840.*

I said a mass of thanksgiving at the foot of this mountain, surrounded by my savages, who intoned chants to the praise of God, and installed myself in the land in the name of our holy founder. . . .

During all my stay in the mountains, I said the holy mass regularly Sundays and feast-days, as well as on days when the Indians did not break camp in the morning; the altar was made of willows; my blanket made an altar cloth, and all the lodge was adorned with images and wild flowers; the Indians knelt without in a circle of about 200 feet, surrounded by little pines and cedars, set out expressly; they took assiduous part with the greatest modesty, attention and devotion, and since various nations were among them, they chanted the praises of God in the Flathead, Nez Percé and Iroquois languages. The Canadians, my Fleming and I sang chants in French, English and Latin. The Flatheads had already had for some years a custom of never breaking camp on Sunday, but of passing that day in devotional exercises.

On the 24th of July, the camp crossed the mountain and moved

510

from Henry's lake to Mosquito [Red Rock] lake.* Until the 8th of August, we were still traveling through a great variety of country. Now we would find ourselves in open, smiling valleys, now in sterile lands beyond lofty mountains and narrow defiles, sometimes in extensive high plains, profusely covered with blocks and fragments of granite.

On the 10th we camped on Jefferson river. The bottom is rich in lovely pasture lands and wooded with trees of thin growth. We went down it, making twelve to fifteen miles a day, and on the 21st of the same month we came to the junction of the three forks of the Missouri, where that river first takes this name; we camped on the middle branch [Madison Fork]. In this great and beautiful plain were buffalo in numberless herds. From Green river to this place, our Indians had made their food of roots and the flesh of such animals as the red and black-tailed deer, elk, gazelle, bighorn or mountain sheep, grizzly and black bear, badger, rabbit and panther, killing also occasionally such feathered game as grouse, prairie-hens (a kind of pheasant), swans, geese, cranes and ducks. Fish abounded besides in the rivers, particularly salmon trout. But cow-meat † is the favorite dish of all the hunters, and as long as they can find it, they never kill any other animals. Finding themselves therefore in the midst of abundance, the Flatheads prepared to lay in their winter supply; they raised willow scaffolds about their lodges for drying meat, and every one made ready his fire-arm, his bow and his arrows. Four hundred horsemen, old and young, mounted on their best horses, started early in the morning for their great hunt. I chose to accompany them in order to watch this striking spectacle from near at hand. At a given signal, they rode at full gallop among the herds; soon everything appeared confusion and flight all over the plain; the hunters pursued the fattest cows, discharged their guns and let fly their arrows, and in three hours they killed more than 500. Then the women, the old men and the children came up, and with the aid of horses carried off the hides and the meat, and soon all the scaffolds were full and gave the camp the aspect of a vast butcher-shop. The buffalo are hard to kill; they must be wounded in the vital parts. A ball that strikes a bull's forehead produces no other effect than

---

* With this move the party entered what is now Montana.
† Buffalo meat; the flesh of cows was favored because it was tender.

a movement of the head and a greater exasperation; on the other hand, one that strikes the forehead of a cow penetrates. Several bulls, mortally wounded in this hunt, defended themselves furiously.

. . .

The 27th of August [1840] was the day I had set for my departure. Seventeen warriors, selected braves of the two nations, stood early in the morning at the entrance to my lodge with three chiefs. The council of the elders had deputed them to serve as my escort for so long as I should find myself in the country of the Blackfeet and Crows, two nations so hostile to the whites,* that the first give them no quarter when they meet them, but massacre them in the cruelest manner; the second take from them everything they have, strip them to the shirt and leave them in the desert to perish of hunger and misery; sometimes they grant them life but make them prisoners. Long before sunrise all the nation was assembled around my Lodge; no one spoke, but grief was painted on each face. The only thing I could say that seemed to console them was a formal promise of a prompt return in the following spring, and of a reinforcement of several missionaries. I performed the morning prayers amid the weeping and sobs of those good savages. They drew from me despite myself the tears that I would gladly have stifled for the moment. I made them see the necessity for my voyage; I urged them to continue serving the Great Spirit with fervor and to put from them every cause of scandal; I recalled to them the principal truths of our holy religion. After this I gave them for their spiritual head a very intelligent Indian, whom I had taken pains to instruct myself in a most particular manner; he was to represent me in my absence, call them together evening and morning, as well as Sundays, say the prayers to them, exhort them to virtue, and anoint the dying, and, in case of need, little children. There was but a single voice, a unanimous assent to all my recommendations. With tears in their eyes they all wished me a fortunate journey. Old Big-Face rose and said: "Black-robe, may the Great Spirit accompany you in your long and dangerous journey. We will offer vows evening and morning that you may arrive safe among your brothers at St. Louis. We will continue to offer

* The Blackfeet were hostile but the Crows consistently friendly to the whites. They would, however, steal horses.

vows until you return to your children of the mountains. When the snows disappear from the valleys, after the winter, when the grass begins to be green again, our hearts, so sad at present, will begin to rejoice. As the grass grows higher, our joy will become greater; but when the flowers appear, we will set out to come and meet you. Farewell."

Full of trust in the Lord who had preserved me thus far, I started with my little band and my faithful Fleming,* who chose to continue sharing my dangers and my labors. . . .

* The Fleming was a lay brother who joined Father DeSmet on this trip and continued to serve him for a long time.

"OUR FATHER"

In the Cree Language

This is the form in which Father DeSmet taught the Roman Catholic prayer, "Our Father," to the Crees of Montana and Alberta. Protestants are familiar with it, with some differences in phrasing, as "The Lord's Prayer." This, of course, is not the accepted phrasing for either Catholic or Protestant churches; the noted Jesuit missionary adapted the wording to phrases which could be expressed by the Indians. Nor is it rendered in "modern" Cree as first compiled in a dictionary by the Rev. E. A. Watkins, Church of England missionary, in 1865. Father DeSmet, twenty years earlier, had to rely upon his own phonetic interpretation. The prayer as given here comes from DeSmet's *Oregon Missions and Travels over the Rocky Mountains* in 1845–46, published in New York in 1847. It is reprinted in *Travels in the Far Northwest*, Vol. II, edited by R. G. Thwaites, published by the Arthur H. Clark Co., Glendale, Calif., in 1906.

Eokosisit   mina,   ewiotawait   mina,   emiosit
Him who has a son, Him who has a Father, Him who is the
            manito,
      beautiful spirit,

owigowionik.   Pitone Ekeesiikik.
in His name.   May it be so.

Notanan   kitsi   kijikok epian pitone mewaitsikatek kiwigowin,
Our Father in the great heaven being seated, may it be honored

pitone   otitamomakad kitibeitsikewin, ispits enatota
Thy name, may it arrive Thy kingdom (reign) like Thee being

kawigan kitsi kisikok,   pitone ekusi iji   waskitaskamik.
followed in the great heaven, may it be the same on earth.

Anots kakijikak   miinanipakweji ganiminan   mina latwaw
Now in this day   give us our   bread   and   in every

kigigake.   Canisi kaiji kasenamawayakik ka   ki   matsitota
day.   As we have remitted to those who to   us have done

koyankik ekusi   iji kasinamawinan eki   matsitotamank.
evil   so likewise remit unto us what we have done evil.

Pisiskeiminan   kitsi   eka matsi mamitoueitamank
Be merciful to us that we fall not into evil,

iekatenamawinan   kamayatok.   Pitone Ekeesiikik.
keep away from us all that is evil. May it be so.

APPENDIX

CHRONOLOGICAL TABLE OF CONTENTS

To assist teachers and students of Montana history, the selections in this book are grouped below under headings which place them within the principal eras of the State's development.

Montana's basic *political* dates are these:

March 9, 1804. The area which is now Montana east of the Rocky Mountains became a part of the United States. The transfer of territory from France which had been negotiated a year before in the Louisiana Purchase became effective on this date.

June 15, 1846. What is now northwestern Montana became a part of the United States. On this date President Polk signed the Oregon boundary convention with Great Britain, establishing the 49th parallel as the international boundary.

May 26, 1864. Montana became a Territory.

Nov. 8, 1889. Montana became a State.

The dates which follow, defining the periods within which the contents of this book have been classified, are *economic* dates.

Until 1877: THE PLAINS INDIANS

There were white men long before this, but not until Chief Joseph's defeat in Montana's last Indian battle and the flight of Sitting Bull's Sioux could they be sure that they were to be permanent tenants!

1805–1860: THE FIRST WHITE MEN

They were explorers (Lewis and Clark, arriving in 1805, were the first white men to see Montana); fur traders (François Larocque of the North-West Company traded for beaverskins that same year along the Yellowstone); and missionaries (Father DeSmet arrived in 1840). Gov. Isaac Stevens' St. Paul-to-Pacific railway survey in 1853 was the last major exploratory venture; the mission era was short because settlement soon brought establishment of parish churches; the fur trade ceased to be a major industry when the last buffalo disappeared in 1883 or 1884.

1852–1906: THE MINERS

The first date is the year gold is believed to have been discovered—by François Finlay, a halfbreed also known as "Benetsee," at Gold Creek near Deer Lodge, and by another, and unidentified, wanderer near Fort Owen in the Bitterroot Valley. The gold rush started in the early 60's and was about over when, in 1881, Marcus Daly discovered copper in the Anaconda mine at Butte. Then came the famed "copper wars," ended February 4, 1906, when F. A. Heinze, young upstart who had beaten the "copper trust" on its own grounds, sold his holdings to his enemy. The Clark copper properties were sold to the Anaconda Company in 1926, but by then the era of mechanized mining was beginning and the brawling days were done.

1866–1910: THE COWBOYS

The first date is that of the first Texas trail drive to Montana, by Nelson Story. Cattle had been brought in earlier, but this was the real beginning of the open range industry. Its life was very brief: it never recovered from the disastrous blizzard of 1886, and another in 1910 which coincided with the arrival of the "nester" and the barbed wire fence finished it.

1910–1931: THE HOMESTEADERS

The tragedy of this period was heightened by its fantastically fortunate beginning—the long cycle of "wet years" which ended abruptly in 1917, to be succeeded by a four-year drought. This ruined most of the luckless newcomers, and another drought, in 1930–31, may be said to have ended the homestead era.

1931–1946: MONTANANS TODAY

Since the mid-30's, and especially throughout the war period, Montana has prospered—economically. Strip farming protects the great wheat ranches in the wind belt; cattle and sheep graze on owned, leased, or cooperatively managed range; irrigation, diversification, the combined grain and livestock operation—these, though not full insurance against disaster, can cushion its shock. The mines are mechanized and Butte has fewer men working underground; gigantic dredges work over the old gold gulches, moving 9,000 tons of dirt a day where the prospector moved five or six tons—with helpers. Still, not all of the prospectors are gone, nor all the cowboys.

INDEX OF AUTHORS, AND ACKNOWLEDGMENTS